Karl Marx:

Essential Writings

edited by
Frederic L. Bender

HARPER TORCHBOOKS
Harper & Row, Publishers
New York, Hagerstown, San Francisco, London

335.4
Mar
6176

The Essential Writings of the Great Philosophers is published under the editorship of Charles M. Sherover.

The author wishes to make acknowledgment to the following firms for allowing the use of copyrighted material in this book:
Doubleday & Company, Inc., for permission to quote from *Writings of the Young Marx on Philosophy and Society,* edited and translated by Loyd D. Easton and Kurt H. Guddat. Copyright © 1967 by Loyd D. Easton and Kurt H. Guddat.
McGraw-Hill Book Company and C.A. Watts & Co., Ltd. for permission to quote from *Karl Marx Early Writings,* translated and edited by T.B. Bottomore. © T.B. Bottomore 1963.
International Publishers Co., Inc. for permission to quote from *Pre-Capitalist Economic Formations,* edited by Eric Hobsbawm.
C. A. Watts & Co. Ltd. for permission to quote from "Marx's Economic and Philosophical Manuscripts" in *Marx's Concept of Man,* translated by T. B. Bottomore, edited by Erich Fromm.

KARL MARX: ESSENTIAL WRITINGS

First HARPER TORCHBOOK edition published 1972.

STANDARD BOOK NUMBER: 06-131558-3

LIBRARY OF CONGRESS CATALOG NUMBER: 70-184651

76 77 78 79 80   12 11 10 9 8 7 6 5 4

Preface

The philosophy of Karl Marx, as it has been both understood and misunderstood, has had enormous consequences in the past century. Two suggestions should be borne in mind while reading the following selections from Marx's work: first, one should be aware of the complex problem of the role and relevance (these may well differ) of Marx's thought as the twentieth century draws to a close; second, because the Marxian legacy is extremely diverse, the problem of understanding and applying Marx's thought is difficult and often prone to oversimplification (both pro and con). It should be obvious that these points closely relate to each other and that they can hardly be separated.

Since Marx's life spanned the central two-thirds of the nineteenth century, much that is to be found in his writings can be fully appreciated only in its historical context. This is not, however, to claim a priori that Marx's thought is "dated" or obsolete; rather, that which was truly alive in his day has grown and developed through the intervening years to the extent that Marx, somewhat surprisingly, retains an air of presence almost entirely lost to other social philosophers of the period. Hegel, Comte, Mill, and Spencer, to name but a few, seem strangely antiquated in our revolutionary age, yet Marx still plays a central role in contemporary struggles and will increasingly do so in the years immediately ahead.

With half of the earth's population governed by men professing to be Marx's followers, and with nearly all the remaining nations possessing active Marxist political groups, it is indeed no exaggeration to claim that ours is the "Age of Marx." It is our task here to determine the characteristics of his day which Marx

grasped as did none of his contemporaries and which are, additionally, basic traits of our own historical situation. Clearly these shall be found in Marx's identification of the process of industrialization as that single condition which was to totally transform the earth during the nineteenth and subsequent centuries, and his refusal to be blinded by the superficially optimistic assessment of this process which was accepted by his contemporaries in social philosophy. The accuracy of Marx's appraisal is, of course, arguable in many details, yet his awareness of, and in fact his role in shaping, many of the problems and movements of the industrial era distinguish him as the outstanding social philosopher of his (and our) time. For this reason, apart from any consideration of his specific views, the serious study of Marx is an indispensable requisite for those who wish to understand and participate in current and future social movements.

With the invention of the steam engine and spinning jenny in 1764, Great Britain was able to establish its world economic supremacy for the following century and to undergo a total social transformation unparalleled in previous history in its scope and rapidity. The other European nations lagged far behind and were largely unable to compete successfully with Britain.

The overwhelming mass of the British population sank into the class of wage laborers (Marx's "proletariat") and suffered conditions of life which were appalling and which remained unrectified until some decades after Marx's death. During Marx's lifetime these abuses cried out for alleviation, but such change was largely impossible until the political power of the working class had been sufficiently developed. Those persons who underwent the consequences of rapid industrialization faced the choice of either accepting continued physical misery (which in many cases entailed outright starvation and in most included debilitation and suffering) or choosing the course of revolution leading to the establishment of socialism. Marx, of course, felt it incumbent to aid the second of these alternatives, and to this task he dedicated his life.

Since Marx's philosophy deals with the problems of a society undergoing rapid industrial development, it should be clear

why his thought still enjoys widespread currency in those regions of the world in which today industrialization is just beginning. Despite his European intellectual heritage, this aspect of his thought remains pertinent to many in the underdeveloped non-Western nations where, under the threat of rapidly expanding population, the alternatives remain sure misery for the masses under the traditional order, increased misery under capitalism, or the hope of alleviating this suffering under revolutionary socialism. There is thus a significant shift of perspective involved here: Marx regarded capitalist development as an essential prerequisite for socialism, but today many find the human costs of capitalism so terrifying that they seek to establish a socialist state prior to entering upon industrialization.

We must further, however, explore the status of Marxist thought in the industrially advanced countries as well. Here, clearly, the alternative is no longer one of starvation versus revolution; rather, it involves the humanistic values which industrial capitalism offers once it has reached the level at which it is capable of meeting the basic physical needs of (most of) the population.

Recent studies of Marx, especially those concentrating on his recently rediscovered early works, have brought to light his particular insight into the processes of alienation which are operative in this type of situation as well as in the earlier stages of industrial development. The alternatives here are either passively accepting the dehumanizing influences of such a society or effecting such social change as will be necessary to achieve a more humanized society.* This is an entirely different focus and complex of problems from those germane to societies still at the threshold of industrialization, yet the Marxist philosophy is literally grounded on the concept of alienation, a concept which *defines* the goal of Marxian communism. Thus, as in the Great Britain of Marx's day, today's industrially advanced countries find themselves in a situation first explored philosophically by Marx and are thus especially susceptible to his analysis.

---

*For details concerning the Marxian significance of the concepts of alienation, dehumanization, and the "truly human" society the reader is referred to the Introduction as well as to Marx's text itself, especially Part II, below.

Before proceeding, it is important to briefly consider the course of development of Marx's thinking, as well as some of the main currents of the subsequent development of his ideas by his followers.

Marx was born in 1818 in the city of Trier, at the time one of the major commercial centers of the Rhineland, an area of Germany which had fallen under Prussian domination following the defeat of Napoleon in 1815. The influence of the French Revolution had been quite strong in Trier during the years of French occupation, and it is in the Revolution's shadow, although quite dimmed, that Marx was raised. After receiving the benefits of an upper-middle-class upbringing, Marx spent the year 1836 at the University of Bonn and subsequently transferred to Berlin, where he engaged in the study of jurisprudence and philosophy. In 1841 he completed his dissertation upon the materialist philosophies of Democritus and Epicurus and received the doctorate in philosophy. He then embarked upon a career as newspaper editor with the liberal *Rheinische Zeitung* (1842–1843). During this period many of his articles dealt with such subjects as German unification, press censorship, and legal and political reform. They led to an increasing concern for problems generated under the social conditions of the day and to a call for the thorough democratization of Prussian institutions. As a result of differences with the government censor, Marx resigned the editorship and, in November, 1843, undertook a voluntary exile in Paris with the avowed purpose of publishing a journal which would be in the forefront of the most politically advanced (i.e., thoroughly democratic) ideas of the day. In collaboration with the Young-Hegelian philosopher Arnold Ruge (1803–1880), the venture, to be known as the *Deutsch-Französische Jahrbücher,* would be an annual journal which would combine the German "head" for philosophy with the French "heart" for political daring.

While spending the year 1844 in Paris, Marx published the one issue of the *Jahrbücher,* containing some of his most important early political essays, entered into socialist circles with the benefit of friendships with Pierre Proudhon (1809–1865) and

the poet Heinrich Heine (1797–1856), and began his lifelong friendship and collaboration with Friedrich Engels (1820–1895). In addition, Marx also devoted a great deal of study to the works of the classical political economists which culminated in his *Economic and Philosophical Manuscripts* of 1844, now regarded as among his major works despite their tentative and fragmentary nature.

Following his expulsion from Paris in late 1844, Marx emigrated to Brussels, where for the next three years he collaborated with Engels on a number of major works. Among these are *The Holy Family* (1845), containing his critique of the liberal idealism espoused by his former teacher Bruno Bauer (1809–1882), and *The German Ideology* (1846), marking his total break with the radical Young-Hegelian school of which he had been a member during 1837–1843, and which included his former philosophical mentors, Bauer and Ludwig Feuerbach (1804–1872). In 1847 Marx published *The Poverty of Philosophy*, his first published foray into the domain of economics, which included his critique of the anarchist socialism of Proudhon; in the following year, with Engels, he published *The Manifesto of the Communist Party*, a pamphlet which played only a minor role in the ensuing uprisings which swept Europe throughout 1848, but which has since had world-wide influence.

Following the defeat of the 1848 revolutions, Marx returned to Cologne to become the editor of the radical *Neue Rheinische Zeitung*, which lasted one year. At that point his political activities generally became less public, as the times had sufficiently changed so as to make direct agitation unproductive. In 1849 Marx left Germany and emigrated to London, where he was to spend the remainder of his life in poverty, dependent upon the largess of Engels and engrossed in the all-consuming task of completing his greatest work, *Capital*, the first volume of which appeared in 1867. Prior to this, however, Marx's critical study of the capitalistic mode of production and of political economy was partially revealed with the publication of the short *A Contribution to the Critique of Political Economy* (1859); it is to be found also in the vast collection of manuscripts of the fifties and

sixties, recently published as the so-called *Grundrisse der Kritik der politischen Ökonomie*. After Marx's death in 1883, Engels edited and published two more volumes of *Capital* (in 1885 and 1894), and the leader of the German Social Democratic party, Karl Kautsky (1854–1938), published more of Marx's economic studies in the four-volume *Theories of Surplus Value* in 1905–1910.

In addition to these economic studies, Marx was in the latter part of his life to play an active role in directing and advising various revolutionary movements, foremost among these being the International Workingmen's Association (the "First International") founded in 1864 and destroyed by Marx in 1872 because of a feud with the Russian anarchist Mikhail Bakunin (1814–1876).

Following Marx's death numerous political movements arose which invoked his name as patron or founder. It is convenient to divide the era following Marx's death into three periods: first, that prior to the Russian Revolution of 1917; second, the interwar period 1918–1945; and last, the postwar period since 1945. During each of these periods Marx's work has been interpreted in different ways, often with different individual works being emphasized.

Marx's associate of four decades, Friedrich Engels, provided the interpretation which was current during the first of these periods through both his activities as Marx's literary executor and his being mentor to the Social Democratic party in Germany, by far the largest socialist party of the period. It is to Engels that Marxism owes its claim to be the (only) faithful interpreter of the physical sciences:* Engels, at this time, adapted the naïve materialism of nineteenth-century physics to the Hegelian dialectical philosophy and created that philosophical system known as "dialectical materialism," which is closely identified with Social Democracy in both Germany and Russia during this period, as well as with Soviet Marxism since 1917.

---

*See especially his *Anti-Dühring* (1878), *Socialism: Utopian and Scientific* (1884), and *Dialectics of Nature* (op. posth.).

Marx, however, having been primarily interested in economic analysis, social criticism, and revolutionary action, had definitely broken with ontological materialism as well as with the Hegelian system by 1845, and had cast his version of the materialist conception of history on the concept of "material" needs (those needs which a society must satisfy for the physical survival of its members) rather than on the unverifiable ontological premise that "all is matter." Engels also cast German Social Democracy into a reform-oriented parliamentary party which, in effect, abandoned its revolutionary heritage while working within the framework of the Prussian-dominated German Empire, although it continued to ritually invoke old revolutionary slogans and concepts.

This disparity between rhetoric and action led Eduard Bernstein (1850–1932) to propose, in 1899, a thorough revision of "orthodox" Marxist dogma in the light of the realities of the situation, thus touching off the famous "revisionist controversy" concerning the philosophical orientation as well as the allegedly "scientific" character of Marxism. The "orthodox" position, as defended by Kautsky, who had inherited the mantle of Engels, largely avoided the ethical issues raised by Bernstein's faction by smothering them with invective. On the eve of the Great War the Russian Social Democrats, as well, adhered to the "orthodox" interpretation of Marxism as "scientific socialism" under the guidance of G. V. Plekhanov (1857–1918), while their prime renegade, Lenin, found himself continually isolated as the leader of the schismatic Bolshevik faction.

In the aftermath of the 1914–1918 war the picture changed considerably. In Germany the Social Democrats gained power in the Weimar Republic and utterly failed to cope with Germany's postwar problems before Hitler's ascent to power in 1933; thus they lost their preeminent position as interpreters of Marxist philosophy. In Russia, however, the revolution led by Aleksandr Kerenski's Social Democrats was successful in deposing the Czar in February, 1917, only to fall to Lenin's coup d'état of October of the same year. Thenceforth it was the Soviet Communist party, itself the creation of Lenin, which established the standards of Marxist "orthodoxy."

The present context is hardly opportune for a detailed examination of the far-reaching revisions of Marx's thought undertaken by Lenin. Suffice it to say that, faced with the immense problems of organizing a sprawling, backward, and chaotic empire caught in a civil war and invaded by foreign powers, and lacking specific guidelines from Marx and Engels concerning the procedures to be followed in the actual establishment of a socialist society, Lenin improvised, often brilliantly. Foremost among these improvisations was the major role now assigned to the Communist party as the "vanguard" of the proletariat. Following Lenin's death in 1924, however, these improvisations became Stalin's dogmas, thus beginning a period of total centralization of authority and the establishment of the party dictatorship which continues today. Under Stalin, industrialization was given first priority and proceeded at an astonishing pace, but at tremendous human cost. Nonetheless, the immense prestige of the Soviet state ensured Marxism-Leninism (as it was now termed) to become accepted as the "legitimate" interpretation of Marxist thought.

In the rapidly changing situation following the Second World War, two new trends have emerged in Marxist thought. The first is the emergence of Marxist movements in those areas of the globe not as yet even begun on the path of industrialization, the foremost among these being China. Second, there has emerged a movement which is characterized by the desire to return to the humanist inspiration of Marx himself, especially in his works of his earlier period, often for the sake of reforming many of the excesses of the Eastern European Communist regimes based on the Stalinist model. The Yugoslav model of an "independent road" to socialism with its emphasis upon decentralization of authority, the Hungarian "revisionist" uprising of 1956, and the "liberalizations" of the Dubcek regime in Czechoslovakia in 1968 (the latter two brutally crushed by Soviet military force) are all cases in point, each attempting to answer to the strivings for a socialist freedom on the part of the populations (especially the youth) of these and other Eastern European nations. Additionally, Marxist thinkers and parties of Western Europe, especially of France and Italy, have been in-

fluential in keeping alive the Western (as opposed to Russian) heritage of Marxist humanism.

From what has been said it should be apparent that "Marxism" is a philosophical and political movement impressive in its diversity; it is certainly a movement in which claims to "orthodoxy" can only indicate a sectarian mentality on the part of the claimant. The wide diversity of situations to which Marxist ideas are applied further reinforces its pluralistic nature. In this light it may be fruitful to consider briefly the possibilities of Marxism in the United States.

First, whatever relevance the Marxian view is to have in this country will obviously stem primarily from the concept of alienation rather than from the "law of the increasing misery" of the proletariat. In this regard there is a great deal to be learned from Marx by Marxists and non-Marxists alike. Second, facing a major revolution in attitudes, it is debatable whether violent revolutionary acts will (for the time being at least) prove to be more productive than the development of an intellectual Marxism alert to, and critical of, numerous contemporary institutions. Third, if it is the case that the industrialized countries are in the early stages of a "humanist revolution," it may be possible that that revolution can be both social and democratic simultaneously, provided that it be developed as an organized political force for significant change. It is our purpose here not to impress the reader with pat Marxist formulas for correcting national ills, but to suggest that he read the selections in this anthology in the light of the notion that Marxism has by no means fully spent its potential in those movements which have borne its name thus far. New conditions and a new national and intellectual context require a new Marxist synthesis, and it is this which may well be achieved on the basis of a detailed and incisive assessment of current conditions plus a careful and critical grasping of *Marx's* contributions to Marxism.

Honolulu, Hawaii   FREDERIC L. BENDER
December, 1970

An Introduction to the Philosophical Study of Marx

It is helpful to conceive of Marx's thought as containing three fundamental arguments. The first, which may be termed the "ethical" argument, refers to Marx's concept of alienation and to the philosophical anthropology upon which it is based. The term "ethical"—which, incidentally, Marx abhorred—is used in this connection simply to refer to the fact that Marx considers any society which alienates man from his nature to be one which *ought to be* overthrown and replaced by one which overcomes this alienation. Second, Marxist philosophy contains a radical critique of the Western philosophical tradition and its supersession in the dialectical philosophy of historical materialism with its attempt to prove that bourgeois society *will be* surpassed. Third, as a corollary to the "historical" argument, there is the "economic" one, which involves demonstrating that the laws underlying the capitalist process of production will lead, dialectically, to capitalism's collapse. Before, however, turning directly to a discussion of these, it is fruitful to examine certain aspects of Hegel's philosophy which formed the intellectual milieu within which Marx's thought developed.

The relation between Marx and Hegel is extemely complex and would require a far more detailed analysis than is possible here. In this context focusing on the question of the *dialectical* aspect of Hegel's philosophy will illustrate the most fundamental sense in which Hegel influenced Marx.

The basic insight of dialectical philosophy lies in its recogni-

tion that a mode of thought which merely states or posits a principle in its attempt to explain reality is *necessarily* abstract, since the stated principle as well as its contradictory is valid. For example, in regard to attempting to adequately know that a certain hard, brown, nearly spherical object with matting on the outside and a liquid inside is a coconut is, to ordinary common sense, quite indisputably the case; to the dialectician, it is necessary to recognize that the object in question both *is* and *is not* a coconut. Dialectical philosophy is in opposition to the *law of noncontradiction,* first enunciated by Aristotle and for twenty-two centuries the cornerstone of Western logic and thus of Western thought. A dialectical logic is based upon a *law of contradiction* which conceives the very nature of reality as that of the presence and actuality of contradiction. These "contradictions" are recognized by the dialectician as aspects of a dynamic equilibrium; that is, reality is comprehended dialectically under the category of *becoming.*

To return to our brown, hard, matted, liquid-filled, spherical object—it both *is* and *is not* a coconut, and it both *is* and *is not* a palm tree, copra, coconut oil, etc., because it is involved in the process of *becoming* all of these. That is to say, dialectical thought comprehends reality as a process generated by "contradictions" within any alleged static relation, whereas common sense (and the Platonic tradition) seeks to grasp reality in terms of what is eternal and unchanging therein. From the perspective of the more traditional logic change must be considered less real (if real at all) than stasis; dialectical thought is considered as quite simply violating the law of noncontradiction and as thus invalid in a universe within which change implies imperfection. From the standpoint of dialectical thinking, however, traditional logic is one-sided and abstract simply because it refuses to recognize that what is real is not eternal and unchanging but is continually being altered. Dialectical thought thus conceives the philosophical task *par excellence* to be the problem of recognizing that direction of change by which we can recognize becoming (=purposeful change) in an apparently meaningless flux. This is the insight of Heraclitus which Plato, with immense consequences, considered applica-

ble only to the inferior world of the senses and not to reality considered in itself and as a whole. To return once more to our coconut: according to the traditional thinker it is merely a hard, brown, etc., object (it is *what it is*); to the dialectician (and to the botanist and commercial grower of coconut palms) it is *what it potentially is*; it is a potential palm tree. To know of this object, then, only what it is, and not to know what it is potentially, is hardly to know the coconut at all. To *fully* comprehend the coconut would require the ability to know not only the natural processes involved in the life cycle of coconut palms, but also myriad details concerning the processing of coconuts, their shipment from the South Pacific to the centers of the world market, the economic relations pertaining in that market which regulate the price and distribution of products manufactured from coconuts, and so on; in other words, fully *adequate* knowledge, to the dialectician, is precisely *knowledge of the whole* and of the particular relations pertaining among all parts of this whole in regard to the object in question (our coconut). Any "knowledge" short of this is, to the dialectician, incomplete and abstract (because abstracted from the total context); and any judgment based thereupon is considered arbitrary and "one-sided." Thus a dialectical philosophy such as that of Hegel or Marx will be essentially a philosophy of becoming which, once translated into terms of human actions, is essentially historical, for it is only in the flux of history that these actions become interrelated.

In general, dialectical change is conceived in three ways: (1) as proceeding through stages of thesis, antithesis and synthesis perhaps best illustrated by the alteration of political institutions, in a given nation, as e. g. in the Old Regime of France, the revolutionary period 1789—1799, and the period of the Napoleonic Empire; (2) as proceeding through numerous stages each of which is conceived as the "negation" of the one previous (the so-called negation and negation of the negation); and (3) as the resultant effect of the play of opposing forces acting either within an entity, state, type of society, etc. or between that entity and others within its environment. In any given case one or more of these conceptions may be used in the attempt to

understand the dynamic process underlying the change in question.

Another sense in which both Hegel and Marx understand dialectics lies in recognizing the importance of the *interaction* between any given object and all others (although the degree of interaction will be vanishingly small for most "other" objects, it will be quite significant in the case of those objects with which the given object interacts in terms of its natural processes). To return to our example, obviously the coconut, once placed in the soil, is involved in a series of interactions with that soil, the wind and rain, insects, bacteria, man, etc. To fully comprehend the coconut involves an adequate grasp of all these specific interactions. In a more interesting case, that of the growth of a child, the dialectician would reject as one-sided both the approach that the child is simply "unfolding his nature" as well as that which understands the child solely in terms of the all-pervasive influence of his "environment." Rather, for the dialectician, the child is a purposeful being (i.e., his growth is a process) and the psychologist must understand the way in which the environment has *significance* for the child (i.e., he neither unfolds his "potentialities" as in a vacuum nor does he merely passively accept stimuli; rather he plays an active role in reacting to and integrating meaningful experiences).

Thus far we have seen how a dialectical philosophy involves the use of concepts which essentially refer to becoming; Hegel's philosophy is essentially an attempt to formulate and interrelate all these dialectical concepts (cf. his *Science of Logic*) and, in the realm of history, to trace the stages through which human culture has developed from forms based upon farther to closer approximations to the (dialectical) concept of human freedom. Hegel's concept of freedom consists essentially in the unity achieved by the dialectical interaction of the individual person with (1) his cultural heritage—that is, the development of the entire human race, although Hegel focuses specifically upon that of the people (nation); (2) his fellow-man through the role he plays as a participant in both economic and political life; and (3) nature. The historical development of humanity is examined by Hegel in terms of the the development of political institu-

tions, art, religion, and philosophy, and it is his conclusion that the principles of the modern bourgeois-democratic state are sufficient to enable mankind finally to become free. Thus, it follows that Hegel regards the attainment of bourgeois democracy (as typified in the ideals of the French Revolution but as modified by his own stress upon the value of tradition and order) as the culmination of mankind's struggle to attain its freedom, because he recognizes that *in principle* the freedom of all is guaranteed in such a state (which he describes as a limited monarchy in his *Philosophy of Right*). A fundamental ambiguity in Hegel's thought lies, however, in his own assessment of the need to challenge the existing state of affairs which only incompletely exemplifies this principle of the freedom of all. As Hegel became older (and also the recipient of more honors from the Prussian monarchy) his views tended to reflect a belief that the current situation was indeed such a near-perfect instantiation that it required little change. It was on the grounds of Hegel's later conservatism in political and theological matters, as well as the idealist nature of his dialectic, that Marx was to struggle to divest himself of a close identification with the Hegelian philosophy, to offer in 1844 a penetrating general critique of Hegel, and two years later to develop (with Friedrich Engels) his realist philosophy of historical materialism.

Ten years after Hegel's death in 1831, Ludwig Feuerbach published *The Essence of Christianity*, a work which decisively developed the Hegelian philosophy in a radical direction, offering as it did an analysis of religious psychology developed along the lines of Hegel's concept of the alienation of self-consciousness. Hegel had conceived "spiritual" life to be a process wherein self-consciousness "alienates" itself into an external object—thus providing the grounds of the very being of that object—and then reappropriates that object as its own. That is to say, the existence of an object is only quasi-independent, awaiting the moment of its reintegration into self-consciousness. Thus, objects indeed exist, but they become fully themselves in the process of their being reappropriated by

self-consciousness (= man) in the act of *knowing*. As used by Feuerbach and later by Marx, the concept of alienation no longer refers to a process which describes the development of spirit as the ontological entity *par excellence* toward its ultimate goal of "absolute knowledge," but rather as the process and the result of converting the products of human and social activity, as well as man's attributes and capacities, into something both independent of and dominating him. Feuerbach's interest lies in his exploring the way in which man alienates his own nature in religion and philosophy, thereby denying himself the chance and even the desire of full actualization in his earthly existence. Marx, on the other hand, applies the concept of alienation to a whole range of human activities (e.g., man's relation to nature, his social activity, his labor) and is careful to emphasize the ways in which alienation is closely bound to the specific (and changing) character of the historical and social situation of the alienated individual or group of individuals in question.

Feuerbach's questions, then, were: Why do Christian doctrines take the specific forms they do? Why do millions of Christians hold these as the objects of the most profound reverence? His answers lay in the analysis of religion as being the process of the projection of human nature into an object in a transcendent realm which is then worshiped by man as all-powerful, all-knowing, and otherwise perfect in every way. This process, needless to say, does not occur consciously, and it is Feuerbach's contention that in its being exposed to the light of self-consciousness, the compelling character it still retains for millions will be lost. Whereas Hegel had accepted the idealist viewpoint that objects are indeed constituted through consciousness' self-projection, Feuerbach, adopting the realist viewpoint that real external objects had their existence in themselves, considered the objects of religious experience to be merely a projection of the self and thus, qua projection, unreal. The attributes of the Divinity are thus the idealized attributes of human nature which, as men come eventually to realize, cannot be actualized on earth and which must then be projected into another world and another time for their actualization. Man has been able to accept his very imperfect earthly existence only because he is

promised (or unself-consciously promises himself) perfection in another existence. This is the key to the riddle as to why religion is so vital in making life bearable and why it is a universal phenomenon; and it is only on the basis of reunifying this fragmented self, of reunifying the actual and the ideal human nature, that human fulfillment can be attained. But, since the process is not one which is performed self-consciously, it cannot be simply eliminated by an act of willing; what is necessary is rather the overcoming of those conditions which make this fantastic projection necessary in the first place.

At this point we must realize that Feuerbach conceives of man as essentially a "species-being," that is, as one who recognizes that his fulfillment lies in his proper integration into the common life of mankind as a whole, rather than in asserting his individuality to the detriment of his fellows. This is the basis of Feuerbach's ethics of community, on the basis of which he developed his "philosophy of the future" as the authentic expression of humanity based upon love.

Without following Feuerbach's argument in detail here, we note that he argues that Christianity is the highest form of religion, because it seeks to reunite all mankind by means of the bonds of love. But, he argues, even this is only an imperfect and indirect reunification, because the unity of mankind can be achieved by Christianity only through the mediation of the God-who-becomes-man and the institution which has been established to further his work, rather than directly. What is necessary, argues Feuerbach, is to de-alienate the human race by promoting the direct establishment of an authentic community on the basis of the love of each for all.

Following Feuerbach's analysis of religion in terms of human self-alienation, Marx applies a similar method to the study of political institutions. In his *Critique of Hegel's Philosophy of Right*, of which only fragments remain, he reaches the position that, just as religion is a fantastic projection of human nature into an object to whom men are in thrall, so too the State is the alienated form of the human community which is accorded nearly total power over human affairs. Whereas man, as a "species-being"—a being who is directly aware of his kinship with

his fellow-men—could be expected to live according to his nature in a communal relationship with all men, we find to the contrary that the political state has everywhere been allowed to serve as an artificial mediator of human affairs, and men, in turn, have become accustomed to regarding their fellows as a threat to their safety, property, or privacy. Further, just as the power of the Divine Being is fully derived from the alienation of human potential in religion, so too the power of the State, the existence of which testifies to the nearly universal slavery of mankind, derives simply from the fact that men are incapable or unwilling (or both) to face directly the problems confronting them in their mutual social interactions. Rather than a community of free men, there exists the political state supposedly protecting men from the "bestiality" allegedly characteristic of a stateless condition. The State, like God, is an alien being, a fetish with ever greater power over men's lives simply because they allow it to become that way. Further, the ideologues of the State would convince its subjects that a true and direct community would be unworkable and that the State is a necessary condition of existence.

In 1844, in his famous *Economic and Philosophical Manuscripts*, Marx carries the analysis of alienation even further. Not only is the State an alienated form of social life, but that social life itself—the life of men as active in the process of appropriating nature (industry) and in the distribution of the products of this activity (commerce) under the conditions of wage labor characteristic of bourgeois civil society—is one of the complete alienation of labor for the vast majority of mankind. In industrial labor, which incidentally was just beginning its tremendous growth at the time of Marx's youth, the situation is typically as follows:

The wage laborer is alienated from the *product* of his labor. This arises out of the peculiarity of capitalist enterprise that the product legally belongs not to he who makes it but to the capitalist who hires the laborer for wages. These products, however, act as further constraints upon the laborer, for they then serve as objects of desire for which the laborer must continue to work so as to acquire sufficient money for their purchase. In addition,

on those periodic occasions when a surplus of products has been produced so as to make for speedy and profitable sale impossible, the product of the laborer's activity forces him out of work and leaves him idle and starving.

The wage laborer is alienated from his *activity* itself, for the actions he performs while in the hire of the capitalist reflect the desires of the latter, not his own. Thus the laborer is reduced to a tool; his lot is not to use his capacity for judgment or to involve himself in any way with the decisions as to what, how much, by what means, for whom to produce; he is simply required to do as he is told. Considering that a major portion of a man's waking hours are spent at his job (twelve to sixteen hours per day in Marx's era), we can see that this procedure robs him of most of his "humanity," i.e., his potentiality to develop himself into the kind of human being he chooses.

In terms of the types of human beings that are developed under the conditions of capitalist society, we find that the wage laborer is traditionally trained in only one operation, that he is left in the state of illiteracy, and that he does not participate at all in the benefits and achievements which have been attained through the centuries of human culture. That is to say, he is a stunted and warped creature hardly fit to be called human, and in this sense he may be considered as alienated from what is truly within the *potential* of human nature in general.

The foregoing aspects of the alienated process of wage labor would hardly be accepted voluntarily by the worker. However, in a society in which he has the choice of hiring himself out or starving—that is, in a society completely dominated by a money economy—it is small wonder that there is an inexhaustible supply of willing labor. But as a direct result of this all men become competitors, as capitalist against other capitalists, as worker against worker, as well as capitalist against worker. Thus each individual struggles against the rest of humanity in the purely private effort to ensure the survival of himself and his family. Under the conditions of bourgeois society, each man is radically alienated from *all other men.* This should be contrasted with Feuerbach's notion of man as a "species-being" adopted by Marx, whereby man (ideally) considers himself a part of, and

dedicates his life activity to working for the benefit of, humanity.

In general, Marx's concept of alienation reflects the insight of Hegel that man is free only when he creates himself in accordance with the full potential of human nature. This concept of human nature is not conceived in terms of some alleged rationality, but rather in terms of the actual historical accomplishments of the human species in such fields as social and political life, art, religion, and philosophy. What has once been attained now becomes the common potential of all. But, in glaring contrast to the full range of such potentialities, bourgeois society thoroughly undermines and perverts human labor—man's very life activity—and thus deforms and destroys mankind.

Thus we see that Marx's thought, even at this early stage, contains the normative dimension based upon the shortcomings of bourgeois society with respect to concrete human potentialities. But it is important to note that this norm is not presented, as in traditional ethics, as an obligation to certain actions incumbent upon the *individual* moral agent. Rather, Marx develops it in the direction of the *telos* of history, as he seeks to discern in the flux of historical transition the law of development whereby the current, alienated, *social* order will be superseded.

Thus, in sum, Marx's theory of alienation contains the following dimensions:

1. the so-called fetishism—that is, the transcendent projection of human nature into an external object—(e.g., religion, the State, money);
2. the alienation of man from man—as opposed to the norm of participation in a genuine community;
3. the alienation from the wealth of human potentialities brought about by the rigid division of labor characteristic of the capitalist process of production;
4. the alienation of labor—the alienation from the freedom to direct one's activities towards ends which are of intrinsic value to ones own life style and goals;
5. the alienation of man from nature as accentuated under

capitalism by the overwhelming use of machinery both in the process of production and in the daily lives of individuals and in the assumption that nature exists to be exploited for profit.

Following his critiques of Hegel's philosophical idealism, of the mechanical materialism of the English and French writers from Bacon to Helvetius and even of the "anthropological materialism" of Feuerbach (under whose influence he had earlier developed his theory of alienation), Marx (with Engels) set out to decisively supersede traditional philosophy with the theory of historical materialism, a view of the development of human history that has as its "first premise" not thought or consciousness, but "real human individuals." Especially in contrast to Hegel's spiritual philosophy of history, Marx and Engels sought a radically human-oriented view, and took their point of departure from "real men" as social beings who must obtain or produce certain articles (e.g., food, clothing, shelter) in order simply to survive. That is, Marx and Engels assume the logical (not temporal) priority of economic (i.e., productive) factors over any "spiritual" ones such as law, art, religion, philosophy, etc. It is important to note that this is not to imply that there has ever existed a society which was entirely devoted to economic ends, or that economic concerns can be fully understood if they are divorced from the entire complex of factors operative in any given society; it is only to state that the way in which a society organizes its productive life is the most fundamental factor influencing the ways in which all the other aspects of human affairs within that society will develop. Furthermore, Marx and Engels do not contemplate a rigid economic determinism here (although this has developed in some quarters as a "Marxist" dogma); rather they conceive the economic "base" as being in an extremely complex dialectical relationship with all the factors commonly called the "superstructure." For example, although it is indeed obvious that economic factors play a major role in the development of laws and of political institutions it is certainly also the case that the influence of law and politics upon economic life is also, if not equally, profound. It is the task of dialectical sociology to study and sort out all the

various modes of interaction involved in any given society. The main contribution of Marx and Engels was in recognizing that economic factors are more important (i.e., have a more pervasive influence) than any of the others.

Beginning, then, with the basic role of economic factors in influencing the composition of society, Marx and Engels further note that the development of any type of society (e.g., feudal, capitalist) depends primarily upon the economic relations obtaining within that society, and then find that these relations can be best sociologically comprehended as *conflicts* among the various *classes* active within that society. It is this "contradiction" of opposing interests (i.e., the "class struggle") which provides the dialectical impetus to social change; and a radical transformation of society occurs when a hitherto subordinate class is able to impose its interests upon society in place of those of the previously dominant class. As such transformations have previously occurred whenever conditions were such as to make possible the seizure of power by an exploited class, and as the productive relations of capitalism tend to increase the size, strength and misery of the proletariat, so too will this class someday transform bourgeois society into socialism.

Having thus briefly examined the philosophical bases of what we have called Marx's "ethical" and "historical" arguments, it would also seem incumbent upon us to dwell briefly upon his analysis of the workings of the capitalist economy which purport to demonstrate the dialectically inevitable demise of bourgeois society. It will be, however, somewhat less confusing for the reader to have this discussion deferred until Part VI below, where the editor shall attempt in his selection headnotes to guide the reader in following Marx's often highly technical argument.

tion is at the same time its loss, that what it combats outside is its own inner defect, that just in this combat philosophy itself falls into the faults which it combats in its opponent, and that it transcends these faults only by falling victim to them. . . .

1. Philosophy as Criticism and Practice

This short selection is taken from a note to Marx's doctoral dissertation (1841) entitled "Philosophy After Its Completion." It is his first discussion of the "overcoming" of philosophy in practice. Even at this early stage, he considers philosophy to be a theoretical activity which essentially reflects the status quo, and opposes to this the view that philosophy reaches its fulfillment as *criticism* of that status quo.

THE PRACTICE [*Praxis*] OF philosophy . . . is itself *theoretical*. It is *criticism* which measures individual existence against essence, particular actuality against the Idea. But this *direct realization* of philosophy is burdened with contradictions in its innermost essence, and this essence manifests itself in appearance and puts its stamp thereon.

While philosophy, as will, turns toward the apparent world, the system is reduced to an abstract totality, that is, it becomes one side of the world facing another. Its relation to the world is reflexive relation. Enthusiastic in its drive to realize itself, it enters into tension with everything else. The inner self-contentedness and roundedness is broken down. The former inner light becomes a consuming flame turning outward. The consequence, hence, is that the world's becoming philosophical is at the same time philosophy's becoming worldly, that its realiza-

From *Writings of the Young Marx on Philosophy and Society,* trans. and ed. by L. D. Easton and K. H. Guddat (New York: Doubleday-Anchor, 1967). Used by permission.

Young-Hegelians, led by David Friedrich Strauss, Bruno Bauer, and Ludwig Feuerbach, whose attacks against the established "Christian State" were embodied in a series of scathing critiques of the New Testament accounts of the life and ministry of Jesus of Nazareth. Under the prevailing conditions of censorship, direct social criticism was impossible and political criticism was possible only as theological criticism. The political ideas of the Young-Hegelians (whose circle Marx never fully joined because he considered them personally frivolous) were predominantly cast in the mode of the liberalism of eighteenth-century France and of the French Revolution.

Marx's own development prior to 1844 followed a similar path: first, opposition to the prevailing conservative interpretation of the Hegelian philosophy; second, adoption of a democratic-liberal stance in the face of Prussian absolutism; and, finally, a break with liberalism because of his conviction that such a philosophy was only the façade, the mere form, of liberty. Marx, at the beginning of 1844, concluded that the rational state of freedom could not be achieved by the merely political form of democracy; it must rather overcome the duality of political man and economic man, that is, of man as citizen distinct from man as a member of civil society.

This development of his is traced in the following selections from the *Rheinische Zeitung* and the *Deutsch-Französische Jahrbücher*.

I.

The Young Marx on Philosophy,
Religion, and the State (1841–1843)

Marx's academic training culminated in his dissertation *On the Difference Between Democritean and Epicurean Natural Philosophy*, for which he received the doctorate in philosophy in 1841. To avoid what he regarded as the stultified life of a German academician, he resolved upon a career as a journalist, and served as editor of the radical newspaper *Rheinische Zeitung* from 1842 until being forced into exile late in 1843. Marx then chose to reside in Paris, the center of the political ferment which was beginning to sweep Europe. Upon his arrival he established and edited the first and only number of the proposed annual journal the *Deutsch-Französische Jahrbücher*.

This period of Marx's youth began within the framework of the Hegelian philosophy (which at the time enjoyed unchallenged hegemony in Germany) which he progressively transformed into radical democracy. Although Hegel had been greatly influenced by the French Revolution at the time of his own youth, by the year of his death, 1831, his philosophy had become symbolic of the reactionary Prussian monarchy.

The 1830s were a decade of the supremacy of the Hegelian philosophy primarily represented by thinkers, most of whom were politically and theologically conservative, known collectively as the Old Hegelians. In this milieu Marx received his academic training, and it was against this kind of Hegelian orthodoxy that he reacted in the direction of democracy and atheism. The last years of the decade saw the emergence of the

Contents

2. On Censorship of the Press

Taken from an article written in February, 1842, entitled "Comments on the Latest Prussian Censorship Instruction," this selection shows Marx's contrasting morality and religion, as well as inveighing against a censorship instruction which is clearly designed as a carte blanche for government harassment of dissenting writers. The relation between Christianity and the law follows from the Prussian monarchy's claim to be a "Christian State," thereby making criticism of religious dogmas tantamount to a civil offense. The article was first published in Switzerland in February, 1843.

THE *orthodoxy* OF the new Censorship Instruction comes into conflict with the *rationalism* of the old Censorship Edict in an additional way. The Edict also includes within the purpose of censorship the suppression of "whatever offends morality and good conduct." . . . But although the *commentary* makes additions in regard to religion, it contains omissions in regard to morality. To offend *morality* and *good conduct* is now to injure "discipline, morals, and outward loyalty." One observes that *morality as morality*, as the *principle of a world* with its own laws, has *disappeared;* external manifestations such as *police-regulated honorability* and *conventional good manners* have taken its place. Credit where credit is due: this shows real con-

From *Writings of the Young Marx on Philosophy and Society,* trans. and ed. by L. D. Easton and K. H. Guddat (New York: Doubleday-Anchor, 1967). Used by permission.

sistency. The specifically Christian legislator *cannot recognize morality* as an independent sphere sanctified in itself, for he derives the inner universal essence of morality from religion. Independent morality offends the basic principles of religion, and particular concepts of religion are opposed to morality. Morality recognizes only its own universal and rational religion, and religion only its own particular and positive morality. Following the Instruction, censorship will have to repudiate such intellectual heroes of morality as Kant, Fichte, Spinoza for being irreligious and threatening discipline, morals, and outward loyalty. All of these moralists proceed from a principled opposition between morality and religion, because *morality,* they claim, is based on the *autonomy,* and *religion* on the *heteronomy* of the human spirit. . . .

According to [the new censorship edict] the writer is subject to the *most horrible terrorism,* to *jurisdiction based on suspicion. Tendentious* laws, laws without objective norms, are laws of terrorism, such as those created by Robespierre because of emergencies in the state and by Roman emperors because of the rottenness of the state. Laws that make the *sentiment* of the acting person the main criterion, and not the *act as such,* are nothing but *positive sanctions of lawlessness.* . . .

Only by *expressing* myself and by entering the sphere of actuality do I enter the legislator's sphere. As far as the law is concerned I do not exist and am not subject to law except in .*my* acts. They alone concern the law; only because of them do I demand the right to exist, a *right of actuality* that makes me subject to *actual law.* But a tendentious law does not punish me for my acts, but for my *motive.* It is an insult to the honor of the citizen, a mockery directed against my existence.

I may turn and twist myself as much as possible—the evidence is not important. My existence is suspect; my innermost being, my individuality, is considered to be *evil,* and I am *punished* for that. The law does not penalize me for wrongs I commit but rather for wrongs I do not commit. In fact, I am punished because my actions are *not illegal,* for in this way alone a mild and well-meaning judge is compelled to consider

my *evil sentiment,* which I am clever enough not to bring out
into the open.

A law like that is *not a law of the state* for the *citizenry,* but
a *law of a party against another party.* The tendentious law
cancels the equality of the citizens before the law. It divides
rather than unites; and all dividing laws are reactionary. It is not
a law; it is a *privilege.* One person may do what another person
may not do, and not because the latter lacks the objective capa-
bility for the action, say like a child who cannot draw up con-
tracts, but rather because his intentions are suspect. In an
ethical state the view of the state is subordinated to its members, even if they *oppose an organ of the state* or the *government.* But a society in which *one* organ thinks of itself as the
only, exclusive possessor of reason and morality on the state
level, a government that in principle opposes the people and
assumes that *their subversive attitude* is universal and normal,
the evil conscience of a faction—such a government invents
tendentious laws, *laws of revenge,* against an attitude existing
only in the members of the government themselves. Such laws
are based on a lack of character and on an unethical and materialistic view of the state. They are indiscreet outcries of bad
conscience. And how can a law of this sort be enforced?
Through means more outrageous than the law itself: through
spies or through a priori decisions saying that entire literary
movements must be considered suspect, in which case one must
find out to which movement an individual belongs. In a tendentious law the *legal form contradicts* the *content;* the *government* issuing it passionately denounces the very thing it
represents itself, a subversive attitude. Similarly such a government constitutes, so to speak, an institution *opposed* to its own
laws, using two yardsticks. Lawfulness on the one side is unlaw-
fulness on the other. *Such laws are the opposite of what they
proclaim to be law.*

The *new Censorship Instruction* is entangled in this dialectic. It is contradictory to force the censors to do the very thing
that is condemned as subversive when it takes place in the
press. . . .

The real *cure* would be the *abolition of censorship*. It is a bad institution, but institutions are more powerful than men. It makes no difference whether we are right or wrong, for the Prussian writers will *gain* something *from the new Instruction:* either in *real freedom* or in *ideal freedom,* in **awareness**.

Rara temporum felicitas, ubi quae vilis sentire et quae sentias dicere licet.

[How rare the fortunate times in which you can think what you wish and say what you think. (Tacitus)]

3. Religion and Authority

In an article in the *Rheinische Zeitung* (July, 1842) entitled "On the Leading Article in No. 179 of the *Kölnische Zeitung:* Religion, Free Press, and Philosophy," we find Marx again utilizing the philosophical critique of religion as a means with which to criticize the Prussian state. Claiming that "philosophy demands that the state be the state of human [not divine] nature," he implies that the religious state (i.e., Prussia as the "Christian State") is an irrational state and thus one in need of significant reform.

NEXT THE question is raised: "Should philosophy discuss religious matters even in newspaper articles?"

We can answer this question only by criticizing it.

Philosophy, above all German philosophy, has a tendency toward solitude, toward systematic seclusion, toward dispassionate self-examination which from the outset puts it in opposition to and estranges it from the ready-tongued, alive-to-events newspapers whose only satisfaction is information. In its systematic development philosophy is unpopular, and to the untutored eye its secret weaving within itself seems to be an occupation as overstrained as it is impractical. It is taken to be a professor of magic whose incantations sound pompous because they are incomprehensible.

From *Writings of the Young Marx on Philosophy and Society*, trans. and ed. by L. D. Easton and K. H. Guddat (New York: Doubleday-Anchor, 1967). Used by permission.

In accordance with its character philosophy has never taken the first step toward replacing its ascetic priestly vestments by the light conventional garb of the newspapers. But philosophers do not grow out of the earth like mushrooms; they are the fruit of their time, of their people whose most subtle, precious and invisible sap circulates in philosophical ideas. The same spirit that builds philosophical systems in the brain of the philosophers builds railroads by the hands of the workers. Philosophy does not stand outside the world any more than man's brain is outside him because it is not in his stomach; but philosophy, to be sure, is in the world with its brain before it stands on the earth with its feet, while many other human spheres have long been rooted in the earth and pluck the fruits of the world long before they realize that the "head" also belongs to this world or that this world is the world of the head.

Since every genuine philosophy is the spiritual quintessence of its time, the time must come when philosophy comes into contact and mutual reaction with the actual world not only internally by its content but also externally through its appearance. Then philosophy ceases to be a specific system compared with other specific systems, it becomes philosophy in general compared with the world, it becomes the philosophy of the present world. . . .

If you presume to stand so far above religion as to have the right to separate the general spirit of religion from its positive *embodiments,* what reproach do you have for the philosophers if they want to make this separation complete and not halfway, if they call the human rather than Christian spirit the universal spirit of religion?

Christians live in states with differing constitutions, some in a republic, others in an absolute monarchy, and still others in a constitutional monarchy. Christianity does not decide on the *quality* of constitutions since it knows no distinction among them. It teaches as religion must: Submit to authority, for *every authority* is ordained by God. The justice of state constitutions is therefore to be decided not on the basis of Christianity, not on the basis of the state's own nature and essence, not from the nature of Christian society but from the nature of human society. . . .

There is a dilemma which "sound" common sense cannot withstand.

Either the Christian state corresponds to the concept of the state as the actualization of rational freedom, and then nothing else can be demanded for it to be Christian than that it be rational; then it suffices to develop the state from reason in human relations, a task philosophy accomplishes. Or, the state of rational freedom cannot be developed out of Christianity; then you will yourselves concede that this development does not lie in the tendency of Christianity, since Christianity does not want a bad state and any state is a bad state which is not the actualization of rational freedom.

Answer the dilemma as you will, you must admit that the state is not to be derived from religion but from the rationale of freedom. Only the crassest ignorance can maintain that the theory which makes the state-concept independent is a passing fancy of modern philosophers. . . .

If it is true that no legislature can decree what is ethical, it is even truer that no legislature can recognize it as legal. Statute law is based on an intellectual abstraction intrinsically lacking content, an abstraction which absorbs the natural, legal, and ethical content as external matter, as matter intrinsically lawless, and then attempts to shape, modify, and arrange this spiritless and lawless matter for an external purpose. Statute law does not treat the objective world according to its innate principles but according to capricious, subjective whims and intentions that have nothing to do with the matter itself. The Prussian jurists showed precious little insight into the nature of statute law. They criticized in particular manifestations of its existence but not its essential nature. They were hostile to its reforming tendency but not to the form and method of the new proposed divorce law. They believed they might find proof of bad laws in bad ethics. Above all else we demand that the criticism be critical of itself and not overlook the difficulty of its subject.

4. Law and Morality

In the *Rheinische Zeitung* of December 19, 1842, in an article entitled "On a Proposed Divorce Law," Marx argued along Hegelian lines that statute law (i.e., law made by men) is only an imperfect approximation to the true notion *(Begriff)* of law. Since Hegel had held that both marriage and the state (as "ethical substances") transcend the caprices of their members, the significance of this article goes far beyond the question of divorce. This article is noteworthy for expressing Marx's espousal of the openly democratic stand that the only safeguard against tyrannical laws (since all laws are imperfect) lies in their being the "conscious expression of the will of the people."

WHEN THE opponents of the [proposed divorce law] point to one of these deficiencies, we agree with them but can in no way approve their unconditional apology for the old system. Let us again reiterate the statement made earlier: "If the legislature cannot decree what is ethical, it can even less recognize what is unethical as legal." When we ask about the basis of the argument of *these* opponents (not the opponents of the ecclesiastical view and critics of the other deficiencies noted), they always talk of the misery of spouses bound to each other against their will. They take an eudaemonistic view. They think only of two

From *Writings of the Young Marx on Philosophy and Society,* trans. and ed. by L. D. Easton and K. H. Guddat (New York: Doubleday-Anchor, 1967). Used by permission.

individuals and forget the *family*. They forget that nearly every dissolution of a marriage is the dissolution of a family and that the children and what belongs to them should not be dependent on arbitrary whims, even from a purely legal point of view. If marriage were not the basis of the family, it would not be subject to legislation, just as friendship is not. Those opponents, therefore, take into account *only* individual will, or rather the *caprice* of the spouses; they do not consider the *will of marriage*, the ethical substance of this relationship. The legislator, however, must consider himself a naturalist. He does not *make* laws; he does not invent them; he only formulates them. He expresses the inner principles of spiritual relationships in conscious, positive laws. The legislator would have to be accused of gross arbitrariness if he permitted his whims to replace the nature of things. But it is his right to regard it as gross arbitrariness if private persons want their whims to prevail against the nature of things. Nobody is forced to enter into a marriage, but everybody must be forced to make up his mind that he will obey the laws of marriage when he enters into it. A person entering into marriage does not *make* or *invent* it just as a swimmer does not invent nature and the laws of water and gravity. Marriage, therefore, cannot yield to his arbitrariness; rather, his arbitrariness must yield to marriage. Anyone who arbitrarily breaks a marriage maintains that arbitrariness, *lawlessness, constitutes the law of marriage*, for no reasonable person would be so presumptuous as to consider his acts privileged acts, acts appropriate for *him alone*. Instead, he will pass them off as legal acts *appropriate for all*. What do you oppose then? Legislation by arbitrariness. But you certainly won't want to turn arbitrariness into law at the very moment you accuse the legislator of arbitrariness.

Hegel says: *Implicitly* and in accordance with its concept, marriage should be indissoluble, but *only* implicitly, that is, only in accordance with its concept. This says nothing which is *peculiar* to marriage. All ethical relationships are by *their very concept* indissoluble, as one can easily find by assuming their *truth*. A *true* state, a *true* marriage, a *true* friendship is indissoluble; but there is no state, no marriage, no friendship that completely corresponds to its concept. Actual friendship even within the family is *dissoluble;* the actual state in world history is dissoluble; and so is actual marriage in the state. No ethical *existence* corresponds to its *essence,* or at least does not *have to* correspond to it. In nature itself there is dissolution and death when a particular existent no longer fully corresponds to its essential determination. World history decides whether a state is so much at odds with the idea of the state that it no longer deserves to continue. Similarly the state decides under which conditions an *existing* marriage has ceased to be a marriage. Divorce is nothing but the declaration that a marriage is *dead* and that its existence is only pretense and deception. It is obvious that neither the arbitrariness of the legislator nor that of private persons can decide whether or not a marriage is dead. Only the *nature of things* can do that, for a *death certificate,* as is well known, depends on factual evidence and not on the *wishes* of the interested parties. Now, as precise unmistakable proof is required for *physical* death, the legislator can declare an *ethical* death only in the presence of the most indubitable symptoms, since to conserve the life of ethical relationships is not only his right but also his *duty,* the duty of his self-preservation.

The *guarantee,* however, that the *conditions* will be fairly substantiated under which the *existence* of an ethical relationship no longer corresponds to its *essence* and is no longer commensurate with reliable knowledge and universal insight—this guarantee will be present only when law is the conscious expression of the will of the people, created with and through it. Let us add a word about making divorce easier or more difficult: Do you consider a natural body healthy, sound, and truly organized if any external shock, any injury, would destroy it? Wouldn't you feel offended if it were an established axiom that your friendship could not withstand the smallest accidents and *would have to* dissolve on account of any crotchet? In regard to marriage, however, the legislator can only determine when it *may* be dissolved, though essentially it already is *dissolved.*

The judicial dissolution can be only the recording of the inner dissolution. The viewpoint of the legislator is the viewpoint of necessity. Believing marriage to be strong enough to withstand many collisions without harm, the legislator shows *reverence* for marriage and recognizes its deeply ethical nature. Compliance with the wishes of individuals would become harshness against their essential nature, against their ethical rationality which is embodied in ethical relationships. . . .

5. The Social Base of Politics

In January, 1843, Marx openly began advocating the cause of the economically distressed vintagers of the Mosel region. We note with interest a short passage from his article "Defense of the Mosel Correspondent: Economic Distress and Freedom of the Press," in which, for the first time, he begins to speak of the effect of economic conditions in determining certain courses of political action. This is the kernel of the theory of historical materialism to be subsequently developed.

IN THE investigation of *political* conditions one is too easily tempted to overlook *the objective nature of the relationships* and to explain everything from the *will* of the persons acting. There are *relationships*, however, which determine the actions of private persons as well as those of individual authorities, and which are as independent as are the movements in breathing. Taking this objective standpoint from the outset, one will not presuppose an exclusively good or bad will on either side. Rather, one will observe relationships in which only persons appear to act at first. As soon as it is demonstrated that something was *necessitated* by conditions, it will not be difficult to figure out under which *external* circumstances this thing *actually* had to come into being, and under which other circum-

From *Writings of the Young Marx on Philosophy and Society,* trans. and ed. by L. D. Easton and K. H. Guddat (New York: Doubleday-Anchor, 1967). Used by permission.

stances it could not have come about although a need for it was present. One can determine this with almost the same certainty as a chemist determines under which *external* circumstances some substances will form a compound. . . .

6. In Praise of Democracy

In his first major (although unpublished) work, *Critique of Hegel's Philosophy of Right* (1843), Marx takes up the defense of democracy against all other forms of the state, on the basis of the principle that "the state is an abstraction, only the people is a concrete fact." In the short excerpts to follow we see Marx combating monarchy (as advocated by Hegel) in the name of democracy, and bureaucracy in the name of the citizenry who, in a truly rational state, would participate by voting in *all* the state's decisions and thus make the bureaucracy superfluous. The reader should take note of the crucial distinction made by Marx between civil society (the domain of individual interests) and the political state (the domain of collective, or "universal," interests).

IN MONARCHY, the whole, the people, is subsumed under one of its particular modes of existence, under political constitution. In democracy the *constitution itself* appears only as *one* determination, and indeed the self-determination of the people. In monarchy we have the people of the constitution; in democracy the constitution of the people. Democracy is the solution of the *problem* of all constitutions. In democracy the constitution is always based on its actual foundation, on *actual man* and the *actual people*, not only *implicitly* and in its essence, but in its

From *Writings of the Young Marx on Philosophy and Society*, trans. and ed. by L. D. Easton and K. H. Guddat (New York: Doubleday-Anchor, 1967). Used by permission.

existence and actuality. Here the constitution is man's and the people's *own* work. The constitution appears as what it is: the free product of man. One could say that in some respect this is true also of constitutional monarchy, but the specific difference in democracy is that here the *constitution* is only *one* particular moment of the people and that the *political constitution* in itself does not form the state.

Hegel proceeds from the state and makes man into the state subjectivized. Democracy proceeds from man and makes the state into man objectivized. Just as religion does not create man, but man creates religion, so the constitution does not create the people, but the people create the constitution. In some respects democracy is related to all other forms of state, as Christianity is related to all other religions. Christianity is . . . the *essence of religion*, deified man as a *particular* religion. Similarly democracy is the *essense of every* constitution, socialized man as a *particular* constitution. Democracy is related to other constitutions as a species is related to its modifications. Only, in democracy the species itself is existent as a *particular* modification distinct from existences that do not correspond to their essence. Democracy is the Old Testament of all other forms of state. Man does not exist for the law, but the law exists for man. In democracy there is *particular human existence*, while in other forms of state man is the *particular juridical existence*. This is the basic uniqueness of democracy.

All other *state formations* are a certain, definite, *particular form of state*. In democracy the *formal* principle is at the same time the *material* principle. Only democracy, therefore, is the true unity of the general and the particular. In monarchy, for example, and in a republic as only a particular form of state, political man has his particular existence alongside unpolitical man, private man. Property, contract, marriage, civil society here appear as *particular* modes of existence alongside the *political* state. . . . They appear as the *content* related to the *political state* as the *organizing form*, actually only as determining, limiting understanding, contentless in itself, at one time affirmative, at another time negative. . . .

Hegel is right, therefore, when he says: the political state is the constitution, that is, the material state is not political. There is only an external identity here; a mutual determination takes place. Of the various phases in a people's life the most difficult was the formation of the political state, the constitution. It emerged as universal reason in contrast to other spheres, and as the aspect most removed from these spheres. The historical problem then was their revindication, but the particular spheres are not aware that their private nature coincides with the distant nature of the constitution or political state, and the far removed existence of the political state is nothing but the affirmation of their own alienation. Up to now the *political constitution* has been the *religious sphere*, the *religion* of the people's life, the heaven of their universality in contrast to the particular *mundane existence* of their actuality. . . . *Political life* in the modern sense of the word is the *scholasticism* of a people's life. *Monarchy* is the completed expression of this alienation. The *republic* is the negation of alienation within alienation. It is obvious that a political constitution as such is formed only where the private spheres have achieved independent existence. Where trade and property are unfree and still not independent, the political constitution also is unfree and still not independent. . . .

The abstraction of the *state as such* belongs only to modern times because the abstraction of private life belongs only to these times. The abstraction of the *political state* is a modern product.

In the Middle Ages there was the serf, the fief, the guild, the scholastic corporation, etc., that is to say, in the Middle Ages property, trade, society, man was *political*. The material content of the state was set by its form. Each private sphere had a political character or was one political sphere, and politics was characteristic of the private spheres. In the Middle Ages the political constitution was the constitution of private property but only because the constitution of private property was political. In the Middle Ages the life of the people and the life of the state were identical. Man was the actual principle of the state, but it was man as *unfree*. Thus it was the *democracy of unfreedom*, perfected alienation. The abstract, reflected antithesis belongs only to the modern world. The Middle Ages is *actual* dualism; the modern period is *abstract* dualism. . . .

Bureaucracy is the imaginary state beside the real state, the spiritualism of the state. Hence everything has a double meaning, a real and a bureaucratic meaning, just as knowledge and also the will are something double, real, and bureaucratic. What is real is dealt with in its bureaucratic nature, in its otherworldly spiritual essence. Bureaucracy possesses the state's essence, the spiritual essence of society, as its *private property*. The universal spirit of bureaucracy is the *secret*, the mystery sustained within bureaucracy itself by hierarchy and maintained on the outside as a closed corporation. The open spirit and sentiment of patriotism, hence, appear to bureaucracy as a *betrayal* of this mystery. So *authority* is the principle of its knowledge, and the deification of authority is its *sentiment*. But within bureaucracy *spiritualism* becomes a *crass materialism*, the materialism of passive obedience, of faith in authority, of the *mechanism* of fixedly formal activity, fixed principles, views, and traditions. For the individual bureaucrat the state's purpose becomes his private purpose of *hunting for higher positions* and *making a career* for himself. In one respect he views actual life as something *material*, for *the spirit of this life has its separate existence* in bureaucracy. Bureaucracy, therefore, must aim to make life as material as possible. . . .

In bureaucracy the identity of the state's interest and particular private purpose is established in such a way that the *state's interest* becomes a *particular* private purpose opposed to other private purposes.

The transcendence of bureaucracy can mean only that the universal interest becomes the particular interest *in actuality* and not, as with Hegel, merely in thought and *abstraction*. This is possible only when the *particular* interest becomes *universal*. Hegel proceeds from an unreal antithesis and hence develops it only to an imaginary identity really antithetical to itself. Such an identity is the bureaucracy. . . .

Hegel has the "state proper," the "governing power," move

into the "service" of the "state's universal interest and of legality, etc." within civil society through "deputies." According to him these "governing deputies" are particularly the "executive civil servants," the *true "representation of the state"* not "of," but "against civil society." Thus the antithesis of state and society is fixed. The state does not reside in but outside civil society. The state makes contact with civil society only through its *"deputies,"* to whom *"service of the state"* is entrusted within this area. The antithesis is not transcended through these "deputies," but becomes a "legal" and "fixed" antithesis. With the deputies against civil society the "state" amounts to something apart from and alien to the *nature* of civil society. "Police," "courts," and "administration" are not deputies of civil society itself, which maintains its *own* universal interest in them and through them, but they are deputies of the state to safeguard the state against civil society.

What counts in the genuine state is not the chance of any citizen to devote himself to the universal class as something special, but the capacity of the universal class to be actually universal, that is, to be the class of every citizen. But Hegel proceeds from the premise of a pseudo-universal, an illusory-universal class, from the premise of universality as a particular class.

The identity Hegel has set up between civil society and the state is the identity of *two hostile armies,* where any soldier has the "chance" to join the "enemy" through "desertion." Thus does Hegel correctly describe the existing empirical situation.

. . . Before we discuss the category of *election* as the political act by which civil society decides upon its political representation, let us look at some additional definitions taken from the Remark on this paragraph.

"The idea that all as individuals should participate in deliberating and deciding on political matters of general concern because everyone is a member of the state, because the state's concerns are the concern of *all,* and because they have a *right* to participate with their knowledge and will—this idea resulted in the intention to put the *democratic* element *without any rational form* into the organism of the state which would need such a form to be an organism. This idea occurs so readily because it stops at the *abstract* definition of being a member of the state; and superficial thinking clings to abstractions."

First of all, Hegel calls "being a member of the state an *abstract* definition," although it is the highest and *most concrete* social definition of the legal person, of the member of the state —and this even in accordance with the *Idea*, the *meaning* of his own development. To stop at the "definition of being a member of the state" and to conceive of the individual in terms of this definition does not after all seem to be the "superficial thinking that clings to abstraction." However, it is not the fault of this thinking that the "definition of being a member of the state" is *"abstract";* it is the fault of Hegel's train of thought and of actual modern conditions which presuppose the separation of actual life from political life and turn the quality of the state into an "abstract definition" of actual political participation.

The immediate participation of *all* in deliberating and deciding on political matters of general concern according to Hegel incorporates "the *democratic* element *without any rational form* into the organism of the state which would *need* such a form to be an organism." In other words, only a state organism that is merely the formalism of the state can incorporate the democratic element as a *formal* element. But the democratic element should be the actual element that acquires its *rational form* within the state organism as a *whole*. If this element enters the state organism or state formalism as a *"particular"* element, then . . . it would appear only as a *formal* principle.

We have already indicated that Hegel develops merely a *state formalism*. For him the only *material* principle is the *Idea*, the abstract thought-*form* of the state as subject, the absolute Idea lacking any passive, any *material* aspect. In contrast to this abstract Idea, the definitions of the actual, empirical state-formalism appear as *content*. Thus the *actual* content (here actual man, actual society, etc.) appears as formless, inorganic matter. . . .

In a really rational state one could answer, "It is not the case that *all as individuals* should participate in deliberating and deciding on political matters of general concern," for the "individuals" participate in deliberating and deciding on political matters of *general concern* as "all," that is, within society and as parts of society. Not all as individuals, but the individuals as all. . . .

The *question* whether civil society is to participate in legislative power *either* through *deputies* or immediately through "all as individuals" is itself a question within the *abstraction of the political state* or within the *abstract political state;* it is an *abstract* political question. . . .

The contradiction essentially is: the *individuals participate as all,* or the *individuals* participate as *few, not all.* In either case the allness is only the *external* multiplicity or totality of individuals. The allness is no essential, no spiritual, no actual quality of the individual. The allness is not something that could deprive the individual of abstract individuality; rather it is only the *sum* total of *individuality. One* individuality, *many* individualities, *all* individualities. The one, the mass, the all— none of these qualifications alters the *essence* of the subject, individuality.

"All" should "as individuals . . . participate in deliberating and deciding on political matters of general concern." On this basis, then, *all* should not participate as all, but as "individuals." . . .

The issue seems to contradict itself in two respects.

The political matters of general concern are the state's concern, the state as *actual concern.* Deliberations and decisions are the *effectuation* of the state as actual concern. It seems obvious that all members of the state have a *relationship* to the state as their *actual concern.* The term *member of the state* already implies being a *part* of the state and the state's including it as *its part.* However, if the member of the state is an *integral part* of the state, its social presence obviously is already *its actual participation* in the state. They *are* not only integral with the state, but the state is integral *with them.* To be consciously integral with something means to take part in it consciously, to be consciously integral with it. Without this consciousness the member of the state would be an *animal.*

With the phrase, "political matters of general concern," it

appears as though the "matters of general concern" and the "state" are something *different*. But the *state* is the "matter of general concern," hence really, "matters of general concern."

To take part in the political matters of general concern and to take part in the state are identical. It is a *tautology* to say that a member of the state, a part of the state, takes part in the state, and this taking part can appear only in the form of deliberation or decision, or some such forms, and to say at the same time that every member of the state participates in *deliberating* and *deciding* on political matters of general concern (if these functions are conceived as functions of the *actual* participation of the state). If Hegel speaks of *actual* members of the state, he cannot speak of this participation as something that *should be*. Otherwise he would speak of subjects that *should* be or *want* to be *members of the state* but really *are* not. . . .

The question whether *"all as individuals* participate in deliberating and deciding on political matters of general concern" arises from the separation of the political state from civil society.

We have seen how the state exists *only* as *political state*. The totality of the political state is the *legislative power*. To take part in this legislative power is therefore to take part in the political state, to prove and actualize one's *existence* as a *member of the political state* or as a *member of the state*. The fact that *all as individuals* wish to take part in legislative power is nothing but the will of *all* to be actual (active) *members of the state*, to give themselves a *political existence*, or to prove and effectuate their *political* existence. . . . The invasion of civil society *en masse*, where possible *totally*, into legislative power and its will to substitute itself an actual for a *fictitious* legislative power—this is nothing but the drive of civil society to give itself *political* existence or to make its *political existence* actual. The drive of *civil society* to become political or to make *political* society *actual* is evident as a drive toward participation in *legislative power* as *universal* as possible. . . .

. . . The question as to whether all as individuals should be members of the legislative power or whether they should enter it through deputies throws into question the *representative* principle within the principle of representation and within the fundamental perspective of the political state existing in constitutional monarchy. 1. The view of the political state as an abstraction is the view that the *legislative power* is the *totality* of the political state. Since this *one* act is the only *political* act of civil society, *all* should and want to participate in it at once. 2. *All* as *individuals.* In the *element pertaining to estates* the legislative activity is not viewed as *social* or a function of *sociality,* but rather as the act in which individuals assume an actually and *consciously social* function, that is, a political function. The *legislative power* is here no outcome, no function of society, but only its *formation.* The formation into legislative power demands that *all* members of civil society regard themselves as *individuals* and act as such. "To be members of the state" is their "abstract definition," a definition which is not realized in living actuality.

There are two possibilities: (1) The political state and civil society are separated. In that case it is not possible that *all as individuals* participate in legislative power. The existence of the political state is *separated* from that of civil society. If all were to be legislators, civil society would have to abolish itself. On the other hand, the political state distinct from civil *society* can only tolerate it in a form that satisfies its *criterion.* Or the participation of civil society in the political state through *deputies* is precisely the *expression* of the separation and merely dualistic unity.

(2) The reverse may occur: Civil society is *actual* political society. Then it would be nonsense to make a claim which has emerged only from the notion of the political state as an existence separated from civil society and from the *theological* notion of the political state. In this situation the significance of *legislative* power as a *representative* power disappears altogether. The legislative power is here representation in the sense that *every* function is representative, as the cobbler, for example, is my representative when he meets a social need; as every specific social activity in a field represents only that field or a specification of my own nature; and as every man is the representative of others. He is the representative not through

something else that he appears to be, but through what he *is* and *does*.

"Legislative" power is something to be aimed at not because of its *content*, but because of its *formal* political significance. Concretely, the goal of popular desire has to be *governmental power* much more than the legislative, *metaphysical* political function. The legislative function is will, not in its practical but in its theoretical energy. Here *will* should not *displace law*, but the *discovery* and *formulation* of actual law is the important thing. . . .

Within the representative constitution . . . it is not a question whether civil society should exercise legislative power through deputies or through all as individuals. Rather it is a question of the *extent* and greatest possible *universalization* of *voting*, of *active* as well as *passive* suffrage. This is the real bone of contention of political *reform*, in France as well as in England.

If *voting* is immediately put into the context of *princely* or *governmental power*, it is not viewed philosophically, not in its own special nature. *Voting* is the *actual relationship* of *actual civil society* to the *civil society* of the *legislative power*, to the *representative element*. Or, *voting* is the *immediate, direct* relationship of civil society to the political state, not *only in appearance but in existence*. Hence it is obvious that *voting* is the paramount political interest of actual civil society. Only in *unlimited voting*, active as well as passive, does civil society *actually* rise to an abstraction of itself, to *political* existence as its true universal and essential existence. But the realization of this abstraction is also the transcendence of the abstraction. By making its *political existence* actual as its *true* existence, civil society also makes its civil existence *unessential* in contrast to its political existence. And with the one thing separated, the other, its opposite, falls. Within the *abstract political state* the reform of voting is the *dissolution* of the state, but likewise the *dissolution of civil society*.

7. Critical Philosophy and Social Reform

The following three selections are all taken from the one published issue of the *Deutsch-Französische Jahrbücher*, edited by Marx in Paris in January, 1844. As a whole they document Marx's growing disenchantment with democratic ideals and his gradual approach to the point where, during the rest of 1844, he was to progressively adopt socialistic ideas.

The first of these three selections from the *Jahrbücher* is the complete text of a letter from Marx to Arnold Ruge written in the course of Marx's journey into exile in Paris, where he was to establish the *Jahrbücher* with Ruge's financial backing. This letter is noteworthy in containing Marx's first evaluation of the primitive communist movements of the day, and especially for the significant insight that their advocacy of the mere "dissolution of private property . . . is in no way identical with communism" as Marx understands it. He goes on to criticize these movements for their alleged one-sided conception of human nature, an error which Marx was to fully excoriate later in 1844 in his important *Economic and Philosophical Manuscripts*.

Kreuznach, in September 1843

I AM glad that you are determined and turn your thoughts from retrospect on the past toward a new undertaking. Hence to

From *Writings of the Young Marx on Philosophy and Society,* trans and ed. by L. D. Easton and K. H. Guddat (New York: Doubleday-Anchor, 1967). Used by permission.

Paris, the old high school of philosophy, *absit omen!* and the new capital of the new world. Whatever is necessary comes to pass. I do not doubt, therefore, that all obstacles, whose weight I do not underestimate, can be removed.

The undertaking may come about or not. At any rate I shall be in Paris at the end of this month, because the air here makes me a serf and I see no room at all for free activity in Germany.

In Germany everything is suppressed by force. A real anarchy of the mind, the regime of stupidity itself, has set in, and Zurich obeys the orders coming from Berlin. It is becoming clearer and clearer, therefore, that a new gathering point for the really thinking and independent minds must be sought. I am convinced that a real demand will be met by our plan, and it must be possible really to fulfill the real demand. I have no doubts about the undertaking, once we mean business.

Even greater than the external obstacles seem to be the inner ones. Even though there is no doubt about the "whence," there does prevail all the more confusion about the "whither." It is not only the fact that a general anarchy has broken out among the reformers; each one will have to admit to himself that he has no exact idea of what is to happen. But that is exactly the advantage of the new direction, namely, that we do not anticipate the world dogmatically, but rather wish to find the new world through criticism of the old. Until now the philosophers had the solution to all riddles in their desks, and the stupid outside world simply had to open its mouth so that the roasted pigeons of absolute science might fly into it. Philosophy has become secularized, and the most striking proof for this is the fact that the philosophical consciousness itself is drawn into the torment of struggle, not only outwardly but inwardly as well. Even though the construction of the future and its completion for all times is not our task, what we have to accomplish at this time is all the more clear: *relentless criticism of all existing conditions,* relentless in the sense that the criticism is not afraid of its findings and just as little afraid of the conflict with the powers that be.

I am not for setting up a dogmatic standard. On the contrary, we must attempt to help the dogmatists make their dogmas clear to themselves. Especially *communism* thus is a dogmatic abstraction; I have in mind the actually existing communism, as Cabet, Dézamy, Weitling, etc., teach it, not some other imagined or possible one. This communism is itself only a separate phenomenon of the humanistic principle, infected by its opposite, private advantage. Dissolution of private property, therefore, is in no way identical with communism, and communism saw the origin of other socialistic doctrines like those of Fourier, Proudhon, etc., not accidentally but necessarily in opposition to itself, because communism itself is only a special, one-sided realization of the socialistic principle.

And the entire socialistic principle, in turn, is only one side of the *reality* of true human nature. We have to be concerned just as much with the other side, the theoretical life of man. Hence, we have to make religion, science, etc., the object of our criticism. Moreover, we wish to influence our contemporaries, our German contemporaries. The question is how to go about it. Two facts cannot be denied; religion and politics are matters now forming focal points of Germany's interest. No matter how these may be, we must begin with them, not oppose them with any one fixed system, as for example the *Voyage to Icaria* [by Etienne Cabet].

Reason has always existed, but not always in rational form. The critic, therefore, can start with any form of theoretical and practical consciousness and develop the true actuality out of the forms *inherent* in existing actuality as its ought-to-be and goal. As far as actual life is concerned, the *political state* especially contains in all its *modern* forms the demands of reason, even where the political state is not yet conscious of socialistic demands. And the political state does not stop here. Everywhere it claims reason as realized. Equally, however, it everywhere gets into the contradiction between its ideal character and its real presuppositions.

Social truth, therefore, can be developed everywhere out of this conflict of the political state with itself. Just as *religion* is the table of contents of the theoretical struggles of mankind, the *political state* is that of the practical ones. The political state, therefore, expresses all social struggles, needs, and truths within its form *sub specie rei publicae.* By no means, then, is the most specific political problem—such as the difference between the estate system and the representative system—to be the object of our critique on account of the *hauteur des principes*. For this question merely expresses in a *political* way the differences between the control of man and the control of private property. The critic not only can but must enter into these political problems, which crass socialists regard as below their dignity. By developing the advantage of the representative system over the estate system the critic gets a large party *interested practically*. By elevating the representative system from its political context to a general context and by claiming the true significance that is due to it, he at the same time forces this party to go beyond itself, for its victory is simultaneously its loss.

Nothing prevents us, therefore, from starting our criticism with criticism of politics, with taking sides in politics, hence with *actual* struggles, and identifying ourselves with them. Then we do not face the world in doctrinaire fashion with a new principle, declaring, "Here is truth, kneel here!" We develop new principles for the world out of the principles of the world. We do not tell the world, "Cease your struggles, they are stupid; we want to give you the true watchword of the struggle." We merely show the world why it actually struggles; and the awareness of this is something the world *must* acquire even if it does not want to.

The reform of consciousness exists *merely* in the fact that one makes the world aware of its consciousness, that one awakens the world out of its own dream, that one *explains* to the world its own acts. Our entire purpose consists in nothing else (as is also the case in Feuerbach's criticism of religion) but bringing the religious and political problems into the self-conscious human form.

Our slogan, therefore, must be: Reform of consciousness, not through dogmas, but through analysis of the mystical consciousness that is unclear about itself, whether in religion or politics. It will be evident, then, that the world has long dreamed of something of which it only has to become conscious in order to possess it in actuality. It will be evident that there is not a big blank between the past and the future, but rather that it is a matter of *realizing* the thoughts of the past. It will be evident, finally, that mankind does not begin any *new* work but performs its old work consciously.

Therefore, we can express the aim of our periodical in *one* phrase: A self-understanding (critical philosophy) of the age concerning its struggles and wishes. This is a task for the world and for us. It must be the work of united forces. It is a *confession*, nothing else. To have its sins forgiven, mankind has only to declare them for what they are.

8. Philosophy and the Proletariat

The article "Toward a Contribution to the Critique of Hegel's *Philosophy of Right,*" which appeared in the *Deutsch-Französische Jahrbücher,* is Marx's second critique of this major work of Hegel. The argument, however, focuses upon the relation between philosophy, especially German philosophy, and the practical movement toward "universal human emancipation," rather than on Hegel's text itself. Among many significant insights into the current backwardness of Germany, this article also contains Marx's first discussion of the role to be played by the proletariat in this movement. He closes with a ringing appeal for the unity of theory and practice, of philosophy and the proletariat, in carrying forward this struggle.

FOR GERMANY, the *criticism of religion* has been largely completed; and the criticism of religion is the premise of all criticism.

. . . Man, who has found in the fantastic reality of heaven, where he sought a supernatural being, only his own reflection, will no longer be tempted to find only the *semblance* of himself —a non-human being—where he seeks and must seek his true reality.

The basis of irreligious criticism is this: *man makes religion; religion does not make man.* Religion is indeed man's self-con-

From *Karl Marx: Early Writings,* ed. by T. B. Bottomore, (New York: McGraw-Hill, 1963). Used by permission.

sciousness and self-awareness so long as he has not found himself or has lost himself again. But *man* is not an abstract being, squatting outside the world. Man is *the human world*, the state, society. This state, this society, produce religion which is an *inverted world consciousness*, because they are an *inverted world*. Religion is the general theory of this world, its encyclopedic compendium, its logic in popular form, its spiritual *point d'honneur*, its enthusiasm, its moral sanction, its solemn complement, its general basis of consolation and justification. It is *the fantastic realization* of the human being inasmuch as the *human being* possesses no true reality. The struggle against religion is, therefore, indirectly a struggle against *that world* whose spiritual *aroma* is religion.

Religious suffering is at the same time an *expression* of real suffering and a *protest* against real suffering. Religion is the sigh of the oppressed creature, the sentiment of a heartless world, and the soul of soulless conditions. It is the *opium* of the people.

The abolition of religion as the *illusory* happiness of men, is a demand for their *real* happiness. The call to abandon their illusions about their condition is a *call to abandon a condition which requires illusions*. The criticism of religion is, therefore, *the embryonic criticism of this vale of tears* of which religion is the *halo*.

Criticism has plucked the imaginary flowers from the chain, not in order that man shall bear the chain without caprice or consolation but so that he shall cast off the chain and pluck the living flower. The criticism of religion disillusions man so that he will think, act and fashion his reality as a man who has lost his illusions and regained his reason; so that he will revolve about himself as his own true sun. Religion is only the illusory sun about which man revolves so long as he does not revolve about himself.

It is the *task of history*, therefore, once the *other-world of truth* has vanished, to establish the *truth of this world*. The immediate *task of philosophy*, which is in the service of history, is to unmask human self-alienation in its *secular form* now that it has been unmasked in its *sacred form*. Thus the criticism of heaven is transformed into the criticism of earth, the *criticism of religion* into the *criticism of law,* and the *criticism of theology* into the *criticism of politics.* . . .

Just as the nations of the ancient world lived their prehistory in the imagination, in mythology, so we Germans have lived our post-history in thought, in *philosophy.* We are the *philosophical* contemporaries of the present day without being its *historical* contemporaries. German philosophy is the *ideal prolongation* of German history. When, therefore, we criticize, instead of the *oeuvres incomplètes* of our real history, the *oeuvres posthumes* of our ideal history—*philosophy,* our criticism stands at the center of the problems of which the present age says: *that is the question.* That which constitutes, for the advanced nations, a *practical* break with modern political conditions, is in Germany where these conditions do not yet exist, virtually a *critical* break with their philosophical reflection. . . .

As the determined adversary of the previous form of German political consciousness, the criticism of the speculative philosophy of right does not remain within its own sphere, but leads on to *tasks* which can only be solved by *means of practical activity.*

The question then arises: can Germany attain a practical activity *à la hauteur des principes;* that is to say, a revolution which will raise it not only to the *official level* of the modern nations, but to the *human level* which will be the immediate future of those nations.

It is clear that the arm of criticism cannot replace the criticism of arms. Material force can only be overthrown by material force; but theory itself becomes a material force when it has seized the masses. Theory is capable of seizing the masses when it demonstrates *ad hominem,* and it demonstrates *ad hominem* as soon as it becomes radical. To be radical is to grasp things by the root. But for man the root is man himself. What proves beyond doubt the radicalism of Germany theory, and thus its practical energy, is that it begins from the resolute *positive* abolition of religion. The criticism of religion ends with the doctrine that *man is the supreme being for man.* It ends, therefore, with the *categorical imperative to overthrow all those con-*

ditions in which man is an abased, enslaved, abandoned, contemptible being—conditions which can hardly be better described than in the exclamation of a Frenchman on the occasion of a proposed tax upon dogs: "Wretched dogs! They want to treat you like men!"

Even from the historical standpoint theoretical emancipation has a specific practical importance for Germany. In fact Germany's *revolutionary* past is theoretical—it is the *Reformation*. In that period the revolution originated in the brain of a monk, today in the brain of the philosopher.

Luther, without question, overcame servitude through devotion but only by substituting servitude through *conviction*. He shattered the faith in authority by restoring the authority of faith. He transformed the priests into laymen by turning laymen into priests. He liberated man from external religiosity by making religiosity the innermost essence of man. He liberated the body from its chains because he fettered the heart with chains.

But if Protestantism was not the solution it did at least pose the problem correctly. It was no longer a question, thereafter, of the layman's struggle against the priest outside himself, but of his struggle against his *own internal priest*, against his own *priestly nature*. And if the Protestant metamorphosis of German laymen into priests emancipated the lay popes—the *princes* together with their clergy, the privileged and the philistines—the philosophical metamorphosis of the priestly Germans into men will emancipate the *people*. But just as emancipation will not be confined to princes, so the *secularization* of property will not be limited to the *confiscation of church property*, which was practiced especially by hypocritical Prussia. At that time, the Peasant War, the most radical event in German history, came to grief because of theology.

Today, when theology itself has come to grief, the most unfree phenomenon in German history—our *status quo*—will be shattered by philosophy. On the eve of the Reformation official Germany was the most abject servant of Rome. On the eve of its revolution Germany is the abject servant of those who are far inferior to Rome; of Prussia and Austria, of petty squires and philistines.

But a *radical* revolution in Germany seems to encounter a major difficulty.

Revolutions need a *passive* element, a *material* basis. Theory is only realized in a people so far as it fulfills the needs of the people. Will there correspond to the monstrous discrepancy between the demands of German thought and the answers of German reality a similar discrepancy between civil society and the state, and within civil society itself? Will theoretical needs be directly practical needs? It is not enough that thought should seek to realize itself; reality must also strive toward thought. . . .

It is not *radical* revolution, *universal human* emancipation, which is a Utopian dream for Germany, but rather a partial, *merely* political revolution which leaves the pillars of the building standing. What is the basis of a partial, merely political revolution? Simply this: a *section of civil society* emancipates itself and attains universal domination; a determinate class undertakes, from its *particular situation,* a general emancipation of society. This class emancipates society as a whole, but only on condition that the whole of society is in the same situation as this class; for example, that it possesses or can easily acquire money or culture.

No class in civil society can play this part unless it can arouse, in itself and in the masses, a moment of enthusiasm in which it associates and mingles with society at large, identifies itself with it, and is felt and recognized as the *general representative* of this society. Its aims and interests must genuinely be the aims and interests of society itself, of which it becomes in reality the social head and heart. It is only in the name of general interests that a particular class can claim general supremacy. In order to attain this liberating position, and the political direction of all spheres of society, revolutionary energy and consciousness of its own power do not suffice. For a *popular revolution* and the *emancipation of a particular class* of civil society to coincide, for *one* class to represent the whole of society, another class must concentrate in itself all the evils of society, a particular class must embody and represent a general obstacle and limitation. A particular social sphere must be regarded as the *notorious crime* of the whole society, so that emancipation from this sphere appears as a general emancipation. For *one* class to be the liberating class *par excellence*, it is necessary that another class should be openly the oppressing class. The negative significance of the French nobility and clergy produced the positive significance of the bourgeoisie, the class which stood next to them and opposed them.

But in Germany every class lacks the logic, insight, courage and clarity which would make it a negative representative of society. Moreover, there is also lacking in every class the generosity of spirit which identifies itself, if only for a moment, with the popular mind; that genius which pushes material force to political power, that revolutionary daring which throws at its adversary the defiant phrase: *I am nothing and I should be everything.* . . .

[In Germany] each sphere of civil society suffers a defeat before gaining the victory; it erects its own barrier before having destroyed the barrier which opposes it; it displays the narrowness of its views before having displayed their generosity, and thus every opportunity of playing an important role has passed before it properly existed, and each class, at the very moment when it begins its struggle against the class above it, remains involved in a struggle against the class beneath. For this reason, the princes are in conflict with the monarch, the bureaucracy with the nobility, the bourgeoisie with all of them, while the proletariat is already beginning its struggle with the bourgeoisie. The middle class hardly dares to conceive the idea of emancipation from its own point of view before the development of social conditions, and the progress of political theory, show that this point of view is already antiquated, or at least disputable. . . .

Where is there, then, a *real* possibility of emancipation in Germany?

This is our reply. A class must be formed which has *radical chains*, a class in civil society which is not a class of civil society, a class which is the dissolution of all classes, a sphere of society which as a universal character because its sufferings are universal, and which does not claim a *particular redress* because the wrong which is done to it is not a *particular wrong* but *wrong in general*. There must be formed a sphere of society which claims no *traditional* status but only a human status, a sphere which is not opposed to particular consequences but is totally opposed to the assumptions of the German political system; a sphere, finally, which cannot emancipate itself without emancipating itself from all the other spheres of society, without, therefore, emancipating all these other spheres, which is, in short, a *total loss* of humanity and which can only redeem itself by a *total redemption of humanity*. This dissolution of society, as a particular class, is the *proletariat*.

The proletariat is only beginning to form itself in Germany, as a result of the industrial movement. For what constitutes the proletariat is not *naturally existing* poverty, but poverty *artificially produced*, is not the mass of people mechanically oppressed by the weight of society, but the mass resulting from the *disintegration* of society and above all from the disintegration of the middle class. Needless to say, however, the numbers of the proletariat are also increased by the victims of natural poverty and of Christian-Germanic serfdom.

When the proletariat announces the *dissolution of the existing social order*, it only declares the *secret of its* own existence, for it *is* the *effective* dissolution of this order. When the proletariat demands the *negation of private property* it only lays down as a *principle for society* what society has already made a principle *for the proletariat*, and what the *latter* already involuntarily embodies as the negative result of society. Thus the proletarian has the same right, in relation to the new world which is coming into being, as the *German king* has in relation to the existing world when he calls the people *his* people or a horse *his* horse. In calling the people his private property the king simply declares that the owner of private property is king.

Just as philosophy finds its *material* weapons in the proletariat, so the proletariat finds its *intellectual* weapons in philosophy. And once the lightning of thought has penetrated deeply into this virgin soil of the people, the *Germans* will emancipate themselves and become *men*.

Let us sum up these results. The emancipation of Germany is only possible *in practice* if one adopts the point of view of that theory according to which man is the highest being for man. Germany will not be able to emancipate itself from the *Middle Ages* unless it emancipates itself at the same time from the *partial* victories over the Middle Ages. In Germany *no* type of enslavement can be abolished unless *all* enslavement is destroyed. Germany, which likes to get to the bottom of things, can only make a revolution which upsets *the whole order* of things. The *emancipation of Germany* will be an *emancipation of man*. *Philosophy* is the *head* of this emancipation and the *proletariat* is its *heart*. Philosophy can only be realized by the abolition of the proletariat, and the proletariat can only be abolished by the realization of philosophy.

9. *Political Rights* versus *Human Emancipation*

This third selection from the *Deutsch-Französische Jahr-bücher* is Marx's reply to an article by Bruno Bauer demand-ing equal political rights for German Jews as well as Christians. The often difficult argument is essentially this: Bauer had advocated civil equality for both Jews and Christians, that is, the abolition of the "Christian State," hence of German feudalism, in opposition to conservatives who held that the Jews, because of their separate ecclesiastical status, should continue to be denied civil and political rights, that these be reserved only for Christians. Bauer's argument is predicated on the democratic notion of the equality of all persons, as persons, before the law, regardless of religion or any other such factors. Marx, however, takes Bauer's argu-ment one step further (and thus goes beyond the presupposi-tions of liberal democracy), by holding that the real problem lies not on the level of political rights, but on the more funda-mental level of civil society. In other words, *political* emanci-pation is not tantamount to *human* emancipation (Marx's more far-reaching goal) in any society whose conditions make possible the development of the religious psychology of es-cape from "this" world, that is, from the reality of human interaction in "civil society." We thus again see Marx rein-forcing the distinction between civil society (the "material life" of men) and life in the political community (man's "spe-cies-life"), such that (and this point is new for Marx) the politi-cal state is "in relation to civil society just as spiritual as is heaven to earth." The reader may be interested in referring back to the Introduction for a discussion of the concept of religious alienation.

THE GERMAN Jews seek emancipation. What kind of emancipation do they want? *Civil, political* emancipation.

Bruno Bauer replies to them: In Germany no one is politically emancipated. We ourselves are not free. How then could we liberate you? You Jews are *egoists* if you demand for yourselves, as Jews, a special emancipation. You should work, as Germans, for the political emancipation of Germany, and as men, for the emancipation of mankind. You should feel the particular kind of oppression and shame which you suffer, not as an exception to the rule but rather as a confirmation of the rule.

Or do the Jews want to be placed on a footing of equality with the *Christian subjects?* If they recognize the *Christian state* as legally established they also recognize the regime of general enslavement. Why should their particular yoke be irksome when they accept the general yoke? Why should the German be interested in the liberation of the Jew, if the Jew is not interested in the liberation of the German?

The *Christian* state recognizes nothing but *privileges.* The Jew himself, in this state, has the privilege of being a Jew. As a Jew he possesses rights which the Christians do not have. Why does he want rights which he does not have but which the Christians enjoy?

In demanding his emancipation from the Christian state he asks the Christian state to abandon its *religious* prejudice. But does he, the Jew, give up *his* religious prejudice? Has he then the right to insist that someone else should forswear his religion? . . .

Bauer demands, on the one hand, that the Jew should renounce Judaism, and in general that man should renounce religion, in order to be emancipated as a citizen. On the

From *Karl Marx: Early Writings,* ed. by T. B. Bottomore (New York: McGraw-Hill, 1963). Used by permission.

other hand, he considers, and this follows logically, that the political abolition of religion is the abolition of all religion. The state which presupposes religion is not yet a true or actual state. . . .

At this point we see that the Jewish question is considered only from one aspect.

It was by no means sufficient to ask: who should emancipate? who should be emancipated? The critic should ask a third question: *what kind of emancipation* is involved? What are the essential conditions of the emancipation which is demanded? The criticism of *political emancipation* itself was only the final criticism of the Jewish question and its genuine resolution into the *"general question of the age."*

Bauer, since he does not formulate the problem at this level, falls into contradictions. He establishes conditions which are not based upon the nature of *political* emancipation. He raises questions which are irrelevant to his problem, and he resolves problems which leave his question unanswered. . . . We see his own error in the fact that he subjects *only* the "Christian state," and not the "state as such" to criticism, that he does not examine *the relation between political emancipation and human emancipation,* and that he, therefore, poses conditions which are only explicable by his lack of critical sense in confusing political emancipation and universal human emancipation. Bauer askes the Jews: Have you, from your standpoint, the right to demand *political emancipation?* We ask the converse question: from the standpoint of *political* emancipation can the Jew be required to abolish Judaism, or man be asked to abolish religion?

The Jewish question presents itself differently according to the state in which the Jew resides. In Germany, where there is no political state, no state as such, the Jewish question is purely *theological.* The Jew finds himself in *religious* opposition to the state, which proclaims Christianity as its foundation. This state is a theologian *ex professo.* Criticism here is criticism of theology; a double-edged criticism, of Christian and of Jewish theology. And so we move always in the domain of theology, however *critically* we may move therein.

In France, which is a *constitutional* state, the Jewish question is a question of constitutionalism, of the incompleteness *of political emancipation*. Since the *semblance* of a state religion is maintained here, if only in the insignificant and self-contradictory formula of a *religion of the majority*, the relation of the Jews to the state also retains a semblance of religious, theological opposition.

It is only in the free states of North America, or at least in some of them, that the Jewish question loses its *theological* significance and becomes a truly *secular* question. Only where the state exists in its completely developed form can the relation of the Jew, and of the religious man in general, to the political state appear in a pure form, with its own characteristics. The criticism of this relation ceases to be theological criticism when the state ceases to maintain a *theological* attitude toward religion, that is, when it adopts the attitude of a state, i.e. a *political* attitude. Criticism then becomes *criticism of the political state*. And at this point, where the question ceases to be *theological*, Bauer's criticism ceases to be critical.

"There is not, in the United States, either a state religion or a religion declared to be that of a majority, or a predominance of one religion over another. The state remains aloof from all religions." There are even some states in North America in which "the constitution does not impose any religious belief or practice as a condition of political rights." And yet, "no one in the United States believes that a man without religion can be an honest man" [Beaumont]. And North America is preeminently the country of religiosity, as Beaumont, Tocqueville and the Englishman, Hamilton, assure us in unison. However, the states of North America only serve as an example. The question is: what is the relation between *complete* political emancipation and religion? If we find in the country which has attained full political emancipation, that religion not only continues to *exist* but is *fresh* and *vigorous*, this is proof that the existence of religion is not at all opposed to the perfection of the state. But since the existence of religion is the existence of a defect, the source of this defect must be sought in the *nature* of the state itself. Religion no longer appears as the basis, but as the *mani-*

festation of secular narrowness. That is why we explain the religious constraints upon the free citizens by the secular constraints upon them. We do not claim that they must transcend their religious narrowness in order to get rid of their secular limitations. We claim that they will transcend their religious narrowness once they have overcome their secular limitations. We do not turn secular questions into theological questions; we turn theological questions into secular ones. History has for long enough been resolved into superstition; but we now resolve superstition into history. The question of the *relation between political emancipation and religion* becomes for us a question of the *relation between political emancipation and human emancipation*. We criticize the religious failings of the political state by criticizing the political state in its *secular* form, disregarding its religious failings. We express in human terms the contradiction between the state and a *particular religion*. . . .

The *political* emancipation of the Jew or the Christian—of the *religious* man in general—is the *emancipation of* the state from Judaism, Christianity, and *religion* in general. The *state* emancipates itself from religion in its own particular way, in the mode which corresponds to its nature, by emancipating itself from the *state religion;* that is to say, by giving recognition to no religion and affirming purely and simply as a state. To be *politically* emancipated from religion is not to be finally and completely emancipated from religion, because political emancipation is not the final and absolute form of *human* emancipation.

The limits of political emancipation appear at once in the fact that the *state* can liberate itself from a constraint without man himself being *really* liberated; that a state may be a free state without man himself being a *free man*. . . .

Thus the state my have emancipated itself from religion, even though the *immense majority* of people continue to be religious. And the immense majority do not cease to be religious by virtue of being religious *in private*. . . .

Furthermore, by emancipating himself *politically*, man emancipates himself in a *devious way*, through an intermediary, however *necessary* this intermediary may be. Finally, even when he proclaims himself an atheist though the intermediary of the state, that is, when he declares the state to be an atheist, he is still engrossed in religion, because he only recognizes himself as an atheist in a roundabout way, through an intermediary. Religion is simply the recognition of man in a roundabout fashion; that is, through an intermediary. The state is the intermediary between man and human liberty. Just as Christ is the intermediary to whom man attributes all his own divinity and all his religious *bonds,* so the state is the intermediary to which man confides all his nondivinity and all his *human freedom.* . . .

The perfected political state is, by its nature, the *species-life* of man as *opposed* to his material life. All the presuppositions of this egoistic life continue to exist in *civil society outside* the political sphere, as qualities of civil society. Where the political state has attained to its full development, man leads, not only in thought, in consciousness, but in *reality,* in *life,* a double existence—celestial and terrestial. He lives in the *political community,* where he regards himself as a *communal being,* and in *civil society* where he acts simply as a *private individual,* treats other men as means, degrades himself to the role of a mere means, and becomes the plaything of alien powers. The political state, in relation to civil society, is just as spiritual as is heaven in relation to earth. It stands in the same opposition to civil society, and overcomes it in the same manner as religion overcomes the narrowness of the profane world; i.e., it has always to acknowledge it again, reestablish it, and allow itself to be dominated by it. Man, in his *most intimate* reality, in civil society, is a profane being. . . . In the state, . . . where he is regarded as a species-being, man is the imaginary member of an imaginary sovereignty, divested of his real, individual life, and infused with an unreal universality. . . .

Political emancipation certainly represents a great progress. It is not, indeed, the final form of human emancipation, but it is the final form of human emancipation *within* the framework of the prevailing social order. It goes without saying that we are speaking here of real, practical emancipation.

Man emancipates himself *politically* from religion by expelling it from the sphere of public law to that of private law. Religion is no longer the spirit of the *state*, in which man behaves, albeit in a specific and limited way and in a particular sphere, as a species-being, in community with other men. It has become the spirit of *civil society*, of the sphere of egoism and of the *bellum omnium contra omnes*. It is no longer the essence of *community*, but the essence of *differentiation*. It has become what it was at the *beginning*, an expression of the fact that man is *separated* from the *community*, from himself and from other men. It is now only the abstract avowal of an individual folly, a private whim or caprice. The infinite fragmentation of religion in North America, for example, already gives it the *external* form of a strictly private affair. It has been relegated among the numerous private interests and exiled from the life of the community as such. But one should have no illusions about the scope of political emancipation. The division of man into the *public person* and the *private person*, the *displacement* of religion from the state to civil society—all this is not a stage in political emancipation but its consummation. Thus political emancipation does not abolish, and does not even strive to abolish, man's *real* religiosity. . . .

In fact, the perfected Christian state is not the so-called *Christian* state which acknowledges Christianity as its basis, as the state religion, and thus adopts an exclusive attitude toward other religions; it is, rather, the *atheistic* state, the democratic state which relegates religion among the other elements of civil society. The state which is still theological, which still professes officially the Christian creed, and which has not yet dared to declare itself a *state*, has not yet succeeded in expressing in a *human* and *secular* form, in its political *reality*, the human basis of which Christianity is the transcendental expression. The so-called Christian state is simply a *nonstate;* since it is not Christianity as a religion, but only the *human core* of the Christian religion which can realize itself in truly human creations. . . .

The so-called Christian state needs the Christian religion in order to complete itself *as a state*. The democratic state, the real state, does not need religion for its political consummation. On the contrary, it can dispense with religion, because in this case the human core of religion is realized in a profane manner. . . .

But the religious spirit cannot be *really* secularized. For what is it but the *nonsecular* form of a stage in the development of the human spirit? The religious spirit can only be realized if the stage of development of the human spirit which it expresses in religious form, manifests and constitutes itself in its *secular* form. This is what happens in the *democratic* state. The basis of this state is not Christianity but the *human basis* of Christianity. Religion remains the ideal, nonsecular consciousness of its members, because it is the ideal form of the *stage of human development* which has been attained.

The members of the political state are religious because of the dualism between individual life and species-life, between the life of civil society and political life. They are religious in the sense that man treats political life, which is remote from his own individual existence, as if it were his true life; and in the sense that religion is here the spirit of civil society, and expresses the separation and withdrawal of man from man. Political democracy is Christian in the sense that man, not merely one man but every man, is there considered a sovereign being; but it is uneducated, unsocial man, man just as he is in his fortuitous existence, man as he has been corrupted, lost to himself, alienated, subjected to the rule of inhuman conditions and elements, by the whole organization of our society—in short man who is not yet a *real* species-being. Creations of fantasy, dreams, the postulates of Christianity, the sovereignty of man—but of man as an alien being distinguished from the real man—all these become, in democracy, the tangible and present reality, secular maxims. . . .

We have shown, therefore, that political emancipation from religion leaves religion in existence, although this is no longer a privileged religion. The contradiction in which the adherent of a particular religion finds himself in relation to his citizenship is only *one aspect* of the universal *secular contradiction between the political state and* civil society. The consummation of the

Christian state is a state which acknowledges itself simply as a state and ignores the religion of its members. The emancipation of the state from religion is not the emancipation of the real man from religion.

We do not say to the Jews, therefore, as does Bauer: you cannot be emancipated politically without emancipating yourselves completely from Judaism. We say rather: it is because you can be emancipated politically, without renouncing Judaism completely and absolutely, that *political emancipation* itself is not *human* emancipation. If you want to be politically emancipated, without emancipating yourselves humanly, the inadequacy and the contradiction is not entirely in yourselves but in the *nature* and the *category* of political emancipation. . . .

A distinction is made between the rights of man and the rights of the citizen. Who is this *man* distinct from the *citizen?* No one but the *member of civil society.* Why is the member of civil society called "man," simply man, and why are his rights called the "rights of man"? . . . This fact [is] to be explained . . . by the relation between the political state and civil society, and by the nature of political emancipation.

Let us notice first of all that the so-called *rights of man,* as distinct from the *rights of the citizen,* are simply the rights of a *member of civil society,* that is, of egoistic man, of man separated from other men and from the community. The most radical constitution, that of 1793, says: *Declaration of the Rights of Man and of the Citizen:* Article 2. "These rights, etc. (the natural and imprescriptible rights) are: *equality, liberty, security, property.*

What constitutes liberty?

Article 6. "Liberty is the power which man has to do everything which does not harm the rights of others."

Liberty is, therefore, the right to do everything which does not harm others. The limits within which each individual can act without harming others are determined by law, just as the boundary between two fields is marked by a stake. It is a question of the liberty of man regarded as an isolated monad, withdrawn into himself. . . . But liberty as a right of man is not founded upon the relations between man and man, but rather upon the separation of man from man. It is the right of such separation. The right of the *circumscribed* individual, withdrawn into himself.

The practical application of the right of liberty is the right of private property. What constitutes the right of private property?

Article 16 (*Constitution* of 1793). "The right of *property* is that which belongs to every citizen of enjoying and disposing *as he will* of his goods and revenues, of the fruits of his work and industry."

The right of property is, therefore, the right to enjoy one's fortune and to dispose of it as one will; without regard for other men and independently of society. It is the right of self-interest. This individual liberty, and its application, form the basis of civil society. It leads every man to see in other men, not the *realization*, but rather the *limitation* of his own liberty. It declares above all the right "to enjoy and to dispose of *as one will*, one's goods and revenues, the fruits of one's work and industry."

There remain the other rights of man, equality and security.

The term "equality" has here no political significance. It is only the equal right to liberty as defined above; namely that every man is equally regarded as a self-sufficient monad. The Constitution of 1795 defines the concept of liberty in this sense.

Article 5 (*Constitution* of 1795). "Equality consists in the fact that the law is the same for all, whether it protects or punishes."

And security?

Article 8 (*Constitution* of 1793). "Security consists in the protection afforded by society to each of its members for the preservation of his person, his rights, and his property."

Security is the supreme social concept of civil society; the concept of the police. The whole society exists only in order to guarantee for each of its members the preservation of his person, his rights and his property. It is in this sense that Hegel calls civil society "the state of need and of reason."

The concept of security is not enough to raise civil society above its egoism. Security is, rather, the *assurance* of its egoism.

None of the supposed rights of man, therefore, go beyond the egoistic man, man as he is, as a member of civil society; that is, an individual separated from the community, withdrawn into himself, wholly preoccupied with his private interest and acting in accordance with his private caprice. Man is far from being considered, in the rights of man, as a species-being; on the contrary, species-life itself—society—appears as a system which is external to the individual and as a limitation of his original independence. The only bond between men is natural necessity, need and private interest, the preservation of their property and their egoistic persons.

It is difficult enough to understand that a nation which has just begun to liberate itself, to tear down all the barriers between different sections of the people and to establish a political community, should solemnly proclaim (*Declaration* of 1791) the rights of the egoistic man, separated from his fellow-men and from the community, and should renew this proclamation at a moment when only the most heroic devotion can save the nation (and is, therefore, urgently called for), and when the sacrifice of all the interests of civil society is in question and egoism should be punished as a crime. (*Declaration of the Rights of Man, etc.,* 1793.) The matter becomes still more incomprehensible when we observe that the political liberators reduce citizenship, the *political community,* to a mere *means* for preserving these so-called rights of man; and consequently, that the citizen is declared to be the servant of egoistic "man," that the sphere in which man functions as a species-being is degraded to a level below the sphere where he functions as a partial being, and finally that it is man as a bourgeois and not man as a citizen who is considered the *true* and *authentic* man. . . .

But the problem is easily solved.

Political emancipation is at the same time the *dissolution* of the old society, upon which the sovereign power, the alienated political life of the people, rests. Political revolution is a revolution of civil society. What was the nature of the old society? It can be characterized in one word: *feudalism.* The old civil society had a *directly political* character; that is, the elements of civil life such as property, the family, and types of occupation had been raised, in the form of lordship, caste and guilds, to elements of political life. They determined, in this form, the relation of the individual to the *state as a whole;* that is, his *political* situation, or in other words, his separation and exclusion from the other elements of society. For this organization of national life did not constitute property and labor as social elements; it rather succeeded in *separating* them from the body of the state, and made them *distinct* societies within society. Nevertheless, at least in the feudal sense, the vital functions and conditions of civil society remained political. They excluded the individual from the body of the state, and transformed the *particular* relation which existed between his corporation and the state into a general relation between the individual and social life, just as they transformed his specific civil activity and situation into a general activity and situation. As a result of this organization, the state as a whole and its consciousness, will and activity—the general political power—also necessarily appeared as the *private* affair of a ruler and his servants, separated from the people.

The political revolution which overthrew this power of the ruler, which made state affairs the affairs of the people, and the political state a matter of *general* concern, i.e., a real state, necessarily shattered everything—estates, corporations, guilds, privileges—which expressed the separation of the people from community life. The political revolution therefore *abolished* the *political character of civil society.* It dissolved civil society into its basic elements, on the one hand *individuals,* and on the other hand the *material and cultural elements* which formed the life experience and the civil situation of these individuals. It set free the political spirit which had, so to speak, been dissolved, fragmented and lost in the various culs-de-sac of feudal society; it reassembled these scattered fragments, liberated the political spirit from its connection with civil life and made of it the community sphere, the *general* concern of the people, in principle independent of these particular elements of civil life. A *specific* activity and situation in life no longer had any but an individual significance. They no longer constituted the general relation between the individual and the state as a whole. Public affairs as such became the general affair of each individual, and political functions became general functions.

But the consummation of the idealism of the state was at the same time the consummation of the materialism of civil society. The bonds which had restrained the egoistic spirit of civil society were removed along with the political yoke. Political emancipation was at the same time an emancipation of civil society from politics and from even the *semblance* of a general content.

Feudal society was dissolved into its basic element, *man;* but into *egoistic* man who was its real foundation.

Man in this aspect, the member of civil society, is now the foundation and presupposition of the *political* state. He is recognized as such in the rights of man. . . .

Thus man was not liberated from religion; he received religious liberty. He was not liberated from property; he received the liberty to own property. He was not liberated from the egoism of business; he received the liberty to engage in business.

The *formation of the political state,* and the dissolution of civil society into independent *individuals* whose relations are regulated by *law,* as the relations between men in the corporations and guilds were regulated by *privilege,* are accomplished by *one and the same act.* Man as a member of civil society— *nonpolitical* man—necessarily appears as the *natural* man. The rights of man appear as natural rights because *conscious* activity is concentrated upon political *action. Egoistic* man is the *passive, given* result of the dissolution of society, an object of *direct apprehension* and consequently a *natural* object. The *political revolution* dissolves civil society into its elements without *revolutionizing* these elements themselves or subjecting them to criticism. This revolution regards civil society, the sphere of human needs, labor, private interests and civil law, as the *basis of its own existence,* as a self-subsistent *precondition,* and thus as its *natural basis.* Finally, man as a member of civil society is identified with *authentic man, man* as distinct from citizen, because he is man in his sensuous, individual and *im-*

mediate existence, whereas *political* man is only abstract, artificial man, man as an *allegorical, moral* person. Thus man as he really is, is seen only in the form of *egoistic* man, and man in his *true* nature only in the form of the *abstract citizen*. . . .

Every emancipation is a *restoration* of the human world and of human relationships to *man himself.*

Political emancipation is a reduction of man, on the one hand to a member of civil society, an *independent* and *egoistic* individual, and on the other hand, to a *citizen*, to a moral person.

Human emancipation will only be complete when the real, individual man has absorbed into himself the abstract citizen; when as an individual man, in his everyday life, in his work, and in his relationships, he has become a *species-being;* and when he has recognized and organized his own powers *(forces propres)* as *social* powers so that he no longer separates this social power from himself as *political* power.

II.

Alienation and Its Overcoming in Communism (1844)

Marx's now widely known *Economic and Philosophical Manuscripts*, written in Paris in 1844, were never intended for publication. Here he developed his first detailed analysis of the processes of estrangement and alienation characteristic of bourgeois society and capitalist production.

Beginning with the presuppositions of the political economists, Marx examined first the alienated condition of the laborers as seen in (1) their relation to the product of their activity; (2) the process of labor itself; (3) the relation of the laborer to nature; (4) the relation of man to man; and (5) their relation to the human potential for freedom and creation. The basis of this condition Marx located in the private property relationship characterized by the reduction of human activity to wage labor as merely one commodity among others. That is, this represents the nearly total dehumanization of the laborer.

In response to this negation of the potentialities of humanity, Marx examines Communism as a proposed solution to this alienation, distinguishing carefully between "vulgar" Communism (determined by the abstract negation of private property and thus still under its sway) and positive Communism, the "real appropriation of human nature through and for man." He discusses the historical basis of Communism and envisions positive Communism as being quite other than a merely utopian dream. It is, rather, to be realized in history through the revolutionary action of the proletariat.

He also examines the foundation of the capitalist process of production in the division of labor and in the social process of exchange characterized and facilitated by money, the (im)moral implications of which Marx sees in what he terms its "fetish" character. This is to claim that in bourgeois society the traditional values have all been debased and replaced by the simple lust for money.

The selections in Part II are taken from Marx's manuscripts of 1844, most from the so-called Economic and Philosophical Manuscripts first edited by D. Riazanov in 1932, and the concluding selection of "Truly Human Production" from Marx's notes on James Mill's *Treatise on Political Economy*.

10. *Alienated Labor*

The first of the *Economic and Philosophical Manuscripts*, from which this selection is taken, is entitled "Alienated Labor." We see Marx's first expression of the concept which forms the cornerstone of his subsequent critique of the capitalist production process and of the bourgeois political economy which remains within its orbit: political economy is unable to detach itself from acquiescence in the alienation of labor which forms the basis of capitalistic enterprise. The selection portrays the important shift from a discussion of political problems to the more fundamental level of labor (= human activity), as well as Marx's newly developed concern with matters of *Praxis* (activity) in addition to philosophy and political theory.

WE HAVE begun from the presuppositions of political economy. We have accepted its terminology and its laws. We presupposed private property, the separation of labor, capital and land, as also of wages, profit and rent, the division of labor, competition, the concept of exchange value, etc. From political economy itself, in its own words, we have shown that the worker sinks to the level of a commodity, and to a most miserable commodity; that the misery of the worker increases with the power and volume of his production; that the necessary result of competition is the accumulation of capital in a few hands, and thus a

---

From *Marx's Concept of Man*, ed. by Erich Fromm, trans. by T. B. Bottomore (New York: Frederick Ungar, 1961). Used by permission.

restoration of monopoly in a more terrible form; and finally that the distinction between capitalist and landlord, and between agricultural laborer and industrial worker, must disappear and the whole of society divide into the two classes of property *owners* and propertyless *workers*.

Political economy begins with the fact of private property; it does not explain it. It conceives the *material process* of private property, as this occurs in reality, in general and abstract formulas which then serve it as laws. It does not *comprehend* these laws; that is, it does not show how they arise out of the nature of private property. Political economy provides no explanation of the basis of the distinction of labor from capital, of capital from land. When, for example, the relation of wages to profits is defined, this is explained in terms of the interests of capitalists; in other words, what should be explained is assumed. Similarly, competition is referred to at every point and is explained in terms of external conditions. Political economy tells us nothing about the extent to which these external and apparently accidental conditions are simply the expression of a necessary development. We have seen how exchange itself seems an accidental fact. The only moving forces which political economy recognizes are *avarice* and the *war between the avaricious, competition.* . . .

Thus we have now to grasp the real connection between this whole system of alienation—private property, acquisitiveness, the separation of labor, capital and land, exchange and competition, value and the devaluation of man, monopoly and competition—and the system of *money.*

Let us not begin our explanation, as does the economist, from a legendary primordial condition. Such a primordial condition does not explain anything; it merely removes the question into a gray and nebulous distance. It asserts as a fact or event what it should deduce, namely, the necessary relation between two things; for example, between the division of labor and exchange. . . .

We shall begin from a *contemporary* economic fact. The worker becomes poorer the more wealth he produces and the more his production increases in power and extent. The worker

becomes an ever cheaper commodity the more goods he creates. The *devaluation* of the human world increases in direct
relation with the *increase in value* of the world of things. Labor
does not only create goods; it also produces itself and the
worker as a *commodity*, and indeed in the same proportion as
it produces goods.

This fact simply implies that the object produced by labor, its
product, now stands opposed to it as an *alien* bring, as a *power
independent* of the producer. The product of labor is labor
which has been embodied in an object and turned into a physical thing; this product is an *objectification* of labor. The performance of work is at the same time its objectification. The
performance of work appears in the sphere of political
economy as a *vitiatian* of the worker, objectification as a *loss*
and as *servitude* to the object, and appropriation as *alienation*.

So much does the performance of work appear as vitiation
that the worker is vitiated to the point of starvation. So much
does objectification appear as loss of the object that the worker
is deprived of the most essential things not only of life but also
of work. Labor itself becomes an object which he can acquire
only by the greatest effort and with unpredictable interrup-
tions. So much does the appropriation of the object appear as
alienation that the more objects the worker produces the fewer
he can possess and the more he falls under the domination of
his product, of capital.

All these consequences follow from the fact that the worker
is related to the *product of his labor* as to an *alien* object. For
it is clear on this presupposition that the more the worker expends himself in work the more powerful becomes the world
of objects which he creates in face of himself, the poorer he
becomes in his inner life, and the less he belongs to himself. It
is just the same as in religion. The more of himself man attributes to God the less he has left in himself. The worker puts his
life into the object, and his life then belongs no longer to himself
but to the object. The greater his activity, therefore, the less he
possesses. What is embodied in the product of his labor is no
longer his own. The greater this product is, therefore, the more
he is diminshed. The *alienation* of the worker in his product

means not only that his labor becomes an object, assumes an *external* existence, but that it exists independently, *outside himself,* and alien to him, and that it stands opposed to him as an autonomous power. The life which he has given to the object sets itself against him as an alien and hostile force.

Let us now examine more closely the phenomenon of *objectification,* the worker's production and the *alienation* and *loss* of the object it produces, which is involved in it. The worker can create nothing without *nature,* without the *sensuous external world.* The latter is the material in which his labor is realized, in which it is active, out of which and through which it produces things.

But just as nature affords the *means of existence* of labor in the sense that labor cannot *live* without objects upon which it can be exercised, so also it provides the *means of existence* in a narrower sense; namely the means of physical existence for the *worker* himself. Thus, the more the worker *appropriates* the external world of sensuous nature by his labor the more he deprives himself of *means of existence,* in two respects: first, that the sensuous external world becomes progressively less an object belonging to his labor, and secondly, that it becomes progressively less a means of existence in the direct sense, a means for the physical subsistence of the worker.

In both respects, therefore, the worker becomes a slave of the object; first, in that he receives an *object of work,* i.e., receives *work,* and secondly that he receives *means of subsistence.* Thus the object enables him to exist, first as a *worker* and secondly, as a *physical subject.* The culmination of this enslavement is that he can only maintain himself as a *physical subject* so far as he is a *worker,* and that it is only as a *physical subject* that he is a worker.

(The alienation of the worker in his object is expressed as follows in the laws of political economy: the more the worker produces the less he has to consume; the more value he creates the more worthless he becomes; the more refined his product the more crude and misshapen the worker; the more civilized the product the more barbarous the worker; the more powerful the work the more feeble the worker; the more the work manifests intelligence the more the worker declines in intelligence and becomes a slave of nature.)

Political economy conceals the alienation in the nature of labor insofar as it does not examine the direct relationship between the worker (work) and production. Labor certainly produces marvels for the rich, but it produces privation for the worker. It produces palaces, but hovels for the worker. It produces beauty, but deformity for the worker. It replaces labor by machinery, but it casts some of the workers back into a barbarous kind of work and turns the others into machines. It produces intelligence, but also stupidity and cretinism for the workers.

The direct relationship of labor to its products is the relationship of the worker to the objects of his production. The relationship of property owners to the objects of production and to production itself is merely a *consequence* of this first relationship and confirms it. We shall consider this second aspect later.

Thus, when we ask what is the important relationship of labor, we are concerned with the relationship of the *worker* to production.

So far we have considered the alienation of the worker only from one aspect; namely, *his relationship with the products of his labor.* However, alienation appears not only in the result, but also in the *process,* of *production,* within *productive activity* itself. How could the worker stand in an alien relationship to the product of his activity if he did not alienate himself in the act of production itself? The product is indeed only the *résumé* of activity, of production. Consequently, if the product of labor is alienation, production itself must be active alienation—the alienation of activity and the activity of alienation. The alienation of the object of labor merely summarizes the alienation in the work activity itself.

What constitutes the alienation of labor? First, that the work is *external* to the worker, that it is not part of his nature; and that, consequently, he does not fulfill himself in his work but denies himself, has a feeling of misery rather than well-being, does not develop freely his mental and physical energies but is physically exhausted and mentally debased. The worker therefore feels himself at home only during his leisure time, whereas to work he feels homeless. His work is not voluntary but imposed, *forced labor*. It is not the satisfaction of a need, but only a *means* for satisfying other needs. Its alien character is clearly shown by the fact that as soon as there is no physical or other compulsion it is avoided like a plague. External labor, labor in which man alienates himself, is a labor of self-sacrifice, of mortification. Finally, the external character of work for the worker is shown by the fact that it is not his own work but work for someone else, that in work he does not belong to himself but to another person. . . .

We arrive at the result that man (the worker) feels himself to be freely active only in his animal functions—eating, drinking and procreating, or at most also in his dwelling and in personal adornment—while in his human functions he is reduced to an animal. The animal becomes human and the human becomes animal.

Eating, drinking and procreating are of course also genuine human functions. But abstractly considered, apart from the environment of other human activities, and turned into final and sole ends, they are animal functions.

We have now considered the act of alienation of practical human activity, labor, from two aspects: (1) the relationship of the worker to the *product of labor* as an alien object which dominates him. This relationship is at the same time the relationship to the sensuous external world, to natural objects, as an alien and hostile world; (2) the relationship of labor to the *act of production* within *labor*. This is the relationship of the worker to his own activity as something alien and not belonging to him, activity as suffering (passivity), strength as powerlessness, creation as emasculation, the *personal* physical and mental energy of the worker, his personal life (for what is life but activity?) as an activity which is directed against himself, independent of him and not belonging to him. This is *self-alienation* as against the above-mentioned alienation of the *thing*.

We have now to infer a third characteristic of *alienated labor* from the two we have considered.

Man is a species-being not only in the sense that he makes the community (his own as well as those of other things) his object both practically and theoretically, but also (and this is simply another expression for the same thing) in the sense that he treats himself as the present, living species, as a *universal* and consequently free being.

Species-life, for man as for animals, has its physical basis in the fact that man (like animals) lives from inorganic nature, and since man is more universal than an animal so the range of inorganic nature from which he lives is more universal. Plants, animals, minerals, air, light, etc., constitute, from the theoretical aspect, a part of human consciousness as objects of natural science and art; they are man's spiritual inorganic nature, his intellectual means of life, which he must first prepare for enjoyment and perpetuation. So also, from the practical aspect they form a part of human life and activity. In practice man lives only from these natural products, whether in the form of food, heating, clothing, housing, etc. The universality of man appears in practice in the universality which makes the whole of nature into his inorganic body: (1) as a direct means of life; and equally (2) as the material object and instrument of his life activity. Nature is the *inorganic body* of man; that is to say, nature excluding the human body itself. To say that man *lives* from nature means that nature is his *body* with which he must remain in a continuous interchange in order not to die. The statement that the physical life and mental life of man, and nature, are interdependent means simply that nature is interdependent with itself, for man is a part of nature.

Since alienated labor: (1) alienates nature from man; and (2) alienates man from himself, from his own active function, his life activity; so it alienates him from the species. It makes *species-life* into a means of individual life. In the first place it alienates species-life and individual life, and secondly, it turns the latter, as an abstraction, into the purpose of the former, also in its abstract and alienated form.

For labor, *life activity, productive life,* now appear to man only as *means* for the satisfaction of a need, the need to maintain his physical existence. Productive life is, however, species-life. It is life creating life. In the type of life activity resides the whole character of a species, its species-character; and free, conscious activity is the species-character of human beings. Life itself appears only as a *means of life*.

The animal is one with its life activity. It does not distinguish the activity from itself. It is *its activity*. But man makes his life activity itself an object of his will and consciousness. He has a conscious life activity. It is not a determination with which he is completely identified. Conscious life activity distinguishes man from the life activity of animals. Only for this reason is he a species-being. Or rather, he is only a self-conscious being, i.e., his own life is an object for him, because he is a species-being. Only for this reason is his activity free activity. Alienated labor reverses the relationship, in that man because he is a self-conscious being makes his life activity, his *being*, only a means for his *existence*.

The practical construction of an *objective world*, the *manipulation* of inorganic nature, is the confirmation of man as a conscious species-being, i.e., a being who treats the species as his own being or himself as a species-being. Of course, animals also produce. They construct nests, dwellings, as in the case of bees, beavers, ants, etc. But they only produce what is strictly necessary for themselves or their young. They produce only in a single direction, while man produces universally. They produce only under the compulsion of direct physical need, while man produces when he is free from physical need and only truly produces in freedom from such need. Animals produce only themselves, while man reproduces the whole of nature. The products of animal production belong directly to their physical bodies, while man is free in face of his product. Animals construct only in accordance with the standards and needs of the species to which they belong, while man knows how to produce in accordance with the standards of every species and knows how to apply the appropriate standard to the object. Thus man constructs also in accordance with the laws of beauty.

It is just in his work upon the objective world that man really proves himself as a *species-being*. This production is his active species-life. By means of it nature appears as *his* work and his reality. The object of labor is, therefore, the *objectification of man's species-life;* for he no longer reproduces himself merely intellectually, as in consciousness, but actively and in a real sense, and he sees his own reflection in a world which he has constructed. While, therefore, alienated labor takes away the object of production from man, it also takes away his *species-life*, his real objectivity as a species-being, and changes his advantage over animals into a disadvantage in so far as his inorganic body, nature, is taken from him.

Just as alienated labor transforms free and self-directed activity into a means, so it transforms the species-life of man into a means of physical existence.

Consciousness, which man has from his species, is transformed through alienation so that species-life becomes only a means for him.

(3) Thus alienated labor turns the *species-life of man,* and also nature as his mental species-property, into an *alien* being and into a *means* for his *individual existence*. It alienates from man his own body, external nature, his mental life and his *human* life.

(4) A direct consequence of the alienation of man from the product of his labor, from his life activity and from his species-life is that *man* is *alienated* from other *men*. When man confronts himself he also confronts *other* men. What is true of man's relationship to his work, to the product of his work and to himself, is also true of his relationship to other men to their labor and to the objects of their labor.

In general, the statement that man is alienated from his species-life means that each man is alienated from others, and that each of the others is likewise alienated from human life.

Human alienation, and above all the relation of man to himself, is first realized and expressed in the relationship between each man and other men. Thus in the relationship of alienated labor every man regards other men according to the standards and relationships in which he finds himself placed as a worker. . . .

Let us now examine further how this concept of alienated

labor must express and reveal itself in reality. If the product of labor is alien to me and confronts me as an alien power, to whom does it belong? . . .

If the product of labor does not belong to the worker, but confronts him as an alien power, this can only be because it belongs to *a man other than the worker.* If his activity is a torment to him it must be a source of enjoyment and pleasure to another. . . . Only man himself can be this alien power over men.

Consider the earlier statement that the relation of man to himself is first realized, objectified, through his relation to other men. If therefore he is related to the product of his labor, his objectified labor, as to an *alien,* hostile, powerful and independent object, he is related in such a way that another alien, hostile, powerful and independent man is the lord of this object. If he is related to his own activity as to unfree activity, then he is related to it as activity in the service, and under the domination, coercion and yoke, of another man.

Every self-alienation of man, from himself and from nature, appears in the relation which he postulates between other men and himself and nature. . . . In the real world of practice this self-alienation can only be expressed in the real, practical relation of man to his fellow-men. The medium through which alienation occurs is itself a *practical* one. Through alienated labor, therefore, man not only produces his relation to the object and to the process of production as to alien and hostile men; he also produces the relation of other men to his production and his product, and the relation between himself and other men. Just as he creates his own production as a vitiation, a punishment, and his own product as a loss, as a product which does not belong to him, so he creates the domination of the nonproducer over production and its product. As he alienates his own activity, so he bestows upon the stranger an activity which is not his own. . . .

Thus, through alienated labor the worker creates the relation of another man, who does not work and is outside the work process, to this labor. The relation of the worker to work also produces the relation of the capitalist (or whatever one likes to call the lord of labor) to work. *Private property* is therefore the product, the necessary result, of *alienated labor,* of the external relation of the worker to nature and to himself.

Private property is thus derived from the analysis of the concept of *alienated labor;* that is, alienated man, alienated labor, alienated life, and estranged man.

We have, of course, derived the concept of *alienated labor (alienated life)* from political economy, from an analysis of the *movement of private property.* But the analysis of this concept shows that although private property appears to be the basis and cause of alienated labor, it is rather a consequence of the latter, just as the gods are *fundamentally* not the cause but the product of confusions of human reason. At a later stage, however, there is a reciprocal influence.

Only in the final stage of the development of private property is its secret revealed, namely, that it is on one hand the *product* of alienated labor, and on the other hand the *means* by which labor is alienated, the *realization of this alienation.*

This elucidation throws light upon several unresolved controversies:

(1) Political economy begins with labor as the real soul of production and then goes on to attribute nothing to labor and everything to private property. Proudhon, faced by this contradiction, has decided in favor of labor against private property. We perceive, however, that this apparent contradiction is the contradiction of *alienated labor* with itself and that political economy has merely formulated the laws of alienated labor.

We also observe, therefore, that *wages* and *private property* are identical, for wages, like the product or object of labor, labor itself remunerated, are only a necessary consequence of the alienation of labor. In the wage system labor appears not as an end in itself but as the servant of wages. . . .

An enforced *increase in wages* (disregarding the other difficulties, and especially that such an anomaly could only be maintained by force) would be nothing more than a *better remuneration of slaves,* and would not restore, either to the worker or to the work, their human significance and worth.

Even the *equality of incomes* which Proudhon demands

would only change the relation of the present-day worker to his work into a relation of all men to work. Society would then be conceived as an abstract capitalist.

(2) From the relation of alienated labor to private property it also follows that the emancipation of society from private property, from servitude, takes the political form of the *emancipation of the workers;* not in the sense that only the latter's emancipation is involved, but because this emancipation includes the emancipation of humanity as a whole. For all human servitude is involved in the relation of the worker to production, and all the types of servitude are only modifications or consequences of this relation. . . .

11. Forms of Private Property

The Second of the *Economic and Philosophical Manuscripts,* "The Relationship of Private Property," continues the discussion of alienated labor; but it focuses on the nature of the historical transition from the large-scale landownership characteristic of the feudal era to the modern capitalistic ownership based upon movable property and wage labor. Marx contrasts the claims made by both these parties and discusses the reasons for the triumph of the bourgeoisie.

THE WORKER is the subjective manifestation of the fact that capital is man wholly lost to himself, just as capital is the objective manifestation of the fact that labor is man lost to himself. However, the *worker* has the misfortune to be a *living* capital, a capital with needs, which forfeits its interest and consequently its livelihood every moment that it is not at work. As capital, the *value* of the worker varies according to supply and demand, and his *physical existence,* his *life,* was and is considered as a supply of goods, similar to any other goods. The worker produces capital and capital produces him. Thus he produces himself, and man as a *worker,* as a *commodity,* is the product of the whole process. Man is simply a *worker,* and as a worker his human qualities only exist for the sake of capital which is *alien* to him. . . . As soon as it occurs to capital—either necessarily or voluntarily—not to exist any longer for the worker, he no longer

From *Marx's Concept of Man,* ed. by Erich Fromm, trans. by T. B. Bottomore (New York: Frederick Ungar, 1961). By permission.

exists for himself; he has *no* work, *no* wage, and since he exists only as a *worker* and not as a *human being*, he may as well let himself be buried, starve, etc. The worker is only a worker when he exists as capital *for himself*, and he only exists as capital when *capital* is there *for him*. The existence of capital is *his* existence, his life, since it determines the content of his life independently of him. Political economy thus does not recognize the unoccupied worker, the working man so far as he is outside this work relationship. . . . The needs of the worker are thus reduced to the need to maintain him *during work*, so that the race of workers does not die out. Consequently, wages have exactly the same significance as the *maintenance* of any other productive instrument, and as the *consumption of capital* in general so that it can reproduce itself with interest. . . .

Production does not only produce man as a *commodity*, the *human commodity*, man in the form of a *commodity*; in conformity with this situation it produces him as a *mentally* and *physically dehumanized* being. . . . Its product is the *self-conscious* and *self-acting commodity* . . . the human commodity. . . . The true end of production is not the number of workers a given capital maintains, but the amount of interest it earns, the total annual saving. It was . . . a great and logical advance in recent English political economy that, while establishing *labor* as the only principle of political economy, it clearly . . . observed that as a rule the capitalist could *only* increase his gains by the depression of wages and vice versa. The *normal* relation is seen to be not the defraudung of the consumer, but the mutual cheating of capitalist and worker. . . . On the one hand, there is the production of human activity as *labor*, that is, as an activity which is alien to itself, to man and to nature, and thus alien to consciousness and to the realization of human life; the *abstract* existence of man as a mere *working man* who therefore plunges every day from his fulfilled nothingness into absolute nothingness, into social, and thus real, nonexistence. On the other hand, there is the production of objects of human labor as *capital*, in which every natural and social characteristic of the object is *dissolved*, in which private property has lost its natural and social quality (and has thereby lost all political and social disguise and no longer even *appears* to be involved with human relationships), and in which the *same* capital remains the *same* in the most varied natural and social conditions, which have no relevance to its *real* content. . . .

The *distinction* between capital and land, profit and ground rent, and the distinction of both from wages, *industry, agriculture, immovable and movable* private property, is a *historical* distinction, not one inscribed in the nature of things. It is a *fixed* stage in the formation and development of the antithesis between capital and labor. In industry, etc., as opposed to immovable landed property, only the mode of origin and the antithesis to agriculture through which industry has developed, is expressed. As a *particular* kind of labor, as a more *significant, important and comprehensive* distinction it exists only so long as industry (town life) is established in opposition to landed property (aristocratic feudal life) and still bears the characteristics of this contradiction in itself in the form of monopolies, crafts, guilds, corporations, etc. In such a situation, labor still appears to have a *social* meaning, still has the significance of *genuine* communal life, and has not yet progressed to *neutrality* in relation to its content, to full self-sufficient being, i.e., to abstraction from all other existence and thus to *liberated* capital.

But the necessary *development* of labor is liberated *industry*, constituted for itself alone, and *liberated capital*. The power of industry over its opponent is shown by the rise of *agriculture* as a real industry, whereas formerly most of the work was left to the soil itself and to the *slave* of the soil through whom the land cultivated itself. With the transformation of the slave into a *free* worker, i.e., into a *hireling*, the landowner himself is transformed into a lord of industry, a capitalist. . . .

Recollecting their contrasting origins and descent the landowner recognizes the capitalist as his insubordinate, liberated and enriched slave of yesterday, and sees himself as a *capitalist* who is threatened by him. The capitalist sees the landowner as the idle, cruel and egotistical lord of yesterday; he knows that he injures him as a capitalist, and yet that industry is responsible for his present social significance, for his possession and pleasures. He regards the landowner as the antithesis of *free* enterprise and of *free capital* which is independent of every natural limitation. This opposition is extremely bitter and each side expresses the truth about the other. . . . The landowner emphasizes the noble lineage of his property, feudal souvenirs, reminiscences, the poetry of recollection, his open-hearted character, his political importance, etc., and when he talks in economic terms asserts that agriculture *alone* is productive. At the same time he portrays his opponent as a sly, bargaining, deceitful, mercenary, rebellious, heartless and soulless individual, an extortionate, pimping, servile, smooth, flattering, desiccated rogue, without honor, principles, poetry or anything else, who is alienated from the community which he freely trades away, and who breeds, nourishes and cherishes competition and along with it poverty, crime and the dissolution of all social bonds. . . .

Movable property, for its part, points to the miracle of modern industry and development. It is the child, the legitimate, native-born son, of the modern age. It pities its opponent as a simpleton, *ignorant* of his own nature (and this is entirely true), who wishes to replace moral capital and free labor by crude, immoral coercion and serfdom. It depicts him as a Don Quixote who, under the appearance of *directness, decency,* the *general interest,* and *stability,* conceals his incapacity for development, greedy self-indulgence, selfishness, sectional interest and evil intention. It exposes him as a cunning *monopolist;* it pours cold water upon his reminiscences, his poetry and his romanticism, by a historical and satirical recital of the baseness, cruelty, degradation, prostitution, infamy, anarchy and revolt, of which the romantic castles were the workshops.

It (movable property) claims to have won political freedom for the people, to have removed the chains which bound civil society, to have linked together different worlds, to have established commerce which promotes friendship between peoples, to have created a pure morality and an agreeable culture. It has given the people, in place of their crude wants, civilized needs and the means of satisfying them. But the landowner—this idle grain speculator—raises the price of the people's basic necessities of life and thereby forces the capitalist to raise wages without being able to increase productivity, so hindering and ultimately arresting the growth of national income and the accumulation of capital upon which depends the creation of work for the people and of wealth for the country. He brings about a general decline, and parasitically exploits *all* the advantages of modern civilization without making the least contribution to it, and without abandoning any of his feudal prejudices. . . . Everything which he can really bring forward in justification is true only of the *cultivator of the land* (the capitalist and the laborers) of whom the landowner is rather the *enemy;* thus he testifies against himself. *Without* capital, landed property is lifeless and worthless matter. It is indeed the civilized victory of movable property to have discovered and created human labor as the source of wealth, in place of the lifeless thing. . . .

From the *real* course of development . . . there follows the necessary victory of the *capitalist,* i.e., of developed private property, over undeveloped, immature private property, the *landowner.* In general, movement must triumph over immobility, overt self-conscious baseness over concealed, unconscious baseness, *avarice* over *self-indulgence,* the avowedly restless and able self-interest of *enlightenment* over the local, worldly-wise, simple, idle and fantastic *self-interest of superstition,* and *money* over the other forms of private property. . . .

12. *Private Property* versus *Communism*

The Third Manuscript of the *Economic and Philosophical Manuscripts,* a discussion of "Private Property and Communism." is one of the most important works of Marx's developmental period in that he here, for the first time, takes up in depth the concept of Communism as the solution to the historically given problem of the alienation of labor. The basis of the discussion is soon revealed to be that of actualizing the nature of man (which Marx terms "socialist man") as one who recognizes in world history the process of his own self-creation. Thus the problem of man's actualization becomes one to be directly faced in a concrete historical context. Considering the fact that the conditions of alienated labor create a deformed subhuman type, the solution is posed in terms of a communism which is not merely the "abstract" negation of private property (a fault of which Marx accuses the communists of his day), but of the positive supersession, or the "negation of the negation," of private property. Thus, we see that for Marx Communism is not merely another political or economic doctrine; it is rather proposed as the practical solution to the problem of actualizing the potential of human nature itself in terms of the conditions of labor in their given historical situation.

THE SUPERSESSION of self-estrangement follows the same course as self-estrangement. *Private property* is first considered

From *Marx's Concept of Man,* ed. by Erich Fromm, trans. by T. B. Bottomore (New York: Frederick Ungar, 1961). Used by permission.

only from its objective aspect, but with labor conceived as its essence. . . . Fourier, in accord with the Physiocrats, regards *agricultural labor* as being at least the exemplary kind of labor. Saint-Simon asserts on the contrary that *industrial labor* as such is the essence of labor, and consequently he desires the *exclusive* rule of the industrialists and an amelioration of the condition of the workers. Finally, *communism* is the *positive* expression of the abolition of private property, and in the first place of universal private property. In taking this relation in its *universal aspect* communism is (1) in its first form, only the generalization and fulfillment of the relation. As such it appears in a double form; the domination of material property looms so large that it aims to destroy everything which is incapable of being possessed by everyone as private property. It wishes to eliminate talent, etc., by *force.* Immediate physical possession seems to it the unique goal of life and existence. The role of *worker* is not abolished, but is extended to all men. The relation of private property remains the relation of the community to the world of things. Finally, this tendency to oppose general private property to private property is expressed in an animal form; *marriage* (which is incontestably a form of *exclusive private property*) is contrasted with the community of women, in which women become communal and common property. One may say that this idea of the *community of women* is the *open secret* of this entirely crude and unreflective communism. Just as women are to pass from marriage to universal prostitution, so the whole world of wealth (i.e., the objective being of man) is to pass from the relation of exclusive marriage with the private owner to the relation of universal prostitution with the community. This communism, which negates the *personality* of man in every sphere, is only the logical expression of private property, which is this negation. Universal *envy* setting itself up as a power is only a camouflaged form of cupidity which reestablishes itself and satisfies itself in a different way. The thoughts of every individual private property are *at least* directed against any *wealthier* private property, in the form of envy and the desire to reduce everything to a common level; so that this envy and leveling in fact constitute the essence of competition. Crude communism is only the culmination of such envy and leveling-down on the basis of a *preconceived* minimum. How little this abolition of private property represents a genuine appropriation is shown by the abstract negation of the whole world of culture and civilization, and the regression to the *unnatural* simplicity of the poor and wantless individual who has not only not surpassed private property but has not yet even attained to it.

The community is only a community of *work* and of *equality of wages* paid out by the communal capital, by the *community* as universal capitalist. The two sides of the relation are raised to a *supposed* universality; *labor* as a condition in which everyone is placed, and *capital* as the acknowledged universality and power of the community.

In the relationship with *woman,* as the prey and the handmaid of communal lust, is expressed the infinite degradation in which man exists for himself; for the secret of this relationship finds its *unequivocal,* incontestable, *open* and revealed expression in the relation of man to woman and in the way in which the *direct* and *natural* species relationship is conceived. The immediate, natural and necessary relation of human being to human being is also the *relation* of *man* to *woman.* In this *natural* species relationship man's relation to nature is directly his relation to man, and his relation to man is directly his relation to nature, to his own *natural* function. Thus, in this relation is *sensuously revealed,* reduced to an observable *fact,* the extent to which human nature has become nature for man and to which nature has become human nature for him. From this relationship man's whole level of development can be assessed. It follows from the character of this relationship how far *man* has become, and has understood himself as, a *species-being,* a *human being.* The relation of man to woman is the *most natural* relation of human being to human being. It indicates, therefore, how far man's *natural* behavior has become *human,* and how far his *human* essence has become a *natural* essence for him, how far his *human nature* has become *nature* for *him.* It also shows how far man's *needs* have become *human* needs, and consequently how far the other person, as a person, has become one of his needs, and to what extent he is in his individual existence at the same time a social being. The first positive annulment of private property, crude communism, is therefore only a *phenomenal form* of the infamy of private property representing itself as positive community.

(2) Communism (a) still political in nature, democratic or despotic; (b) with the abolition of the state, yet still incomplete and influenced by private property, that is, by the alienation of man. In both forms communism is already aware of being the reintegration of man, his return to himself, the supersession of man's self-alienation. But since it has not yet grasped the positive nature of private property, or the *human* nature of needs, it is still captured and contaminated by private property. It has well understood the concept, but not the essence.

(3) *Communism* is the *positive* abolition of *private property,* of *human self-alienation,* and thus the real *appropriation* of *human* nature through and for man. It is, therefore, the return of man himself as a *social,* i.e., really human, being, a complete and conscious return which assimilates all the wealth of previous development. Communism as a fully developed naturalism is humanism and as a fully developed humanism is naturalism. It is the *definitive* resolution of the antagonsim between man and nature, and between man and man. It is the true solution of the conflict between existence and essence, between objectification and self-affirmation, between freedom and necessity, between individual and species. It is the solution of the riddle of history and knows itself to be this solution.

Thus the whole historical development, both the *real* genesis of communism (the birth of its empirical existence) and its thinking consciousness, is its comprehended and conscious process of becoming; whereas the other, still undeveloped communism seeks in certain historical forms opposed to private property, a *historical* justification founded upon what already exists, and to this end tears out of their context isolated elements of this development. . . .

It is easy to understand the necessity which leads the whole revolutionary movement to find its empirical, as well as its theoretical, basis in the development of *private property,* and more precisely of the economic system.

This material, directly *perceptible* private property is the material and sensuous expression of *alienated human* life. Its movement—production and consumption—is the *sensuous* manifestation of the movement of all previous production, i.e., the realization or reality of man. Religion, the family, the state, law, morality, science, art, etc., are only *particular* forms of production and come under its general law. The positive supersession of *private property* as the appropriation of *human* life is therefore the *positive* supersession of all alienation, and the return of man from religion, the family, the state, etc., to his *human*, i.e., *social* life. Religious alienation as such occurs only in the sphere of *consciousness*, in the inner life of man, but economic alienation is that of *real life* and its supersession therefore affects both aspects. Of course, the development in different nations has a different beginning according to whether the actual and *established* life of the people is more in the realm of mind or more in the external world, is a real or ideal life. Communism begins where atheism begins (Owen), but atheism is at the outset still far from being communism; indeed it is still for the most part an abstraction. Thus the philanthropy of atheism is at first only an abstract *philosophical* philanthropy, whereas that of communism is at once *real* and oriented towards *action.*

We have seen how, on the assumption that private property has been positively superseded, man produces man, himself and then other men; how the object which is the direct activity of his personality is at the same time his existence for other men and their existence for him. Similarly, the material of labor and man himself as a subject are the starting point as well as the result of this movement (and because there must be this starting point private property is a historical necessity). Therefore, the *social* character is the universal character of the whole movement; *as* society itself produces *man* as *man*, so it is *produced* by him. Activity and mind are social in their content as well as in their *origin;* they are *social* acitivty and *social* mind. The *human* significance of nature only exists for *social* man, because only in this case is nature a *bond* with other *men*, the basis of his existence for others and of their existence for him. Only then is nature the *basis* of his own *human* experience and a vital element of human reality. The *natural* existence of man has here become his *human* existence and nature itself has become human for him. Thus *society* is the accomplished union of man with nature, the veritable resurrection of nature, the realized naturalism of man and the realized humanism of nature.

Social activity and social mind by no means exist *only* in the form of activity or mind which is directly communal. Nevertheless, communal activity and mind, i.e., activity and mind which express and confirm themselves directly in a *real association* with other men, occur everywhere where this *direct* expression of sociability arises from the content of the activity or corresponds to the nature of mind.

Even when I carry out *scientific* work, etc., an activity which I can seldom conduct in direct association with other men, I perform a *social,* because *human,* act. It is not only the material of my activity—such as the language itself which the thinker uses—which is given to me as a social product. *My own existence* is a social activity. For this reason, what I myself produce I produce for society, and with the consciousness of acting as a social being. . . .

It is above all necessary to avoid postulating "society" once again as an abstraction confronting the individual. The individual *is* the *social being.* The manifestation of his life—even when it does not appear directly in the form of a communal manifestation, accomplished in association with other men—is therefore a manifestation and affirmation of *social life.* Individual human life and species-life are not *different things,* even though the mode of existence of individual life is necessarily either a more *specific* or a more *general* mode of species-life, or that of species-life a more *specific* or more *general* mode of individual life.

In his *species-consciousness* man confirms his real *social life,* and reproduces his real existence in thought; while conversely, species-life confirms itself in species-consciousness and exists for itself in its universality as a thinking being. Though man is a unique individual—and it is just his particularity which makes him an individual, a really *individual* communal being—he is equally the *whole*, the ideal whole, the subjective existence of society as thought and experienced. He exists in reality as the representation and the real mind of social existence, and as the sum of human manifestation of life.

Thought and being are indeed *distinct*, but they also form a unity. *Death* seems to be a harsh victory of the species over the individual and to contradict their unity; but the particular individual is only a *determinate species-being* and as such he is mortal.

(4) Just as *private property* is only the sensuous expression of the fact that man is at the same time an *objective* fact for himself and becomes an alien and nonhuman object for himself; just as his manifestation of life is also his alienation of life and his self-realization a loss of reality, the emergence of an *alien* reality; so the positive supersession of private property, i.e., the *sensuous* appropriation of the human essence and of human life, of objective man and of human *creations*, by and for man, should not be taken only in the sense of *immediate*, exclusive *enjoyment*, or only in the sense of *possession* or *having*. Man appropriates his manifold being in an all-inclusive way, and thus as a whole man. All his *human* relations to the world—seeing, hearing, smelling, testing, touching, thinking, observing, feeling, desiring, acting, loving—in short all the organs of his individuality, like the organs which are directly communal in form are, in their objective action (their *action in relation to the object*) the appropriation of this object, the appropriation of human reality. The way in which they react to the object is the confirmation of *human reality*.[1] It is human effectiveness and human *suffering*, for suffering humanly considered is an enjoyment of the self for man.

Private property has made us so stupid and partial that an object is only *ours* when we have it, when it exists for us as capital or when it is directly eaten, drunk, worn, inhabited, etc., in short, *utilized* in some way; although private property itself

1. It is therefore just as varied as the determinations of human nature and activities are diverse.

only conceives these various forms of possession as *means of life*, and the life for which they serve as means is the *life* of *private property*—labor and creation of capital.

Thus *all* the physical and intellectual senses have been replaced by the simple alienation of *all* these senses; the sense of *having*. The human being had to be reduced to this absolute poverty in order to be able to give birth to all his inner wealth. . . .

The supersession of private property is therefore the complete *emancipation* of all the human qualities and senses. It is this emancipation because these qualities and senses have become *human*, from the subjective as well as the objective point of view. The eye has become a *human* eye when its *object* has become a *human*, social object, created by man and destined for him. The senses have therefore become directly theoreticians in practice. They relate themselves to the thing for the sake of the thing, but the thing itself is an *objective human* relation to itself and to man, and vice versa.[2] Need and enjoyment have thus lost their *egoistic* character, and nature has lost its mere *utility* by the fact that its utilization has become *human* utilization.

Similarly, the senses and minds of other men have become my *own* appropriation. Thus besides these direct organs, *social* organs are constituted, in the form of society; for example, activity in direct association with others has become an organ for the manifestation of life and a mode of appropriation of *human* life.

It is evident that the human eye appreciates things in a different way from the crude, nonhuman eye, the human *ear* differently from the crude ear. As we have seen, it is only when the object becomes a *human* object, or objective *humanity*, that man does not become lost in it. This is only possible when the object becomes a *social* object, and when he himself becomes a social being and society becomes a being for him in this object.

On the one hand, it is only when objective reality everywhere

---

2. In practice I can only relate myself in a human way to a thing when the thing is related in a human way to man.

becomes for man in society the reality of human faculties, human reality, and thus the reality of his own faculties, that all *objects* become for him the *objectification of himself*. The objects then confirm and realize his individuality, they are *his own* objects, i.e., man himself becomes the object. *The manner in which* these objects become his own depends upon the *nature of the object* and the nature of the corresponding faculty; for it is precisely the *determinate character* of this relation which constitutes the specific *real* mode of affirmation. The object is not the same for the *eye* as for the *ear,* for the ear as for the eye. The *distinctive character* of each faculty is precisely its *characteristic* essence and thus also the characteristic mode of its objectification, of its *objectively real*, living *being*. It is therefore not only in thought, but through *all* the senses that man is affirmed in the objective world.

Let us next consider the subjective aspect. Man's musical sense is only awakened by music. The most beautiful music has no meaning for the nonmusical ear, is not an object for it, because my object can only be the confirmation of one of my own faculties. It can only be so for me in so far as my faculty exists for itself as a subjective capacity, because the meaning of an object for me extends only as far as the sense extends (only makes sense for an appropriate sense). For this reason, the *senses* of social man are *different* from those of nonsocial man. It is only through the objectively deployed wealth of the human being that the wealth of subjective *human* sensibility (a musical ear, an eye which is sensitive to the beauty of form, in short, senses which are capable of human satisfaction and which confirm themselves as human faculties) is cultivated or created. For it is not only the five senses, but also the so-called spritual senses, the practical senses (desiring, loving, etc.), in brief, human sensibility and the human character of the senses, which can only come into being through the existence of *its* object, through humanized nature. The cultivation of the five senses is the work of all previous history. Sense which is subservient to crude needs has only a restricted meaning. For a starving man the human form of food does not exist, but only its abstract character as food. It could just as well exist in the most crude form, and it is impossible to say in what way this feeding-activity would differ from that of animals. The needy man, burdened with cares, has no appreciation of the most beautiful spectacle. The dealer in minerals sees only their commercial value, not their beauty or their particular characteristics; he has no mineralogical sense. Thus, the objectification of the human essence, both theoretically and practically, is necessary in order to *humanize* man's *senses*, and also to create the *human senses* corresponding to all the wealth of human and natural being.

Just as society at its beginnings finds, through the development of *private property* with its wealth and poverty (both intellectual and material), the materials necessary for this *cultural development, so* the fully constituted society produces man in all the plenitude of his being, the wealthy man endowed with all the senses, as an enduring reality. It is only in a social context that subjectivism and objectivism, spiritualism and materialism, activity and passivity, cease to be antinomies and thus cease to exist as such antinomies. The resolution of the *theoretical* contradictions is possible *only* through *practical* means, only through the practical energy of man. Their resolution is not by any means, therefore, only a problem of knowledge, but is a *real* problem of life which philosophy was unable to solve precisely because it saw there a purely theoretical problem.

It can be seen that the history of *industry* and industry as it *objectively* exists is an open book of the *human faculties*, and a human *psychology* which can be sensuously apprehended. This history has not so far been conceived in relation to human *nature*, but only from a superficial utiltarian point of view, since in the condition of alienation it was only possible to conceive real human faculties and *human* species-action in the form of general human existence, as religion, or as history in its abstract, general aspect as politics, art and literature, etc. *Everyday material industry* (which can be conceived as part of that general development; or equally, the general development can be conceived as a *specific* part of industry since all human activity up to the present has been labor, i.e., industry, self-alienated activity) shows us, in the form of *sensuous useful objects*, in an alienated form, the *essential human faculties* transformed into objects. No psychology for which this book, i.e., the most sensibly present and accessible part of history, remains closed, can become a *real* science with a genuine content. What is to be thought of a science which stays aloof from this enormous field of human labor and which does not feel its own inadequacy even though this great wealth of human activity means nothing to it except perhaps what can be expressed in the single phrase —"need," "common need"?

The *natural sciences* have developed a tremendous activity and have assembled an ever-growing mass of data. But philosophy has remained alien to these sciences just as they have remained alien to philosophy. Their momentary *rapprochement* was only a *fantastic* illusion. There was a desire for union but the power to effect it was lacking. Historiography itself only takes natural science into account incidentally, regarding it as a factor making for enlightenment, for practical utility and for particular great discoveries. But natural science has penetrated all the more *practically* into human life through industry. It has transformed human life and prepared the emancipation of humanity even though its immediate effect was to accentuate the dehumanization of man. *Industry* is the actual historical relationship of nature, and thus of natural science, to man. If industry is conceived as the *exoteric* manifestation of the essential human *faculties*, the *human* essence of nature and the *natural* essence of man can also be understood. Natural science will then abandon its abstract materialist, or rather idealist, orientation, and will become the basis of a *human* science, just as it has already become—though in an alienated form—the basis of actual human life. One basis for life and another for science is *a priori* a falsehood. Nature, as it develops in human history, in the act of genesis of human society, is the *actual* nature of man; thus nature, as it develops through industry, though in an *alienated* form, is truly *anthropological* nature.

Sense experience (see Feuerbach) must be the basis of all science. Science is *only genuine* science when it proceeds from sense experience, in the two forms of *sense perception* and *sensuous* need; i.e., only when it proceeds from nature. The whole of history is a preparation for "man" to become an object of *sense perception*, and for the development of human needs (the needs of man as such). History itself is a *real* part of *natural history*, of the development of nature into man. Natural science will one day incorporate the science of man, just as the science of man will incorporate natural science; there will be a *single* science.

Man is the direct object of natural science, because directly *perceptible nature* is for man directly human sense experience (an identical expression) as the *other person* who is directly presented to him in a sensuous way. His own sense experience only exists as human sense experience for himself through the *other person*. But *nature* is the direct object of the *science of man*. The first object for man—man himself—is nature, sense experience; and the particular sensuous human faculties, which can only find objective realization in *natural* objects, can only attain self-knowledge in the science of natural being. The element of thought itself, the element of the living manifestation of thought, *language*, is sensuous in nature. The *social* reality of nature and *human* natural science or the *natural science of man*, are identical expressions.

It will be seen from this how, in place of the *wealth* and *poverty* of political economy, we have the *wealthy* man and the plenitude of *human* need. The wealthy man is at the same time one who *needs* a complex of human manifestations of life, and whose own self-realization exists as an inner necessity, a *need*. Not only the *wealth* but also the *poverty* of man acquires, in a socialist perspective, a *human* and thus a social meaning. Poverty is the passive bond which leads man to experience a need for the greatest wealth, the *other* person. The sway of the objective entity within me, the sensuous outbreak of my life-activity, is the passion which here becomes the *activity* of my being.

(5) A being does not regard himself as independent unless he is his own master, and he is only his own master when he owes his existence to himself. A man who lives by the favor of another considers himself a dependent being. But I live completely by another person's favor when I owe to him not only the continuance of my life but also *its creation;* when he is its *source.* My

life has necessarily such a cause outside itself if it is not my own creation. The idea of *creation* is thus one which it is difficult to eliminate from popular consciousness. This consciouness is *unable to conceive* that nature and man exist on their own account, because such an existence contradicts all the tangible facts of practical life. . . .

But it is easy indeed to say to the particular individual what Aristotle said: You are engendered by your father and mother, and consequently it is the coitus of two human beings, a human species-act, which has produced the human being. You see therefore that even in a physical sense man owes his existence to man. Consequently, it is not enough to keep in view only one of the two aspects, the *infinite* progression, and to ask further: who engendered my father and my grandfather? You must also keep in mind the *circular movement* which is perceptible in that progression, according to which man, in the act of generation, reproduces himself; thus *man* always remains the subject. But you will reply: I grant you this circular movement, but you must in turn concede the progression, which leads even further to the point where I ask: who created the first man and nature as a whole? I can only reply: your question is itself a product of abstraction. Ask yourself how you arrive at that question. Ask yourself whether your question does not arise from a point of view to which I cannot reply because it is a perverted one. Ask yourself whether that progression exists as such for rational thought. If you ask a question about the creation of nature and man you abstract from nature and man. You suppose them *nonexistent* and you want me to demonstrate that they *exist*. I reply: give up your abstraction and at the same time you abandon your question. Or else, if you want to maintain your abstraction, be consistent, and if you think of man and nature as nonexistent think of yourself too as nonexistent, for you are also man and nature. Do not think, do not ask me any questions, for as soon as you think and ask questions your *abstraction* from the existence of nature and man becomes meaningless. Or are you such an egoist that you conceive everything as nonexistent and yet want to exist yourself?

You may reply: I do not want to conceive the nothingness of

nature, etc.; I only ask you about the act of its creation, just as I ask the anatomist about the formation of bones, etc.

Since, however, for socialist man, the *whole of what is called world history* is nothing but the creation of man by human labor, and the emergence of nature for man, he therefore has the evident and irrefutable proof of his *self-creation*, of his *origins*. Once the essence of man and of nature, man as a natural being and nature as a human reality, has become evident in practical life, in sense experience, the quest for an *alien* being, a being above man and nature (a quest which is an avowal of the unreality of man and nature) becomes impossible in practice. *Atheism*, as a denial of this unreality, is no longer meaningful, for atheism is a *negation of God* and seeks to assert by this negation the *existence of man*. Socialism no longer requires such a roundabout method; it begins from the *theoretical* and *practical sense perception* of man and nature as essential beings. It is positive human *self-consciousness*, no longer a self-consciousness attained through the negation of religion; just as the *real life* of man is positive and no longer attained through the negation of private property, through *communism*. Communism is the phase of negation of the negation and is, consequently, for the next stage of historical development, a real and necessary factor in the emancipation and rehabilitation of man. Communism is the necessary form and the dynamic principle of the immediate future, but communism is not itself the goal of human development—the form of human society.

13. The Perversion of Human Needs

Directly following the preceding selection, Marx enters into a discussion of "Needs, Production, and Division of Labor," in which he elaborates upon the perverse nature of social relations under capitalism and briefly contrasts it with a communistic form of association. He then discusses the political economists' treatment of the division of labor and of their facile way of ignoring its dehumanizing effects.

WE HAVE seen what importance should be attributed, in a socialist perspective, to the *wealth of* human needs, and consequently also to a *new mode of production* and to a new *object* of production. A new manifestation of *human* powers and a new enrichment of the human being. Within the system of private property it has the opposite meaning. Every man speculates upon creating a *new* need in another in order to force him to a new sacrifice, to place him in a new dependence, and to entice him into a new kind of pleasure and thereby into economic ruin. Everyone tries to establish over others an *alien* power in order to find there the satisfaction of his own egoistic need. With the mass of objects, therefore, there also increases the realm of alien entities to which man is subjected. Every new product is a new *potentiality* of mutual deceit and robbery. Man becomes increasingly poor as a man; he has increasing need of *money* in order to take possession of the hostile being.

From *Marx's Concept of Man*, ed. by Erich Fromm, trans. by T. B. Bottomore (New York: Frederick Ungar, 1961). Used by permission.

The power of his *money* diminishes directly with the growth of the quantity of production, i.e., his need increases with the increasing *power* of money. The need for money is therefore the real need created by the modern economy, and the only need which it creates. The *quantity* of money becomes increasingly its only important quality. Just as it reduces every entity to its abstraction, so it reduces itself in its own development to a *quantitative* entity. Excess and immoderation become its true standard. This is shown subjectively, partly in the fact that the expansion of production and of needs becomes an *ingenious* and always *calculating* subservience to inhuman, depraved, unnatural, and *imaginary* appetites. Private property does not know how to change crude need into *human* need; its *idealism* is *fantasy, caprice* and *fancy*. No eunuch flatters his tyrant more shamefully or seeks by more infamous means to stimulate his jaded appetite, in order to gain some favor, than does the eunuch of industry, the entrepreneur, in order to acquire a few silver coins or to charm the gold from the purse of his dearly beloved neighbor. (Every product is a bait by means of which the individual tries to entice the essence of the other person, his money. Every real or potential need is a weakness which will draw the bird into the lime. Universal exploitation of human communal life. As every imperfection of man is a bond with heaven, a point from which his heart is accessible to the priest, so every want is an opportunity for approaching one's neighbor, with an air of friendship, and saying, "Dear friend, I will give you what you need, but you know the *conditio sine qua non*. You know what ink you must use in signing yourself over to me. I shall swindle you while providing your enjoyment.") The entrepreneur accedes to the most depraved fancies of his neighbor, plays the role of pander between him and his needs, awakens unhealthy appetites in him, and watches for every weakness in order, later, to claim the remuneration for this labor of love.

This alienation is shown in part by the fact that the refinement of needs and of the means to satisfy them produces as its counterpart a bestial savagery, a complete, primitive and abstract simplicity of needs; or rather, that it simply reproduces itself in its opposite sense. For the worker even the need for fresh air ceases to be a need. Man returns to the cave dwelling again, but it is now poisoned by the pestilential breath of civilization. The worker has only a *precarious* right to inhabit it, for it has become an alien dwelling which may suddenly not be available, or from which he may be evicted if he does not pay the rent. He has to *pay* for this mortuary. The dwelling full of light which Prometheus, in Aeschylus, indicates as one of the great gifts by which he has changed savages into men, ceases to exist for the worker. Light, air, and the simplest *animal* cleanliness cease to be human needs. *Filth,* this corruption and putrefaction which runs in the *sewers* of civilization (this is to be taken literally) becomes the *element in which man lives.* Total and *unnatural* neglect, putrified nature, becomes the *element in which he lives.* None of his senses exist any longer, either in a human form, or even in a *nonhuman,* animal form. The crudest *methods* and (and *instruments*) of human labor reappear; thus the *tread-mill* of the Roman slaves has become the mode of production and mode of existence of many English workers. It is not enough that man should lose his human needs; even animal needs disappear. The Irish no longer have any need but that of *eating—eating potatoes.* But France and England already possess in every industrial town a *little* Ireland. Savages and animals have at least the need for hunting, exercise and companionship. But the simplification of machinery and of work is used to make workers out of those who are just growing up, who are still immature, *children,* while the worker himself has become a child deprived of all care. Machinery is adapted to the weakness of the human being, in order to turn the weak human being into a machine.

The fact that the growth of needs and of the means to satisfy them results in a lack of needs and of means is demonstrated in several ways by the economist (and by the capitalist; in fact, it is always *empirical* businessmen we refer to when we speak of economists, who are their *scientific* self-revelation and existence). First, by reducing the needs of the worker to the miserable necessities required for the maintenance of his physical existence, and by reducing his activity to the most abstract mechanical movements, the economist asserts that man has no needs, for activity or enjoyment, beyond that; and yet he declares that this kind of life is a *human* way of life. Secondly, by reckoning as the general standard of life (general because it is applicable to the mass of men) the *most impoverished* life conceivable, he turns the worker into a being who has neither senses nor needs, just as he turns his acitivty into a pure abstraction from all activity. Thus all working class *luxury* seems to him blameworthy, and everything which goes beyond the most abstract need (whether it be a passive enjoyment or a manifestation of personal activity) is regarded as a *luxury*. Political economy, the science of *wealth*, is therefore, at the same time, the science of renunciation, of privation and of saving, which actually succeeds in depriving man of fresh *air* and of physical *activity*. This science of a marvelous industry is at the same time the science of *asceticism*. Its true ideal is the *ascetic* but *usurious* miser and the *ascetic* but *productive* slave. Its moral ideal is the *worker* who takes a part of his wages to the savings bank. It has even found a servile art to embody this favorite idea, which has been produced in a sentimental manner on the stage. Thus, despite its worldly and pleasure-seeking appearance, it is a truly moral science, the most moral of all sciences. Its principal thesis is the renunciation of life and of human needs. The less you eat, drink, buy books, go to the theatre or to balls, or to the public house, and the less you think, love, theorize, sing, paint, fence, etc., the more you will be able to save and the *greater* will become your treasure which neither moth nor rust will corrupt—your *capital*. The less you *are*, the less you express your life, the more you *have*, the greater is your *alienated* life and the greater is the saving of your alienated being. Everything which the economist takes from you in the way of life and humanity, he restores to you in the form of *money* and *wealth*. And everything which you are unable to do, your money can do for you; it can eat, drink, go to the ball and to the theatre. It can acquire art, learning, historical treasures, political power; and it can travel. It *can* appropriate all these things for you, can purchase everything; it is the true *opulence*. . . .

You must not only be abstemious in the satisfaction of your direct senses, such as eating, etc., but also in your participation in general interests, your sympathy, trust, etc., if you wish to be economical and to avoid being ruined by illusions.

Everything which you own must be made *venal,* i.e., useful. Suppose I ask the economist: am I acting in accordance with economic laws if I earn money by the sale of my body, by prostituting it to another person's lust (in France, the factory workers call the prostitution of their wives and daughters the nth hour of work, which is literally true); or if I sell my friend to the Moroccans (and the direct sale of men occurs in all civilized countries in the form of trade in conscripts)? He will reply: you are not acting contrary to my laws, but you must take into account what Cousin Morality and Cousin Religion have to say. My *economic* morality and religion have no objection to make, but. . . . But whom then should we believe, the economist or the moralist? The morality of political economy is *gain,* work, thrift and sobriety—yet political economy promises to satisfy my needs. The political economy of morality is the riches of a good conscience, of virtue, etc., but how can I be virtuous if I am not alive and how can I have a good conscience if I am not aware of anything? The nature of alienation implies that each sphere applies a different and contradictory norm, that morality does not apply the same norm as political economy, etc., because each of them is a particular alienation of man; each is concentrated upon a specific area of alienated activity and is itself alienated from the other[s]. . . .

The bearing of political economy upon morals is either arbitrary and accidental and thus lacking any scientific basis or character, a mere *sham,* or it is *essential* and can then only be a relation between economic laws and morals. . . . Moreover, the antithesis between morals and political economy is itself only *apparent;* there is an antithesis and equally no antithesis. Political economy expresses, *in its own fashion,* the moral laws.

The absence of needs, as the principle of political economy, is shown in the most *striking* way in its *theory of population.* There are *too many* men. The very existence of man is a pure luxury, and if the worker is *"moral"* he will be *economical* in procreation. (Mill proposes that public commendation should be given to those who show themselves abstemious in sexual relations, and public condemnation to those who sin against the sterility of marriage. Is this not the moral doctrine of asceticism?) The production of men appears as a public misfortune.

The significance which production has in relation to the wealthy is *revealed* in the significance which it has for the poor. . . . The *crude* need of the worker is a much greater source of profit than the *refined* need of the wealthy. The cellar dwellings in London bring their landlords more than do the palaces; i.e., they constitute *greater wealth* as far as the landlord is concerned and thus, in economic terms, greater *social* wealth.

Just as industry speculates upon the refinement of needs so also it speculates upon their *crudeness*, and upon their artificially produced crudeness whose true soul therefore is *self-stupefaction*, the *illusory* satisfaction of needs, a civilization *within* the crude barbarism of need. The English gin-shops are therefore *symbolical* representations of private property. Their *luxury* reveals the real relation of industrial luxury and wealth to man. They are therefore rightly the only Sunday enjoyment of the people. . . .

We have already seen how the ecomomist establishes the unity of labor and capital in various ways: (1) capital is *accumulated* labor; (2) the purpose of capital within production —partly the reproduction of capital with profit, partly capital as raw material (material of labor), partly capital as itself a *working instrument* (the machine is fixed capital which is identical with labor)—is *productive work;* (3) the worker is capital; (4) wages form part of the costs of capital; (5) for the worker, labor is the reproduction of his life-capital; (6) for the capitalist, labor is a factor in the activity of his capital.

Finally (7) the economist postulates the original unity of capital and labor as the unity of capitalist and worker. This is the original paradisaical condition. How these two factors, as two persons, spring at each other's throats is for the economist a *fortuitous* occurrence, which therefore requires only to be explained by external circumstances. . . .

If we now characterize *communism* itself (for as negation of the negation, as the appropriation of human existence which mediates itself with itself through the negation of private property, it is not the *true*, self-originating position, but rather one which begins from private property) . . .[1] The alienation of human life remains and a much greater alienation remains the more one is conscious of it as such can only be accomplished by the establishment of communism. In order to supersede the *idea* of private property communist *ideas* are sufficient but *genuine* communist activity is necessary in order to supersede *real* private property. History will produce it, and the development which we already recognize in *thought* as self-transcending will in reality involve a severe and protracted process. We must, however, consider it an advance that we have previously acquired an awareness of the limited nature and the goal of the historical development and can see beyond it.

When communist *artisans* form associations teaching and propaganda are their first aims. But their association itself creates a new need—the need for society—and what appeared to be a means has become an end. The most striking results of this practical development are to be seen when French socialist workers meet together. Smoking, eating and drinking are no longer simply means of bringing people together. Society, association, entertainment which also has society as its aim, is sufficient for them; the brotherhood of man is no empty phrase but a reality, and the nobility of man shines forth upon us from their toilworn bodies. . . .

We said above that man is regressing to the *cave dwelling*, but in an alienated, malignant form. The savage in his cave (a natural element which is freely offered for his use and protection) does not feel himself a stranger; on the contrary he feels as much at home as a *fish* in water. But the cellar dwelling of the poor man is a hostile dwelling, "an alien, constricting power which only surrenders itself to him in exchange for blood and sweat." He cannot regard it as his home, as a place where he might at last say, "here I am at home." Instead, he finds himself

---

1. A part of the page is torn away here, and there follow fragments of six lines which are insufficient to reconstruct the passage.—*Tr. Note*

in *another person's* house, the house of a *stranger* who lies in wait for him every day and evicts him if he does not pay the rent. He is also aware of the contrast between his own dwelling and a human dwelling such as exists in *that other world,* the heaven of wealth.

Alienation is apparent not only in the fact that *my* means of life belong to *someone else,* that *my* desires are the unattainable possession of *someone else,* but that everything is *something different* from itself, that my activity is *something else,* and finally (and this is also the case for the capitalist) that *an inhuman power* rules over everything. There is a kind of wealth which is inactive, prodigal and devoted to pleasure, the beneficiary of which *behaves* as an *ephemeral,* aimlessly active individual who regards the slave labor of others, human *blood and sweat,* as the prey of his cupidity and sees mankind, and himself, as a sacrificial and superfluous being. Thus he acquires a contempt for mankind, expressed in the form of arrogance and the squandering of resources which would support a hundred human lives, and also in the form of the infamous illusion that his unbridled extravagance and endless unproductive consumption is a condition for the *labor* and *subsistence* of others. He regards the realization of the *essential powers* of man only as the realization of his own disorderly life, his whims and his capricious, bizarre ideas. Such wealth, however, which sees wealth merely as a means, as something to be consumed, and which is therefore both master and slave, generous and mean, capricious, presumptuous, conceited, refined, cultured, and witty, has not yet discovered *wealth* as a wholly *alien power* but sees in it its own power and enjoyment rather than wealth. . . .

Society, as it appears to the economist, is *civil society,* in which each individual is a totality of needs and only exists for another person, as another exists for him, in so far as each becomes a means for the other. The economist (like politics in its *rights of man*) reduces everything to man, i.e., to the individual, whom he deprives of all characteristics in order to classify him as a capitalist or a worker.

The *division of labor* is the economic expression of the *social character of labor* within alienation. Or, since *labor* is only an expression of human activity within alienation, of life activity as alienation of life, the *division of labor* is nothing but the *alienated* establishment of human activity as a *real species-activity* or *the activity of man as a species-being.* . . .

The whole of modern political economy is agreed, however, upon the fact that division of labor and wealth of production, division of labor and accumulation of capital, are mutually determining; and also that liberated and autonomous private property alone can produce the most effective and extensive division of labor.

Adam Smith's argument may be summarized as follows: the division of labor confers upon labor an unlimited capacity to produce. It arises from the *propensity to exchange and barter,* a specifically human propensity which is probably not fortuitous but determined by the use of reason and speech. The motive of those who engage in exchange is not humanity but *egoism.* The diversity of human talents is more the effect than the cause of the division of labor, i.e., of exchange. Furthermore, it is only the latter which makes this diversity useful. The particular qualities of the different tribes within an animal species are by nature more pronounced than the differences between the aptitudes and activities of human beings. But since animals are not able to exchange, the diversity of qualities in animals of the same species but of different tribes is of no benefit to any individual animal. Animals are unable to combine the various qualities of their species, or to contribute to the *common* advantage and comfort of the species. It is otherwise with *men,* whose most diverse talents and forms of activity are useful to each other, *because* they can bring their *different* products together in a common stock, from which each man can buy. As the division of labor arises from the propensity to *exchange,* so it develops and is limited by the *extent of exchange,* by the *extent of the market.* In developed conditions every man is a *merchant* and society is a *commercial association.* Say regards *exchange* as fortuitous and not fundamental. Society could exist without it. It becomes indispensable in an advanced state of society. Yet *production* cannot take place *without it.* The division of labor is a *convenient* and *useful* means, a skillful deployment of human powers for social wealth, but it diminishes the *capacity of each person* taken *individually*. The last remark is an advance on the part of Say. . . .

The consideration of *division of labor* and *exchange* is of the greatest interest, since they are the *perceptible, alienated* expression of human *activity* and *capacities* as the activity and capacities *proper to a species*. . . .

The *division of labor* and *exchange* are the two *phenomena* which lead the economist to vaunt the social character of his science, while in the same breath he unconsciously expresses the contradictory nature of his science—the establishment of society through unsocial, particular interests.

The factors we have to consider are as follows: the *propensity to exchange*—whose basis is egoism—is regarded as the cause of the reciprocal effect of the division of labor. Say considers exchange as being not *fundamental* to the nature of society. Wealth and production are explained by the division of labor and exchange. The impoverishment and denaturing of individual activity through the division of labor are admitted. Exchange and division of labor are recognized as the sources of the great *diversity of human talents*, a diversity which in turn becomes useful as a result of exchange. . . . Further, the division of labor is limited by the *market*. Human labor is simple *mechanical motion;* the major part is done by the material properties of the objects. The smallest possible number of operations must be allocated to each individual. Fission of labor and concentration of capital; the nullity of individual production and the mass production of wealth. Meaning of free private property in the division of labor.

14. The Destructive Power of Money

Marx advances the thesis that money is the alienated form of labor process as well as a "disruptive power," which undermines all social relations. This argument is presented in the present selection, the first part of which is taken from Marx's notes of 1844 on James Mill's *Treatise of Political Economy*, and the second part is from the Third of the *Economic and Philosophical Manuscripts* of the same year.

THE ESSENCE of money is not primarily that it externalizes property, but that the *mediating activity* or process—the *human* and social act in which man's products reciprocally complement one another—becomes *alienated* and takes on the quality of a *material thing*, money, external to man. By externalizing this mediating activity, man is active only as he is lost and dehumanized. The very *relationship* of things and the human dealings with them become an operation beyond and above man. Through this *alien mediation* man regards his will, his activity, and his relationships to others as a power independent of himself and of them—instead of man himself being the mediator for man. His slavery thus reaches a climax. It is clear that this *mediator* becomes an *actual god*, for the mediator is

First part from *Writings of the Young Marx on Philosophy and Society*, trans. and ed. by L. D. Easton and K. H. Guddat (New York: Doubleday-Anchor, 1967). Used by permission. Second part from *Marx's Concept of Man*, ed. by Erich Fromm, trans. by T. B. Bottomore (New York: Frederick Ungar, 1961). Used by permission.

the *actual power* over that which he mediates to me. His worship becomes an end in itself. Apart from this mediation, objects lose their value. They have value only insofar as they *represent* it while originally it appeared that the mediation would have value only insofar as *it* represents *objects*. This inversion of the original relationship is necessary. The *mediation,* therefore, is the lost, alienated *essence* of private property, exteriorated and *externalized* private property, just as it is the *externalized exchange* of human production with human production, the *externalized* species-activity of man. All qualities involved in this activity are transmitted to the mediator. Man as separated from this mediator thus becomes so much the poorer as the mediator becomes *richer*. . . .

Why must private property end up in *money?* Because man as a social being must resort to *exchange* and because exchange —under the presupposition of private property—must end up in value. The mediating process of man making exchanges is no social, no *human process,* no human relationship; rather, it is the *abstract relationship* of private property to private property, and this *abstract* relationship is the *value* whose actual existence as value is primarily *money*. Because men making exchanges do not relate to one another as men, *things* lose the significance of being human and personal property. The social relationship of private property to private property is a relationship in which private property has alienated itself. The reflexive existence of this relationship, money, is thus the externalization of private property, an abstraction from its *specific* and personal nature. . . .

[. . . Money is] the *pander* between need and object, between human life and the means of subsistence. But *that which* mediates *my* life mediates also the existence of other men for me. It is for me the *other* person.

> "Why, Zounds! Both hands and feet are, truly—
> And head and virile forces—thine:
> Yet all that I indulge in newly,

Is't thence less wholly mine?
If I've six stallions in my stall,
Are not their forces also lent me?
I speed along completest man of all,
As though my feet were four-and-twenty.
                    (Goethe, *Faust*—Mephistopheles)[1]

Shakespeare in *Timon of Athens:*

Gold? yellow, glittering, precious gold? No, gods,
I am no idle votarist: roots, you clear heavens!
Thus much of this will make black, white; foul, fair;
Wrong, right; base, noble; old, young; coward, valiant.
.... Why this
Will lug your priests and servants from your sides;
Pluck stout men's pillows from below their heads:
This yellow slave
Will knit and break religions; bless th' accurst;
Make the hoar leprosy ador'd; place thieves,
And give them title, knee, and approbation,
With senators on the bench: this is it
That makes the wappen'd widow wed again;
She whom the spital-house and ulcerous sores
Would cast the gorge at, this embalms and spices
To th'April day again. Come, damned earth,
Thou common whore of mankind, that putt'st odds
Among the rout of nations, I will make thee
Do thy right nature."[2]

And later on:

"O thou sweet king-killer, and dear divorce
'Twixt natural son and sire! Thou bright defiler
Of Hymen's purest bed! thou valiant Mars!
Thou ever young, fresh, loved, and delicate wooer,
Whose blush doth thaw the consecrated snow
That lies on Dian's lap! thou visible god,
That solder'st close impossibilities,

---

1. Goethe, *Faust.* Part I, Scene 4. This passage is taken from the translation by Bayard Taylor; the Modern Library, New York, 1950.—*Tr. Note*
2. Shakespeare, *Timon of Athens.* Act IV, Scene 3. Marx quotes from the Schlegel-Tieck translation.—*Tr. Note*

And mak'st them kiss! that speak'st with every tongue,
To every purpose! O thou touch of hearts!
Think, thy slave man rebels; and by the virtue
Set them into confounding odds, that beasts
May have the world in empire!"[3]

Shakespeare portrays admirably the nature of *money*. To understand him, let us begin by expounding the passage from Goethe.

That which exists for me through the medium of *money*, that which I can pay for (i.e., which money can buy), that I *am*, the possessor of the money. My own power is as great as the power of money. The properties of money are my own (the possessor's) properties and faculties. What I *am* and *can do* is, therefore, not at all determined by my individuality. I *am* ugly, but I can buy the *most beautiful* woman for myself. Consequently, I am not *ugly*, for the effect of *ugliness*, its power to repel, is annulled by money. As an individual I am *lame*, but money provides me with twenty-four legs. Therefore, I am not lame. I am a detestable, dishonorable, unscrupulous and stupid man, but money is honored and so also is its possessor. Money is the highest good, and so its possessor is good. Besides, money saves me the trouble of being dishonest; therefore, I am presumed honest. I am *stupid*, but since money is the *real mind* of all things, how should its possessor be stupid? Moreover, he can buy talented people for himself, and is not he who has power over the talented more talented than they? I who can have, through the power of money, *everything* for which the human heart longs, do I not possess all human abilities? Does not my money, therefore, transform all my incapacities into their opposites?

If *money* is the bond which binds me to *human* life, and society to me, and which links me with nature and man, is it not the bond of all *bonds?* Is it not, therefore, also the universal agent of separation? It is the real means of both *separation* and *union*, the galvano-*chemical* power of society.

Shakespeare emphasizes particularly two properties of money: (1) it is the visible deity, the transformation of all human

3. *Ibid.*

and natural qualities into their opposites, the universal confusion and inversion of things; it brings incompatibles into fraternity; (2) it is the universal whore, the universal pander between men and nations.

The power to confuse and invert all human and natural qualities, to bring about fraternization of incompatibles, the *divine* power of money, resides in its *character* as the alienated and self-alienating species-life of man. It is the alienated *power* of *humanity*.

What I as a *man* am unable to do, and thus what all my individual faculties are unable to do, is made possible for me by *money*. Money, therefore, turns each of these faculties into something which it is not, into its *opposite*.

If I long for a meal, or wish to take the mail coach because I am not strong enough to go on foot, money provides the meal and the mail coach; i.e., it transforms my desires from representations into *realities*, from imaginary being into *real being*. In mediating thus, money is a *genuinely creative* power.

Demand also exists for the individual who has no money, but his demand is a mere creature of the imagination which has no effect, no existence for me, for a third party . . . and which thus remains *unreal* and *without object*. The difference between effective demand, supported by money, and ineffective demand, based upon my need, my passion, my desire, etc., is the difference between *being* and *thought*, between the merely *inner* representation and the representation which exists outside myself as a *real object*.

If I have no money for travel I have no *need*—no real and self-realizing need—for travel. If I have a *vocation* for study but no money for it, then I have *no* vocation, i.e., no *effective*, *genuine* vocation. Conversely, if I really have *no* vocation for study, but have money and the urge for it, then I have an *effective* vocation. *Money* is the external, universal *means* and *power* (not derived from man as man or from human society as society) to change *representation* into *reality* and *reality* into *mere representation*. It transforms *real human and natural faculties* into mere abstract representations, i.e., *imperfections* and tormenting chimeras; and on the other hand, it transforms *real imperfections and fancies,* faculties which are really impotent and which exist only in the individual's imagination, into *real faculties and powers.* In this respect, therefore, money is the general inversion of *individualities,* turning them into their opposites and associating contradictory qualities with their qualities.

Money, then, appears as a *disruptive* power for the individual and for the social bonds, which claim to be self-subsistent *entities.* It changes fidelity into infidelity, love into hate, hate into love, virtue into vice, vice into virtue, servant into master, stupidity into intelligence and intelligence into stupidity.

Since money, as the existing and active concept of value, confounds and exchanges everything, it is the universal *confusion and transposition* of all things, the inverted world, the confusion and transposition of all natural and human qualities.

He who can purchase bravery is brave, though a coward. Money is not exchanged for a particular quality, a particular thing, or a specific human faculty, but for the whole objective world of man and nature. Thus, from the standpoint of its possessor, it exchanges every quality and object for every other, even though they are contradictory. It is the fraternization of incompatibles; it forces contraries to embrace.

Let us assume *man* to be *man,* and his relation to the world to be a human one. Then love can only be exchanged for love, trust for trust, etc. If you wish to enjoy art you must be an artistically cultivated person; if you wish to influence other people you must be a person who really has a stimulating and encouraging effect upon others. Every one of your relations to man and to nature must be a *specific expression,* corresponding to the object of your will, of your *real individual* life. If you love without evoking love in return, i.e., if you are not able, by the *manifestation* of yourself as a loving person, to make yourself a *beloved person,* then your love is impotent and a misfortune.

15. *Alienated Labor* versus *Truly Human Production*

This selection is also taken from Marx's notes and comments on Mill's *Treatise;* it directly contrasts alienated labor under capitalism with the concept of labor which would not be so alienated. This is a crucial discussion, for it explores in more detail than elsewhere the positive nature of Marx's communist ideal.

. . .THE *EXCHANGE* OF human activity within production itself as well as the exchange of *human products* with one another is equivalent to the *generic activity* and generic spirit whose actual, conscious, and authentic existence is *social* activity and *social* satisfaction. As *human* nature is the *true common life* [*Gemeinwesen*] of man, men through the activation of their *nature create* and produce a human *common life*, a social essence which is no abstractly universal power opposed to the single individual, but is the essence or nature of every single individual, his own activity, his own life, his own spirit, his own wealth. *Authentic common life* arises not through reflection; rather it comes about from the *need* and *egoism* of individuals, that is, immediately from the activation of their very existence. It is not up to man whether this common life exists or not. However, so long as man does not recognize himself as man and does not organize the world humanly, this *common life* appears

From *Writings of the Young Marx on Philosophy and Society*, trans. and ed. by L. D. Easton and K. H. Guddat (New York: Doubleday-Anchor, 1967). Used by permission.

in the form of *alienation*, because its *subject*, man, is a being alienated from itself. Men as actual, living, particular individuals, not in an abstraction, *constitute* this common life. It is, therefore, *what* men are. To say that *man* alienates himself is the same as saying that the *society* of this alienated man is the caricature of his *actual common life*, of his true generic life. His activity, therefore, appears as torment, his own creation as a force alien to him, his wealth as poverty, the *essential bond* connecting him with other men as something unessential so that the separation from other men appears as his true existence. His life appears as the sacrifice of his life, the realization of his nature as the diminution of his life, his production as the production of his destruction, his power over the object as the power of the object over him; the master of his creation appears as its slave.

Political economy understands the *common life of man*, the self-activating *human* essence and mutual redintegration toward generic and truly human life, in the form of *exchange* and *commerce*. Society, says Destutt de Tracy, is a *series of multilateral exchanges*. It is constituted by this movement of multilateral integration. *Society*, says Adam Smith, is a *commercial enterprise*. Each of its members is a *merchant*. It is evident that political economy *establishes* an *alienated* form of social intercourse as the *essential*, *original*, and definitive human form.

Economics—like the actual process itself—proceeds from the *relationship of man to man* and from the relationship of one *property owner to another*. Let us presuppose man as *property owner*, that is, an exclusive possessor who maintains his personality and distinguishes himself from other men and relates himself to them through this exclusive possession. Private property is his personal existence, his *distinguishing* and hence essential existence. The *loss* or *relinquishing* of private property, then, is an *externalization of man* as well as of *private property*. We are concerned here only with the latter. When I yield my private property to another person, it ceases being mine. It becomes something independent of me and *outside* my sphere, something *external* to me. I *externalize* my private property. So far as I am concerned, it is *externalized* private property. I see it only as something generally *externalized;* I only transcend my *personal* relationship to it; and I return it to the *elemental* forces of nature when I externalize it only in relation to myself. It only becomes externalized *private property* as it ceases being *my* private property without ceasing to be *private property* in general, that is, when it acquires the same relationship to *another* man *outside* of me, as it had to me—in a word, when it becomes the *private property* of *another* man. Apart from the situation of *force,* what causes me to externalize *my* private property to another person? Economics answers correctly: *need* and *want.* The other person is also a property owner, but of *another* object which I lack and which I neither can nor want to be without, an object which to me seems to be something *needed* for the redintegration of my existence and the realization of my nature.

The bond relating the two property owners to each other is the *specific nature of the object.* The fact that either property owner desires and wants objects makes him aware that he has another *essential* relationship to objects outside of property and that he is not the particular being he takes himself to be but rather a *total* being whose wants have a relationship of *inner* property to the products of the labor of the other person. For the need of an object is the most evident and irrefutable proof that the object belongs to *my* nature and that the existence of the object for me and its *property* are the property appropriate to my essence. Both owners are thus impelled to relinquish their property, but in such a way that at the same time they reaffirm that property; or they are impelled to relinquish that property within the relationship of private property. Each thus externalizes a part of his property in the other person.

The *social* relationship of both owners is thus the *mutuality of externalization,* the relationship of externalization on both sides—or *externalization* as the relationship of both owners—while in simple private property *externalization* takes place only one-sidedly, in relationship to itself.

Exchange or *barter,* therefore, is the social, generic act, the common essence, the social intercourse and integration of man within *private property,* and the external, the *externalized* generic act. For that very reason it appears as *barter*. And hence it is likewise the opposite of the *social* relationship.

Through the mutual externalization or alienation of private property, *private property* itself has been determined as *externalized* private property. First of all it has ceased being the product of labor and being the exclusive, distinctive personality of its owner because the owner has externalized it; it has been removed from the owner whose product it was and has acquired a personal significance for the person who did *not* produce it. It has lost its personal significance for the owner. In the second place it has been related to and equated with another private property. A private property of a *different* nature has taken its place, just as it itself takes the position of a private property of a *different* nature. On both sides, then, private property appears as a representative of private property of a different nature, as the *equivalence* of another natural product. Both sides are so related that each represents the existence of the *other* and they mutually serve as *substitutes* for themselves and the other. The existence of private property as such has thus become a *substitute*, an *equivalent*. Instead of its immediate self-unity it exists only in relationship to *something else*. As an *equivalent* its existence is no longer something peculiarly appropriate to it. It has become *value* and immediately *exchange value*. Its existence as *value* is a determination of *itself*, different from its immediate existence, outside of its specific nature, and *externalized*—only a *relative* existence. . . .

The relationship of exchange being presupposed, *labor immediately* becomes *wage-labor*. This relationship of alienated labor reaches its apex only by the fact (1) that on the one side *wage-labor*, the product of the laborer, stands in no *immediate* relationship to his need and to his *status* but is rather determined in both directions through social combinations alien to the laborer; (2) that the *buyer* of the product is not himself productive but exchanges what has been produced by others. In the crude form of *externalized* private property, *barter*, each of the two private owners produces what his need, his inclination, and the existing raw material induces him to produce. They exchange only the surplus of their production. To be sure, labor was for each one the immediate *source of his subsistence;* at the same time, however, it was also the confirmation of his *individual existence.* Through exchange, his *labor* has partly become his *source of income.* The purpose and existence of labor have changed. The product is created as *value, exchange value,* and an *equivalent* and no longer because of its immediate personal relationship to the producer. The more varied production becomes—in other words, the more varied the needs become on the one hand and the more one-sided the producer's output becomes on the other—the more does his labor fall into the category of *wage-labor,* until it is eventually nothing but wage-labor and until it becomes entirely *incidental* and *unessential* whether the producer immediately enjoys and needs his product and whether the *activity,* the action of labor itself, is his self-satisfaction and the realization of his natural dispositions and spiritual aims.

The following elements are contained in *wage-labor:* (1) the chance relationship and alienation of labor from the laboring subject; (2) the chance relationship and alienation of labor from its object; (3) the determination of the laborer through social needs which are an alien compulsion to him, a compulsion to which he submits out of egoistic need and distress—these social needs are merely a source of providing the necessities of life for him, just as he is merely a slave for them; (4) the maintenance of his individual existence appears to the worker as the *goal* of his activity and his real action is only a means; he lives to acquire the means of *living.*

The greater and the more articulated the social power is within the relationship of private property, the more *egoistic* and asocial man becomes, the more he becomes alienated from his own nature.

Just as the mutual exchange of products of *human activity* appears as *trading* and *bargaining,* so does the mutual redintegration and exchange of the activity itself appear as the *division of labor* making man as far as possible an abstract being, an automaton, and transforming him into a spiritual and physical monster.

Precisely the unity of human labor is regarded as being its

division because its social nature comes into being only as its opposite, in the form of alienation. The *division of labor* increases with civilization.

Within the presupposition of the division of labor, the product and material of private property gradually acquire for the individual the significance of an *equivalent*. He no longer exchanges his *surplus*, and he can become *indifferent* to the object of his production. He no longer immediately exchanges his product for the product he *needs*. The equivalent becomes an equivalent in *money* which is the immediate result of wage-labor and the *medium* of exchange.

The complete domination of the alienated object *over* man is evident in *money* and the complete disregard of the nature of the material, the specific nature of private property as well as the personality of the proprietor.

What formerly was the domination of one person over another has now become the general domination of the *thing* over the *person*, the domination of the product over the producer. Just as the determination of the *externalization* of private property lay in the *equivalent* and in value, so is *money* the sensuous, self-objectified existence of this *externalization*.. . .

It is the basic presupposition of private property that man *produces* only in order to *own*. The purpose of production is to *own*. It not only has such a *useful* purpose; it also has a *selfish* purpose. Man only produces in order to *own* something for himself. The object of his production is the objectification of his *immediate*, selfish *need*. Man—in his wild, barbaric condition—determines his production by the *extent* of his immediate need whose content is the *immediately* produced object itself.

In that condition man produces *no more* than he immediately needs. The *limit of his need* is the *limit of his production*. Demand and supply coincide. Production is *determined* by need. Either no exchange takes place or the exchange is reduced to the exchange of man's labor for the product of his labor, and this exchange is the latent form (the germ) of real exchange.

As soon as exchange occurs, there is an overproduction beyond the immediate boundary of ownership. But this overproduction does not exceed selfish need. Rather it is only an *indirect* way of satisfying a need which finds its objectification in the production of another person. Production has become a *source of income*, labor for profit. While formerly need determined the extent of production, now production, or rather the *owning of the product*, determines how far needs can be satisfied.

I have produced for myself and not for you, just as you have produced for yourself and not for me. The result of my production as such has as little direct connection with you as the result of your production has with me, that is, our production is not production of man for man as man, not *socialized* production. No one is gratified by the product of another. Our mutual production means nothing for us as human beings. Our exchange, therefore, cannot be the mediating movement in which it would be acknowledged that my product means anything for you because it is an *objectification* of your being, your need. *Human nature* is not the bond of our production for each other. Exchange can only set in *motion* and confirm the *relationship* which each of us has to his own product and to the production of the other person. Each of us sees in his product only his *own* objectified self-interest and in the product of another person, *another* self-interest which is independent, alien, and objectified.

As a human being, however, you do have a human relation to my product; you *want* my product. It is the object of your desire and your will. But your want, desire, and will for my product are impotent. In other words, your *human* nature, necessarily and intimately related to my human production, is not your *power*, not your sharing in this production, because the *power* of human nature is not acknowledged in my production. Rather it is in the *bond* which makes you dependent upon me because it makes you dependent on my product. It is far from being the *means* of giving you *power* over my production; rather it is the *means* of giving me power over you.

When I produce *more* than I can consume, I subtly *reckon*

with your need. I produce only the *semblance* of a surplus of
the object. In truth I produce a *different* object, the object of
your production which I plan to exchange for this surplus, an
exchange already accomplished in thought. My *social* relationship with you and my labor for your want is just plain *deception*
and our mutual redintegration is *deception* just as well. Mutual
pillaging is its base. Its background is the intent to pillage, to
defraud. Since our exchange is selfish on your side as well as
mine and since every self-interest attempts to surpass that of
another person, we necessarily attempt to defraud each other.
The power I give my object over yours, however, requires your
acknowledgment to become real. Our mutual acknowledgment
of the mutual power of our objects is a battle and the one with
more insight, energy, power, and cleverness is the winner. If
my physical strength suffices, I pillage you directly. If there is
no physical power, we mutually dissemble and the more adroit
comes out on top. It makes no difference for the *entire* relationship who the winner is, for the *ideal* and *intended* victory takes
place on both sides; in his own judgment each of the two has
overcome the other.

On both sides exchange necessarily requires the *object* of
mutual production and mutual ownership. The ideal relationship to the mutual objects of our production is our mutual need.
But the *real* and *truly effective* relationship is only the mutually
exclusive ownership of mutual production. It is your *object*, the
equivalent of my object, that gives your want for my object
value, dignity, and *efficacy* for me. Our mutual product, therefore, is the *means,* the *intermediary,* the *instrument,* the *acknowledged power* of our mutual needs. Your *demand* and the
equivalent of your property are terms which for me are *synonymous* and equally valid, and your demand is effective only
when it has an effect on me. Without this effect your demand
is merely an unsatisfied effort on your part and without consequence for me. You have no relationship to my object as a
human being because I *myself* have no human relation to it.
But the *means* is the *real power* over an object, and we mutually regard our product as the *power* each one has over the
other and over himself. In other words, our own product is

turned against us. It appeared to be our property, but actually we are its property. We ourselves are excluded from *true* property because our *property* excludes the other human being.

Our objects in their relation to one another constitute the only intelligible language we use with one another. We would not understand a human language, and it would remain without effect. On the one hand, it would be felt and spoken as a plea, as begging, and as *humiliation* and hence uttered with shame and with a feeling of supplication; on the other hand, it would be heard and rejected as *effrontery* or *madness*. We are so much mutually alienated from human nature that the direct language of this nature is an *injury to human dignity* for us, while the alienated language of objective values appears as justified, self-confident, and self-accepted human dignity.

To be sure, from your point of view your product is an *instrument*, a *means* for the appropriation of my product and for the satisfaction of your need. But from my point of view it is the *goal* of our exchange. I regard you as a means and instrument for the production of this object, that is, my goal, and much more so than I regard you as related to my object. But (1) each of us actually *does* what the other thinks he is doing. You actually made yourself the means, the instrument, and the producer of *your* own object in order to appropriate mine; (2) for you, your own object is only the *sensuous shell* and *concealed form* of my object; its production *means* and *expressly* is the *acquisition* of my object. You indeed become the *means* and *instrument* of your object; your greed is the *slave* of this object, and you performed slavish services so that the object is never again a remission of your greed. This mutual servitude to the object is actually manifested to us at the beginning of its development as the relationship of *lordship* and *slavery*, and is only the *crude* and *frank* expression of our *essential* relationship.

Our *mutual* value is the *value* of our mutual objects for us. Man himself, therefore, is mutually *valueless* for us.

Suppose we had produced things as human beings: in his production each of us would have *twice affirmed* himself and the other. (1) In my *production* I would have objectified my *individuality* and its *particularity*, and in the course of the activity I would have enjoyed an individual *life;* in viewing the object I would have experienced the individual joy of knowing my personality as an *objective, sensuously perceptible,* and *indubitable* power. (2) In your satisfaction and your use of my product I would have had the *direct* and conscious satisfaction that my work satisfied a *human* need, that it objectified *human* nature, and that it created an object appropriate to the need of another *human* being. (3) I would have been the *mediator* between you and the species and you would have experienced me as a redintegration of your own nature and a necessary part of your self; I would have been affirmed in your thought as well as your love. (4) In my individual life I would have directly created your life; in my individual activity I would have immediately *confirmed* and *realized* my true *human* and *social* nature.

Our productions would be so many mirrors reflecting our nature.

What happens so far as I am concerned would also apply to you.

Let us summarize the various factors in the supposition above:

My labor would be a *free manifestation of life* and an *enjoyment* of *life.* Under the presupposition of private property it is an *externalization of life* because I work *in order to live* and provide for myself the *means* of living. Working *is not* living.

Furthermore, in my labor the *particularity* of my individuality would be affirmed because my *individual* life is affirmed. Labor then would be *true, active property.* Under the presupposition of private property my individuality is externalized to the point where I *hate* this *activity* and where it is a *torment* for me. Rather it is then only the *semblance* of an activity, only a *forced* activity, imposed upon me only by *external* and accidental necessity and *not* by an *internal* and *determined* necessity.

My labor can appear in my object only according to its nature; it cannot appear as something *different* from itself. My labor, therefore, is manifested as the objective, sensuous, perceptible, and indubitable expression of my *self-loss* and my *powerlessness.*

III.

Critique of the Philosophical Tradition (1844–1846)

During the year 1844–1845, Marx made what he considered to be his final break with the Western philosophical tradition, as represented by (a) the idealist Hegel, who claimed to synthesize in his thought the aspirations to "Absolute Knowledge" characteristic of the Platonic-idealistic tradition; (b) the naïve materialists of France since Descartes and of England since Bacon; and (c) Feuerbach, the one thinker who had seriously attempted—and succeeded—with the *philosophical* unification of these two standpoints in his "anthropological materialism."

It is with the "abstract" and de facto conservative quality of even Feuerbach that philosophy has demonstrated—to Marx—its inability to deal in a progressive manner with the ongoing process of history, that is, with mankind's continual appropriation of the natural and social worlds. As will be indicated in Part IV, which focuses on Marx's historical materialism, philosophy had become for Marx synonymous with mere speculation, at best an ideological recapitulation of past and present from the viewpoint of the masters of the present; that is, philosophy is essentially retrospective, a static "view" which is irrelevant to the problem of guiding a concrete futurity. Thus, philosophy (along with religion, political ideals, and other forms of ideology) became, for Marx, nothing more than an "illusion of its epoch."

The selections which follow are taken from Marx's *Critique of Hegel's Dialectic and General Philosophy* (1844), *The Holy Family* (written with Engels, 1844–1845), the *Theses on Feuerbach* (1845), and *The German Ideology* (written with Engels, 1845–1846).

16. Critique of Hegel

Examination of Marx's relation to the Western philosophical tradition begins with his most fundamental critique of Hegel, which appeared in a section of the *Economic and Philosophical Manuscripts* entitled "Critique of Hegel's Dialectic and General Philosophy." Marx first comments on the role played by Feuerbach in founding "genuine materialism" on the basis of the Hegelian dialectic. Within a year of these manuscripts, as illustrated in Selection 19 below, Marx is to find Feuerbach's materialism too abstract. In this present selection, however, Marx criticizes Hegel for his idealism, that is, for his (allegedly) beginning his philosophical enterprise not with "real, concrete man" but with consciousness. Thus, Marx sees Hegel's system as itself but another form of alienation of human nature, although he does recognize the "dialectics of negativity" as the "outstanding achievement" of Hegel's *Phenomenology of Spirit*. Marx then enters into a discussion of man as a "natural being" and a "species-being," presenting his ontology as explicitly as we shall ever see it. The entire argument is based upon the contrast of man as understood by Hegel (and the Idealists) as self-consciousness and Marx's own, more concrete, understanding of man as his self-creative (hence, historical) activity (=labor). While directed at Hegel, this essay is therefore more than a critique of Hegel's philosophy; it is a critique of idealist philosophy in general.

From *Marx's Concept of Man*, ed. by Erich Fromm, trans. by T. B. Bottomore (New York: Frederick Ungar, 1961). Used by permission.

THIS IS perhaps an appropriate point at which to explain and substantiate what has been said, and to make some general comments upon Hegel's dialectic, especially as it is expounded in the *Phenomenology* and *Logic*, and upon its relation to the modern critical movement.

Modern German criticism was so much concerned with the past, and was so hampered by its involvement with its subject matter, that it had a wholly uncritical attitude to the methods of criticism and completely ignored the partly formal, but in fact *essential* question—how do we now stand with regard to the Hegelian *dialectic*? . . .

Feuerbach is the only person who has a *serious* and *critical* relation to Hegel's dialectic, who has made real discoveries in this field, and above all, who has vanquished the old philosophy. The magnitude of Feuerbach's achievement and the unassuming simplicity with which he presents his work to the world are in striking contrast with the behavior of others.

Feuerbach's great achievement is: (1) to have shown that philosophy is nothing more than religion brought into thought and developed by thought, and that it is equally to be condemned as another form and mode of existence of human alienation; (2) to have founded *genuine materialism* and *positive science* by making the social relationship of "man to man" the basic principle of his theory; (3) to have opposed to the negation of the negation which claims to be the absolute positive, a self-subsistent principle positively founded on itself. . . .

In conceiving the negation of the negation, from the aspect of the positive relation inherent in it, as the only true positive, and from the aspect of the negative relation inherent in it, as the only true act and self-confirming act of all being, Hegel has merely discovered an *abstract, logical* and *speculative* expression of the historical process, which is not yet the *real* history of man as a given subject, but only the history of the *act of creation*, of the *genesis of man*. . . .

Hegel's *Encyclopaedia* begins with logic, with *pure specula-*

tive thought, and ends with *absolute knowledge,* the self-conscious and self-conceiving philosophical or absolute mind, i.e., the superhuman, abstract mind. The whole of the *Encyclopaedia* is nothing but the *extended being* of the philosophical mind, its self-objectification; and the philosophical mind is nothing but the alienated world mind thinking within the bounds of its self-alienation, i.e., conceiving itself in an abstract manner. *Logic* is the money of the mind, the speculative thought-*value* of man and of nature, their essence indifferent to any real determinate character and thus unreal; *thought* which is *alienated* and abstract and which ignores real nature and man. *The external character of this abstract thought . . . nature* as it exists for this abstract thought. Nature is external to it, loss of itself, and is only conceived as something external, as abstract thought, but alienated abstract thought. Finally, spirit, this thought which returns to its own origin and which, as anthropological, phenomenological, psychological, customary, artistic-religious spirit, is not valid for itself until it discovers itself and relates itself to itself as absolute knowledge in the absolute (i.e., abstract) spirit, and so receives its conscious and fitting existence. For its real mode of existence is *abstraction.*

Hegel commits a double error. The first appears most clearly in the *Phenomenology,* the birthplace of his philosophy. When Hegel conceives wealth, the power of the state, etc., as entities alienated from the human being, he conceives them only in their thought form. They are entities of thought and thus simply an alienation of *pure* (i.e., abstract philosophical) thought. The whole movement, therefore, ends in absolute knowledge. It is precisely abstract thought from which these objects are alienated, and which they confront with their presumptuous reality. The *philosopher,* himself an abstract form of alienated man, sets himself up as the *measure* of the alienated world. The whole *history of alienation,* and of the *retraction* of alienation, is therefore only the *history of the production* of abstract thought, i.e., of absolute, logical, speculative thought. *Estrangement,* which thus forms the real interest of this alienation and of the supersession of this alienation, is the opposition of *in itself* and *for itself,* of *consciousness* and *self-consciousness,* of *object* and *subject,* i.e., the opposition in thought itself between abstract thought and sensible reality or real sensuous existence. All other contradictions and movements are merely the *appearance,* the *cloak,* the *exoteric* form of these two opposites which are alone important and which constitute the *significance* of the other, profane contradictions. It is not the fact that the human being *objectifies* himself *inhumanly,* in opposition to himself, but that he *objectifies* himself by *distinction* from and in *opposition* to abstract thought, which constitutes alienation as its exists and as it has to be transcended.

The appropriation of man's objectified and alienated faculties is thus, in the first place, only an *appropriation* which occurs in *consciousness,* in *pure thought,* i.e., in *abstraction.* It is the appropriation of these objects as *thoughts* and as *movements of thought.* For this reason, despite its thoroughly negative and critical appearance, and despite the genuine criticism which it contains and which often anticipates later developments, there is already implicit in the *Phenomenology,* as a germ, as a potentiality and a secret, the uncritical positivism and uncritical idealism of Hegel's later works—the philosophical dissolution and restoration of the existing empirical world. *Secondly,* the vindication of the objective world for man (for example, the recognition that *sense* perception is not *abstract* sense perception but *human* sense perception, that religion, wealth, etc., are only the alienated reality of *human* objectification, of *human* faculties put to work, and are therefore a *way* to genuine *human* reality), this appropriation, or the insight into this process, appears in Hegel as the recognition of *sensuousness, religion,* state power, etc., as *mental* phenomena, for *mind* alone is the *true* essence of man, and the true form of mind is thinking mind, the logical, speculative mind. The *human character* of nature, of historically produced nature, of man's products, is shown by their being *products* of abstract mind, and thus phases of *mind, entities of thought.* The *Phenomenology* is a concealed, unclear and mystifying criticism, but in so far as it grasps the *alienation* of man (even though man appears only as mind) *all* the elements of criticism are contained in it, and are often *presented* and *worked out* in a manner which goes far beyond Hegel's own point of view. The sections devoted to the "unhappy consciousness," the "honest consciousness," the struggle between the "noble" and the "base" consciousness, etc., etc., contain the *critical* elements (though still in an alienated form) of whole areas such as religion, the state, civil life, etc. Just as the *entity,* the *object,* appears as an entity of thought, so also the *subject* is always *consciousness* or *self-consciousness;* or rather, the object appears only as *abstract* consciousness and man as *self-consciousness.* Thus the distinctive forms of alienation which are manifested are only different forms of consciousness and self-consciousness. Since abstract consciousness (the form in which the object is conceived) is in *itself* merely a distinctive moment of self-consciousness, the outcome of the movement is the identity of self-consciousness and consciousness—absolute knowledge—the movement of abstract thought not directed outwards but proceeding within itself; i.e., the dialectic of pure thought is the result.

The outstanding achievement of Hegel's *Phenomenology*— the dialectic of negativity as the moving and creating principle —is, first, that Hegel grasps the self-creation of man as a process, objectification as loss of the object, as alienation and transcendence of this alienation, and that he therefore grasps the nature of *labor,* and conceives objective man (true, because real man) as the result of his *own labor.* The *real,* active orientation of man to himself as a species-being, or the affirmation of himself as a real species-being (i.e., as a human being) is only possible so far as he really brings forth all his *species-powers* (which is only possible through the cooperative endeavors of mankind and as an outcome of history) and treats these powers as objects, which can only be done at first in the form of alienation. . . .

For the present, let us make these preliminary observations: Hegel's standpoint is that of modern political economy. He conceives *labor* as the *essence,* the self-confirming essence of man; he observes only the positive side of labor, not its negative side. Labor is *man's coming to be for himself* within *alienation,* or as an *alienated* man. Labor as Hegel understands and recognizes it is *abstract mental* labor. Thus, that which above all constitutes the *essence* of philosophy, the *alienation of man knowing himself,* or *alienated* science *thinking* itself, Hegel grasps as its essence. Consequently he is able to bring together the separate elements of earlier philosophy and to present his own as *the* philosophy. . . .

For Hegel, *human life, man,* is equivalent to *self-consciousness.* All alienation of human life is therefore *nothing* but *alienation of self-consciousness.* The alienation of self-consciousness is not regarded as the *expression,* reflected in knowledge and thought, of the *real* alienation of human life. Instead, *actual* alienation, that which appears real, is in its *innermost* hidden nature (which philosophy first discloses) only the *phenomenal being* of the alienation of real human life, of *self-consciousness.* The science which comprehends this is therefore called *Phenomenology.* All reappropriation of alienated objective life appears therefore as an incorporation in self-consciousness. The person who takes possession of his being is only the self-consciousness which takes possession of objective being; the return of the object into the Self is therefore the reappropriation of the object. . . .

When real, corporeal *man,* with his feet firmly planted on the solid ground, inhaling and exhaling all the powers of nature, *posits* his real objective *faculties,* as a result of his alienation, as alien objects, the *positing* is not the subject of this act but the subjectivity of *objective* faculties whose action must also therefore be *objective.* An objective being acts objectively, and it would not act objectively if objectivity were not part of its essential being. It creates and establishes *only objects because* it is established by objects, and because it is fundamentally *natural.* In the act of establishing it does not descend from its "pure activity" to the *creation of objects;* its *objective* product simply confirms its *objective* activity, its activity as an objective, natural being.

We see here how consistent naturalism or humanism is distinguished from both idealism and materialism, and at the same time constitutes their unifying truth. We see also that only naturalism is able to comprehend the process of world history.

Man is directly a *natural being.* As a natural being, and as a living natural being he is, on the one hand, endowed with *natu-*

ral powers and *faculties,* which exist in him as tendencies and abilities, as *drives.* On the other hand, as a natural, embodied, sentient, objective being he is a *suffering,* conditioned and limited being, like animals and plants. The *objects* of his drives exist outside himself as *objects* independent of him, yet they are *objects* of his *needs,* essential *objects* which are indispensable to the exercise and confirmation of his faculties. The fact that man is an *embodied,* living, real, sentient, objective being with natural powers, means that he has *real, sensuous objects* as the objects of his being, or that he can only express his being in real, sensuous objects. *To be* objective, natural, sentient and at the same time to have object, nature and sense outside oneself, or to be oneself object, nature and sense for a third person, is the same thing. *Hunger* is a natural *need;* it requires therefore a *nature* outside itself, an *object* outside itself, in order to be satisfied and stilled. Hunger is the objective need of a body for an *object* which exists outside itself and which is essential for its integration and the expression of its nature. The sun is an *object,* a necessary and life-assuring object, for the plant, just as the plant is an object for the sun, an *expression* of the sun's life-giving power and *objective* essential powers.

A being which does not have its nature outside itself is not a *natural* being and does not share in the being of nature. A being which has no object outside itself is not an objective being. A being which is not itself an object for a third being has no being for its *object,* i.e., it is not objectively related and its being is not objective.

A nonobjective being is a *nonbeing.* Suppose a being which neither is an object itself nor has an object. In the first place, such a being would be the *only* being; no other being would exist outside itself and it would be solitary and alone. For as soon as there exist objects outside myself, as soon as I am not *alone,* I am *another, another reality* from object outside me. For this third object I am thus an *other reality* than itself, i.e., *its object.* To suppose a being which is not the object of another being would be to suppose that *no* objective being exists. As soon as I have an object, this object has me for its object. But a *nonobjective* being is an unreal, nonsensuous, merely conceived being; i.e., a merely imagined being, an abstraction. To be *sensuous,* i.e., real, is to be an object of sense or *sensuous* object, and thus to have sensuous objects outside oneself, objects of one's sensations. To be sentient is to *suffer* (to experience).

Man as an objective sentient being is a *suffering* being, and since he feels his suffering, a *passionate* being. Passion is man's faculties striving to attain their object.

But man is not merely a natural being; he is a *human* natural being. He is a being for himself, and therefore a *species-being;* and as such he has to express and authenticate himself in being as well as in thought. Consequently, *human* objects are not natural objects as they present themselves directly, nor is *human sense,* as it is immediately and objectively *given, human* sensibility and human objectivity. Neither objective nature nor subjective nature is directly presented in a form adequate to the *human* being. And as everything natural must have its *origin so man* has his process of genesis, *history,* which is for him, however, a conscious process and thus one which is consciously self-transcending. . . .

We have now to consider the *positive* moments of Hegel's dialectic, within the condition of alienation.

(a) *Supersession* as an objective movement which *reabsorbs* alienation into itself. This is the insight, expressed within alienation, into the *appropriation* of the objective being through the supersession of its alienation. It is the alienated insight into the *real objectification* of man, into the real appropriation of his objective being by the destruction of the *alienated* character of the objective world, by the annulment of its alienated mode of existence. In the same way, atheism as the annulment of God is the emergence of theoretical humanism, and communism as the annulment of private property is the vindication of real human life as man's property. The latter is also the emergence of practical humanism, for atheism is humanism mediated to itself by the annulment of religion, while communism is humanism mediated to itself by the annulment of private property. It is only by the supersession of this mediation (which is, however, a necessary precondition) that the self-originating *positive* humanism can appear.

But atheism and communism are not flight or abstraction from, or loss of, the objective world which men have created by the objectification of their faculties. They are not an impoverished return to unnatural, primitive simplicity. They are rather the first real emergence, the genuine actualization, of man's nature as something real.

Thus Hegel, in so far as he sees the *positive* significance of the self-referring negation (though in an alienated mode), conceives man's self-estrangement, alienation of being, loss of objectivity and reality, as self-discovery, change of nature, objectification and realization. In short, Hegel conceives labor as man's *act of self-creation* (though in abstract terms); he grasps man's relation to himself as an alien being and the emergence of *species-consciousness* and *species-life* as the demonstration of his alien being.

(b) But in Hegel, apart from, or rather as a consequence of, the inversion we have already described, this act of genesis appears, in the first place, as one which is merely *formal,* because it is abstract, and because human nature itself is treated as merely *abstract, thinking nature,* as self-consciousness.

Secondly, because the conception is *formal* and *abstract* the annulment of alienation becomes a confirmation of alienation. For Hegel, this movement of *self-creation* and *self-objectification* in the form of *self-estrangement* is the *absolute* and hence final *expression of human life,* which has its end in itself, is at peace with itself and at one with its own nature.

This movement, in its abstract form as dialectic, is regarded therefore as *truly human life,* and since it is nevertheless an abstraction, an alienation of human life, it is regarded as a *divine process* and thus as the divine process of mankind; it is a process which man's abstract, pure, absolute being, as distinguished from himself, traverses.

Thirdly, this process must have a bearer, a subject; but the subject first emerges as a result. This result, the subject knowing itself as absolute self-consciousness, is therefore *God, absolute spirit, the self-knowing and self-manifesting idea.* Real man and real nature become mere predicates, symbols of this concealed unreal man and unreal nature. Subject and predicate have therefore an inverted relation to each other; a *mystical subject-object*, or a *subjectivity reaching beyond the object*, the *absolute subject* as a *process of self-alienation* and of return from alienation into itself, and at the same time of reabsorption of this alienation, the *subject* as this process; pure, *unceasing* revolving within itself.

First, the formal and abstract conception of man's act of self-creation or self-objectification.

Since Hegel equates man with self-consciousness, the alienated object, the alienated real being of man, is simply *consciousness,* merely the thought of alienation, its abstract and hence vacuous and unreal expression, the *negation.* The annulment of alienation is also, therefore, merely an abstract and vacuous annulment of this empty abstraction, the *negation of the negation.* The replete, living, sensuous, concrete activity of self-objectification is therefore reduced to a mere abstraction, *absolute negativity,* an abstraction which is then crystallized as such and is conceived as an independent activity, as activity itself. Since this so-called negativity is merely the *abstract, vacuous* form of that real living act, its content can only be a *formal* content produced by abstraction from all content. These are, therefore, general, abstract *forms of abstraction* which refer to any content and are thus neutral toward, and valid for, any content; forms of thought, logical forms which are detached from *real* spirit and *real* nature. . . .

But *nature* too, taken abstractly, for itself, and rigidly separated from man, is *nothing* for man. It goes without saying that the abstract thinker who has committed himself to intuition, intuits nature abstractly. As nature lay enclosed in the thinker in a form which was obscure and mysterious even to himself, as absolute idea, as an entity of thought, so in truth, when he let it emerge from himself it was still only *abstract nature,* nature as an *entity of thought,* but now with the significance that it is the other being of thought, is real, intuited nature, distinguished from abstract thought. Or, to speak in human language, the abstract thinker discovers from intuiting nature that the entities which he thought to create out of nothing, out of pure abstraction, to create in the divine dialectic as the pure products of thought endlessly shuttling back and forth in itself and never regarding external reality, are simply *abstractions* from *natural characteristics*. The whole of nature, therefore, reiterates to him the logical abstractions, but in a sensuous, external form. He *analyzes* nature and these abstractions again. His intuition of nature is therefore simply the act of confimation of his abstraction from the intuition of nature. . . .

Externality should not be understood here as the *self-externalizing world of sense,* open to the light and to man's senses. It has to be taken here in the sense of alienation, an error, a defect, that which ought not to be. For that which is true is still the idea. Nature is merely the *form* of its *other-being.* And since abstract thought is *being,* that which is external to it is by its nature a merely *external thing.* The abstract thinker recognizes at the same time that *sensuousness, externality* in contrast to thought which shuttles back and forth *within itself,* is the essence of nature. But at the same time he expresses this antithesis in such a way that this *externality of nature,* and its *contrast* with thought, appears as a *deficiency,* and that nature distinguished from abstraction appears as a deficient being. A being which is deficient, not simply for me or in my eyes, but in itself, has something outside itself which it lacks. That is to say, its being is something other than itself. For the abstract thinker, nature must therefore supersede itself, because it is already posited by him as a potentially *superseded* being. . . .

17. Critique of Idealism

Early in 1845 Marx began his first collaborative effort with Friedrich Engels, on a polemical work entitled *The Holy Family*, in which the authors broke with the "Critical" school of philosophy over the issue of the practical versus the merely theoretical role to be played by philosophy. Most of the book is devoted to excoriating Bruno Bauer and his circle of "Critical" philosophers (compare Marx's own "critical" period of 1842–1843); it also contains some important passages on Hegel as well as a section devoted to a critique of French and English materialism from Descartes and Bacon through the Utopian Socialists.

The two passages which constitute the selection continue and amplify Marx's critique of Hegel (see Selection 16).

[As HEGEL] puts *self-consciousness* in the place of *man*, the *most varied* human relaity appears only as a *definite* form, as a *determination of self-consciousness*. But a mere determination of self-consciousness is a *"pure category,"* a mere "thought" which I can consequently also abolish in "pure" thought and overcome through pure thought. In Hegel's *Phenomenology* the *material, perceptible, objective* bases of the various estranged forms of human self-consciousness are *left as they are.* Thus the whole destructive work results in the *most conservative philosophy* because it thinks it has overcome the *objective world*, the sensuously real world, by merely transforming it into

From *The Holy Family*, trans. by R. Dixon (Moscow, 1956).

a "thing of thought," a mere *determination* of *self-consciousness* and can therefore dissolve its opponent, which has become *ethereal*, in the *"ether of pure thought." Phenomenology* is therefore quite logical when in the end it replaces human reality by *"Absolute Knowledge"—Knowledge*, because this is the only mode of existence of self-consciousness, because self-consciousness is considered as the only mode of existence of man; *absolute* knowledge for the very reason that self-consciousness knows *itself alone* and is no more disturbed by any objective world. Hegel makes man *the man of self-consciousness* instead of making self-consciousness the *self-consciousness of man*, of real man, man living in a real objective world and determined by that world. He stands the world *on its head* and can therefore dissolve *in the head* all the limitations which naturally remain in existence for *evil sensuousness*, for *real* man. . . . The whole of *Phenomenology* is intended to prove that *self-consciousness* is the *only reality* and *all reality*.

If from real apples, pears, strawberries and almonds I form the general idea *"Fruit,"* if I go further and *imagine* that my abstract idea "Fruit," derived from real fruit, is an entity existing outside me, is indeed the *true* essence of the pear, the apple, etc.; then, in the *language of speculative philosophy* I am declaring that "Fruit" is the *substance* of the pear, the apple, the almond, etc. I am saying, therefore, that to be a pear is not essential to the pear, that to be an apple is not essential to the apple; that what is essential to these things is not their real being, perceptible to the senses, but the essence that I have extracted from them and then foisted on them, the essence of my idea—"Fruit." I therefore declare apples, pears, almonds, etc., to be mere forms of existence, *modi,* of "Fruit." My finite understanding supported by my senses does, of course, *distinguish* an apple from a pear and a pear from an almond; but my speculative reason declares these sensuous differences unessential, indifferent. It sees in the apple *the same* as in the pear, and in the pear the same as in the almond, namely "Fruit." Particular real fruits are no more than semblances whose true essence is "the Substance"—"Fruit." . . .

Having reduced the different real fruits to the *one* fruit of abstraction—"Fruit," speculation must, in order to attain some appearance of real content, try somehow to find its way back from "Fruit," from *Substance* to the *different* profane real fruits, the pear, the apple, the almond, etc. It is as hard to produce real fruits from the abstract idea "Fruit" as it is easy to produce this abstract idea from real fruits. Indeed it is impossible to arrive at the *opposite* of an abstraction without *relinquishing* the abstraction. . . .

If apples, pears, almonds and strawberries are really nothing but "Substance," "Fruit," the question arises: Why does "Fruit" manifest itself to me sometimes as an apple, sometimes as a pear, sometimes as an almond? Why this *appearance of diversity* which so strikingly contradicts my speculative conception of *"Unity"*; "Substance"; "Fruit"?

This, answers the speculative philosopher, is because fruit is not dead, undifferentiated, motionless, but living, self-differentiating, moving. The diversity of profane fruits is significant not only to *my* sensuous understanding, but also to "Fruit" itself and to speculative reasoning. The different profane fruits are different manifestations of the life of the *one* "Fruit"; they are crystallizations of "Fruit" itself. In the apple "Fruit" gives itself an apple-like existence, in the pear a pear-like existence. We must therefore no longer say as from the standpoint of Substance: a pear is "Fruit," an apple is "Fruit," an almond is "Fruit," but "Fruit" presents itself as a pear, "Fruit" presents itself as an apple, "Fruit" presents itself as an almond; and the differences which distinguish apples, pears and almonds from one another are the self-differentiations of "Fruit" making the particular fruits subordinate members of the life-process of "Fruit." . . .

But the apples, pears, almonds and raisins that we get in the speculative world are nothing but *semblances* of apples, *semblances* of pears, *semblances* of almonds and *semblances* of raisins; they are moments in the life of "Fruit," that abstract *being of reason,* and therefore themselves abstract *beings of reason.* Hence what you enjoy in speculation is to find all the real fruits there, but as fruits which have a higher mystic significance, which are grown out of the ether of your brain and not out of the material earth, which are incarnations of "Fruit," *the Absolute Subject*. When you return from the abstraction, the *preternatural* being of reason, "Fruit," to real *natural* fruits, you give, contrariwise, the natural fruits a preternatural significance and transform them into so many abstractions. Your main interest is then to point out the *unity* of "Fruit" in all the manifestations of its life—the apple, the pear, the almond—that is, the *mystical interconnection* between these fruits, how in each one of them "Fruit" develops *by degrees* and *necessarily* progresses, for instance, from its existence as a raisin to its existence as an almond. The value of profane fruits *no longer* consists in their *natural* qualities *but* in their *speculative* quality which gives each of them a definite place in the life-process of "Absolute Fruit."

The ordinary man does not think he is saying anything extraordinary when he states that there are apples and pears. But if the philosopher expresses those existences in the speculative way he says something *extraordinary*. He works a *wonder* by producing the real *natural being,* the apple, the pear, etc., out of the unreal *being of reason* "Fruit," i.e., by *creating* those fruits out of *his own abstract reason,* which he considers as an Absolute Subject outside himself, represented here as "Fruit." And in every existence which he expresses he accomplishes an act of creation. . . .

18. Critique of Materialism

This selection, also from *The Holy Family*, clarifies Marx's relation to earlier materialist philosophies. While regarding these as certainly superior to idealist speculation, he nonetheless is aware of the "one-sided" (i.e. non-dialectical) character of the materialistic tradition dominant in France and England—ultimately traceable to Hobbes—a point that has often been overlooked by Soviet Marxists in their rush to be even more emphatic than the positivists in their worship of modern scientific advances and the general technologization of society. Rather, this materialist tradition leads only to the social philosophies of the utopians Fourier and Owen, and the utilitarians Helvetius and Bentham. We shall see in Part IV below how different Marx's historical materialism is from these.

THE FRENCH Enlightenment of the eighteenth century, in particular *French materialism*, was not only a struggle against the existing political institutions and the existing religion and theology; it was just as much an *open* struggle against *metaphysics* of the *seventeenth century*, and against all metaphysics, in particular that of *Descartes, Malebranche, Spinoza and Leibnitz*. *Philosophy* was opposed to *metaphysics* as *Feuerbach*, in his first decisive attack on *Hegel* opposed *sober philosophy* to *drunken speculation*. Seventeenth-century *metaphysics*, beaten off the field by the French Enlightenment, to be precise, by *French materialism* of the eighteenth century, was given a

From *The Holy Family*, trans. by R. Dixon (Moscow, 1956).

victorious and solid restoration in *German philosophy,* particularly in *speculative German philosophy* of the nineteenth century. After *Hegel* linked it in so masterly a fasion with all subsequent metaphysics and with German idealism and founded a metaphysical universal kingdom, the attack on *speculative metaphysics* and *metaphysics in general* again corresponded, as in the eighteenth century, to the attack on theology. It will be defeated for ever by *materialism* which has now been perfected by the work of *speculation* itself and coincides with *humanism.* As *Feuerbach* represented *materialism* in the *theoretical* domain, French and English *socialism* and *communism* in the *practical* field represent *materialism* which now *coincides* with *humanism.*

"Speaking *exactly* and in the *prosaic* sense," there are *two trends* in *French materialism;* one traces its origin to *Descartes,* the other to *Locke.* The latter is *mainly* a *French* development and leads direct to *socialism.* The former, *mechanical* materialism, merges with what is properly French *natural science.* The two trends cross in the course of development. We have no need here to go deep into French materialism, which comes direct from *Descartes,* any more than into the French *Newton* school or the development of French natural science in general.

We shall therefore just note the following:

Descartes in his *physics* endowed *matter* with self-creative power and conceived *mechanical* motion as the act of its life. He completely separated his *physics* from his *metaphysics. Within* his physics *matter* is the only *substance,* the only basis of being and of knowledge.

Mechanical French materialism followed *Descartes' physics* in opposition to his metaphysics. His followers were by profession *anti-metaphysicists, i.e., physicists.*

The school begins with the *physician Leroy,* reaches its zenith with the physician *Cabanis,* and the physician *Lamettrie* is its center. Descartes was still living when Leroy, like Lamettrie in the eighteenth century, transposed the Cartesian structure of *animals* to the human soul and affirmed that the soul is a *modus of the body* and *ideas* are *mechanical motions.* Leroy even thought Descartes had kept his real opinion secret. Descartes protested. At the end of the eighteenth century *Cabanis* perfected Cartesian materialism in his treatise: *Rapport du Physique et du Moral de l'homme.*

Cartesian materialism still exists today in France. It had great success in *mechanical natural science* which, "speaking *exactly* in the *prosaic* sense" will be least of all reproached with *romanticism.*

Metaphysics of the seventeenth century, represented in France by *Descartes,* had *materialism* as its *antagonist* from its very birth. It personally opposed Descartes in *Gassendi,* the restorer of *epicurean* materialism. French and English materialism was always closely related to *Democritus* and *Epicurus.* Cartesian metaphysics had another opponent in the *English* materialist *Hobbes.* Gassendi and Hobbes were victorious over their opponent long after their death when metaphysics was already officially dominant in all French schools. . . .

The downfall of seventeenth-century metaphysics can be explained by the materialistic theory of the eighteenth century only as far as that theoretical movement itself is explained by the practical nature of French life at the time. That life was turned to the immediate present, worldly enjoyment and worldly interests, the *earthly* world. Its anti-theological, anti-metaphysical and materialistic practice demanded corresponding anti-theological, anti-metaphysical and materialistic theories. Metaphysics had *in practice* lost all credit. Here we have only to indicate briefly the *theoretical* process.

In the seventeenth century metaphysics (cf. Descartes, Leibnitz, and others) still had an element of *positive,* profane content. It made discoveries in mathematics, physics and other exact sciences which seemed to come within its pale. This appearance was done away with as early as the beginning of the eighteenth century. The positive sciences broke off from it and determined their own separate fields. The whole wealth of metaphysics was reduced to beings of thought and heavenly things, although this was the very time when real beings and earthly things began to be the center of all interest. Metaphysics had gone stale. . . .

The man who deprived seventeenth-century metaphysics of all *credit* in the domain of *theory* was *Pierre Bayle.* His weapon was *skepticism* which he forged out of metaphysics' own magic formulas. He at first proceeded from Cartesian metaphysics. As *Feuerbach* was driven by the fight against speculative theology to the fight against *speculative philosophy* precisely because he recognized in speculation the last prop of theology, because he had to force theology to turn back from pretended science to *coarse*, repulsive *faith*, so Bayle too was driven by religious doubt to doubt about metaphysics which was the support of that faith. He therefore critically investigated metaphysics from its very origin. He became its historian in order to write the history of its death. He mainly refuted *Spinoza* and *Leibnitz*.

Pierre Bayle did not only prepare the reception of materialism and the philosophy of common sense in France by shattering metaphysics with his skepticism. He heralded *atheistic society*, which was soon to come to existence, by *proving* that a society consisting only of atheists is *possible*, that an atheist *can* be a respectable man and that it is not by atheism but by superstition and idolatry that man debases himself. . . .

Besides the negative refutation of seventeenth-century theology and metaphysics, a *positive, anti-metaphysical* system was required. A book was needed which would systematize and theoretically justify the practice of life of the time. *Locke's* treatise on the origin of human reason came from across the Channel as if in answer to a call. It was welcomed enthusiastically like a long-awaited guest. . . .

Materialism is the son *of Great Britain by birth.* Even Britain's scholastic *Duns Scotus* wondered: *"Can matter think?"*

In order to bring about that miracle he had recourse to God's omnipotence, i.e., he forced *theology* itself to preach *materialism*. In addition he was a *nominalist.* Nominalism is a main component of *English* materialism and is in general the *first expression* of materialism.

The real founder of *English materialism* and all *modern experimental* science was *Bacon.* For him natural science was true science and *physics* based on perception was the most excellent part of natural science. *Anaxagoras* with his *homoeomeria* and *Democritus* with his atoms are often the authorities he refers to. According to his teaching the *senses* are infallible and are the *source* of all knowledge. Science is *experimental* and consists in applying a *rational method* to the data provided by the senses. Induction, analysis, comparison, observation and experiment are the principal requisites of rational method. The first and most important of the inherent qualities of *matter* is *motion*, not only *mechanical* and *mathematical* movement, but still more *impulse, vital life-spirit, tension*. ... The primary forms of matter are the living, individualizing *forces of being* inherent in it and producing the distinctions between the species.

In *Bacon*, its first creator, materialism contained latent and still in a naïve way the germs of all-round development. Matter smiled at man with poetical sensuous brightness. The aphoristic doctrine itself, on the other hand, was full of the inconsistencies of theology.

In its further development materialism became *one-sided*. *Hobbes* was the one who *systematized Bacon's* materialism. Sensuousness lost its bloom and became the abstract sensuousness of the *geometrician*. *Physical* motion was sacrificed to the *mechanical* or *mathematical, geometry* was proclaimed the principal science. Materialism became *hostile* to *humanity*. In order to overcome the *anti-human incorporeal* spirit in its own field, materialism itself was obliged to mortify its flesh and become an *ascetic*. It appeared as a *being of reason*, but it also developed the implacable logic of reason.

If man's senses are the source of all his knowledge, Hobbes argues, proceeding from Bacon, then conception, thought, imagination, etc., are nothing but phantoms of the material world more or less divested of its sensuous form. Science can only give a name to these phantoms. One name can be applied to several phantoms. There can even be names of names. But it would be a contradiction to say, on the one hand, that all ideas have their origin in the world of the senses and to maintain, on the other hand, that a word is more than a word, that besides the beings represented, which are always individual, there exist also general beings. An *incorporeal substance* is just as much a nonsense as an *incorporeal body*. *Body, being, substance*, are one and the same *real* idea. One cannot separate the thought from matter *which* thinks. Matter is the subject of all changes. The word *infinite* is *meaningless* unless it means the capacity of our mind to go on adding without end. Since only what is material is perceptible, knowable, *nothing* is known of the existence of God. I am sure only of my own existence. Every human passion is a mechanical motion ending or beginning. The objects of impulses are what is called good. Man is subject to the same laws as nature; might and freedom are identical.

Hobbes systematized Bacon, but did not give a more precise proof of his basic principle that our knowledge and our ideas have their source in the world of the senses.

Locke proved the principle of Bacon and Hobbes in his essay on the origin of human reason. . . .

We have already mentioned how opportune Locke's work was for the French. Locke founded the philosophy of *bon sens,* of common sense; i.e., he said indirectly that no philosopher can be at variance with the healthy human senses and reason based on them.

Locke's *immediate* follower, *Condillac,* who also translated him into *French,* at once opposed Locke's sensualism to seventeenth-century *metaphysics.* He proved that the French had quite rightly rejected metaphysics as the mere bungling of fancy and theological prejudice. He published a refutation of the systems of *Descartes, Spinoza, Leibnitz* and *Malebranche.*

In his *Essai sur l'origine des connaissances humaines* he expounded Locke's ideas and proved that not only the soul, but the senses too, not only the art of creating ideas, but also the art of sensuous perception are matters of *experience* and *habit.* The whole development of man therefore depends on *education* and *environment.* It was only by *eclectic* philosophy that Condillac was ousted from the French schools.

The difference between *French* and *English* materialism follows from the difference between the two nations. The French imparted to English materialism wit, flesh and blood, and eloquence. They gave it the temperament and grace that it lacked. They *civilized* it.

In *Helvetius,* who also based himself on Locke, materialism became really French. Helvetius conceived it immediately in its application to social life, (Helvetius, *De l'homme, de ses facultés intellectuelles et de son éducation*). Sensuous qualities and self-love, enjoyment and correctly understood personal interests are the bases of moral. The natural equality of human intelligence, the unity of progress of reason and progress of industry, the natural goodness of man and the omnipotence of education are the main points in his system.

In *Lamettrie's* works we find a combination of Descartes' system and English materialism. He makes use of Descartes' physics in detail. His *"Man Machine"* is a treatise after the model of Descartes' beast-machine. The physical part of Holbach's *Système de la nature, ou des lois du monde physique et du monde moral* is also a result of the combination of French and English materialism, while the moral part is based substantially on the moral of Helvetius. *Robinet (De la Nature)*, the French materialist who had the most connection with metaphysics and was therefore praised by Hegel, refers explicitly to *Leibnitz*. . . .

As *Cartesian* materialism merges into *natural science proper,* the other branch of French materialism leads direct to *socialism* and *communism.*

There is no need of any great penetration to see from the teaching of materialism on the original goodness and equal intellectual endowment of men, the omnipotence of experience, habit and education, and the influence of environment on man, the great significance of industry, the justification of enjoyment, etc., how necessarily materialism is connected with communism and socialism. If man draws all his knowledge, sensation, etc., from the world of the senses and the experience gained in it, the empirical world must be arranged so that in it man experiences and gets used to what is really human and that he becomes aware of himself as man. If correctly understood interest is the principle of all moral, man's private interest must be made to coincide with the interest of humanity. If man is unfree in the materialist sense, i.e., is free not through the negative power to avoid this or that, but through the positive power to assert his true individuality, crime must not be punished in the individual, but the anti-social source of crime must be destroyed, and each man must be given social scope for the vital manifestation of his being. If man is shaped by his surroundings, his surroundings must be made human. If man is social by nature, he will develop his true nature only in society, and the power of his nature must be measured not by the power of separate individuals but by the power of society.

This and similar propositions are to be found almost literally even in the oldest French materialists. This is not the place to assess them. *Fable of the Bees, or Private Vices Made Public Benefits,* by *Mandeville,* is typical of the social tendencies of materialism. He proves that in *modern* society vice is *indispensable* and *useful.* This was by no means an apology of modern society.

Fourier proceeds immediately from the teaching of the French materialists. The *Babouvists* were coarse, uncivilized materialists, but mature communism too comes *directly* from *French materialism.* The latter returned to its mother country, *England,* in the form *Helvetius* gave it. *Bentham* based his system of *correctly understood interest* on Helvetius's moral, and *Owen* proceeded from *Betham's* system to found English communism. Exiled to England, the Frenchman *Cabet* came under the influence of communist ideas there and on his return to France became the most popular, although the most superficial, representative of communism. Like Owen, the more scientific French communists . . . developed the teaching of *materialism* as the teaching of *real humanism* and the *logical* basis of *communism.* . . .

19.   *Critique of Feuerbach*

Marx's final break with the philosophical tradition is clearly stated in his famous notes of 1845, subsequently published by Engels as the *Theses on Feuerbach*, which constitute the first part of the selection. This break is further amplified by several passages (which deal directly with Feuerbach) in *The German Ideology*, which was written with Engels in 1845–1846; these passages constitute the second half of the selection. In 1844 Marx had called Feuerbach a "genuine materialist"; now even Feuerbach has been assigned the place of simply another abstract materialist. The *Theses* contain, in a remarkably compact presentation, the basic principles which Marx and Engels elaborate at great length as their *historical materialism*, the "unity of theory and practice," in *The German Idealogy* (see Part IV, below).

I

The chief defect of all hitherto existing materialism (that of Feuerbach included) is that the thing, reality, sensuousness, is conceived only in the form of the *object or of contemplation*, but not as *sensuous human activity, practice*, not subjectively. Hence, in contradistinction to materialism, the *active* side was developed abstractly by idealism—which, of course, does not know real, sensuous activity as such. Feuerbach wants sensuous

From *The German Ideology*, ed. by S. Ryazanskaya (Moscow, 1964).

objects, really distinct from the thought objects, but he does not conceive human activity itself as *objective* activity. Hence, in [*The Essence of Christianity*], he regards the theoretical attitude as the only genuinely human attitude, while practice is conceived and fixed only in its dirty-judaical manifestation. Hence he does not grasp the significance of "revolutionary," of "practical-critical," activity.

II

The question whether objective truth can be attributed to human thinking is not a question of theory but is a *practical question*. Man must prove the truth, i.e., the reality and power, the this-sidedness of his thinking in practice. The dispute over the reality or non-reality of thinking that is isolated from practice is a purely *scholastic* question.

III

The materialist doctrine concerning the changing of circumstances and upbringing forgets that circumstances are changed by men and that it is essential to educate the educator himself. This doctrine must, therefore, divide society into two parts, one of which is superior to society.

The coincidence of the changing of circumstances and of human activity or self-changing can be conceived and rationally understood only as *revolutionary practice*.

IV

Feuerbach starts out from the fact of religious self-alienation, of the duplication of the world into a religious world and a secular one. His work consists in resolving the religious world into its secular basis. But that the secular basis detaches itself from itself and establishes itself as an independent realm in the clouds can only be explained by the cleavages and self-contradictions within this secular basis. The latter must, therefore, in itself be both understood in its contradiction and revolutionized in practice. Thus, for instance, after the earthly family is discovered to be the secret of the holy family, the former must then itself be destroyed in theory and in practice.

V

Feuerbach, not satisfied with *abstract thinking*, wants *contemplation;* but he does not conceive sensuousness as *practical,* human-sensuous activity.

VI

Feuerbach resolves the religious essence into the *human* essence. But the human essence is no abstraction inherent in each single individual. In its reality it is the ensemble of the social relations.

Feuerbach, who does not enter upon a criticism of this real essence, is consequently compelled:

1. To abstract from the historical process and to fix the religious sentiment as something by itself and to presuppose an abstract—*isolated*—human individual.

2. Essence, therefore, can be comprehended only as "genus," as an internal, dumb generality which *naturally* unites the many individuals.

VII

Feuerbach, consequently, does not see that the "religious sentiment" is itself a social product, and that the abstract individual whom he analyses belongs to a particular form of society.

VIII

All social life is essentially *practical.* All mysteries which lead theory to mysticism find their rational solution in human practice and in the comprehension of this practice.

IX

The highest point reached by contemplative materialism, that is, materialism which does not comprehend sensuousness as practical activity, is the contemplation of single individuals and of civil society.

X

The standpoint of the old materialism is civil society; the standpoint of the new is human society, or social humanity.

XI

The philosophers have only *interpreted* the world, in various ways; the point is to *change* it.

Feuerbach is deceiving himself when . . . by virtue of the qualification "common man" he declares himself a communist, transforms the latter into a predicate of "man," and thereby thinks it possible to change the word "communist," which in the real world means the follower of a definite revolutionary party, into a mere category. Feuerbach's whole deduction with regard to the relation of men to one another goes only so far as to prove that men need and *always have needed* each other. He wants to establish consciousness of this fact, that is to say, like the other theorists, merely to produce a correct consciousness about an *existing* fact; whereas for the real communist it is a question of overthrowing the existing state of things. We thoroughly appreciate, moreover, that Feuerbach, in endeavoring to produce consciousness of just *this* fact, is going as far as a theorist possibly can, without ceasing to be a theorist and philosopher. . . . As an example of Feuerbach's acceptance and at the same time misunderstanding of existing reality, which he still shares with our opponents, we recall the passage in the *Philosophy of the Future* where he develops the view that the existence of a thing or a man is at the same time its or his essence, that the conditions of existence, the mode of life and activity of an animal or human individual are those in which its "essence" feels itself satisfied. Here every exception is expressly conceived as an unhappy chance, as an abnormality which cannot be altered. Thus if millions of proletarians feel by no means contented with their living conditions, if their "existence" does not in the least correspond to their "essence," then, according to the passage quoted, this is an unavoidable misfortune, which must be borne quietly. The millions of proletarians and communists, however, think differently and will prove this in time, when they bring their "existence" into harmony with their "essence" in a practical way, by means of a revolution. Feuerbach, therefore, never speaks of the world of man in such cases, but always takes refuge in external nature, and moreover in *nature* which has not yet been subdued by men. But every new invention, every advance made by industry, detaches another piece from this domain, so that the ground which produces examples illustrating such Feuerbachian propositions is steadily shrinking. . . .

. . . In reality and for the *practical* materialist, i.e., the *communist,* it is a question of revolutionizing the existing world, of practically attacking and changing existing things. When occasionally we find such views with Feuerbach, they are never more than isolated surmises and have much too little influence on his general outlook to be considered here as anything else than embryos capable of development. Feuerbach's "conception" of the sensuous world is confined on the one hand to mere contemplation of it, and on the other to mere feeling; he says "Man" instead of "real historical man.". . . He does not see how the sensuous world around him is not a thing given direct from all eternity, remaining ever the same, but the product of industry and of the state of society; and, indeed, in the sense that it is a historical product, the result of the activity of a whole succession of generations, each standing on the shoulders of the preceding one, developing its industry and its intercourse, modifying its social system according to the changed needs.

Even the objects of the simplest "sensuous certainty" are only given him through social development, industry and commercial intercourse. . . .

Incidentally, when we conceive things thus, as they really are and happened, every profound philosophical problem is resolved, as will be seen even more clearly later, quite simply into an empirical fact. For instance, the important question of the relation of man to nature . . . out of which all the "unfathomably lofty works" on "substance" and "self-consciousness" were born, crumbles of itself when we understand that the celebrated "unity of man with nature" has always existed in industry and has existed in varying forms in every epoch according to the lesser or greater development of industry, just like the "struggle" of man with nature, right up to the development of his productive powers on a corresponding basis. Industry and commerce, production and the exchange of the necessities of life, themselves determine distribution, the structure of the different social classes, and are, in turn, determined by it as to the mode in which they are carried on. . . . Feuerbach speaks in particular of the perception of natural science; he mentions secrets which are disclosed only to the eye of the physicist and chemist; but where would natural science be without industry and commerce? Even this "pure" natural science is provided with an aim, as with its material, only through trade and industry, through the sensuous activity of men. . . .

Certainly Feuerbach has a great advantage over the "pure" materialists in that he realizes how man too is an "object of the senses." But apart from the fact that he only conceives him as an "object of the senses," not as "sensuous activity," because he still remains in the realm of theory and conceives of men not in their given social connection, not under their existing conditions of life, which have made them what they are, he never arrives at the really existing active men, but stops at the abstraction "man," and gets no further than recognizing "the true, individual, corporeal man" emotionally, i.e., he knows no other "human relationships" "of man to man" than love and friendship, and even then idealized. He gives no criticism of the present conditions of life. Thus he never manages to conceive the sensuous world as the total living sensuous *activity* of the individuals composing it; and therefore when, for example, he sees instead of healthy men a crowd of scrofulous, overworked and consumptive starvelings, he is compelled to take refuge in the "higher perception" and in the ideal "compensation in the species," and thus to relapse into idealism at the very point where the communist materialist sees the necessity, and at the same time the condition, of a transformation both of industry and of the social structure.

As far as Feuerbach is a materialist he does not deal with history, and as far as he considers history he is not a materialist. With him materialism and history diverge completely. . . .

IV.

The Materialist Conception of History
(1845–1859)

In the face of the demise of all philosophical speculation, Marx and Engels developed their understanding of the scope of human development, that is, the materialist conception of history. This conception, its authors claim, begins from *real* premises, from men in their activity as living, natural beings. Historical materialism may be considered "materialist" in neither the sense that reduces the "stuff" of the universe of a collection of atoms (as was advocated by Democritus in the early fourth century whose position was rejected by Marx as early as the dissertation of 1841) nor in the more modern mechanical materialism which reduces the phenomena of life to a series of motions (rejected by Marx in *The Holy Family* in 1845).

It is vital to note that the historical materialism of Marx is not an ontology; it is decidedly not an attempt at the construction of a speculative metaphysics. (In this regard, one might profit by a comparison of Marx's work with Engel's unfinished *Dialectics of Nature*, which is precisely such an ontology.) The materialistic conception of history is based upon understanding the social groupings of man on the basis of the primacy of their "material" needs (e.g., food, shelter, clothing, water) which must be socially met in order to enable man to survive, and, second, develop his cultural life. Historical materialism focuses upon man's *productive* activities; that is, upon his appropriation and use of nature (including "human nature," i.e., man as he has *created himself* throughout history).

The basic outline of the materialist conception of history is presented, first, in a short selection from the Preface to Marx's *A Contribution to the Critique of Political Economy* of 1859, followed by a major extract from *The German Ideology* (1845–1846) in which Marx and Engels first state their position in depth, and finally in an analysis of "precapitalist economic formations" taken from Marx's *Grundrisse* (Outlines) of 1857–1858, which contain his most detailed investigations into the stages preceding bourgeois society. Further discussion of the historical development of the capitalist process of production will also be found in *The Manifesto of the Communist Party* (see Part V) and the theoretical analysis of capitalism in *Capital* (see Part VI).

20. Outline of the Theory

We depart now from the chronological sequence of Marx's writings to present a passage from the Preface to his *A Contribution to the Critique of Political Economy*, from which the selection is taken. Although published in 1859, it briefly summarizes Marx's conception of historical materialism as he recalls having held it as the beginning of his exile in Brussels (early 1845). At that time he and Engels were in the process of developing the theory for the first time in *The German Ideology*. This passage remains Marx's most succinct formulation of the general thesis of historical materialism and thus will serve as an introduction to the detailed treatment of the subject presented in the two selections which follow.

IN THE social production which men carry on they enter into definite relations that are indispensable and independent of their will; these relations of production correspond to a definite stage of development of their material powers of production. The sum total of these relations of production constitutes the economic structure of society—the real foundation, on which rise legal and political superstructures and to which correspond definite forms of social consciousness. The mode of production in material life determines the general character of the social, political and spiritual processes of life. It is not the consciousness

---

From Marx, *A Contribution to the Critique of Political Economy* (Chicago: Charles Kerr Co., 1904).

of men that determines their existence, but, on the contrary, their social existence determines their consciousness. At a certain stage of their development, the material forces of production in society come in conflict with the existing relations of production, or—what is but a legal expression for the same thing—with the property relations within which they had been at work before. From forms of development of the forces of production these relations turn into their fetters. Then comes the period of social revolution. With the change of the economic foundation the entire immense superstructure is more or less rapidly transformed. In considering such transformations the distinction should always be made between the material transformation of the economic conditions of production which can be determined with the precision of natural science, and the legal, political, religious, aesthetic or philosophic—in short ideological forms in which men become conscious of this conflict and fight it out. Just as our opinion of an individual is not based on what he thinks of himself, so can we not judge of such a period of transformation by its own consciousness; on the contrary, this consciousness must rather be explained from the contradictions of material life, from the existing conflict between the social forces of production and the relations of production. No social order ever disappears before all the productive forces, for which there is room in it, have been developed; and new higher relations of production never appear before the material conditions of their existence have matured in the womb of the old society. Therefore, mankind always takes up only such problems as it can solve; since, looking at the matter more closely, we will always find that the problem itself arises only when the material conditions necessary for its solution already exist or are at least in the process of formation. In broad outlines we can designate the Asiatic, the ancient, the feudal, and the modern bourgeois methods of production as so many epochs in the progress of the economic formation of society. The bourgeois relations of production are the last antagonistic form of the social process of production—antagonistic not in the sense of individual antagonism, but of one arising from conditions surrounding the life of individuals in society; at the same time the productive forces developing in the womb of bourgeois society create the material conditions for the solution of that antagonism. This social formation constitutes, therefore, the closing chapter of the prehistoric stage of human society. . . .

21. Essentials of the Theory

The following presentation of the theory of historical materialism is taken from *The German Idology* by Marx and Engels. Here is found the core of the "Marxist" viewpoint, carrying forward as it does the philosophical criticism of idealism and materialism into a positive world outlook. Present are various aspects of the concept of alienation, together with the principle that overcoming the division of labor is the fundamental prerequisite for the actualization of man as both a "natural being" and a "species-being" in terms of the concrete historical and social conditions attained in any given society.

THE PREMISES from which we begin are not arbitrary ones, not dogmas, but real premises from which abstraction can only be made in the imagination. They are the real individuals, their activity and the material conditions under which they live, both those which they find already existing and those produced by their activity. These premises can thus be verified in a purely empirical way.

The first premise of all human history is, of course, the existence of living human individuals. Thus the first fact to be established is the physical organization of these individuals and their consequent relation to the rest of nature. Of course, we cannot here go either into the actual physical nature of man, or into the natural conditions in which man finds himself—geological, orohydorgraphical, climatic and so on. The writing of history

From *The German Ideology*, ed. by S. Ryazanskaya, (Moscow, 1964).

must always set out from these natural bases and their modification in the course of history through the action of men.

Men can be distinguished from animals by consciousness, by religion or anything else you like. They themselves begin to distinguish themselves from animals as soon as they begin to *produce* their means of subsistence, a step which is conditioned by their physical organization. By producing their means of subsistence men are indirectly producing their actual material life.

The way in which men produce their means of subsistence depends first of all on the nature of the actual means of subsistence they find in existence and have to reproduce. This mode of production must not be considered simply as being the reproduction of the physical existence of the individuals. Rather it is a definite form of activity of these individuals, a definite form of expressing their life, a definite *mode of life* on their part. As individuals express their life, so they are. What they are, therefore, coincides with their production, both with *what* they produce and with *how* they produce. The nature of individuals thus depends on the material conditions determining their production.

This production only makes its appearance with the *increase of population*. In its turn this presupposes the *intercourse* [*Verkehr*] of individuals with one another. The form of this intercourse is again determined by production.

The relations of different nations among themselves depend upon the extent to which each has developed its productive forces, the division of labor and internal intercourse. This statement is generally recognized. But not only the relation of one nation to others, but also the whole internal structure of the nation itself depends on the stage of development reached by its production and its internal and external intercourse. How far the productive forces of a nation are developed is shown most manifestly by the degree to which the division of labor has been carried. Each new productive force, insofar as it is not merely a quantitative extension of productive forces already known (for instance the bringing into cultivation of fresh land), causes a further development of the division of labor.

The division of labor inside a nation leads at first to the separation of industrial and commercial from agricultural labor, and hence to the separation of *town* and *country* and to the conflict of their interests. Its further development leads to the separation of commercial from industrial labor. At the same time through the division of labor inside these various branches there develop various divisions among the individuals cooperating in definite kinds of labor. The relative position of these individual groups is determined by the methods employed in agriculture, industry and commerce (patriarchalism, slavery, estates, classes). These same conditions are to be seen (given a more developed intercourse) in the relations of different nations to one another.

The various stages of development in the division of labor are just so many different forms of ownership, i.e., the existing stage in the division of labor determines also the relations of individuals to one another with reference to the material, instrument, and product of labor.

The first form of ownership is tribal ownership. It corresponds to the undeveloped stage of production, at which a people lives by hunting and fishing, by the rearing of beasts or, in the highest stage, agriculture. In the latter case it presupposes a great mass of uncultivated stretches of land. The division of labor is at this stage still very elementary and is confined to a further extension of the natural division of labor existing in the family. The social structure is, therefore, limited to an extension of the family; patriarchal family chieftains, below them the members of the tribe, finally slaves. The slavery latent in the family only develops gradually with the increase of population, the growth of wants, and with the extension of external relations, both of war and of barter.

The second form is the ancient communal and State ownership which proceeds especially from the union of several tribes into a *city* by agreement or by conquest, and which is still accompanied by slavery. Beside communal ownership we already find movable, and later also immovable, private property developing, but as an abnormal form subordinate to communal ownership. The citizens hold power over their laboring slaves only in their community, and on this account alone, therefore, they are bound to the form of communal ownership. It is the communal private property which compels the active citizens to remain in this spontaneously derived form of association over against their slaves. For this reason the whole structure of society based on this communal ownership, and with it the power of the people, decays in the same measure as, in particular, immovable private property evolves. The division of labor is already more developed. We already find the antagonism of town and country; later the antagonism between those states which represent town interests and those which represent country interests, and inside the towns themselves the antagonism between industry and maritime commerce. The class relation between citizens and slaves is now completely developed.

This whole interpretation of history appears to be contradicted by the fact of conquest. Up till now violence, war, pillage, murder and robbery, etc., have been accepted as the driving force of history. Here we must limit ourselves to the chief points and take, therefore, only the most striking example —the destruction of an old civilization by a barbarous people and the resulting formation of an entirely new organization of society. (Rome and the barbarians; feudalism and Gaul; the Byzantine Empire and the Turks.) With the conquering barbarian people war itself is still, as indicated above, a regular form of intercourse, which is the more eagerly exploited as the increase in population together with the traditional and, for it, the only possible, crude mode of production gives rise to the need for new means of production. In Italy, on the other hand, the concentration of landed property (caused not only by buying-up and indebtedness but also by inheritance, since loose living being rife and marriage rare, the old families gradually died out and their possessions fell into the hands of a few) and its conversion into grazing-land (caused not only by by the usual economic forces still operative today but by the importation of plundered and tribute corn and the resultant lack of demand for Italian corn) brought about the almost total disappearance of the free population. The very slaves died out again and again, and had constantly to be replaced by new ones. Slavery remained the basis of the whole productive system. The plebeians, midway between freemen and slaves, never succeeded in becoming more than a proletarian rabble. Rome indeed never became more than a city; its connection with the provinces was almost exclusively political and could, therefore, easily be broken again by political events.

With the development of private property, we find here for the first time the same conditions which we shall find again, only on a more extensive scale, with modern private property. On the one hand, the concentration of private property, which began very early in Rome (as the Licinian agrarian law proves) and proceeded very rapidly from the time of the civil wars and especially under the Emperors; on the other hand, coupled with this, the transformation of the plebeian small peasantry into a proletariat, which, however, owing to its intermediate position between propertied citizens and slaves, never achieved an independent development.

The third form of ownership is feudal or estate property. If antiquity started out from the *town* and its little territory, the Middle Ages started out from the *country*. This different starting-point was determined by the sparseness of the population at that time, which was scattered over a large area and which received no large increase from the conquerors. In contrast to Greece and Rome, feudal development at the outset, therefore, extends over a much wider territory, prepared by the Roman conquests and the spread of agriculture at first associated with them. The last centuries of the declining Roman Empire and its conquest by the barbarians destroyed a number of productive forces; agriculture had declined, industry had decayed for want of a market, trade had died out or been violently suspended, the rural and urban population had decreased. From these conditions and the mode of organization of the conquest determined by them, feudal property developed under the influence of the Germanic military constitution. Like tribal and communal ownership, it is based again on a community; but the directly producing class standing over against it is not, as in the case of the ancient community, the slaves, but the enserfed small peasantry. As soon as feudalism is fully developed, there also arises antagonism to the towns. The hierarchical structure of land-ownership, and the armed bodies of retainers associated with it, gave the nobility power over the serfs. This feudal organization was, just as much as the ancient communal ownership, an association against a subjected producing class; but the form of association and the relation to the direct producers were different because of the different conditions of production.

This feudal system of landownership had its counterpart in the *towns* in the shape of corporative property, the feudal organization of trades. Here property consisted chiefly in the labor of each individual person. The necessity for association against the organized robber-nobility, the need for communal covered markets in an age when the industrialist was at the same time a merchant, the growing competition of the escaped serfs swarming into the rising towns, the feudal structure of the whole country: these combined to bring about the *guilds*. The gradually accumulated small capital of individual craftsmen and their stable numbers, as against the growing population, evolved the relation of journeyman and apprentice, which brought into being in the towns a hierarchy similar to that in the country.

Thus the chief form of property during the feudal epoch consisted on the one hand of landed property with serf labor chained to it, and on the other of the labor of the individual with small capital commanding the labor of journeymen. The organization of both was determined by the restricted conditions of production—the small-scale and primitive cultivation of the land, and the craft type of industry. There was little division of labor in the heyday of feudalism. Each country bore in itself the antithesis of town and country; the division into estates was certainly strongly marked; but apart from the differentiation of princes, nobility, clergy and peasants in the country, and masters, journeymen, apprentices and soon also the rabble of casual laborers in the towns, no division of importance took place. In agriculture it was rendered difficult by the strip-system, beside which the cottage industry of the peasants themselves emerged. In industry there was no division of labor at all in the individual trades themselves, and very little between them.

The separation of industry and commerce was found already in existence in older towns; in the newer it only developed later, when the towns entered into mutual relations.

The grouping of larger territories into feudal kingdoms was a necessity for the landed nobility as for the towns. The organization of the ruling class, the nobility, had, therefore, everywhere a monarch at its head.

The fact is, therefore, that definite individuals who are productively active in a definite way enter into these definite social and political relations. Empirical observation must in each separate instance bring out empirically, and without any mystification and speculation, the connection of the social and political structure with production. The social structure and the State are continually evolving out of the life-process of definite individuals, but of individuals, not as they may appear in their own or other people's imagination, but as they *really* are; i.e., as they operate, produce materially, and hence as they work under definite material limits, presuppositions and conditions independent of their will.

The production of ideas, of conceptions, of consciousness, is at first directly interwoven with the material activity and the material intercourse of men, the language of real life. Conceiving, thinking, the mental intercourse of men, appear at this stage as the direct efflux of their material behavior. The same applies to mental production as expressed in the language of politics, laws, morality, religion, metaphysics, etc., of a people. Men are the producers of their conceptions, ideas, etc.—real, active men, as they are conditioned by a definite development of their productive forces and of the intercourse corresponding to these, up to its furthest forms. Consciousness can never be anything else than conscious existence, and the existence of men is their actual life-process. If in all ideology men and their circumstances appear upside-down as in a *camera obscura*, this phenomenon arises just as much from their historical life-process as the inversion of objects on the retina does from their physical life-process.

In direct contrast to German philosophy which descends from heaven to earth, here we ascend from earth to heaven.

That is to say, we do not set out from what men say, imagine, conceive, nor from men as narrated, thought of, imagined, conceived, in order to arrive at men in the flesh. We set out from real, active men, and on the basis of their real life-process we demonstrate the development of the ideological reflexes and echoes of this life-process. The phantoms formed in the human brain are also, necessarily, sublimates of their material life-process, which is empirically verifiable and bound to material premises. Morality, religion, metaphysics, all the rest of ideology and their corresponding forms of consciousness, thus no longer retain the semblance of independence. They have no history, no development; but men, developing their material production and their material intercourse, alter, along with this their real existence, their thinking and the products of their thinking. Life is not determined by consciousness, but consciousness by life. In the first method of approach the starting-point is consciousness taken as the living individual; in the second method, which conforms to real life, it is the real living individuals themselves, and consciousness is considered solely as *their* consciousness.

This method of approach is not devoid of premises. It starts out from the real premises and does not abandon them for a moment. Its premises are men, not in any fantastic isolation and rigidity, but in their actual, empirically perceptible process of development under definite conditions. As soon as this active life-process is described, history ceases to be a collection of dead facts as it is with the empiricists (themselves still abstract), or an imagined activity of imagined subjects, as with the idealists.

Where speculation ends—in real life—there real, positive science begins: the representation of the practical activity, of the practical process of development of men. Empty talk about consciousness ceases, and real knowledge has to take its place. When reality is depicted, philosophy as an independent branch of knowledge loses its medium of existence. At the best its place can only be taken by a summing-up of the most general results, abstractions which arise from the observation of the historical development of men. Viewed apart from real history, these abstractions have in themselves no value whatsoever. They can only serve to facilitate the arrangement of historical material, to indicate the sequence of its separate strata. But they by no means afford a recipe or schema, as does philosophy, for neatly trimming the epochs of history. On the contrary, our diffiulties begin only when we set about the observation and the arrangement—the real depiction—of our historical material, whether of a past epoch or of the present. The removal of these difficulties is governed by premises which it is quite impossible to state here, but which only the study of the actual life-process and the activity of the individuals of each epoch will make evident. We shall select here some of these abstractions, which we use in contradistinction to the ideologists, and shall illustrate them by historical examples.

Since we are dealing with the Germans, who are devoid of premises, we must begin by stating the first premise of all human existence and, therefore, of all history, the premise, namely, that men must be in a position to live in order to be able to "make history."[1] But life involves before everything else eating and drinking, a habitation, clothing and many other things. The first historical act is thus the production of the means to satisfy these needs, the production of material life itself. And indeed this is a historical act, a fundamental condition of all history, which today, as thousands of years ago, must daily and hourly be fulfilled merely in order to sustain human life. Even when the sensuous world is reduced to a minimum, to a stick as with . . . Bruno [Bauer], it presupposes the action of producing the stick. Therefore in any interpretation of history one has first of all to observe this fundamental fact in all its significance and all its implications and to accord it its due importance. . . .

The second point is that the satisfaction of the first need (the action of satisfying, and the instrument of satisfaction which has been acquired) leads to new needs; and this production of new needs is the first historical act. . . .

1. Marginal note by Marx: *Hegel*. Geological, hydrographical, etc., conditions. Human bodies. Needs, labor.

The third circumstance which, from the very outset, enters into historical development, is that men, who daily remake their own life, begin to make other men, to propagate their kind: the relation between man and woman, parents and children, the *family*. The family, which to begin with is the only social relationship, becomes later, when increased needs create new social relations and the increased population new needs, a subordinate one . . . and must then be treated and analyzed according to the existing empirical data, not according to "the concept of the family," as is the custom in Germany. These three aspects of social activity are not of course to be taken as three different stages, but just as three aspects . . . which have existed simultaneously since the dawn of history and the first men, and which still assert themselves in history today.

The production of life, both of one's own in labor and of fresh life in procreation, now appears as a double relationship: on the one hand as a natural, on the other as a social relationship. By social we understand the cooperation of several individuals, no matter under what conditions, in what manner and to what end. It follows from this that a certain mode of production, or industrial stage, is always combined with a certain mode of cooperation, or social stage, and this mode of cooperation is itself a "productive force." Further, that the multitude of productive forces accessible to men determines the nature of society, hence, that the "history of humanity" must always be studied and treated in relation to the history of industry and exchange. . . .

Only now, after having considered four moments, four aspects of the primary historical relationships, do we find that man also possesses "consciousness";[2] but, even so, not inherent, not "pure" consciousness. From the start the "spirit" is afflicted with the curse of being "burdened" with matter, which here makes its appearance in the form of agitated layers of air, sounds, in short, of language. Language is as old as conscious-

2. Marginal note by Marx: Men have history because they must *produce* their life, and because they must produce it moreover in a *certain* way: this is determined by their physical organization; their consciousness is determined in just the same way.

ness, language *is* practical consciousness that exists also for other men, and for that reason alone it really exists for me personally as well; language, like consciousness, only arises from the need, the necessity, of intercourse with other men. Where there exists a relationship, it exists for me: the animal does not enter into *"relations"* with anything, it does not enter into any relation at all. For the animal, its relation to others does not exist as a relation. Consciousness is, therefore, from the very beginning a social product, and remains so as long as men exist at all. Consciousness is at first, of course, merely consciousness concerning the *immediate* sensuous environment and consciousness of the limited connection with other persons and things outside the individual who is growing self-conscious. At the same time it is consciousness of nature, which first appears to men as a completely alien, all-powerful and unassailable force, with which men's relations are purely animal and by which they are overawed like beasts; it is thus a purely animal consciousness of nature (natural religion).

We see here immediately: this natural religion or this particular relation of men to nature is determined by the form of society and vice versa. Here, as everywhere, the identity of nature and man appears in such a way that the restricted relation of men to nature determines their restricted relation to one another, and their restricted relation to one another determines men's restricted relation to nature, just because nature is as yet hardly modified historically; and, on the other hand, man's consciousness of the necessity of associating with the individuals around him is the beginning of the consciousness that he is living in society at all. This beginning is as animal as social life itself at this stage. It is mere herd-consciousness, and at this point man is only distinguished from sheep by the fact that with him consciousness takes the place of instinct or that his instinct is a conscious one. This sheep-like or tribal consciousness receives its further development and extension through increased productivity, the increase of needs, and, what is fundamental to both of these, the increase of population. With these there develops the division of labor, which was originally nothing but the division of labor in the sexual act, then that division of labor which develops spontaneously or "naturally" by virtue of natural predisposition (e.g., physical strength), needs, accidents, etc., etc. Division of labor only becomes truly such from the moment when a division of material and mental labor appears.[3] From this moment onward consciousness *can* really flatter itself that it is something other than consciousness of existing practice, that it *really* represents something without representing something real; from now on consciousness is in a position to emancipate itself from the world and to proceed to the formation of "pure" theory, theology, philosophy, ethics, etc. But even if this theory, theology, philosophy, ethics, etc., comes into contradiction with the existing relations, this can only occur because existing social relations have come into contradiction with existing forces of production. . . .

Moreover, it is quite immaterial what consciousness starts to do on its own: out of all such muck we get only the one inference that these three moments, the forces of production, the state of society and consciousness, can and must come into contradiction with one another, because the *division of labor* implies the possibility, nay the fact that intellectual and material activity—enjoyment and labor, production and consumption—devolve on different individuals, and that the only possibility of their not coming into contradiction lies in the negation in its turn of the division of labor. . . .

With the division of labor, in which all these contradictions are implicit, and which in its turn is based on the natural division of labor in the family and the separation of society into individual families opposed to one another, is given simultaneously the *distribution*, and indeed the *unequal* distribution, both quantitative and qualitative, of labor and its products, hence property: the nucleus, the first form, of which lies in the family, where wife and children are the slaves of the husband. This latent slavery in the family, though still very crude, is the first property, but even at this early stage it corresponds perfectly to the definition of modern economists who call it the

---

3. Marginal note by Marx: The first form of ideologists, *priests*, is concurrent.

power of disposing the labor power of others. Division of labor and private property are, moreover, identical expressions: in the one the same thing is affirmed with reference to activity as is affirmed in the other with reference to the product of the activity.

Further the division of labor implies the contradiction between the interest of the separate individual or the individual family and the communal interest of all individuals who have intercourse with one another. And indeed, this communal interest does not exist merely in the imagination, as the "general interest," but first of all in reality, as the mutual interdependence of the individuals among whom the labor is divided. And finally, the division of labor offers us the first example of how, as long as man remains in natural society, that is, as long as a cleavage exists between the particular and the common interest, as long, therefore, as activity is not voluntarily, but naturally, divided, man's own deed becomes an alien power opposed to him, which enslaves him instead of being controlled by him. For as soon as the distribution of labor comes into being, each man has a particular, exclusive sphere of activity, which is forced upon him and from which he cannot escape. He is a hunter, a fisherman, a shepherd, or a critical critic, and must remain so if he does not want to lose his means of livelihood; while in communist society, where nobody has one exclusive sphere of activity but each can become accomplished in any branch he wishes, society regulates the general production and thus makes it possible for me to do one thing today and another tomorrow, to hunt in the morning, fish in the afternoon, rear cattle in the evening, criticize after dinner, just as I have a mind, without ever becoming hunter, fisherman, shepherd or critic. This fixation of social activity, this consolidation of what we ourselves produce into an objective power above us, growing out of our control, thwarting our expectations, bringing to naught our calculations, is one of the chief factors in historical development up till now.

And out of this very contradiction between the interest of the individual and that of the community the latter takes an independent form as the *State*, divorced from the real interests of individual and community, and at the same time as an illusory communal life, always based, however, on the real ties existing in every family and tribal conglomeration—such as flesh and blood, language, division of labor on a larger scale and other interests—and especially, as we shall enlarge upon later, on the classes, already determined by the division of labor, which in every such mass of men separate out, and of which one dominates all the others. It follows from this that all struggles within the State, the struggle between democracy, aristocracy, and monarchy, the struggle for the franchise, etc., etc., are merely the illusory forms in which the real struggles of the different classes are fought out among one another. . . . Further, it follows that every class which is struggling for mastery, even when its domination, as is the case with the proletariat, postulates the abolition of the old form of society in its entirety and of domination itself, must first conquer for itself political power in order to represent its interest in turn as the general interest, which in the first moment it is forced to do. Just because individuals seek *only* their particular interest, which for them does not coincide with their communal interest (in fact the general is the illusory form of communal life), the latter will be imposed on them as an interest "alien" to them, and "independent" of them, as in its turn a particular, peculiar "general" interest; or they themselves must remain within this discord, as in democracy. On the other hand, too, the *practical* struggle of these particular interests, which constantly *really* run counter to the communal and illusory communal interests, makes *practical* intervention and control necessary through the illusory "general" interest in the form of the State. The social power, i.e., the multiplied productive force, which arises through the cooperation of different individuals as it is determined by the division of labor, appears to these individuals, since their cooperation is not voluntary but has come about naturally, not as their own united power, but as an alien force existing outside them, of the origin and goal of which they are ignorant, which they thus cannot control, which on the contrary passes through a peculiar series of phases and stages independent of the will and the action of man, nay even being the prime governor of these.

This *"estrangement"* . . . can, of course, only be abolished given two *practical* premises. For it to become an "intolerable" power, i.e., a power against which men make a revolution, it must necessarily have rendered the great mass of humanity "propertyless," and produced, at the same time, the contradiction of an existing world of wealth and culture, both of which conditions presuppose a great increase in productive power, a high degree of its development. And, on the other hand, this development of productive forces (which itself implies the actual empirical existence of men in their *world-historical*, instead of local, being) is an absolutely necessary practical premise because without it *want* is merely made general, and with *destitution* the struggle for necessities and all the old filthy business would necessarily be reproduced; and furthermore, because only with this universal development of productive forces is a *universal* intercourse between men established, which produces in all nations simultaneously the phenomenon of the "propertyless" mass (universal competition), makes each nation dependent on the revolutions of the others, and finally has put *world-historical*, empirically universal individuals in place of local ones. Without this, (1) communism could only exist as a local event; (2) the *forces* of intercourse themselves could not have developed as *universal*, hence intolerable powers: they would have remained home-bred conditions surrounded by superstition; and (3) each extension of intercourse would abolish local communism. Empirically, communism is only possible as the act of the dominant peoples "all at once" and simultaneously, which presupposes the universal development of productive forces and the world intercourse bound up with communism. . . .

Communism is for us not a *state of affairs* which is to be established, an *ideal* to which reality [will] have to adjust itself. We call communism the *real* movement which abolishes the present state of things. The conditions of this movement result from the premises now in existence. Moreover, the mass of *propertyless* workers—the utterly precarious position of labor power on a mass scale cut off from capital or from even a limited satisfaction and, therefore, no longer merely temporarily deprived of work itself as a secure source of life—presupposes the *world market* through competition. The proletariat can thus only exist *world-historically*, just as communism, its activity, can only have a "world-historical" existence. World-historical existence of individuals, i.e., existence of individuals which is directly linked up with world history.

The form of intercourse determined by the existing productive forces at all previous historical stages, and in its turn determining these, is *civil society*. The latter, as is clear from what we have said above, has as its premises and basis the simple family and the multiple, the so-called tribe, and the more precise determinants of this society are enumerated in our remarks above. Already here we see how this civil society is the true source and theatre of all history, and how absurd is the conception of history held hitherto, which neglects the real relationships and confines itself to high-sounding dramas of princes and states.

Civil society embraces the whole material intercourse of individuals within a definite stage of the development of productive forces. It embraces the whole commercial and industrial life of a given stage and, insofar, transcends the State and the nation, though, on the other hand again, it must assert itself in its foreign relations as nationality, and inwardly must organize itself as State. The term "civil society" [*bürgerliche Gesellschaft*][4] emerged in the eighteenth century, when property relationships had already extricated themselves from the ancient and medieval communal society. Civil society as such only develops with the bourgeoisie; the social organization evolving directly out of production and commerce, which in all ages forms the basis of the State and of the rest of the idealistic superstructure, has, however, always been designated by the same name. . . .

In history up to the present it is certainly an empirical fact that separate individuals have, with the broadening of their

4. *"Bürgerliche Gesellschaft"* can mean either "bourgeois society" or "civil society."—*Ed.*

activity into world-historical activity, become more and more enslaved under a power alien to them (a pressure which they have conceived of as a dirty trick on the part of the so-called universal spirit, etc.), a power which has become more and more enormous and, in the last instance, turns out to be the *world market.* But it is just as empirically established that, by the overthrow of the existing state of society by the communist revolution . . . and the abolition of private property which is identical with it, this power . . . will be dissolved; and that then the liberation of each single individual will be accomplished in the measure in which history becomes transformed into world history. From the above it is clear that the real intellectual wealth of the individual depends entirely on the wealth of his real connections. Only then will the separate individuals be liberated from the various national and local barriers, be brought into practical connection with the material and intellectual production of the whole world and be put in a position to acquire the capacity to enjoy this all-sided production of the whole earth (the creations of man). *Allround* dependence, this natural form of the *World-historical* co-operation of individuals, will be transformed by this communist revolution into the control and conscious mastery of these powers, which, born of the action of men on one another, have till now overawed and governed men as powers completely alien to them. Now this view can be expressed again in speculative-idealistic, i.e., fantastic, terms as "self-generation of the species" ("society as the subject"), and thereby the consecutive series of interrelated individuals connected with each other can be conceived as a single individual, which accomplishes the mystery of generating itself. It is clear here that individuals certainly make *one another*, physically and mentally. . . .

This conception of history depends on our ability to expound the real process of production, starting out from the material production of life itself, and to comprehend the form of intercourse connected with this and created by this mode of production (i.e., civil society in its various stages), as the basis of all history; and to show it in its action as State, to explain all the different theoretical products and forms of consciousness, religion, philosophy, ethics, etc., etc., and trace their origins and growth from that basis; by which means, of course, the whole thing can be depicted in its totality (and therefore, too, the reciprocal action of these various sides on one another). It has not, like the idealistic view of history, in every period to look for a category, but remains constantly on the real *ground* of history; it does not explain practice from the idea but explains the formation of ideas from material practice; and accordingly it comes to the conclusion that all forms and products of consciousness cannot be dissolved by mental criticism . . . but only by the practical overthrow of the actual social relations which gave rise to this idealistic humbug; that not criticism but revolution is the driving force of history, also of religion, of philosophy and all other types of theory. It shows that history does not end by being resolved into "self-consciousness" as "spirit of the spirit," but that in it at each stage there is found a material result: a sum of productive forces, a historically created relation of individuals to nature and to one another, which is handed down to each generation from its predecessor; a mass of productive forces, capital funds and conditions, which, on the one hand, is indeed modified by the new generation, but also on the other prescribes for it its conditions of life and gives it a definite development, a special character. It shows that circumstances make men just as much as men make circumstances. This sum of productive forces, capital funds and social forms of intercourse, which every individual and generation finds in existence as something given, is the real basis of what the philosophers have conceived as "substance" and "essence of man," and what they have deified and attacked: a real basis which is not in the least disturbed, in its effect and influence on the development of men, by the fact that these philosophers revolt against it as "self-consciousness" and the "Unique." These conditions of life, which different generations find in existence, decide also whether or not the periodically recurring revolutionary convulsion will be strong enough to overthrow the basis of the entire existing system. And if these material elements of a complete revolution are not present (namely, on the one hand the existing productive forces, on the other the formation of a revolutionary mass, which revolts not only against separate conditions of society up till then, but against the very "production of life" till then, the "total activity" on which it was based), then, as far as practical development is concerned, it is absolutely immaterial whether the *idea* of this revolution has been expressed a hundred times already, as the history of communism proves.

In the whole conception of history up to the present this real basis of history has either been totally neglected or else considered as a minor matter quite irrelevant to the course of history. History must, therefore, always be written according to an extraneous standard; the real production of life seems to be primeval history, while the truly historical appears to be separated from ordinary life, something extra-superterrestrial. With this the relation of man to nature is excluded from history and hence the antithesis of nature and history is created. The exponents of this conception of history have consequently only been able to see in history the political actions of princes and States, religious and all sorts of theoretical struggles, and in particular in each historical epoch have had to *share the illusion of that epoch.* For instance, if an epoch imagines itself to be actuated by purely "political" or "religious" motives, although "religion" and "politics" are only forms of its true motives, the historian accepts this opinion. . . .

History is nothing but the succession of the separate generations, each of which exploits the materials, the capital funds, the productive forces handed down to it by all preceding generations, and thus, on the one hand, continues the traditional activity in completely changed circumstances and, on the other, modifies the old circumstances with a completely changed activity. This can be speculatively distorted so that later history is made the goal of earlier history . . . while what is designated with the words "destiny," "goal," "germ," or "idea" of earlier history is nothing more than an abstraction formed from later history, from the active influence which earlier history exercises on later history.

The further the separate spheres, which act on one another, extend in the course of this development, the more the original isolation of the separate nationalities is destroyed by the developed mode of production and intercourse and the division of labor between various nations naturally brought forth by these, the more history becomes world history. Thus, for instance, if in England a machine is invented, which deprives countless workers of bread in India and China, and overturns the whole form of existence of these empires, this invention becomes a world-historical fact. . . . From this it follows that this transformation of history into world history is not indeed a mere abstract act on the part of the "self-consciousness," the world spirit, or of any other metaphysical specter, but a quite material, empirically verifiable act, an act the proof of which every individual furnishes as he comes and goes, eats, drinks and clothes himself.

The ideas of the ruling class are in every epoch the ruling ideas: i.e., the class which is the ruling *material* force of society, is at the same time its ruling *intellectual* force. The class which has the means of material production at its disposal, has control at the same time over the means of mental production, so that thereby, generally speaking, the ideas of those who lack the means of mental production are subject to it. The ruling ideas are nothing more than the ideal expression of the dominant material relationships, the dominant material relationships grasped as ideas; hence of the relationships which make the one class the ruling one, therefore, the ideas of its dominance. The individuals composing the ruling class possess among other things consciousness, and therefore think. Insofar, therefore, as they rule as a class and determine the extent and compass of an epoch, it is self-evident that they do this in its whole range, hence among other things rule also as thinkers, as producers of ideas, and regulate the production and distribution of the ideas of their age: thus their ideas are the ruling ideas of the epoch. For instance, in an age and in a country where royal power, aristocracy and bourgeoisie are contending for mastery and where, therefore, mastery is shared, the doctrine of the separation of powers proves to be the dominant idea and is expressed as an "eternal law."

The division of labor, which we already saw above as one of

the chief forces of history up till now, manifests itself also in the ruling class as the division of mental and material labor, so that inside this class one part appears as the thinkers of the class (its active, conceptive ideologists, who make the perfecting of the illusion of the class about itself their chief source of livelihood), while the others' attitude to these ideas and illusions is more passive and receptive, because they are in reality the active members of this class and have less time to make up illusions and ideas about themselves. Within this class this cleavage can even develop into a certain opposition and hostility between the two parts, which, however, in the case of a practical collision, in which the class itself is endangered, automatically comes to nothing, in which case there also vanishes the semblance that the ruling ideas were not the ideas of the ruling class and had a power distinct from the power of this class. . . .

If now in considering the course of history we detach the ideas of the ruling class from the ruling class itself and attribute to them an independent existence, if we confine ourselves to saying that these or those ideas were dominant at a given time, without bothering ourselves about the conditions of production and the producers of these ideas, if we thus ignore the individuals and world conditions which are the source of the ideas, we can say, for instance, that during the time that the aristocracy was dominant, the concepts honor, loyalty, etc., were dominant, during the dominance of the bourgeoisie the concepts freedom, equality, etc. The ruling class itself on the whole imagines this to be so. This conception of history, which is common to all historians, particularly since the eighteenth century, will necessarily come up against the phenomenon that increasingly abstract ideas hold sway, i.e., ideas which increasingly take on the form of universality. For each new class which puts itself in the place of one ruling before it, is compelled, merely in order to carry through its aim, to represent its interest as the common interest of all the members of society, that is, expressed in ideal form: it has to give its ideas the form of universality, and represent them as the only rational, universally valid ones. The class making a revolution appears from the very start, if only because it is opposed to a *class*, not as a class but as the representative of the whole of society; it appears as the whole mass of society confronting the one ruling class. It can do this because, to start with, its interest really is more connected with the common interest of all other nonruling classes, because under the pressure of hitherto existing conditions its interest has not yet been able to develop as the particular interest of a particular class. Its victory, therefore, benefits also many individuals of the other classes which are not winning a dominant position, but only insofar as it now puts these individuals in a position to raise themselves into the ruling class. . . . Every new class, therefore, achieves its hegemony only on a broader basis than that of the class ruling previously, whereas the opposition of the nonruling class against the new ruling class later develops all the more sharply and profoundly. . . .

This whole semblance, that the rule of a certain class is only the rule of certain ideas, come to a natural end, of course, as soon as class rule in general ceases to be the form in which society is organized, that is to say, as soon as it is no longer necessary to represent a particular interest as general or the "general interest" as ruling. . . .

The greatest division of material and mental labor is the separation of town and country. The antagonism between town and country begins with the transition from barbarism to civilization, from tribe to State, from locality to nation, and runs through the whole history of civilization to the present day. . . .

The existence of the town implies, at the same time, the necessity of administration, police, taxes, etc., in short, of the municipality, and thus of politics in general. Here first became manifest the division of the population into two great classes, which is directly based on the division of labor and on the instruments of production. The town already is in actual fact the concentration of the population, of the instruments of production, of capital, of pleasures, of needs, while the country demonstrates just the opposite fact, isolation and separation. The antagonism between town and country can only exist within the framework of private property. It is the most crass expression of the subjection of the individual under the division of labor, under a definite activity forced upon him—a subjection which makes one man into a restricted town-animal, the other into a restricted country-animal, and daily creates anew the conflict between their interests. Labor is here again the chief thing, power *over* individuals, and as long as the latter exists, private property must exist. The abolition of the antagonism between town and country is one of the first conditions of communal life, a condition which again depends on a mass of material premises and which cannot be fulfilled by the mere will, as anyone can see at the first glance. . . . The separation of town and country can also be understood as the separation of capital and landed property, as the beginning of the existence and development of capital independent of landed property— the beginning of property having its basis only in labor and exchange.

In the towns which, in the Middle Ages, did not derive ready-made from an earlier period but were formed anew by the serfs who had become free, each man's own particular labor was his only property apart from the small capital he brought with him, consisting almost solely of the most necessary tools of his craft. The competition of serfs constantly escaping into the town, the constant war of the country against the towns and thus the necessity of an organized municipal military force, the bond of common ownership in a particular kind of labor, the necessity of common buildings for the sale of their wares at a time when craftsmen were also traders, and the consequent exclusion of the unauthorized from these buildings, the conflict among the interests of the various crafts, the necessity of protecting their laboriously acquired skill, and the feudal organization of the whole of the country: these were the causes of the union of the workers of each craft in guilds. We have not at this point to go further into the manifold modifications of the guild system, which arise through later historical developments. The flight of the serfs into the towns went on without interruption right through the Middle Ages. These serfs, persecuted by their lords in the country, came separately into the towns, where they found an organized community, against which they were powerless and in which they had to subject themselves to the station assigned to them by the demand for their labor and the interest of their organized urban competitors. These workers, entering separately, were never able to attain to any power, since, if their labor was of the guild type which had to be learned, the guild-masters bent them to their will and organized them according to their interest; or if their labor was not such as had to be learned, and therefore not of the guild type, they became day-laborers and never managed to organize, remaining an unorganized rabble. The need for day-laborers in the towns created the rabble.

These towns were true "associations," called forth by the direct need, the care of providing for the protection of property, and of multiplying the means of production and defense of the separate members. The rabble of these towns was devoid of any power, composed as it was of individuals strange to one another who had entered separately, and who stood unorganized over against an organized power, armed for war, and jealously watching over them. The journeymen and apprentices were organized in each craft as it best suited the interest of the masters. The patriarchal relationship existing between them and their masters gave the latter a double power—on the one hand because of their influence on the whole life of the journeymen, and on the other because, for the journeymen who worked with the same master, it was a real bond which held them together against the journeymen of other masters and separated them from these. And finally, the journeymen were bound to the existing order by their simple interest in becoming masters themselves. While, therefore, the rabble at least carried out revolts against the whole municipal order, revolts which remained completely ineffective because of their powerlessness, the journeymen never got further than small acts of insubordination within separate guilds, such as belong to the very nature of the guild system. The great risings of the Middle Ages all radiated from the country, but equally remained totally ineffective because of the isolation and consequent crudity of the peasants.

In the towns, the division of labor between the individual guilds was as yet [quite naturally derived] and, in the guilds themselves, not at all developed between the individual workers. Every workman had to be versed in a whole round of tasks, had to be able to make everything that was to be made with his tools. The limited commerce and the scanty communication between the individual towns, the lack of population and the narrow needs did not allow of a higher division of labor, and therefore every man who wished to become a master had to be proficient in the whole of his craft. Thus there is found with medieval craftsmen an interest in their special work and in proficiency in it, which was capable of rising to a narrow artistic sense. For this very reason, however, every medieval craftsman was completely absorbed in his work, to which he had a contented, slavish relationship, and to which he was subjected to a far greater extent than the modern worker, whose work is a matter of indifference to him.

Capital in these towns was a naturally derived capital, consisting of a house, the tools of the craft, and the natural, hereditary customers; and not being realizable, on account of the backwardness of commerce and the lack of circulation, it descended from father to son. Unlike modern capital, which can be assessed in money and which may be indifferently invested in this thing or that, this capital was directly connected with the particular work of the owner, inseparable from it and to this extent *estate* capital.

The next extension of the division of labor was the separation of production and commerce, the formation of a special class of merchants; a separation which, in the towns bequeathed by a former period, had been handed down (among other things with the Jews) and which very soon appeared in the newly formed ones. With this there was given the possibility of commercial communications transcending the immediate neighborhood, a possibility, the realization of which depended on the existing means of communication, the state of public safety in the countryside, which was determined by political conditions (during the whole of the Middle Ages, as is well known, the merchants traveled in armed caravans), and on the cruder or more advanced needs (determined by the stage of culture attained) of the region accessible to intercourse.

With commerce the prerogative of a particular class, with the extension of trade through the merchants beyond the immediate surroundings of the town, there immediately appears a reciprocal action between production and commerce. The towns enter into relations *with one another,* new tools are brought from one town into the other, and the separation between production and commerce soon calls forth a new division of production between the individual towns, each of which is soon exploiting a predominant branch of industry. The local restrictions of earlier times begin gradually to be broken down.

In the Middle Ages the citizens in each town were compelled to unite against the landed nobility to save their skins. The extension of trade, the establishment of communications, led the separate towns to get to know other towns, which had asserted the same interests in the struggle with the same antagonist. Out of the many local corporations of burghers there arose only gradually the burgher *class.* The conditions of life of the individual burghers became, on account of their contradiction to the existing relationships and of the mode of labor determined by these, conditions which were common to them all and independent of each individual. The burghers had created the conditions insofar as they had torn themselves free from feudal ties, and were created by them insofar as they were determined by their antagonism to the feudal system which they found in existence. When the individual towns began to enter into associations, these common conditions developed into class conditions. The same conditions, the same contradiction, the same interests necessarily called forth on the whole similar customs everywhere. The bourgeoisie itself, with its conditions, develops only gradually, splits according to the division of labor into various factions and finally absorbs all propertied classes it finds in existence (while it develops the majority of the earlier propertyless and a part of the hitherto propertied classes into a new class, the proletariat) in the measure to which all property found in existence is transformed into industrial or commercial capital. The separate individuals form a class only insofar as they have to carry on a common battle against another class; otherwise they are on hostile terms with each other as competitors. On the other hand, the class in its turn achieves an independent existence over against the individuals, so that the latter find their conditions of existence predestined, and hence have their position in life and their personal development assigned to them by their class, become subsumed under it. This is the same phenomenon as the subjection of the separate individuals to the division of labor and can only be removed by the abolition of private property and of labor itself. We have already indicated several times how this subsuming of individuals under the class brings with it their subjection to all kinds of ideas, etc.

It depends purely on the extension of commerce whether the productive forces achieved in a locality, especially inventions, are lost for later development or not. As long as there exists no commerce transcending the immediate neighborhood, every invention must be made separately in each locality, and mere chances such as irruptions of barbaric peoples, even ordinary wars, are sufficient to cause a country with advanced productive forces and needs to have to start right over again from the beginning. In primitive history every invention had to be made daily anew and in each locality independently. . . . Only when commerce has become world commerce and has as its basis large-scale industry, when all nations are drawn into the competitive struggle, is the permanence of the acquired productive forces assured.

The immediate consequence of the division of labor between the various towns was the rise of manufactures, branches of production which had outgrown the guild system. Manufactures first flourished, in Italy and later in Flanders, under the historical premise of commerce with foreign nations. In other countries, England and France for example, manufactures were at first confined to the home market. Besides the premises already mentioned, manufactures depend on an already advanced concentration of population, particularly in the countryside, and of capital, which began to accumulate in the hands of individuals, partly in the guilds in spite of the guild regulations, partly among the merchants.

That labor which from the first presupposed a machine, even of the crudest sort, soon showed itself the most capable of development. Weaving, earlier carried on in the country by the peasants as a secondary occupation to procure their clothing, was the first labor to receive an impetus and a further development through the extension of commerce. Weaving was the first and remained the principal manufacture. The rising demand for clothing materials, consequent on the growth of population, the growing accumulation and mobilization of natural capital through accelerated circulation, the demand for luxuries called forth by the latter and favored generally by the gradual extension of commerce, gave weaving a quantitative and qualitative stimulus, which wrenched it out of the form of production hitherto existing. Alongside the peasants weaving for their own use, who continued, and still continue, with this sort of work, there emerged a new class of weavers in the towns, whose fabrics were destined for the whole home market and usually for foreign markets too.

Weaving, an occupation demanding in most cases little skill and soon splitting up into countless branches, by its whole nature resisted the trammels of the guild. Weaving was, therefore, carried on mostly in villages and market centers without guild organization, which gradually became towns, and indeed the most flourishing towns in each land.

With guild-free manufacture, property relations also quickly changed. The first advance beyond naturally derived estate capital was provided by the rise of merchants whose capital was from the beginning movable, capital in the modern sense as far as one can speak of it, given the circumstances of those times. The second advance came with manufacture, which again made mobile a mass of natural capital, and altogether increased the mass of movable capital as against that of natural capital.

At the same time, manufacture became a refuge of the peasants from the guilds which excluded them or paid them badly, just as earlier the guild towns had [served] as a refuge for the peasants from [the oppressive landed nobility]. . . .

With the advent of manufactures, the various nations entered into a competitive relationship, the struggle for trade, which was fought out in wars, protective duties and prohibitions, whereas earlier the nations, insofar as they were connected at all, had carried on an inoffensive exchange with each other. Trade had from now on a political significance.

With the advent of manufacture the relationship between worker and employer changed. In the guilds the patriarchal relationship between journeyman and master continued to exist; in manufacture its place was taken by the monetary relation between worker and capitalist—a relationship which in the countryside and in small towns retained a patriarchal tinge, but in the large, the real manufacturing towns, quite early lost almost all patriarchal complexion.[5]

5. Another point which has not yet been sufficiently appreciated in the history of manufacturing industry is the disbanding of the numerous retinues of feudal lords, whose subordinate ranks became vagrants before entering the workshop. The creation of the workshop was preceded by an almost universal vagrancy in the fifteenth and sixteenth centuries. The workshop found, besides, a powerful support in the many peasants who, continually driven from the country owing to the transformation of the fields into pastures and to the progress in agriculture which necessitated fewer hands for the tillage of the soil, went on congregating in the towns during whole centuries.

The growth of the market, the accumulation of capital, the modification in the social position of the classes, a large number of persons being deprived of their sources of income, all these are historical preconditions for the formation of manufacture. It was not, as M. Proundhon says, friendly agreements between equals that brought men together into the workshop. It was not even in the bosom of the old guilds that manufacture was born. It was the merchant that became the head of the modern workshop, and not the old guild master. Almost everywhere there was a desperate struggle between manufacture and crafts.

The accumulation and concentration of instruments and workers preceded the development of the division of labor inside the workshop. Manufacture consisted much more in the bringing together of many workers and many crafts in one place, in one room under the command of one capital, than in the analysis of labor and the adaptation of a special worker to a very simple task.

The utility of a workshop consisted much less in the division of labor as such than in the circumstance that work was done on a much larger scale, that many unnecessary expenses were saved, etc. At the end of the sixteenth and at the beginning of the seventeenth century, Dutch manufacture scarcely knew any division of labor.

The development of the division of labor supposes the assemblage of workers in a workshop. There is not one single example, whether in the sixteenth or in the seventeenth century, of the different branches of one and the same craft being exploited separately to such an extent that it would have sufficed to assemble them all in one place so as to obtain a complete, ready-made workship. But once the men and the instruments had been brought together, the division of labor, such as it had existed in the form of the guilds, was reproduced, necessarily reflected inside the worksop. Marx, *The Poverty of Philosophy* (Moscow, Progress Publishers, 1966), pp. 119–120.

Manufacture and the movement of production in general received an enormous impetus through the extension of commerce which came with the discovery of America and the sea route to the East Indies. The new products imported thence, particularly the masses of gold and silver which came into circulation and totally changed the position of the classes toward one another, dealing a hard blow to feudal landed property and to the workers; the expeditions of adventurers, colonization; and above all the extension of markets into a world market, which had now become possible and was daily becoming more and more a fact, called forth a new phase of historical development, into which in general we cannot here enter further. Through the colonization of the newly discovered countries the commercial struggle of the nations amongst one another was given new fuel and accordingly greater extension and animosity.

The expansion of trade and manufacture accelerated the accumulation of movable capital, while in the guilds, which were not stimulated to extend their production, natural capital remained stationary or even declined. Trade and manufacture created the big bourgeoisie; in the guilds was concentrated the petty bourgeoisie, which no longer was dominant in the towns as formerly, but had to bow to the might of the great merchants and manufacturers. Hence the decline of the guilds, as soon as they came into contact with manufacture.

The intercourse of nations took on, in the epoch of which we have been speaking, two different forms. At first the small quantity of gold and silver in circulation involved the ban on the export of these metals; and industry, for the most part imported from abroad and made necessary by the need for employing the growing urban population, could not do without those privileges which could be granted not only, of course, against home competition, but chiefly against foreign. The local guild privilege was in these original prohibitions extended over the whole nation. Customs duties originated from the tributes which the feudal lords exacted as protective levies against robbery from merchants passing through their territories, tributes later imposed likewise by the towns, and which, with the rise of the

modern states, were the Treasury's most obvious means of raising money.

The appearance of American gold and silver on the European
markets, the gradual development of industry, the rapid expansion of trade and the consequent rise of the nonguild bourgeoisie and of money, gave these measures another significance.
The State, which was daily less and less able to do without
money, now retained the ban on the export of gold and silver
out of fiscal considerations; the bourgeois, for whom these
masses of money which were hurled onto the market became
the chief object of speculative buying, were thoroughly content
with this; privileges established earlier became a source of income for the government and were sold for money. . . .

The second period began in the middle of the seventeenth
century and lasted almost to the end of the eighteenth. Commerce and navigation had expanded more rapidly than manufacture, which played a secondary role; the colonies were
becoming considerable consumers; and after long struggles the
separate nations shared out the opening world market among
themselves. . . . The competition of the nations among themselves was excluded as far as possible by tariffs, prohibitions and
treaties; and in the last resort the competitive struggle was
carried on and decided by wars (especially naval wars). The
mightiest maritime nation, the English, retained preponderance in trade and manufacture. . . .

Manufacture was all the time sheltered by protective duties
in the home market, by monopolies in the colonial market, and
abroad as much as possible by differential duties. The working-
up of home-produced material was encouraged (wool and linen
in England, silk in France), the export of home-produced raw
material forbidden (wool in England), and the [working-up] of
imported material neglected or suppressed (cotton in England)
The nation dominant in sea trade and colonial power naturally
secured for itself also the greatest quantitative and qualitative
expansion of manufacture. Manufacture could not be carried on
without protection, since, if the slightest change takes place
in other countries, it can lose its market and be ruined;
under reasonably favorable conditions it may easily be intro-

duced into a country, but for this very reason can easily be destroyed. . . . [so] that no country dare jeopardize its existence by permitting free competition. Insofar as it manages to export, it therefore depends entirely on the extension or restriction of commerce, and exercises a relatively very small reaction [on the latter]. Hence its secondary [importance] and the influence of [the merchants] in the eighteenth century. It was the merchants and especially the shippers who more than anybody else pressed for State protection and monopolies; the manufacturers also demanded and indeed received protection, but all the time were inferior in political importance to the merchants. The commercial towns, particularly the maritime towns, became to some extent civilized and acquired the outlook of the big bourgeoisie, but in the factory towns an extreme petty-bourgeois outlook persisted. . . .

This period is also characterized by the cessation of the bans on the export of gold and silver and the beginning of the trade in money; by banks, national debts, paper money; by speculation in stocks and shares and stockjobbing in all articles; by the development of finance in general. Again capital lost a great part of the natural character which had still clung to it.

The concentration of trade and manufacture in one country, England, developing irresistibly in the seventeenth century, gradually created for this country a relative world market, and thus a demand for the manufactured products of this country, which could no longer be met by the industrial productive forces hitherto existing. This demand, outgrowing the productive forces, was the motive power which, by producing big industry—the application of elemental forces to industrial ends, machinery and the most complex division of labor—called into existence the third period of private ownership since the Middle Ages. There already existed in England the other preconditions of this new phase: freedom of competition inside the nation, the development of theoretical mechanics, etc. (Indeed, the science of mechanics perfected by Newton was altogether the most popular science in France and England in the eighteenth century.) (Free competition inside the nation itself had everywhere to be conquered by a revolution—1640 and 1688 in England, 1789 in France.) Competition soon compelled every country that wished to retain its historical role to protect its manufactures by renewed customs regulations (the old duties were no longer any good against big industry) and soon after to introduce big industry under protective duties. Big industry universalized competition in spite of these protective measures (it is practical free trade; the protective duty is only a palliative, a measure of defense *within* free trade), established means of communication and the modern world market, subordinated trade to itself, transformed all capital into industrial capital, and thus produced the rapid circulation (development of the financial system) and the centralization of capital. By universal competition it forced all individuals to strain their energy to the utmost. It destroyed as far as possible ideology, religion, morality, etc., and where it could not do this, made them into a palpable lie. It produced world history for the first time, insofar as it made all civilized nations and every individual member of them dependent for the satisfaction of their wants on the whole world, thus destroying the former natural exclusiveness of separate nations. It made natural science subservient to capital and took from the division of labor the last semblance of its natural character. It destroyed natural growth in general, as far as this is possible while labor exists, and resolved all natural relationships into money relationships. In the place of naturally grown towns it created the modern, large industrial cities which have sprung up overnight. Wherever it penetrated, it destroyed the crafts and all earlier stages of industry. It completed the victory of the commercial town over the countryside. [Its first premise] was the automatic system. [Its development] produced a mass of productive forces, for which private [property] became just as much a fetter as the guild had been for manufacture and the small, rural workshop for the developing craft. These productive forces received under the system of private property a one-sided development only, and became for the majority destructive forces; moreover, a great multitude of such forces could find no application at all within this system. Generally speaking, big industry created everywhere the same relations between the classes of society, and thus destroyed the peculiar individuality of the various nationalities. And finally, while the bourgeoisie of each nation still retained separate national interests, big industry created a class, which in all nations has the same interest and with which nationality is already dead; a class which is really rid of all the old world and at the same time stands pitted against it. Big industry makes for the worker not only the relation to the capitalist, but labor itself, unbearable.

It is evident that big industry does not reach the same level of development in all districts of a country. This does not, however, retard the class movement of the proletariat, because the proletarians created by big industry assume leadership of this movement and carry the whole mass along with them, and because the workers excluded from big industry are placed by it in a still worse situation than the workers in big industry itself. The countries in which big industry is developed act in a similar manner upon the more or less nonindustrial countries, insofar as the latter are swept by universal commerce into the universal competitive struggle.[6] . . .

In big industry and competition the whole mass of conditions of existence, limitations, biases of individuals, are fused together into the two simplest forms: private property and labor. With money every form of intercourse, and intercourse itself, is considered fortuitous for the individuals. Thus money implies that all previous intercourse was only intercourse of individuals under particular conditions, not of individuals as individuals. These conditions are reduced to two: accumulated labor or private property, and actual labor. If both or one of these ceases, then intercourse comes to a standstill. . . . On the other hand,

---

6. Competition separates individuals from one another, not only the bourgeois but still more the workers, in spite of the fact that it brings them together. Hence it is a long time before these individuals can unite, apart from the fact that for the purposes of this union—if it is not to be merely local—the necessary means, the great industrial cities and cheap and quick communications, have first to be produced by big industry. Hence every organized power standing over against these isolated individuals, who live in relationships daily reproducing this isolation, can only be overcome after long struggles. To demand the opposite would be tantamount to demanding that competition should not exist in this definite epoch of history, or that the individuals should banish from their minds relationships over which in their isolation they have no control.

the individuals themselves are entirely subordinated to the division of labor and hence are brought into the most complete dependence on one another. . . .

Thus two facts are here revealed. First the productive forces appear as a world for themselves, quite independent of and divorced from the individuals, alongside the individuals: the reason for this is that the individuals, whose forces they are, exist split up and in opposition to one another, while, on the other hand, these forces are only real forces in the intercourse and association of these individuals. Thus, on the one hand, we have a totality of productive forces, which have, as it were, taken on a material form and are for the individuals no longer the forces of the individuals but of private property, and hence of the individuals only insofar as they are owners of private property themselves. Never, in any earlier period, have the productive forces taken on a form so indifferent to the intercourse of individuals *as* individuals, because their intercourse itself was formerly a restricted one. On the other hand, standing over against these productive forces, we have the majority of the individuals from whom these forces have been wrested away, and who, robbed thus of all real life-content, have become abstract individuals, but who are, however, only by this fact put into a position to enter into relation with one another *as individuals.*

The only connection which still links them with the productive forces and with their own existence—labor—has lost all semblance of self-activity and only sustains their life by stunting it. While in the earlier periods self-activity and the production of material life were separated, in that they devolved on different persons, and while, on account of the narrowness of the individuals themselves, the production of material life was considered as a subordinate mode of self-activity, they now diverge to such an extent that altogether material life appears as the end, and what produces this material life, labor (which is now the only possible but, as we see, negative form of self-activity), as the means.

Thus things have now come to such a pass that the individuals must appropriate the existing totality of productive forces, not only to achieve self-activity, but, also, merely to safeguard their very existence. This appropriation is first determined by the object to be appropriated, the productive forces, which have been developed to a totality and which only exist within a universal intercourse. From this aspect alone, therefore, this appropriation must have a universal character corresponding to the productive forces and the intercourse. The appropriation of these forces is itself nothing more than the development of the individual capacities corresponding to the material instruments of production. The appropriation of a totality of instruments of production is, for this very reason, the development of a totality of capacities in the individuals themselves. This appropriation is further determined by the persons appropriating. Only the proletarians of the present day, who are completely shut off from all self-activity, are in a position to achieve a complete and no longer restricted self-activity, which consists in the appropriation of a totality of productive forces and in the thus postulated development of a totality of capacities. All earlier revolutionary appropriations were restricted; individuals, whose self-activity was restricted by a crude instrument of production and a limited intercourse, appropriated this crude instrument of production, and hence merely achieved a new state of limitation. Their instrument of production became their property, but they themselves remained subordinate to the division of labor and their own instrument of production. In all expropriations up to now, a mass of individuals remained subservient to a single instrument of production; in the appropriation by the proletarians, a mass of instruments of production must be made subject to each individual, and property to all. Modern universal intercourse can be controlled by individuals, therefore, only when controlled by all.

This appropriation is further determined by the manner in which it must be effected. It can only be effected through a union, which by the character of the proletariat itself can again only be a universal one, and through a revolution, in which, on the one hand, the power of the earlier mode of production and intercourse and social organization is overthrown, and, on the other hand, there develops the universal character and the energy of the proletariat, without which the revolution cannot be accomplished; and in which, further, the proletariat rids itself of everything that still clings to it from its previous position in society.

Only at this stage does self-activity coincide with material life, which corresponds to the development of individuals into complete individuals and the casting-off of all natural limitations. The transformation of labor into self-activity corresponds to the transformation of the earlier limited intercourse into the intercourse, of individuals as such. With the appropriation of the total productive forces through united individuals, private property comes to an end. While previously in history a particular condition always appeared as accidental, now the isolation of individuals and the particular private gain of each man have themselves become accidental. . . .

Finally, from the conception of history we have sketched we obtain these further conclusions: (1) In the development of productive forces there comes a stage when productive forces and means of intercourse are brought into being, which, under the existing relationships, only cause mischief, and are no longer productive but destructive forces (machinery and money); and connected with this a class is called forth, which has to bear all the burdens of society without enjoying its advantages, which, ousted from society, is forced into the most decided antagonism to all other classes; a class which forms the majority of all members of society, and from which emanates the consciousness of the necessity of a fundamental revolution, the communist consciousness, which may, of course, arise among the other classes too through the contemplation of the situation of this class. (2) The conditions under which definite productive forces can be applied are the conditions of the rule of a definite class of society, whose social power, deriving from its property, has its *practical*-idealistic expression in each case in the form of the State; and, therefore, every revolutionary struggle is directed against a class, which till then has been in power. (3) In all revolutions up till now the mode of activity always remained unscathed and it was only question of a different distribution of this activity, a new distribution of labor to other persons, while the communist revolution is directed against the preceding *mode* of activity, does away with *labor,* and abolishes the rule of all classes with the classes themselves, because it is carried through by the class which no longer counts as a class in society, is not recognized as a class, and is in itself the expression of the dissolution of all classes, nationalities, etc., within present society; and (4) both for the production on a mass scale of this communist consciousness, and for the success of the cause itself, the alteration of men on a mass scale is necessary, an alteration which can only take place in a practical movement, a *revolution;* this revolution is necessary, therefore, not only because the *ruling* class cannot be overthrown in any other way, but also because the class *overthrowing* it can only in a revolution succeed in ridding itself of all the muck of ages and become fitted to found society anew.

Communism differs from all previous movements in that it overturns the basis of all earlier relations of production and intercourse, and for the first time consciously treats all natural premises as the creatures of hitherto existing men, strips them of their natural character and subjugates them to the power of the united individuals. Its organization is, therefore, essentially economic, the material production of the conditions of this unity; it turns existing conditions into conditions of unity. The reality, which communism is creating, is precisely the true basis for rendering it impossible that anything should exist independently of individuals, insofar as reality is only a product of the preceding intercourse of individuals themselves. Thus the communists in practice treat the conditions created up to now by production and intercourse as inorganic conditions, without, however, imagining that it was the plan or the destiny of previous generations to give them material, and without believing that these conditions were inorganic for the individuals creating them. The difference between the individual as a person and what is accidental to him is not a conceptual difference but a historical fact. This distinction has a different significance at different times—e.g., the estate as something accidental to the individual in the eighteenth century, the family more or less too. It is not a distinction that we have to make for each age, but one which each age makes itself from among the different elements which it finds in existence, and indeed not according to any theory, but compelled by material collisions in life. What appears accidental to the later age as opposed to the earlier—and this applies also to the elements handed down by an earlier age—is a form of intercourse which corresponded to a definite stage of development of the productive forces. The relation of the productive forces to the form of intercourse is the relation of the form of intercourse to the occupation or activity of the individuals. (The fundamental form of this activity is, of course, material, on which depend all other forms—mental, political, religious, etc. The various shaping of material life is of course, in every case dependent on the needs which are already developed, and the production, as well as the satisfaction, of these needs is a historical process. . . .) The conditions under which individuals have intercourse with each other, so long as the above-mentioned contradiction is absent, are conditions appertaining to their individuality, in no way external to them; conditions under which these definite individuals, living under definite relationships, can alone produce their material life and what is connected with it, are thus the conditions of their self-activity and are produced by this self-activity. The definite condition under which they produce thus corresponds, as long as the contradiction has not yet appeared, to the reality of their conditioned nature, their one-sided existence, the one-sidedness of which only becomes evident when the contradiction enters on the scene and thus exists for the later individuals. Then this condition appears as an accidental fetter, and the consciousness that it is a fetter is imputed to the earlier age as well.

These various conditions, which appear first as conditions of self-activity, later as fetters upon it, form in the whole evolution of history a coherent series of forms of intercourse, the coherence of which consists in this: in the place of an earlier form of intercourse, which has become a fetter, a new one is put, corresponding to the more developed productive forces and, hence, to the advanced mode of the self-activity of individuals—a form which in its turn becomes a fetter and is then replaced by another. Since these conditions correspond at every stage to the simultaneous development of the productive forces, their history is at the same time the history of the evolving productive forces taken over by each new generation, and is, therefore, the history of the development of the forces of the individuals themselves.

Since this evolution takes place naturally, i.e., is not subordinated to a general plan of freely combined individuals, it proceeds from various localities, tribes, nations, branches of labor, etc., each of which to start with develops independently of the others and only gradually enters into relation with the others. Furthermore, it takes place only very slowly; the various stages and interests are never completely overcome, but only subordinated to the prevailing interest and trail along beside the latter for centuries afterward. It follows from this that within a nation itself the individuals, even apart from their pecuniary circumstances, have quite different developments, and that an earlier interest, the peculiar form of intercourse of which has already been ousted by that belonging to a later interest, remains for a long time afterward in possession of a traditional power in the illusory community (State, law), which has won an existence independent of the individuals; a power which in the last resort can only be broken by a revolution. This explains why, with reference to individual points which allow of a more general summing-up, consciousness can sometimes appear further advanced than the contemporary empirical relationships, so that in the struggles of a later epoch one can refer to earlier theoreticians as authorities. . . .

Nothing is more common than the notion that in history up till now it has only been a question of *taking*. The barbarians *take* the Roman Empire, and this fact of taking is made to explain the transition from the old world to the feudal system. In this taking by barbarians, however, the question is, whether the nation which is conquered has evolved industrial productive forces, as is the case with modern peoples, or whether their productive forces are based for the most part merely on their association and on the community. Taking is further determined by the object taken. A banker's fortune, consisting of paper, cannot be taken at all, without the taker's submitting to the conditions of production and intercourse of the country taken. Similarly the total industrial capital of a modern industrial country. And finally, everywhere there is very soon an end to taking, and when there is nothing more to take, you have to set about producing. From this necessity of producing, which very soon asserts itself, it follows that the form of community adopted by the settling conquerors must correspond to the stage of development of the productive forces they find in existence; or, if this is not the case from the start, it must change according to the productive forces. By this, too, is explained the fact, which people profess to have noticed everywhere in the period following the migration of the peoples, namely, that the servant was master, and that the conquerors very soon took over language, culture and manners from the conquered. The feudal system was by no means brought complete from Germany, but had its origin, as far as the conquerors were concerned, in the martial organisation of the army during the actual conquest, and this only evolved after the conquest into the feudal system proper through the action of the productive forces found in the conquered countries. To what an extent this form was determined by the productive forces is shown by the abortive attempts to realise other forms derived from reminiscences of ancient Rome (Charlemagne, etc.).

Thus all collisions in history have their origin, according to our view, in the contradiction between the productive forces and the form of intercourse.

The transformation, through the division of labor, of personal powers (relationships) into material powers, cannot be dispelled by dismissing the general idea of it from one's mind, but can only be abolished by the individuals again subjecting these material powers to themselves and abolishing the division of labor. This is not possible without the community. Only in community [with others has each] individual the means of cultivating his gifts in all directions; only in the community, therefore, is personal freedom possible. In the previous substitutes for the community, in the State, etc., personal freedom has existed only for the individuals who developed within the relationships of the ruling class, and only insofar as they were individuals of this class. The illusory community, in which individuals have up till now combined, always took on an independent existence in relation to them, and was at the same time, since it was the combination of one class over against another, not only a completely illusory community, but a new fetter as well. In the real community the individuals obtain their freedom in and through their association.

It follows from all we have been saying up till now that the communal relationship into which the individuals of a class entered, and which was determined by their common interests over against a third party, was always a community to which these individuals belonged only as average individuals, only insofar as they lived within the conditions of existence of their class—a relationship in which they participated not as individuals but as members of a class. With the community of revolutionary proletarians, on the other hand, who take their conditions of existence and those of all members of society under their control, it is just the reverse; it is as individuals that the individuals participate in it. It is just this combination of individuals (assuming the advanced stage of modern productive forces, of course) which puts the conditions of the free development and movement of individuals under their control—conditions which were previously abandoned to chance and had won an independent existence over against the separate individuals just because of their separation as individuals, and because of the necessity of their combination which had been determined by the division of labor, and through their separation had become a bond alien to them. Combination up till now . . . was an agreement upon these conditions, within which the individuals were free to enjoy the freaks of fortune. . . . This right to the undisturbed enjoyment, within certain conditions of fortuity and chance has up till now been called personal freedom. . . .

This subsuming of individuals under definite classes cannot be abolished until a class has taken shape, which has no longer any particular class interest to assert against the ruling class.

Individuals have always built on themselves, but naturally on themselves within their given historical conditions and relationships, not on the "pure" individual in the sense of the ideologists. But in the course of historical evolution, and precisely through the inevitable fact that within the division of labor social relationships take on an independent existence, there appears a division within the life of each individual, insofar as it is personal and insofar as it is determined by some branch of labor and the conditions pertaining to it. (We do not mean it to be understood from this that, for example, the rentier, the capitalist, etc., cease to be persons; but their personality is conditioned and determined by quite definite class relationships, and the division appears only in their opposition to another class and, for themselves, only when they go bankrupt.) In the estate (and even more in the tribe) this is as yet concealed: for instance, a nobleman always remains a nobleman, a commoner always a commoner, apart from his other relationships, a quality inseparable from his individuality. The division between the personal and the class individual, the accidental nature of the conditions of life for the individual, appears only with the emergence of the class, which is itself a product of the bourgeoisie. This accidental character is only engendered and developed by competition and the struggle of individuals among themselves. Thus, in imagination, individuals seem freer under the dominance of the bourgeoisie than before, because their conditions of life seem accidental; in reality, of course, they are less free, because they are more subjected to the violence of things. . . .

For the proletarians . . . the condition of their existence, labor, and with it all the conditions of existence governing modern society, have become something accidental, something over which they, as separate individuals, have no control, and over which no *social* organization can give them control. The contradiction between the individuality of each separate proletarian and labor, the condition of life forced upon him, becomes evident to him himself, for he is sacrificed from youth upward and, within his own class, has no chance of arriving at the conditions which would place him in the other class.

Thus, while the refugee serfs only wished to be free to develop and assert those conditions of existence which were already there, and hence, in the end, only arrived at free labor, the proletarians, if they are to assert themselves as individuals, will have to abolish the very condition of their existence hitherto (which has, moreover, been that of all society up to the present), namely labor. Thus they find themselves directly opposed to the form in which, hitherto, the individuals, of which society consists, have given themselves collective expression, that is, the State. In order, therefore, to assert themselves as individuals, they must overthrow the State.

22. Details of the Theory

This last selection dealing with the theory of historical materialism is taken from the collection of Marx's manuscripts on economics dating from the late 1850s, recently published under the title *Grundrisse zur Kritik der politischen Ökonomie.* In a section bearing the title "Pre-capitalist Economic Formations," parts of which are presented here, Marx takes up in more detail first the description of, and later the transitions between, the various historical stages prior to the establishment of the capitalistic stage of production originally outlined in *The Germany Ideology* (cf. Selection 21). Although the text is somewhat disorganized (Marx never intended it for publication in this form), the reader will readily see that the factual basis supporting the thesis of historical materialism is a good deal more secure than might first appear only from *The German Ideology* and as popularized in *The Manifesto of the Communist Party* (cf. Selection 25, below).

THE FIRST prerequisite of this earliest form of landed property appears as a human community, such as emerges from spontaneous evolution *(naturwüchsig):* the family, the family expanded into a tribe, or the tribe created by the intermarriage of families or combination of tribes. We may take it for granted that pastoralism, or more generally a migratory life, is the first form of maintaining existence, the tribe not settling in a fixed

From *Pre-Capitalist Economic Formations,* ed. by Eric Hobsbawm, trans. by Jack Cohen (London: Lawrence & Wishart, 1964). Used by permission.

place but using up what it finds locally and then passing on. Men are not settled by nature (unless perhaps in such fertile environments that they could subsist on a single tree like the monkeys; otherwise they would roam, like the wild animals). Hence the tribal community, the natural common body, appears not as the consequence, but as the precondition of the joint (temporary) appropriation and use of the soil.

Once men finally settle down, the way in which to a smaller degree this original community is modified will depend on various external, climatic, geographical, physical, etc., conditions as well as on their special natural make-up—their tribal character. The spontaneously evolved tribal community, or, if you will, the herd—the common ties of blood, language, custom, etc.—is the first precondition of the appropriation of the objective conditions of life, and of the activity which reproduces and gives material expression to, or objectifies *(vergegenständlichenden)* it (activity as herdsmen, hunters, agriculturalists, etc.). The earth is the great laboratory, the arsenal which provides both the means and the materials of labor, and also the location, the *basis* of the community. Men's relation to it is naïve: they regard themselves as its *communal proprietors,* and as those of the community which produces and reproduces itself by living labor. Only in so far as the individual is a member—in the literal and figurative sense—of such a community, does he regard himself as an owner or possessor. . . .

Where the fundamental relationship is the same, this form can realize itself in a variety of ways. For instance, as is the case in most Asiatic fundamental forms it is quite compatible with the fact that the *all-embracing unity* which stands above all these small common bodies may appear as the higher or *sole proprietor,* the real communities only as *hereditary* possessors. Since the *unity* is the real owner, and the real precondition of common ownership, it is perfectly possible for it to appear as something separate and superior to the numerous real, particular communities. The individual is then in fact propertyless, or property—i.e., the relationship of the individual to the *natural* conditions of labor and reproduction, the inorganic nature which he finds and makes his own, the objective body of his subjectivity—appears to be mediated by means of a grant *(Ablassen)* from the total unity to the individual through the intermediary of the particular community. The despot here appears as the father of all the numerous lesser communities, thus realizing the common unity of all. It therefore follows that the surplus product (which, incidentally, is legally determined in terms of the real appropriation through labor) belongs to this highest unity. Oriental despotism therefore appears to lead to a legal absence of property. In fact, however, its foundation is tribal or common property, in most cases created through a combination of manufacture and agriculture within the small community which thus becomes entirely self-sustaining and contains within itself all conditions of production and surplus production.

Part of its surplus labor belongs to the higher community, which ultimately appears as a *person*. This surplus labor is rendered both as tribute and as common labor for the glory of the unity, in part that of the despot, in part that of the imagined tribal entity of the god. In so far as this type of common property is actually realized in labor, it can appear in two ways. The small communities may vegetate independently side by side, and within each the individual labors independently with his family on the land allotted to him. (There will also be a certain amount of labor for the common store—for insurance as it were —on the one hand; and on the other for defraying the costs of the community as such, i.e., for war, religious worship, etc. The dominion of lords, in its most primitive sense, arises only at this point. . . . Here lies the transition to serfdom, etc.) Secondly, the unity can involve a common organization of labor itself, which in turn can constitute a veritable system, as in Mexico, and especially Peru, among the ancient Celts, and some tribes of India. Furthermore, the communality within the tribal body may tend to appear either as a representation of its unity through the head of the tribal kinship group, or as a relationship between the heads of families. Hence either a more despotic or a more democratic form of the community. The communal conditions for real appropriation through labor, such as irrigation systems (very important among the Asian peoples), means of communication, etc., will then appear as the work of the higher unity—the despotic government which is poised above the lesser communities. Cities in the proper sense arise by the side of these villages only where the location is particularly favorable to external trade, or where the head of the state and his satraps exchange their revenue (the surplus product) against labor, which they expend as labor-funds.

The second form (of property) has, like the first, given rise to substantial variations, local, historical, etc. It is the product of a more dynamic historical life, of the fate and modification of the original tribes. The *community* is here also the first precondition, but unlike our first case, it is not here the substance of which the individuals are mere accidents or of which they form mere spontaneously natural parts. The basis here is not the land, but the city as already created seat (center) of the rural population (landowners). The cultivated area appears as the territory of the city; not, as in the other case, the village as a mere appendage to the land. However great the obstacles the land may put in the way of those who till it and really appropriate it, it is not difficult to establish a relationship with it as the inorganic nature of the living individual, as his workshop, his means of labor, the object of his labor and the means of subsistence of the subject. The difficulties encountered by the organized community can arise only from other communities which have either already occupied the land or disturbed the community in its occupation of it. War is therefore the great all-embracing task, the great communal labor, and it is required either for the occupation of the objective conditions for living existence or for the protection and perpetuation of such occupation. The community, consisting of kinship groups, is therefore in the first instance organized on military lines, as a warlike, military force, and this is one of the conditions of its existence as a proprietor. Concentration of settlement in the city is the foundation of this warlike organization. The nature of tribal structure leads to the differentiation of kinship groups into higher and lower, and this social differentiation is developed further by the mixing of conquering and conquered tribes, etc. Common land—as state property, *ager publicus*—is here separate from private property. The property of the individual, unlike our first case, is here not direct communal property, where the individual is not an owner in separation from the community, but rather its occupier. Circumstances arise in which individual property does not require communal labor for its valorization (e.g., as it does in the irrigation systems of the Orient); the purely primitive character of the tribe may be broken by the movement of history or migration; the tribe may remove from its original place of settlement and occupy *foreign* soil, thus entering substantially new conditions of labor and developing the energies of the individual further. The more such factors operate—and the more the communal character of the tribe therefore appears, and must appear, rather as a negative unity as against the outside world—the more do conditions arise which allow the individual to become a *private proprietor* of land—of a particular plot—whose special cultivation belongs to him and his family.

The community—as a state—is, on the one hand, the relationship of these free and equal private proprietors to each other, their combination against the outside world—and at the same time their safeguard. The community is based on the fact that its members consist of working owners of land, cultivators; but in the same measure the independence of the latter consists in their mutual relation as members of the community, in the safeguarding of the *ager publicus* (common land) for common needs and common glory, etc. To be a member of the community remains the precondition for the appropriation of land, but in his capacity as member of the community the individual is a private proprietor. His relation to his private property is both a relation to the land and to his existence as a member of the community, and his maintenance as a member is the maintenance of the community, and vice versa, etc. Since the community, though it is here not merely a de facto *product of history,* but one of which men are conscious as such, has therefore *had an origin,* we have here the precondition for *property* in land —i.e., for the relation of the working subject to the natural conditions of his labor as belonging to him. But this "belonging" is mediated through his existence as a member of the state, through the existence of the state—hence through a *precondition* which is regarded as divine, etc. There is concentration in the city, with the land as its territory; small-scale agriculture producing for immediate consumption; manufacture as the domestic subsidiary, labor of wives and daughters (spinning and weaving) or achieving independent existence in a few craft occupations." . . . The precondition for the continued existence of the community is the maintenance of equality among its free self-sustaining peasants, and their individual labor as the condition of the continued existence of their property. Their relation to the natural conditions of labor are those of proprietors; but personal labor must continuously establish these conditions as real conditions and objective elements of the personality of the individual, of his personal labor.

On the other hand the tendency of this small warlike community drives it beyond these limits, etc. (Rome, Greece, Jews, etc.). As Niebuhr says: "When the auguries had assured Numa of the divine approval for his election, the first preoccupation of the pious monarch was not the worship of the gods, but a human one. He distributed the land conquered in war by Romulus and left to be occupied: he founded the worship of Terminus (the god of boundary-stones). All the ancient law-givers and above all Moses founded the success of their arrangements for virtue, justice and good morals *(Sitte)* upon landed property, or at least on secure hereditary possession of land, for the greatest possible number of citizens." . . . The individual is placed in such condition of gaining his life as to make not the acquiring of wealth his object, but self-sustenance, its own reproduction as a member of the community; the reproduction of himself as a proprietor of the parcel of ground and, in that quality, as a member of the commune. The continuation of the commune is the reproduction of all its members as self-sustaining peasants, whose surplus time belongs precisely to the commune, the labor of war, etc. Ownership of one's labor is mediated through the ownership of the conditions of labor—the plot of land, which is itself guaranteed by the existence of the community, which in turn is safeguarded by the surplus labor of its members in the form of military service, etc. The member of the community reproduces himself not through cooperation in wealth-producing labor, but in cooperation in labor for the (real or imaginary) communal interests aimed at sustaining the union against external and internal stress. Property formally belongs to the Roman citizen, the private owner of land is such only by virtue of being Roman, but any Roman is also a private landowner.

Another form of the property of working individuals, self-sustaining members of the community, in the natural conditions of their labor, is the *Germanic*. Here the member of the community as such is not, as in the specifically oriental form, co-owner of the communal property. (Where property exists *only* as communal property, the individual member as such is only the *possessor* of a particular part of it, hereditary or not, for any fraction of property belongs to no member for himself, but only as the direct part of the community, consequently as someone in direct unity with the community and not as distinct from it. The individual is therefore only a possessor. What exists is only *communal* property and *private possession*. Historic and local, etc., circumstances may modify the character of this possession in its relation to the communal property in very different ways, depending on whether labor is performed in isolation by the private possessor or is in turn determined by the community, or by the unity standing above the particular community.) Neither is the land occupied by the community as in the Roman, Greek (in brief, the ancient classical) form as Roman land. Part of it remains with the community as such, as distinct from the members, *ager publicus* (common land) in its various forms; the remainder is distributed, each plot of land being Roman by virtue of the fact that it is the private property, the domain, of a Roman, the share of the laboratory which is his; conversely he is Roman only, in so far as he possesses this sovereign right over part of the Roman soil. . . .

The Germanic community is not concentrated in the city; a concentration—the city the center of rural life, the domicile of the land workers, as also the center of warfare—which gives the

community as such an external existence, distinct from that of
its individual members. Ancient classical history is the history
of cities, but cities based on landownership and agriculture;
Asian history is a kind of undifferentiated unity of town and
country (the large city, properly speaking, must be regarded
merely as a princely camp, superimposed on the real economic
structure); the Middle Ages (Germanic period) starts with the
countryside as the locus of history, whose further development
then proceeds through the opposition of town and country;
modern (history) is the urbanization of the countryside, not, as
among the ancients, the ruralization of the city.

Union in the city gives the community as such an economic
existence; the mere *presence* of the town as such is different
from a mere mutiplicity of separate houses. Here the whole
does not consist of its separate parts. It is a form of independent
organism. Among the Germans, where single heads of families
settle in the forests, separated by long distances, even on an
external view the community exists merely by virtue of every
act of union of its members, although their unity *existing in
itself* is embodied in descent, language, common past and history, etc. The *community* therefore appears as an *association,*
not as a *union,* as an agreement, whose independent subjects
are the landowners, and not as a unity. In fact, therefore, the
community has no existence as a *state,* a *political entity* as
among the ancients, because it has no existence as a *city.* If the
community is to enter upon real existence, the free landowners
must hold an *assembly,* whereas, e.g., in Rome it *exists* apart
from such assemblies, in the presence of the *city itself* and the
officials placed at its head, etc.

True, the *ager publicus,* the common land or peoples' land,
occurs among the Germans also, as distinct from the property
of individuals. It consists of hunting grounds, common pastures
or woodlands, etc., as that part of the land which cannot be
partitioned if it is to serve as a means of production in this
specific form. However, unlike the Roman case, the *ager publicus* does not appear as the particular economic being of the
state, by the side of the private owners—who are properly
speaking private proprietors as such in so far as they have been

excluded from or deprived of the use of the *ager publicus*, like the Plebeians. The *ager publicus* appears rather as a mere supplement to individual property among the Germans, and figures as property only in so far as it is defended against hostile tribes as the common property of one tribe. The property of the individual does not appear mediated through the community, but the existence of the community and of communal property as mediated through—i.e., as a mutual relation of—the independent subjects.

At bottom every individual household contains an entire economy, forming as it does an independent center of production (manufacture merely the domestic subsidiary labor of the women, etc.). In classical antiquity the city with its attached territory formed the economic whole, in the Germanic world, the individual home, which itself appears merely as a point in the land belonging to it; there is no concentration of a multiplicity of proprietors, but the family as an independent unit. In the Asiatic form (or at least predominantly so) there is no property, but only individual possession; the community is properly speaking the real proprietor—hence property only as *communal property* in land. In antiquity (Romans as the classic example, the thing in its purest and most clearly marked form), there is a contraditory form of state landed property and private landed property, so that the latter is mediated through the former, or the former exists only in this double form. The private landed proprietor is therefore simultaneously an urban citizen. Economically citizenship may be expressed more simply as a form in which the agriculturalist lives in a city. In the Germanic form the agriculturalist is not a citizen, i.e., not an inhabitant of cities, but its foundation is the isolated, independent family settlement, guaranteed by means of its association with other such settlements by men of the same tribe, and their occasional assembly for purposes of war, religion, the settlement of legal disputes, etc., which establishes their mutual surety. Individual landed property does not here appear as a contradictory form of communal landed property, nor as mediated by the community, but the other way around. The community exists only in the mutual relation of the individual landowners as such. Communal property as such appears only as a communal accessory to the individual kin settlements and land appropriations. The community is neither the substance, of which the individual appears merely as the accident, nor is it the general, which *exists and has being* as such in men's minds, and in the reality of the city and its urban requirements, distinct from the separate economic being of its members. It is rather on the one hand, the common element in language, blood, etc., which is the premise of the individual proprietor; but on the other hand, it has real being only in its *actual assembly* for communal purposes; and, in so far as it has a separate economic existence, in the communally used hunting grounds, pastures, etc., it is used thus by every individual proprietor as such, and not in his capacity as the representative of the state (as in Rome). It is genuinely the common property of the individual owners, and not of the union of owners, possessing an existence of its own in the city, distinct from that of the individual members.

The crucial point here is this: in all these forms, where landed property and agriculture form the basis of the economic order and consequently the economic object is the production of use values, i.e., the *reproduction of the individual* in certain definite relationships to his community, of which it forms the basis, we find the following elements:

1. Appropriation of the natural conditions of labor, of the *earth* as the original instrument of labor, both laboratory and repository of its raw materials; however, appropriation not by means of labor, but as the preliminary condition of labor. The individual simply regards the objective conditions of labor as his own, as the inorganic nature of his subjectivity, which realizes itself through them. The chief objective condition of labor itself appears not as the *product* of labor, but occurs as *nature*. On the one hand we have the living individual, on the other the earth, as the objective condition of his reproduction.

2. The *attitude* to the land, to the earth as the property of the working individual, means that a man appears from the start as something more than the abstraction of the "working individ-

ual," but has an *objective mode of existence* in his ownership of the earth, which is *antecedent* to his activity and does not appear as its mere consequence, and is as much a precondition of his activity as his skin, his senses, for whole skin and sense organs are also developed, reproduced, etc., in the process of life, they are also presupposed by it. What immediately mediates this attitude is the more or less naturally evolved, more or less historically evolved and modified existence of the individual as a member of a community—his primitive existence as part of a tribe, etc.

An isolated individual could no more possess property in land than he could speak. At most he could live off it as a source of supply, like the animals. The relation to the soil as property always arises through the peaceful or violent occupation of the land by the tribe or the community in some more or less primitive or already historically developed form. The individual here can never appear in the total isolation of the mere free laborer. If the objective conditions of his labor are presumed to belong to him, he himself is subjectively presumed to belong to a community which mediates his relationship to the objective conditions of labor. Conversely, the real existence of the community is determined by the specific form of its ownership of the objective conditions of labor. The property mediated by its existence in a community may appear as *communal property*, which gives the individual only possession and no private property in the soil; or else it may appear in the dual form of state and private property which coexist side by side, but in such a way as to make the former the precondition of the latter, so that only the citizen is and must be a private proprietor, while on the other hand his property *qua* citizen also has a separate existence. Lastly, communal property may appear merely as a supplement to private property, which in this case forms the basis; in this case the community has no existence except in the *assembly* of its members and in their association for common purposes.

These different forms of relationship of communal tribal members to the tribal land—to the earth upon which it has settled—depend partly on the natural character of the tribe, partly on the economic conditions in which the tribe really exercises its ownership of the land, i.e., appropriates its fruits by means of labor. And this in turn will depend on the climate, the physical properties of the soil, the physically conditioned mode of its utilization, the relationships to hostile or neighboring tribes, and such modifications as are introduced by migrations, historical events, etc. If the community as such is to continue in the old way, the reproduction of its members under the objective conditions already assumed as given, is necessary. Production itself, the advance of population (which also falls under the head of production), in time necessarily eliminates these conditions, destroying instead of reproducing them etc., and as this occurs the community decays and dies, together with the property relations on which it was based.

The Asiatic form necessarily survives longest and most stubbornly. This is due to the fundamental principle on which it is based, that is, that the individual does not become independent of the community; that the circle of production is self-sustaining, unity of agriculture and craft manufacture, etc. If the individual changes his relation to the community, he modifies and undermines both the community and its economic premise; conversely, the modification of this economic premise—produced by its own dialectic, pauperization, etc. Note especially the influence of warfare and conquest. While, e.g., in Rome this is an essential part of the economic conditions of the community itself, it breaks the real bond on which the community rests.

In all these forms the basis of evolution is the *reproduction* of relations between individual and community *assumed as given* —they may be more or less primitive, more or less the result of history, but fixed into tradition—and a *definite, predetermined objective* existence, both as regards the relation to the conditions of labor and the relation between one man and his co-workers, fellow-tribesmen, etc. Such evolution is therefore from the outset *limited,* but once the limits are transcended, decay and disintegration ensue. Evolution of slavery, concentration of landed property, exchange, a monetary economy, conquest, etc., as among the Romans. All these appeared nevertheless up to a point to be compatible with the base, and merely innocent extensions of it, or else mere abuses arising from it. Considerable developments are thus possible within a given sphere. Individuals may appear to be great. But free and full development of individual or society is inconceivable here, for such evolution stands in contradiction to the original relationship.

Among the ancients we discover no single inquiry as to which form of landed property, etc., is the most productive, which creates maximum wealth. Wealth does not appear as the aim of production, although Cato may well investigate the most profitable cultivation of fields, or Brutus may even lend money at the most favorable rate of interest. The inquiry is always about what kind of property creates the best citizens. Wealth as an end in itself appears only among a few trading peoples—monopolists of the carrying trade—who live in the pores of the ancient world like the Jews in medieval society. Wealth is on the one hand a thing, realized in things, in material products as against man as a subject. On the other hand, in its capacity as value, it is the mere right to command other people's labor, not for the purpose of dominion, but of private enjoyment, etc. In all its forms it appears in the form of objects, whether of things or of relationships by means of things, which lie outside of, and as it were accidentally beside, the individual.

Thus the ancient conception, in which man always appears (in however narrowly national, religious or political a definition) as the aim of production, seems very much more exalted than the modern world, in which production is the aim of man and wealth the aim of production. In fact, however, when the narrow bourgeois form has been peeled away, what is wealth, if not the universality of needs, capacities, enjoyments, productive powers, etc., of individuals, produced in universal exchange? What, if not the full development of human control over the forces of nature—those of his own nature as well as those of so-called nature? What, if not the absolute elaboration of his creative dispositions, without any preconditions other than antecedent historical evolution which makes the totality of this evolution—i.e., the evolution of all human powers as such, un-

measured by any *previously established* yardstick—an end in
itself? What is this, if not a situation where man does not reproduce himself in any determined form, but produces his totality? Where he does not seek to remain something formed by
the past, but is in the absolute movement of becoming? In
bourgeois political economy—and in the epoch of production to
which it corresponds—this complete elaboration of what lies
within man, appears as the total alienation, and the destruction
of all fixed, one-sided purposes as the sacrifice of the end in itself
to a wholly external compulsion. Hence in one way the childlike
world of the ancients appears to be superior; and this is so, in
so far as we seek for closed shape, form and established limitation. The ancients provide a narrow satisfaction, whereas the
modern world leaves us unsatisfied, or, where it appears to be
satisfied with itself, is *vulgar* and *mean*.

What M. Proudhon calls the *extra-economic* origin of property—by which he means landed property—is the *prebourgeois*
relationship of the individual to the objective conditions of labor, and in the first instance to the *natural* objective conditions
of labor. For, just as the working subject is a natural individual,
a natural being, so the first objective condition of his labor
appears as nature, earth, as an inorganic body. He himself is not
only the organic body, but also inorganic nature as a subject.
This condition is not something he has produced, but something
he finds to hand; something existing in nature and which he
presupposes. . . . In other words, the *extra-economic origin* of
property merely means the historic origin of the bourgeois
economy, of the forms of production to which the categories of
political economy give theoretical or ideal expression. But to
claim that prebourgeois history and each phase of it, has its own
economy and an *economic base* of its movement, is at bottom
merely to state the tautology that human life has always rested
on some kind of production—*social* production—whose relations are precisely what we call economic relations.

The original conditions of production cannot initially be
themselves produced—they are not the results of production.
(Instead of original conditions of production we might also say:
for if this reproduction appears on one hand as the appropria-

tion of the objects by the subjects, it equally appears on the other as the molding, the subjection, of the objects by and to a subjective purpose; the transformation of the objects into results and repositories of subjective activity.) What requires explanation is not the *unity* of living and active human beings with the natural, inorganic conditions of their metabolism with nature, and therefore their appropriation of nature; nor is this the result of a historic process. What we must explain is the *separation* of these inorganic conditions of human existence from this active existence, a separation which is only fully completed in the relationship between wage labor and capital.

In the relationship of slavery and serfdom there is no such separation; what happens is that one part of society is treated by another as the mere *inorganic and natural* condition of its own reproduction. The slave stands in no sort of relation to the objective conditions of his labor. It is rather *labor* itself, both in the form of the slave as of the serf, which is placed among the other living things *as inorganic condition* of production, alongside the cattle or as an appendage of the soil. In other words: the original conditions of production appear as natural prerequisites, *natural conditions of existence of the producer,* just as his living body, however reproduced and developed by him, is not originally established by himself, but appears as his *prerequisite;* his own (physical) being is a natural prerequisite, not established by himself. These *natural conditions of existence,* to which he is related as to an inorganic body, have a dual character: they are (1) subjective and (2) objective. The producer occurs as part of a family, a tribe, a grouping of his people, etc.—which acquires historically differing shapes as the result of mixture and conflict with others. It is as such a communal part that he has his relation to a determined (piece of) nature (let us still call it earth, land, soil), as his own inorganic being, the condition of his production and reproduction. As the natural part of the community he participates in the communal property and takes a separate share into his own possession; just so, as a Roman citizen by birth, he has (at least) ideally a claim to the *ager publicus* and a real claim to so and so many units of land, etc. His *property,* i.e., his relation to the natural prerequisites of his production as *his own,* is mediated by his natural membership of a community. . . .

Among nomadic pastoral tribes—and all pastoral peoples are originally migratory—the earth, like all other conditions of nature, appears in its elementary boundlessness, e.g., in the Asian steppes and the Asian high plateaus. It is grazed, etc., consumed by the herds, which provide the nomadic peoples with their subsistence. They regard it as their property, though never fixing that property. This is the case with the hunting grounds of the wild Indian tribes of America: the tribe considers a certain region as its hunting territory and maintains it by force against other tribes, or seeks to expel other tribes from the territory they claim. Among the nomadic pastoral tribes the community is in fact always united, a traveling party, caravan, horde, and the forms of higher and lower rank develop out of the conditions of this mode of life. What is *appropriated* and *reproduced* is here only the herd and not the soil, which is always used in temporary commonalty wherever the tribe breaks its wanderings.

Let us pass on to the consideration of settled peoples. The only barrier which the community can encounter in its relations to the natural conditions of production *as its own*—to the land—is some *other community,* which has already laid claim to them as its inorganic body. War is therefore one of the earliest tasks of every primitive community of this kind, both for the defense of property and for its acquisition. (It will be sufficient to speak of original property in land, for among pastoral peoples property in such natural products of the earth as, e.g., sheep is at the same time property in the pastures they pass through. In general, property in land includes property in its organic products.) Where man himself is captured as an organic accessory of the land and together with it, he is captured as one of the conditions of production, and this is the origin of slavery and serfdom, which soon debase and modify the original forms of all communities, and themselves become their foundation. As a result the simple structure is thereby determined negatively.

Thus originally *property* means no more than man's attitude to his natural conditions of production as belonging to him, as the *prerequisites of his own existence;* his attitude to them as *natural prerequisites* of himself, which constitute, as it were, a prolongation of his body. In fact he stands in no relation to his conditions of production, but has a double existence, subjectively as himself and objectively in these natural inorganic conditions of his being. The forms of these *natural conditions of production* have a double character: (1) his existence as part of a community, which in its original form is a tribal community, more or less modified; (2) his relation to the *land* as to *his own*, in virtue of the community, communal landed property, at the same time *individual possession* for the individual, or in such a manner that the soil and its cultivation remain in common and only its products are divided. (However, *dwellings*, etc. . . . nevertheless appear to be always in the possession of individuals.) Membership of a *naturally evolved society*, a tribe, etc., is a natural condition of production for the living individual. Such membership is, e.g., already a condition of his language, etc. His own productive existence is only possible under this condition. His subjective existence as such is conditioned by it as much as it is conditioned by the relationship to the earth as to his laboratory. . . .

Property therefore means *belonging to a tribe* (community) (to have one's subjective/objective existence within it), and by means of the relationship of this community to the land, to the earth as its inorganic body, there occurs the relationship of the individual to the land, to the external primary condition of production—for the earth is at the same time raw material, tool and fruit—as the preconditions belonging to his individuality, as its modes of existence. We *reduce this property to the relationship to the conditions of production*. Why not to those of consumption, since originally the act of producing by the individual is confined to the reproduction of his own body through the appropriation of ready-made objects prepared by nature for consumption? But even where these have merely to be *found* and *discovered*, effort, labor—as in hunting, fishing, the care of flocks—and the production (i.e., the development) of certain capacities by the subject, are soon required. Moreover, conditions in which man need merely reach for what is already available, without any tools (i.e., without products of labor already designed for production), etc., are very transitory, and can nowhere be regarded as normal; not even as normal in the most primitive state. In addition, the original conditions of production automatically include matter directly consumable without labor, such as fruit, animals, etc.; consequently, the fund of consumption itself appears as a part of the *original fund of production.*

The fundamental condition of property based on tribalism . . . is to be a member of the tribe. Consequently a tribe conquered and subjugated by another becomes *propertyless* and part of the *inorganic conditions* of the conquering tribe's reproduction, which that community regards as its own. Slavery and serfdom are therefore simply further developments of property based on tribalism. They necessarily modify all its forms. This they are least able to do in the Asiatic form. In the self-sustaining unity of manufactures and agriculture on which this form is based, conquest is not so essential a condition as where *landed property, agriculture,* predominate exclusively. On the other hand, since the individual in this form never becomes an owner but only a possessor, he is at bottom himself the property, the slave of that which embodies the unity of the community. Here slavery neither puts an end to the conditions of labor, nor does it modify the essential relationship.

It is therefore now evident that:

In so far as property is merely a conscious attitude to the conditions of production as to *one's own*—an attitude established by the community for the individual, proclaimed and guaranteed as law; in so far as the existence of the producer therefore appears as an existence within the objective conditions *belonging to him,* it is realized only through production. Actual appropriation takes place not through the relationship to these conditions as expressed in thought, but through the active, real relationship to them; in the process of positing them as the conditions of man's subjective activity.

But this also clearly means that *these conditions change.* What makes a region of the earth into a hunting-ground is being hunted over by tribes; what turns the soil into a prolongation of the body of the individual is agriculture. Once the *city of Rome* had been built and its surrounding land cultivated by its citizens, the conditions of the community were different from what they had been before. The object of all these communities is preservation, *i.e., the production of the individuals which constitute them as proprietors, i.e., in the same objective mode of existence, which also forms the relationship of the members to each other, and therefore forms the community itself. But this reproduction is at the same time necessarily new production and the destruction of the old form. . . .* The act of reproduction itself changes not only the objective conditions—e.g. transforming village into town, the wilderness into agricultural clearings, etc.—but the producers change with it, by the emergence of new qualities, by transforming and developing themselves in production, forming new powers and new conceptions, new modes of intercourse, new needs, and new speech.

We have an original unity between a specific form of community or tribal unit and the property in nature connected with it, or the relation to the objective conditions of production as naturally existing, as the objective being of the individual by means of the community. Now this unity, which in one sense appears as the particular form of property, has its living reality in a specific *mode of production* itself, and this mode appears equally as the relationship of the individuals to one another and as their specific daily behavior towards inorganic nature, their specific mode of labor (which is always family labor and often communal labor). The community itself appears as the first great force of production; special kinds of conditions of production (e.g. animal husbandry, agriculture) lead to the evolution of a special mode of production and special forces of production, both objective and subjective, the latter appearing as qualities of the individuals.

In the last instance the community and the property resting upon it can be reduced to a specific stage in the development of the forces of production of the laboring subjects—to which correspond specific relations of these subjects with each other and with nature. Up to a certain point, reproduction. Thereafter, it turns into dissolution.

Property—and this applies to its Asiatic, Slavonic ancient classical and Germanic forms—therefore originally signifies a relation of the working (producing) subject (or a subject reproducing himself) to the conditions of his production or reproduction as his own. Hence, according to the conditions of production, property will take different forms. The object of production itself is to reproduce the producer in and together with these objective conditions of his existence.

It is of course easy to imagine a powerful, physically superior person, who first captures animals and then captures men in order to make them catch animals for him; in brief, one who uses man as a naturally occurring condition for his reproduction like any other living natural thing; his own labor being exhausted in the act of domination. But such a view is stupid, though it may be correct from the point of view of a given tribal or communal entity; for it takes the *isolated* man as its starting-point. But man is only individualized through the process of history. He originally appears as a *generic being, a tribal being, a herd animal*—though by no means as a "political animal" in the political sense. Exchange itself is a major agent of this individualization. It makes the herd animal superflous and dissolves it. Once the situation is such, that man as an isolated person has relation only to himself, the means of establishing himself as an isolated individual have become what gives him his general communal character. In such a community the objective existence of the individual as a proprietor, say a landed proprietor, is presupposed, though he is a proprietor under certain conditions which chain him to the community, or rather constitute a link in his chain. . . .

All the forms in which the community imputes to the subjects a specific objective unity with the conditions of their production, or in which a specific subjective existence imputes the community itself as condition of production, necessarily correspond only to a development of the forces of production which is limited both in fact and in principle. (These forms are of course more or less naturally evolved, but at the same time also the results of a historic process.) The evolution of the forces of production dissolves them, and their dissolution is itself an evolution of the human forces of production.*

*Men make their own history, but they do not make it just as they please; they

What we are concerned with here is this: the relationship of labor to capital, or to the objective conditions of labor as capital, presupposes a historic process which dissolves the different forms, in which the laborer is an owner and the owner labors. This means first and foremost:

(1) A *dissolution* of the relation to the earth—to land or soil —as a natural condition of production which man treats as his own inorganic being, the laboratory of his forces and the domain of his will. All forms in which this property is found assume a *communal entity* whose members, whatever the formal distinctions between them, are *proprietors* by virtue of being its members. Hence the original form of this property is *direct communal property*. . . .

(2) *Dissolution of the relations* in which man appears as the *proprietor of the instrument*. As the above form of landed property assumes a *real community*, so this ownership of the tool by the laborer assumes a particular form of development of manufacture—namely, in the form of *handicraft labor*. Guild and corporative institutions are bound up with this. (The manufacturing activities of the ancient Orient may be included under our heading (1) above.) Here labor itself is still half the expression of artistic creation, half its own reward, etc. The institution of the "master craftsman." The capitalist himself still a master craftsman. Special craft skill itself ensures the ownership of the instrument, etc., etc. In a sense, the mode of labor becomes hereditary together with the organization of labor and its instrument. Medieval town life. Labor still belongs to a man; a certain self-sufficient development of specialized (*einseitige*) capacities, etc.

(3) Included in both is the fact that man possesses means of consumption prior to production, necessary in order to enable him to keep alive as producer—i.e., in the course of production, *before* its completion. As a landowner, he appears to be directly

---

do not make it under circumstances chosen by themselves, but under circumstances directly encountered, given and transmitted from the past. The tradition of all the dead generations weighs like a nightmare on the brain of the living. Marx, *The Eighteenth Brumaire of Louis Bonaparte* (Moscow, n.d.), p. 15.

provided with the necessary fund for consumption. As a master artisan he had inherited, earned or saved this fund, and as a youngster he is still an *apprentice,* he does not yet appear as an independent worker in the strict sense, but shares the master's food in the patriarchal manner. As a (genuine) journeyman there is a certain common utilitzation of the fund of consumption which is in the master's possession. Though this is not the journeyman's *property,* the laws and customs, etc., of the guild at least make him into a co-possessor.

(4) On the other hand *dissolution* both of the relations under which the *laborers themselves,* the *living units of labor power* are still a *direct part of the objective conditions of production* and are appropriated as such—and are therefore slaves or serfs. For capital the worker does not constitute a condition of production, but only labor. If this can be performed by machinery, or even by water or air, so much the better. And what capital appropriates is not the laborer, but his labor—and not directly, but by means of exchange.

These, then, on the one hand, are historic prerequisites without which the laborer cannot occur as free laborer, as objective-less, purely subjective capacity for laboring, confronting the objective conditions of production as his *nonproperty,* as *someone else's property,* as *value* existing for itself, as capital. . . .

V.

The Politics of Revolution (1844—1875)

The transformation from capitalism into communism is not one which can be expected to occur automatically. Central to Marx's understanding of historical transitions between stages of development is the active reappropriation of the means of production by a new class—in this case by the revolutionary proletariat. The selections comprising this section illustrate various phases of the workers' struggle as it developed through four decades of the nineteenth century.

In Selection 23, written in 1844, Marx makes the fundamental distinction between political and social revolution and applies this to the German situation which, at the time, was taken as an example of an almost entirely undeveloped and ununified collection of feudal principalities. There follows a major selection from the famous pamphlet *The Manifesto of the Communist Party*, written with Engels on the eve of the continent-wide uprisings of 1848. With the defeat of these workers' risings, or the betrayal of their partial success by the bourgeois democrats, the tactics of the decimated German Communist League changed, and in his *Address of the Central Committee to the Communist League* of 1850, Marx outlines the new policies to be adopted in the face of the emerging industrialization and growing national consciousness which is to characterize Bismarck's nascent German Empire. Twenty-five years later, amid rapidly expanding industrialization, the two largest workers' parties in Germany issued a unity program following a congress at Gotha, which Marx excoriated in his *Critique of the Gotha Program* (1875); he here sharply attacks the new rhetoric of "social democracy" and outlines the notion of the revolutionary dictatorship of the proletariat which is to be the form of state implemented by the victorious workers. The final selection deals with the Paris Commune, taken from Marx's *The Civil War in France* (1871), in which he describes this first government which is truly "of the people and for the people" and which has served as a model to be emulated for subsequent generations of Marx's followers.

23. Revolution: Social or Political?

The representative sampling of Marx's more specifically political writings spans most of his career as an active revolutionary. The first of these is a selection from an article written in 1844 replying to Arnold Ruge's article "The King of Prussia and Social Reform," which dealt with the aftermath of the Silesian weavers' rising of that year. In his "Critical Notes to 'The King of Prussia and Social Reform'" Marx makes the distinction between social and political revolution; for the first time also he claims that the state owes its very existence to a class conflict within civil society which the state is designed to control in favor of the most powerful class. Read in the light of his other writings of 1844, we can see that by the time this article was written Marx was in full possession of his socialist viewpoint, and recognized that, from the point of view of the proletariat, a social revolution was the only feasible route to the establishment of a socialistic community.

THE *STATE* AND the *organization of society* are not, from the *political* standpoint, *two* different things. The state is the organization of society. So far as the state admits the existence of *social* evils, it attributes them either to *natural laws*, which no human power can change, or to *private life*, which is independent of the state, or to the *inadequacy of administration*, which

From *Writings of the Young Marx on Philosophy and Society*, trans. and ed. by L.D. Easton and K.H. Guddat (New York: Doubleday-Anchor, 1967). Used by permission.

is dependent on it. Thus England finds poverty rooted in the *natural law* according to which population continuously exceeds the means of subsistence. From another side, England explains *pauperism* as a consequence of the *ill will of the poor*, just as the King of Prussia explains it by the *unchristian spirit of the rich* and the Convention explains it by the *counterrevolutionary and equivocal attitude of property owners*. Hence England punishes the poor, the King of Prussia admonishes the rich, and the Convention decapitates property owners.

In the end, *every* state seeks the cause of its ills in *accidental* or *intentional defects* of *administration* and therefore seeks the remedy in *reprimand* of the administration. Why? Simply because the *administration* is the *organizing* activity of the state.

The state cannot transcend the *contradiction* between the aim and good intentions of the administration on the one hand and its means and resources on the other without transcending itself, for it *is based* on this contradiction. It is based on the contradiciton between *public* and *private life*, on the contradiction between *general interests* and *particular interests*. The *administration*, therefore, must confine itself to a *formal* and *negative* activity because its power ceases where civil life and its work begin. Indeed, as against the consequences which spring from the unsocial nature of this civil life, of private property, trade, industry, and the mutual plundering of different civil groups, as against these consequences *impotence* is the *natural law* of administration. This dismemberment, this debasement, this *slavery of civil society* is the natural foundation on which the *modern* state rests, just as the *civil society of slavery* was the foundation of the state in *antiquity*. The existence of the state and the existence of slavery are indivisible. The state and slavery of antiquity—open *classical* antitheses— were not more closely *joined* than are the modern state and the modern world of bargaining—sanctimonious *Christian* antitheses. If the modern state would want to transcend the *impotence* of its administration, it would have to transcend the present mode of *private life*. If it wanted to transcend this private life, it would have to transcend itself, for it exists *only* in contrast to that life. No *living person,* however, believes that the defect of his specific existence is rooted in the *principle* or essence of his life, but rather in circumstances *outside* his life. *Suicide* is unnatural. Thus the state cannot believe in the *innate* impotence of its administration, that is, of its own self. It can notice *only* formal, accidental defects of administration and seek to remedy them. If these modifications are fruitless, then the social ill is a natural imperfection independent of mankind, a *law of God,* or else the will of private individuals is too corrupted to advance the good aims of the administration. And what perverse private individuals! They grumble against the government whenever it restricts freedom, and they demand that the government prevent the necessary consequences of this freedom.

The more powerful the state and hence the more *political* a country is, the less is it inclined to seek the basis and grasp the *general* principle of *social* ills in the *principle of the state* itself, thus in the *existing organization of society* of which the state is the active, self-conscious, and official expression. *Political* thought is *political* precisely because it takes place *within* the bounds of politics. The more acute, the more vigorous it is, the more it is *incapable* of comprehending social ills. The *classical* period of political thought is the *French Revolution.* Far from perceiving the source of social defects in the principle of the state, the heroes of the French Revolution rather saw the source of political evils in social defects. Thus *Robespierre* saw in great poverty and great wealth only an obstacle to *pure democracy.* Hence he wanted to establish a general *Spartan* frugality. The principle of politics is *will.* The more one-sided and thus the more perfected *political* thought is, the more it believes in the *omnipotence* of will, the blinder it is to *natural* and spiritual *restrictions* on the will, and the more incapable it is of discovering the source of social ills. . . .

It must be granted that the German proletariat is the *theorist* of the European proletariat, just as the English proletariat is its *economist* and the French proletariat its *politician.* It must be admitted that Germany, though incapable of *political* revolution, has a *classical* summons to *social* revolution. As the impotence of the German bourgeoisie is the *political* impotence of Germany, the talent of the German proletariat—even apart from German theory—is the *social* talent of Germany. The disparity between philosophical and political development in Germany is no *abnormality*. It is a necessary disparity. Only in socialism can a philosophical people find its suitable practice, thus only in the *proletariat* can it find the active element of its emancipation. . . . The more developed and general the *political* intelligence of a people is, the more the *proletariat*—at least at the beginning of the movement—wastes its energies in irrational and useless uprisings which are suppressed in blood. Because it thinks politically, it sees the cause of all evils in *will* and all remedies in *force* and the *overthrow* of a *particular* form of the state. As evidence, consider the first outbreaks of the *French* proletariat. The workers of Lyons believed that they were pursuing only political aims, that they were only soldiers of the Republic, while actually they were soldiers of socialism. Thus their political understanding clouded the roots of their social misery, distorted their insight into their actual aims, and *deceived* their *social instinct*.

Do not *all* uprisings without exception, however, break out *in the disastrous isolation of men from the community?* Doesn't *every* uprising necessarily presuppose this isolation? Would the Revolution of 1789 have occurred without the disastrous isolation of the French citizens from the community? Its aim, after all, was to end this isolation.

But the *community* from which the worker is *isolated* is a community of a very different order and extent than the *political* community. This community, from which *his own labor* separates him, is *life* itself, physical and spiritual life, human morality, human activity, human enjoyment, *human* existence. *Human existence* is the *real community* of man. As the disastrous isolation from this existence is more final, intolerable, terrible, and contradictory than isolation from the political community, so is the ending of this isolation. And even a partial reaction, a *revolt* against it, means all the more, as *man* is more than *citizen* and *human life* more than *political life*. Hence, however *partial* the *industrial* revolt may be, it conceals within itself a *universal* soul: no matter how universal a *political* revolt may be, it conceals a *narrow-minded* spirit under the *most colossal* form. . . .

We have seen that a *social* revolution involves the standpoint of the *whole* because it is a protest of man against dehumanized life even if it occurs in only *one* factory district, because it proceeds from the *standpoint* of the *single actual individual*, because the *community* against whose separation from himself the individual reacts is the *true* community of man, *human* existence. The *political soul* of a revolution, on the other hand, consists in the *tendency* of politically uninfluential classes to end their *isolation* from the *state* and from *power*. Its standpoint is that of the state, an *abstract* whole, which exists *only* through the separation from actual life and which is *unthinkable* without the *organized* antithesis between the universal idea and the individual existence of man. Hence a revolution of the *political soul* also organizes, in accordance with the *narrow* and *split* nature of this soul, a ruling group in society at the expense of society. . . .

A *"social"* revolution with a *political* soul is either a compounded absurdity if the "Prussian" [Ruge] means by "social" revolution a "social" revolution in *contrast* to a political one and nevertheless attributes to this social revolution a political rather than a social soul. Or a *"social revolution with a political soul"* is nothing but a *paraphrase* of what used to be called a *"political revolution"* or a *"revolution pure and simple."* Any revolution breaks up the *old society;* to that extent it is *social*. Any revolution overthrows the *old ruling power;* to that extent it is *political*. . . .

But though it is . . . senseless to speak of a *social revolution* with a *political soul*, it is sensible to talk about a *political revolution* with a *social* soul. *Revolution* in general—the *overthrow* of the existing ruling power and the *dissolution* of the old conditions—is a *political act*. Without *revolution*, however, *socialism* cannot come about. It requires this *political act* so far as it needs *overthrow* and *dissolution*. But where its *organizing activity* begins, where its *own aim* and *spirit* emerge, there socialism throws the *political* hull away. . . .

24. The Revolutionary Proletariat

In a short passage taken from the concluding pages of *The Poverty of Philosophy* (1847) Marx adopted one of the basic tenets of the anarchism of Pierre Proudhon whose work *The Philosophy of Poverty* was being polemicized by Marx, in that Marx declares that upon the victory of the proletariat "there will be no more political power properly so called." Based upon his doctrine of the state as indivisible from the existence of slavery (cf. Selection 23), this step is seen to be an integral part of Marx's philosophy and essential to the realization of the goals of Communsim and humanism.

ECONOMIC CONDITIONS had first transformed the mass of the people of the country into workers. The combination of capital has created for this mass a common situation, common interests. This mass is thus already a class as against capital, but not yet for itself. In the struggle, of which we have noted only a few phases, this mass becomes united, and constitutes itself as a class for itself. The interests it defends become class interests. But the struggle of class against class is a political struggle. . . .

An oppressed class is the vital condition for every society founded on the antagonism of classes. The emancipation of the oppressed class thus implies necessarily the creation of a new society. For the oppressed class to be able to emancipate itself it is necessary that the productive powers already acquired and the existing social relations should no longer be capable of exist-

From *The Poverty of Philosophy* (Moscow, 1966).

ing side by side. Of all the instruments of production, the greatest productive power is the revolutionary class itself. The organization of revolutionary elements as a class supposes the existence of all the productive forces which could be engendered in the bosom of the old society.

Does this mean that after the fall of the old society there will be a new class domination culminating in a new political power? No.

The condition for the emancipation of the working class is the abolition of every class, just as the condition for the liberation of the third estate, of the bourgeois order, was the abolition of all estates and all orders.

The working class, in the course of its development, will substitute for the old civil society an association which will exclude classes and their antagonism, and there will be no more political power properly so called, since political power is precisely the official expression of antagonism in civil society.

Meanwhile the antagonsim between the proletariat and the bourgeoisie is a struggle of class against class, a struggle which carried to its highest expression is a total revolution. Indeed, is it at all surprising that a society founded on the opposition of classes should culminate in brutal *contradiction*, the shock of body against body, as its final *denouement?*

Do not say that social movement excludes political movement. There is never a political movement which is not at the same time social.

It is only in an order of things in which there are no more classes and class antagonisms that *social evolutions* will cease to be *political revolutions*. Till then, on the eve of every general reshuffling of society, the last word of social science will always be: *"Le combat ou la mort; la lutte sanguinaire ou le néant. C'est ainsi que la question est invinciblement posée"* (George Sand).

25. The Manifesto

This selection comprises the first two parts of *The Manifesto of the Communist Party*, written by Marx and Engels in January, 1848. It remains the classic popular expression of their program and must be counted as among the handful of most influential books ever published. For our purpose it illustrates Marx's position on the development and significance of modern industry (i.e., it may be considered as complementing the selection on precapitalist stages of development in Selection 23) and of the historical roles played by the bourgeoisie and the proletariat. One should carefully note the dialectical relationship described as holding between these two classes, for a great deal of Marx's political argument depends upon the thesis that as capitalism develops so too must the proletariat necessarily develop along with it. The second part of the *Manifesto*, concerned with the program of the infant Communist party of Germany in 1848, has served as a model for all subsequent Communist movements.

A SPECTER IS haunting Europe—the specter of Communism. All the Powers of old Europe have entered into a holy alliance to exorcise this specter: Pope and Czar, Metternich and Guizot, French Radicals and German police spies.

Where is the party in opposition that has not been decried as Communistic by its opponents in power? Where the Opposition

From *The Manifesto of the Communist Party*, trans. by Samuel Moore (Moscow: Foreign Languages Publishing House, n.d.).

that has not hurled back the branding reproach of Communism, against the more advanced opposition parties, as well as against its reactionary adversaries?

Two things result from this fact.

I. Communism is already acknowledged by all European Powers to be itself a Power.

II. It is high time that Communists should openly, in the face of the whole world, publish their views, their aims, their tendencies, and meet this nursery tale of the Specter of Communism with a Manifesto of the party itself.

To this end, Communists of various nationalities have assembled in London, and sketched the following Manifesto, to be published in the English, French, German, Italian, Flemish and Danish languages.

I

BOURGEOIS AND PROLETARIANS

The history of all hitherto existing society is the history of class struggles.

Freeman and slave, patrician and plebeian, lord and serf, guild-master and journeyman, in a word, oppressor and oppressed, stood in constant opposition to one another, carried on an uninterrupted, now hidden, now open fight, a fight that each time ended, either in a revolutionary reconstitution of society at large, or in the common ruin of the contending classes.

In the earlier epochs of history, we find almost everywhere a complicated arrangement of society into various orders, a manifold gradation of social rank. In ancient Rome we have patricians, knights, plebeians, slaves; in the Middle Ages, feudal lords, vassals, guild-masters, journeymen, apprentices, serfs; in almost all of these classes, again, subordinate gradations. The modern bourgeois society that has sprouted from the ruins of feudal society has not done away with class antagonisms. It has but established new classes, new conditions of oppression, new forms of struggle in place of the old ones.

Our epoch, the epoch of the bourgeoisie, possesses, however, this distinctive feature: it has simplified the class antagonisms.

Society as a whole is more and more splitting up into two great hostile camps, into two great classes directly facing each other: Bourgeoisie and Proletariat.

From the serfs of the Middle Ages sprang the chartered burghers of the earliest towns. From these burgesses the first elements of the bourgeoisie were developed.

The discovery of America, the rounding of the Cape, opened up fresh ground for the rising bourgeoisie. The East Indian and Chinese markets, the colonization of America, trade with the colonies, the increase in the means of exchange and in commodities generally, gave to commerce, to navigation, to industry, an impulse never before known, and thereby, to the revolutionary element in the tottering feudal society, a rapid development.

The feudal system of industry, under which industrial production was monopolized by closed guilds, now no longer sufficed for the growing wants of the new markets. The manufacturing system took its place. The guild-masters were pushed on one side by the manufacturing middle class; division of labor between the different corporate guilds vanished in the face of division of labor in each single workshop.

Meantime the markets kept ever growing, the demand ever rising. Even manufacture no longer sufficed. Thereupon, steam and machinery revolutionized industrial production. The place of manufacture was taken by the giant, Modern Industry, the place of the industrial middle class, by industrial millionaires, the leaders of whole industrial armies, the modern bourgeois.

Modern industry has established the world market, for which the discovery of America paved the way. This market has given an immense development to commerce, to navigation, to communication by land. This development has, in its turn, reacted on the extension of industry; and in proportion as industry, commerce, navigation, railways extended, in the same proportion the bourgeoisie developed, increased its capital, and pushed into the background every class handed down from the Middle Ages.

We see, therefore, how the modern bourgeoisie is itself the product of a long course of development, of a series of revolutions in the modes of production and of exchange.

Each step in the development of the bourgeoisie was accompanied by a corresponding political advance of that class. An oppressed class under the sway of the feudal nobility, an armed and self-governing association in the medieval commune; here independent urban republic (as in Italy and Germany), there taxable "third estate" of the monarchy (as in France), afterward, in the period of manufacture proper, serving either the semifeudal or the absolute monarchy as a counterpoise against the nobility, and, in fact, cornerstone of the great monarchies in general, the bourgeoisie has at last, since the establishment of Modern Industry and of the world market, conquered for itself, in the modern representative State, exclusive political sway. The executive of the modern State is but a committee for managing the common affairs of the whole bourgeoisie.

The bourgeoisie, historically, has played a most revolutionary part.

The bourgeoisie, wherever it has got the upper hand, has put an end to all feudal, patriarchal, idyllic relations. It has pitilessly torn asunder the motley feudal ties that bound man to his "natural superiors," and has left remaining no other nexus between man and man than naked self-interest, than callous "cash payment." It has drowned the most heavenly ecstasies of religious fervor, of chivalrous enthusiasm, of philistine sentimentalism, in the icy water of egotistical calculation. It has resolved personal worth into exchange value, and in place of the numberless indefeasible chartered freedoms, has set up that single, unconscionable freedom—Free Trade. In one word, for exploitation, veiled by religious and political illusions, it has substituted naked, shameless, direct, brutal exploitation.

The bourgeoisie has stripped of its halo every occupation hitherto honored and looked up to with reverent awe. It has converted the physician, the lawyer, the priest, the poet, the man of science, into its paid wage laborers.

The bourgeoisie has torn away from the family its sentimental veil, and has reduced the family relation to a mere money relation.

The bourgeoisie has disclosed how it came to pass that the brutal display of vigor in the Middle Ages, which Reactionists so much admire, found its fitting complement in the most slothful indolence. It has been the first to show what man's activity can bring about. It has accomplished wonders far surpassing Egyptian pyramids, Roman aqueducts, and Gothic cathedrals; it has conducted expeditions that put in the shade all former Exoduses of nations and crusades.

The bourgeoisie cannot exist without constantly revolutionizing the instruments of production, and thereby the relations of production, and with them the whole relations of society. Conservation of the old modes of production in unaltered form was, on the contrary, the first condition of existence for all earlier industrial classes. Constant revolutionizing of production, uninterrupted disturbance of all social conditions, everlasting uncertainty and agitation distinguish the bourgeois epoch from all earlier ones. All fixed, fast-frozen relations, with their train of ancient and venerable prejudices and opinions are swept away, all new-formed ones become antiquated before they can ossify. All that is solid melts into air, all that is holy is profaned, and man is at last compelled to face with sober senses his real conditions of life, and his relations with his kind.

The need of a constantly expanding market for its products chases the bourgeoisie over the whole surface of the globe. It must nestle everywhere, settle everywhere, establish connections everywhere.

The bourgeoisie has through its exploitation of the world market given a cosmopolitan character to production and consumption in every country. To the great chagrin of Reactionists, it has drawn from under the feet of industry the national ground on which it stood. All old-established national industries have been destroyed or are daily being destroyed. They are dislodged by new industries, whose introduction becomes a life and death question for all civilized nations, by industries that no longer work up indigenous raw material, but raw material drawn from the remotest zones; industries whose products are consumed, not only at home, but in every quarter of the globe. In place of the old wants, satisfied by the productions of the country, we find new wants, requiring for their satisfaction the products of distant lands and climes. In place of the old local and national seclusion and self-sufficiency, we have intercourse in every direction, universal interdependence of nations. And as in material, so also in intellectual production. The intellectual creations of individual nations become common property. National one-sidedness and narrow-mindedness become more and more impossible, and from the numerous national and local literatures, there arises a world literature.

The bourgeoisie, by the rapid improvement of all instruments of production, by the immensely facilitated means of communication, draws all, even the most barbarian, nations into civilization. The cheap prices of its commodities are the heavy artillery with which it batters down all Chinese walls, with which it forces the barbarians' intensely obstinate hatred of foreigners to capitulate. It compels all nations, on pain of extinction, to adopt the bourgeois mode of production; it compels them to introduce what it calls civilization into their midst, i.e., to become bourgeois themselves. In one word, it creates a world after its own image.

The bourgeoisie has subjected the country to the rule of the towns. It has created enormous cities, has greatly increased the urban population as compared with the rural, and has thus rescued a considerable part of the population from the idiocy of rural life. Just as it has made the country dependent on the towns, so it has made barbarian and semibarbarian countries dependent on the civilized ones, nations of peasants on nations of bourgeois, the East on the West.

The bourgeoisie keeps more and more doing away with the scattered state of the population, of the means of production, and of property. It has agglomerated population, centralized means of production, and has concentrated property in a few hands. The necessary consequence of this was political centralization. Independent, or but loosely connected, provinces with separate interests, laws, governments and systems of taxation, became lumped together into one nation, with one government, one code of laws, one national class-interest, one frontier and one customs tariff.

The bourgeoisie, during its rule of scarce one hundred years, has created more massive and more colossal productive forces than have all preceding generations together. Subjection of

Nature's forces to man, machinery, application of chemistry to industry and agriculture, steam navigation, railways, electric telegraphs, clearing of whole continents for cultivation, canalization of rivers, whole populations conjured out of the ground —what earlier century had even a presentiment that such productive forces slumbered in the lap of social labor?

We see then: the means of production and of exchange, on whose foundation the bourgeoisie built itself up, were generated in feudal society. At a certain stage in the development of these means of production and of exchange, the conditions under which feudal society produced and exchanged, the feudal organization of agriculture and manufacturing industry, in one word, the feudal relations of property became no longer compatible with the already developed productive forces; they became so many fetters. They had to be burst asunder; they were burst asunder.

Into their place stepped free competition, accompanied by a social and political constitution adapted to it, and by the economical and political sway of the bourgeois class.

A similar movement is going on before our own eyes. Modern bourgeois society with its relations of production, of exchange and of property, a society that has conjured up such gigantic means of production and of exchange, is like the sorcerer, who is no longer able to control the powers of the nether world whom he has called up by his spells. For many a decade past, the history of industry and commerce is but the history of the revolt of modern productive forces against modern conditions of production, against the property relations that are the conditions for the existence of the bourgeoisie and of its rule. It is enough to mention the commercial crises that by their periodical return put on its trial, each time more threateningly, the existence of the entire bourgeois society. In these crises a great part not only of the existing products, but also the previously created productive forces, are periodically destroyed. In these crises there breaks out an epidemic that, in all earlier epochs, would have seemed an absurdity—the epidemic of overproduction. Society suddenly finds itself put back into a state of momentary barbarism; it appears as if a famine, a universal war of devastation had cut off the supply of every means of subsistence; industry and commerce seem to be destroyed; and why? Because there is too much civilization, too much means of subsistence, too much industry, too much commerce. The productive forces at the disposal of society no longer tend to further the development of the conditions of bourgeois property; on the contrary, they have become too powerful for these conditions, by which they are fettered, and so soon as they overcome these fetters, they bring disorder into the whole of bourgeois society, endanger the existence of bourgeois property. The conditions of bourgeois society are too narrow to comprise the wealth created by them. And how does the bourgeoisie get over these crises? On the one hand by enforced destruction of a mass of productive forces; on the other, by the conquest of new markets, and by the more thorough exploitation of the old ones. That is to say, by paving the way for more extensive and more destructive crises, and by diminishing the means whereby crises are prevented.

The weapons with which the bourgeoisie felled feudalism to the ground are now turned against the bourgeoisie itself.

But not only has the bourgeoisie forged the weapons that bring death to itself; it has also called into existence the men who are to wield those weapons—the modern working class—the proletarians.

In proportion as the bourgeoisie, i.e., capital, is developed, in the same proportion is the proletariat, the modern working class, developed—a class of laborers, who live only so long as they find work, and who find work only so long as their labor increases capital. These laborers, who must sell themselves piecemeal, are a commodity, like every other article of commerce, and are consequently exposed to all the vicissitudes of competition, to all the fluctuations of the market.

Owing to the extensive use of machinery and to division of labor, the work of the proletarians has lost all individual character, and, consequently, all charm for the workman. He becomes an appendage of the machine, and it is only the most simple, most monotonous, and most easily acquired knack that is required of him. Hence, the cost of production of a workman is restricted, almost entirely, to the means of subsistence that he requires for his maintenance, and for the propagation of his race. But the price of a commodity, and therefore also of labor, is equal to its cost of production. In proportion, therefore, as the repulsiveness of the work increases, the wage decreases. Nay more, in proportion as the use of machinery and division of labor increases, in the same proportion the burden of toil also increases, whether by prolongation of the working hours, by increase of the work exacted in a given time or by increased speed of the machinery, etc.

Modern industry has converted the little workshop of the patriarchal master into the great factory of the industrial capitalist. Masses of laborers, crowded into the factory, are organized like soldiers. As privates of the industrial army they are placed under the command of a perfect hierarchy of officers and sergeants. Not only are they slaves of the bourgeois class, and of the bourgeois State; they are daily and hourly enslaved by the machine, by the overlooker, and, above all, by the individual bourgeois manufacturer himself. The more openly this despotism proclaims gain to be its end and aim, the more petty, the more hateful and the more embittering it is.

The less the skill and exertion of strength implied in manual labor, in other words, the more modern industry becomes developed, the more is the labor of men superseded by that of women. Differences of age and sex have no longer any distinctive social validity for the working class. All are instruments of labor, more or less expensive to use, according to their age and sex.

No sooner is the exploitation of the laborer by the manufacturer, so far, at an end, that he receives his wages in cash, than he is set upon by the other portions of the bourgeoisie, the landlord, the shopkeeper, the pawnbroker, etc.

The lower strata of the middle class—the small tradespeople, shopkeepers, and retired tradesmen generally, the handicraftsmen and peasants—all these sink gradually into the proletariat, partly because their diminutive capital does not suffice for the scale on which Modern Industry is carried on, and is swamped in the competition with the large capitalists, partly because their specialized skill is rendered worthless by new methods of production. Thus the proletariat is recruited from all classes of the population.

The proletariat goes through various stages of development. With its birth begins its struggle with the bourgeoisie. At first the contest is carried on by individual laborers, then by the workpeople of a factory, then by the operatives of one trade, in one locality, against the individual bourgeois who directly exploits them. They direct their attacks not against the bourgeois conditions of production, but against the instruments of production themselves; they destroy imported wares that compete with their labor, they smash to pieces machinery, they set factories ablaze, they seek to restore by force the vanished status of the workman of the Middle Ages.

At this stage the laborers still form an incoherent mass scattered over the whole country, and broken up by their mutual competition. If anywhere they unite to form more compact bodies, this is not yet the consequence of their own active union, but of the union of the bourgeoisie, which class, in order to attain its own political ends, is compelled to set the whole proletariat in motion, and is moreover yet, for a time, able to do so. At this stage, therefore, the proletarians do not fight their enemies, but the enemies of their enemies, the remnants of absolute monarchy, the landowners, the nonindustrial bourgeois, the petty bourgeoisie. Thus the whole historical movement is concentrated in the hands of the bourgeoisie; every victory so obtained is a victory for the bourgeoisie.

But with the development of industry the proletariat not only increases in number; it becomes concentrated in greater masses, its strength grows, and it feels that strength more. The various interests and conditions of life within the ranks of the proletariat are more and more equalized, in proportion as machinery obliterates all distinctions of labor, and nearly everywhere reduces wages to the same low level. The growing competition among the bourgeois, and the resulting commercial crises, make the wages of the workers ever more fluctuating. The unceasing improvement of machinery, ever more rapidly developing, makes their livelihood more and more precarious; the collisions between individual workmen and individual bourgeois take more and more the character of collisions between two classes. Thereupon the workers begin to form combinations (Trades' Unions) against the bourgeois; they club together in order to keep up the rate of wages; they found permanent associations in order to make provision beforehand for these occasional revolts. Here and there the contest breaks out into riots.

Now and then the workers are victorious, but only for a time. The real fruit of their battles lies, not in the immediate result, but in the ever-expanding union of the workers. This union is helped on by the improved means of communication that are created by modern industry and that place the workers of different localities in contact with one another. It was just this contact that was needed to centralize the numerous local struggles, all of the same character, into one national struggle between classes. But every class struggle is a political struggle. And that union, to attain which the burghers of the Middle Ages, with their miserable highways, required centuries, the modern proletarians thanks to railways, achieve in a few years.

This organization of the proletarians into a class, and consequently into a political party, is continually being upset again by the competition between the workers themselves. But it ever rises up again, stronger, firmer, mightier. It compels legislative recognition of particular interests of the workers, by taking advantage of the divisions among the bourgeoisie itself. Thus the ten-hours' bill in England was carried.

Altogether collisions between the classes of the old society further, in many ways, the course of development of the proletariat. The bourgeoisie finds itself involved in a constant battle. At first with the aristocracy; later on, with those portions of the bourgeoisie itself, whose interests have become antagonistic to the progress of industry; at all times, with the bourgeoisie of foreign countries. In all these battles it sees itself compelled to appeal to the proletariat, to ask for its help, and thus, to drag it into the political arena. The bourgeoisie itself, therefore, supplies the proletariat with its own elements of political and general education, in other words, it furnishes the proletariat with weapons for fighting the bourgeoisie.

Futher, as we have already seen, entire sections of the ruling classes are, by the advance of industry, precipitated into the proletariat, or are at least threatened in their conditions of existence. These also supply the proletariat with fresh elements of enlightenment and progress.

Finally, in times when the class struggle nears the decisive hour, the process of dissolution going on within the ruling class, in fact within the whole range of old society, assumes such a violent, glaring character that a small section of the ruling class cuts itself adrift, and joins the revolutionary class, the class that holds the future in its hands. Just as, therefore, at an earlier period, a section of the nobility went over to the bourgeoisie, so now a portion of the bourgeoisie goes over to the proletariat, and in particular, a portion of the bourgeois ideologists, who have raised themselves to the level of comprehending theoretically the historical movement as a whole.

Of all the classes that stand face to face with the bourgeoisie today, the proletariat alone is a really revolutionary class. The other classes decay and finally disappear in the face of modern industry; the proletariat is its special and essential product.

The lower middle class, the small manufacturer, the shopkeeper, the artisan, the peasant, all these fight against the bourgeoisie, to save from extinction their existence as fractions of the middle class. They are therefore not revolutionary, but conservative. Nay more, they are reactionary, for they try to roll back the wheel of history. If by chance they are revolutionary, they are so only in view of their impending transfer into the proletariat, they thus defend not their present, but their future interests, they desert their own standpoint to place themselves at that of the proletariat.

The "dangerous class," the social scum, that passively rotting mass thrown off by the lowest layers of old society, may, here and there, be swept into the movement by a proletarian revolution; its conditions of life, however, prepare it far more for the part of a bribed tool of reactionary intrigue.

In the conditions of the proletariat, those of old society at large are already virtually swamped. The proletarian is without property; his relation to his wife and children has no longer anything in common with the bourgeois family relations; modern industrial labor, modern subjection to capital, the same in England as in France, in America as in Germany, has stripped him of every trace of national character. Law, morality, religion, are to him so many bourgeois prejudices, behind which lurk in ambush just as many bourgeois interests.

All the preceding classes that got the upper hand sought to fortify their already acquired status by subjecting society at large to their conditions of appropriation. The proletarians cannot become masters of the productive forces of society, except by abolishing their own previous mode of appropriation, and thereby also every other previous mode of appropriation. They have nothing of their own to secure and to fortify; their mission is to destroy all previous securities for, and insurances of, individual property.

All previous historical movements were movements of minorities, or in the interest of minorities. The proletarian movement is the self-conscious, independent movement of the immense majority, in the interest of the immense majority. The proletariat, the lowest stratum of our present society, cannot stir, cannot raise itself up, without the whole superincumbent strata of official society being sprung into the air.

Though not in substance, yet in form, the struggle of the proletariat with the bourgeoisie is at first a national struggle. The proletariat of each country must, of course, first of all settle matters with its own bourgeoisie.

In depicting the most general phases of the development of the proletariat, we traced the more or less veiled civil war, raging within existing society, up to the point where that war breaks out into open revolution, and where the violent overthrow of the bourgeoisie lays the foundation for the sway of the proletariat.

Hitherto, every form of society has been based, as we have already seen, on the antagonism of oppressing and oppressed classes. But in order to oppress a class, certain conditions must be assured to it under which it can, at least, continue its slavish existence. The serf, in the period of serfdom, raised himself to membership in the commune, just as the petty bourgeois, under the yoke of feudal absolutism, managed to develop into a bourgeois. The modern laborer, on the contrary, instead of rising with the progress of industry, sinks deeper and deeper below the conditions of existence of his own class. He becomes a pauper, and pauperism develops more rapidly than population and wealth. And here it becomes evident that the bourgeoisie is unfit any longer to be the ruling class in society, and to impose its conditions of existence upon society as an overriding law. It is unfit to rule because it is incompetent to assure an existence to its slave within his slavery, because it cannot help letting him sink into such a state, that it has to feed him, instead of being fed by him. Society can no longer live under this bourgeoisie, in other words, its existance is no longer compatible with society.

The essential condition for the existence, and for the sway of the bourgeois class, is the formation and augmentation of capital; the condition for capital is wage labor. Wage labor rests exclusively on competition between the laborers. The advance of industry, whose involuntary promoter is the bourgeoisie, replaces the isolation of the laborers, due to competition, by their revolutionary combination, due to association. The development of Modern Industry, therefore, cuts from under its feet the very foundation on which the bourgeoisie produces and appropriates products. What the bourgeoisie, therefore, produces, above all, is its own gravediggers. Its fall and the victory of the proletariat are equally inevitable.

II

PROLETARIANS AND COMMUNISTS

In what relation do the Communists stand to the proletarians as a whole?

The Communists do not form a separate party opposed to other working-class parties.

They have no interests separate and apart from those of the proletariat as a whole.

They do not set up any sectarian principles of their own, by which to shape and mold the proletarian movement.

The Communists are distinguished from the other working-class parties by this only: 1. In the national struggles of the proletarians of the different countries, they point out and bring to the front the common interests of the entire proletariat, independently of all nationality. 2. In the various stages of development which the struggle of the working class against the bourgeoisie has to pass through, they always and everywhere represent the interests of the movement as a whole.

The Communists, therefore, are on the one hand, practically, the most advanced and resolute section of the working-class parties of every country, that section which pushes forward all others; on the other hand, theoretically, they have over the great mass of the proletariat the advantage of clearly understanding the line of march, the conditions, and the ultimate general results of the proletarian movement.

The immediate aim of the Communists is the same as that of all the other proletarian parties: formation of the proletariat into a class, overthrow of the bourgeois supremacy, conquest of political power by the proletariat.

The theoretical conclusions of the Communists are in no way based on ideas or principles that have been invented, or discovered, by this or that would-be universal reformer.

They merely express, in general terms, actual relations springing from an existing class struggle, from a historical movement going on under our very eyes. The abolition of existing property relations is not at all a distinctive feature of Communism.

All property relations in the past have continually been subject to historical change consequent upon the change in historical conditions.

The French Revolution, for example, abolished feudal property in favor of bourgeois property.

The distinguishing feature of Communism is not the abolition of property generally, but the abolition of bourgeois property. But modern bourgeois private property is the final and most complete expression of the system of producing and appropriating products, that is based on class antagonisms, on the exploitation of the many by the few.

In this sense, the theory of the Communists may be summed up in the single sentence: Abolition of private property.

We Communists have been reproached with the desire of abolishing the right of personally acquiring property as the fruit of a man's own labor, which property is alleged to be the groundwork of all personal freedom, activity and independence.

Hard-won, self-acquired, self-earned property! Do you mean the property of the petty artisan and of the small peasant, a form of property that preceded the bourgeois form? There is no need to abolish that; the development of industry has to a great extent already destroyed it, and is still destroying it daily.

Or do you mean modern bourgeois private property?

But does wage labor create any property for the laborer? Not a bit. It creates capital, i.e., that kind of property which exploits wage labor, and which cannot increase except upon condition of begetting a new supply of wage labor for fresh exploitation. Property, in its present form, is based on the antagonism of capital and wage labor. Let us examine both sides of this antagonism.

To be a capitalist is to have not only a purely personal, but a social *status* in production. Capital is a collective product, and only by the united action of many members, nay, in the last restort, only by the united action of all members of society, can it be set in motion.

Capital is, therefore, not a personal, it is a social power.

When, therefore, capital is converted into common property, into the property of all members of society, personal property is not thereby transformed into social property. It is only the social character of the property that is changed. It loses its class character.

Let us now take wage labor.

The average price of wage labor is the minimum wage, i.e., that quantum of the means of subsistence, which is absolutely requisite to keep the laborer in bare existence as a laborer. What, therefore, the wage laborer appropriates by means of his labor, merely suffices to prolong and reproduce a bare existence. We by no means intend to abolish this personal appropriation of the products of labor, an appropriation that is made for the maintenance and reproduction of human life, and that leaves no surplus wherewith to command the labor of others. All that we want to do away with is the miserable character of this appropriation, under which the laborer lives merely to increase capital, and is allowed to live only in so far as the interest of the ruling class requires it.

In bourgeois society, living labor is but a means to increase accumulated labor. In Communist society, accumlated labor is but a means to widen, to enrich, to promote the existence of the laborer.

In bourgeois society, therefore, the past dominates the present; in Communist society, the present dominates the past. In bougeois society capital is independent and has individuality, while the living person is dependent and has no individuality.

And the abolition of this state of things is called by the bourgeois, abolition of individuality and freedom! And rightly so. The abolition of bourgeois individuality, bourgeois independence, and bourgeois freedom is undoubtedly aimed at.

By freedom is meant, under the present bourgeois conditions of production, free trade, free selling and buying.

But if selling and buying disappears, free selling and buying disappears also. This talk about free selling and buying, and all the other "brave words" of our bourgeoisie about freedom in general, have a meaning, if any, only in contrast with restricted selling and buying, with the fettered traders of the Middle Ages, but have no meaning when opposed to the Communistic abolition of buying and selling, of the bougeois conditions of production, and of the bourgeoisie itself.

You are horrified at our intending to do away with private property. But in your existing society, private property is already done away with for nine-tenths of the population; its existence for the few is solely due to its nonexistence in the hands of those nine-tenths. You reproach us, therefore, with intending to do away with a form of property, the necessary condition for whose existence is the nonexistence of any property for the immense majority of society.

In one word, you reproach us with intending to do away with your property. Precisely so; that is just what we intend.

From the moment when labor can no longer be converted into capital, money, or rent, into a social power capable of being monopolized, i.e., from the moment when individual property can no longer be transformed into bourgeois property, into capital, from that moment, you say, individuality vanishes.

You must, therefore, confess that by "individual" you mean no other person than the bourgeois, than the middle-class owner of property. This person must, indeed, be swept out of the way, and made impossible.

Communism deprives no man of the power to appropriate the products of society; all that it does is to deprive him of the power to subjugate the labor of others by means of such appropriation.

It has been objected that upon the abolition of private property all work will cease, and universal laziness will overtake us.

According to this, bourgeois society ought long ago to have gone to the dogs through sheer idleness; for those of its members who work acquire nothing, and those who acquire anything do not work. The whole of this objection is but another expression of the tautology: that there can no longer be any wage labor when there is no longer any capital.

All objections urged against the Communistic mode of producing and appropriating material products, have, in the same way, been urged against the Communistic modes of producing and appropriating intellectual products. Just as, to the bourgeois, the disappearance of class property is the disappearance of production itself, so the disappearance of class culture is to him identical with the disappearance of all culture.

That culture, the loss of which he laments, is, for the enormous majority a mere training to act as a machine.

But don't wrangle with us so long as you apply, to our intended abolition of bourgeois property, the standard of your bougeois notions of freedom, culture, law, etc. Your very ideas are but the outgrowth of the conditions of your bougeois production and bourgeois property, just as your jurisprudence is but the will of your class made into a law for all, a will whose essential character and direction are determined by the economical conditions of existence of your class.

The selfish misconception that induces you to transform into eternal laws of nature and of reason, the social forms springing from your present mode of production and form of property—historical relations that rise and disappear in the progress of production—this misconception you share with every ruling class that has preceded you. What you see clearly in the case of ancient property, what you admit in the case of feudal property, you are of course forbidden to admit in the case of your own bourgeois form of property.

Abolition of the family! Even the most radical flare up at this infamous proposal of the Communists.

On what foundation is the present family, the bourgeois family, based? On capital, on private gain. In its completely developed form this family exists only among the bourgeoisie. But this state of things finds its complement in the practical absence of the family among the proletarians, and in public prostitution.

The bourgeois family will vanish as a matter of course when its complement vanishes, and both will vanish with the vanishing of capital.

Do you charge us with wanting to stop the exploitation of children by their parents? To this crime we plead guilty.

But, you will say, we destroy the most hallowed of relations, when we replace home education by social.

And your education! Is not that also social, and determined by the social conditions under which you educate, by the intervention, direct or indirect, of society, by means of schools, etc? The Communists have not invented the intervention of society in education; they do but seek to alter the character of that intervention, and to rescue education from the influence of the ruling class.

The bourgeois clap-trap about the family and education, about the hallowed co-relation of parent and child, becomes all the more disgusting, the more, by the action of Modern Industry, all family ties among the proletarians are torn asunder, and their children transformed into simple articles of commerce and instruments of labor.

But you Communists would introduce community of women, screams the whole bourgeoisie in chorus.

The bourgeois sees in his wife a mere instrument of production. He hears that the instruments of production are to be exploited in common, and, naturally, can come to no other conclusion than that the lot of being common to all will likewise fall to the women.

He has not even a suspicion that the real point aimed at is to do away with the status of women as mere instruments of production.

For the rest, nothing is more ridiculous than the virtuous indignation of our bourgeois at the community of women which, they pretend, is to be openly and officially established by the Communists. The Communists have no need to introduce community of women; it has existed almost from time immemorial.

Our bourgeois, not content with having the wives and daughters of their proletarians at their disposal, not to speak of common prostitutes, take the greatest pleasure in seducing each other's wives.

Bourgeois marriage is in reality a system of wives in common and thus, at the most, what the Communists might possibly be reproached with, is that they desire to introduce, in substitution for a hypocritically concealed, an openly legalized community of women. For the rest, it is self-evident that the abolition of the present system of production must bring with it the abolition of the community of women springing from that system, i.e., of prostitution both public and private.

The Communists are further reproached with desiring to abolish countries and nationality.

The working men have no country. We cannot take from them what they have not got. Since the proletariat must first of all acquire political supremacy, must rise to be the leading class of the nation, must constitute itself *the* nation, it is, so far, itself national, though not in the bourgeois sense of the word.

National differences and antagonisms between peoples are daily more and more vanishing, owing to the development of the bourgeoisie, to freedom of commerce, to the world market, to uniformity in the mode of production and in the conditions of life corresponding thereto.

The supremacy of the proletariat will cause them to vanish still faster. United action, of the leading civilized countries at least, is one of the first conditions for the emancipation of the proletariat.

In proportion as the exploitation of one individual by another is put an end to, the exploitation of one nation by another will also be put an end to. In proportion as the antagonism between classes within the nation vanishes, the hostility of one nation to another will come to an end.

The charges against Communism made from a religious, a philosophical, and, generally, from an ideological standpoint, are not deserving of serious examination.

Does it require deep intuition to comprehend that man's ideas, views and conceptions, in one word, man's consciousness, changes with every change in the conditions of his material existence, in his social relations and in his social life?

What else does the history of ideas prove, than that intellectual production changes its character in proportion as material production is changed? The ruling ideas of each age have ever been the ideas of its ruling class.

When people speak of ideas that revolutionize society, they do but express the fact that within the old society, the elements of a new one have been created, and that the dissolution of the old ideas keeps even pace with the dissolution of the old conditions of existence.

When the ancient world was in its last throes, the ancient religions were overcome by Christianity. When Christian ideas succumbed in the eighteenth century to rationalist ideas, feudal society fought its death battle with the then revolutionary bourgeoisie. The ideas of religious liberty and freedom of conscience merely gave expression to the sway of free competition within the domain of knowledge.

"Undoubtedly," it will be said, "religious, moral, philosophical and juridical ideas have been modified in the course of historical development. But religion, morality, philosophy, political science, and law constantly survived this change."

"There are, besides, eternal truths, such as Freedom, Justice, etc., that are common to all states of society. But Communism abolishes eternal truths, it abolishes all religion, and all morality, instead of constituting them on a new basis; it therefore acts in contradiction to all past historical experience."

What does this accusation reduce itself to? The history of all past society has consisted in the development of class antagonisms, antagonisms that assumed different forms at different epochs.

But whatever form they may have taken, one fact is common to all past ages, *viz.*, the exploitation of one part of society by the other. No wonder, then, that the social consciousness of past ages, despite all the multiplicity and variety it displays, moves within certain common forms, or general ideas, which cannot completely vanish except with the total disappearance of class antagonisms.

The Communist revolution is the most radical rupture with traditional property relations; no wonder that its development involves the most radical rupture with traditional ideas.

But let us have done with the bourgeois objections to Communism.

We have seen above that the first step in the revolution by the working class is to raise the proletariat to the position of ruling class, to win the battle of democracy.

The proletariat will use its political supremacy to wrest, by degrees, all capital from the bourgeoisie, to centralize all instruments of production in the hands of the State, i.e., of the proletariat organized as the ruling class; and to increase the total of productive forces as rapidly as possible.

Of course, in the beginning, this cannot be effected except by means of despotic inroads on the rights of property, and on the conditions of bourgeois production; by means of measures, therefore, which appear economically insufficient and untenable, but which, in the course of the movement, outstrip themselves, necessitate further inroads upon the old social order, and are unavoidable as a means of entirely revolutionizing the mode of production.

These measures will of course be different in different countries.

Nevertheless in the most advanced countries, the following will be pretty generally applicable.

1. Abolition of property in land and application of all rents of land to public purposes.

2. A heavy progressive or graduated income tax.

3. Abolition of all right of inheritance.

4. Confiscation of the property of all emigrants and rebels.

5. Centralization of credit in the hands of the State, by means of a national bank with State capital and an exclusive monopoly.

6. Centralization of the means of communication and transport in the hands of the State.

7. Extension of factories and instruments of production owned by the State; the bringing into cultivation of wastelands, and the improvement of the soil generally in accordance with a common plan.

8. Equal liability of all to labor. Establishment of industrial armies, especially for agriculture.

9. Combination of agriculture with manufacturing industries; gradual abolition of the distinction between town and country, by a more equable distribution of the population over the country.

10. Free education for all children in public schools. Abolition of children's factory labor in its present form. Combination of education with industrial production, etc., etc.

When, in the course of development, class distinctions have disappeared, and all production has been concentrated in the hands of a vast association of the whole nation, the public power will lose its political character. Political power, properly so called, is merely the organized power of one class for oppressing another. If the proletariat during its contest with the bourgeoisie is compelled, by the force of circumstances, to organize itself as a class, if, by means of a revolution, it makes itself the ruling class, and, as such, sweeps away by force the old conditions of production, then it will, along with these conditions, have swept away the conditions for the existence of class antagonisms and of classes generally, and will thereby have abolished its own supremacy as a class.

In place of the old bourgeois society, with its classes and class antagonisms, we shall have an association in which the free development of each is the condition for the free development of all.

26. Communist Tactics in a Democracy

This selection is taken from the little-known *Address of the Central Council to the Communist League* (1850), in which the Central Council, controlled by Marx and functioning in London, gives instructions to the disorganized remnant of Communists in Germany in the wake of the disastrous rising of 1848–1849. The document has great significance in that it explicitly contains Marx's views concerning the role to be played by a Communist party in such circumstances, that is, in cooperation with, but at the same time working to take the revolutionary initiative from, petit bourgeois democrats and bourgeois liberals struggling against the weakened reactionary elements who have been forced to yield limited concessions to the bourgeoisie. This address was extremely influential upon the way in which Lenin conducted the Bolsheviks during the years between the first Russian Revolution of 1905 and the February Revolution of 1917. The scenario has been repeated scores of times in other countries, as Communists seek to gain control of nationalist (i.e., bourgeois) movements against colonial and neocolonial domination, as well as democratic opposition to bourgeois regimes.

THE PETIT-BOURGEOIS Democratic Party in Germany is very powerful; it comprises not only the great majority of the bourgeois inhabitants of the towns, the small industrial businessmen and guild masters, it numbers among its following the peasants and the rural proletariat, in so far as the latter

From Marx and Engels, *Selected Works*, Vol. II (Moscow, 1935).

has not yet found a support in the independent proletariat of the towns.

The relation of the revolutionary workers' party to petit bourgeois democracy is this: it marches together with it against the section which it aims at overthrowing, it opposes the petit bourgeois in everything by which they desire to establish themselves.

The democratic petit bourgeois, far from desiring to revolutionize all society for the revolutionary proletarians, strive for a change in social conditions by means of which existing society will be made as tolerable and comfortable as possible for them. Hence they demand above all diminution of state expenditure by restricting the bureaucracy and shifting the chief taxes onto the big landowners and bourgeois. Further, they demand the abolition of the pressure of big capital on small, through public credit institutions and laws against usury, by which means it will be possible for them and the peasants to obtain advances, on favorable conditions, from the state instead of from the capitalists; and, further, they demand the establishment of bourgeois property relations in the countryside by the complete abolition of feudalism. In order to accomplish all this, they require a democratic state constitution, whether constitutional or republican, giving a majority to them and their allies, the peasants, as well as a democratic local government which would give them control over municipal property and over a series of functions now performed by the bureaucrats.

The domination and speedy increase of capital is further to be counteracted partly by limiting the right of inheritance and partly by transferring as many works as possible to the state. As far as the workers are concerned, it remains certain above all that they are to remain wage workers as before; the democratic petit bourgeois only desire better wages and a secure existence for the workers and hope to achieve this through partial employment by the state and through charity measures, in short, they hope to bribe the workers by more or less concealed alms and to break their revolutionary force by making their position tolerable for the moment. . . . But these demands can in no wise suffice for the party of the proletariat. While the democratic petit bourgeois wish to bring the revolution to a conclusion as quickly as possible and with the achievement at most of the above demands, it is our interest and our task to make the revolution permanent, until all more or less possessing classes have been displaced from domination, until the proletariat has conquered state power, and the association of proletarians, not only in one country but in all the dominant countries of the world, has advanced so far that competition among the proletarians of these countries has ceased and that at least the decisive productive forces are concentrated in the hands of the proletarians. For us the issue cannot be the alteration of private property but only its abolition, not the smoothing over of class antagonisms but the abolition of classes, not the improvement of existing society but the foundation of a new one. That, during the further development of the revolution, petit bourgeois democracy will for a moment obtain predominating influence in Germany is not open to doubt. The question, therefore, arises as to what the attitude of the proletariat and in particular of the [Communist] League will be in relation to it:

1. During the continuance of the present conditions where the petit bourgeois democrats are likewise oppressed;

2. In the next revolutionary struggle which will give them the upper hand;

3. After this struggle, during the period of preponderance over the overthrown classes and the proletariat.

1. At the present moment, when the democratic petit bourgeois are everywhere oppressed, they preach in general unity and reconciliation to the proletariat, they offer them their hand and strive for the establishment of a large opposition party which will embrace all shades of opinion in the Democratic Party, i.e., they strive to involve the workers in a party organization in which general Social Democratic phrases predominate, behind which their special interests are concealed and in which the particular demands of the proletariat may not be brought forward for the sake of beloved peace. Such a union would turn out solely to their advantage and altogether to the disadvantage of the proletariat. The proletariat would lose its whole independent, laboriously obtained position and once more sink down to being an appendage of official bourgeois democracy. This union

must, therefore, be most decisively rejected. Instead of once again stooping to serve as the applauding chorus of the bourgeois democrats, the workers, and above all the League, must strive to establish an independent, secret and open, organization of the Workers' Party alongside the official democrats and make each local section the central point and nucleus of workers' associations in which the attitude and interests of the proletariat will be discussed independently of bourgeois influences. . . . In the case of a struggle against a common opponent no special union is required. As soon as such an opponent has to be fought directly, the interests of both parties, for the moment, coincide, and, as previously, so also in the future, this union calculated only for the moment will arise of itself. It is self-evident that in the coming bloody conflicts, as in all earlier ones, it is the workers who, in the main, will have to win the victory by their courage, determination and self-sacrifice. As previously, so also in this struggle, the mass of the petit bourgeois will behave as long as possible in a hesitating, undecided and inactive manner, and then, as soon as the victory has been decided, take possession of it for themselves, call upon the workers to maintain tranquillity and return to their work, guard against so-called excesses and exclude the proletariat from the fruits of victory. It is not in the power of the workers to restrain the petit bourgeois democrats from doing this, but it is in their power to make it difficult for them to push forward in the face of the armed proletariat and to dictate such conditions to them that the rule of the bourgeois democrats from the outset bears within it the seeds of its downfall, and their later supplanting by the rule of the proletariat will be considerably facilitated. Above all things, the workers must counteract, as much as is at all possible during the conflict and immediately after the struggle, the bourgeois endeavors to allay the storm, and must compel the democrats to carry out their present terrorist phrases. They must act so as to prevent the immediately revolutionary excitement from being suppressed again immediately after the victory. On the contrary, they must maintain it as long as possible. Far from opposing so-called excesses, instances of popular revenge against hated individuals or public buildings that are only associated with hateful recollections, such instances must not only be tolerated but the leadership of them must be taken in hand. During the struggle and after the struggle the workers must at every opportunity put forward their own demands alongside of the demands of the bourgeois democrats. They must demand guarantees for the workers as soon as the democratic bourgeois set about taking over the government. If necessary they must obtain these guarantees by force and in general they must ensure that the new rulers pledge themselves to all possible concessions and promises—the surest way to compromise them. In general, they must in every way restrain as far as possible the intoxication of victory and the enthusiasm for the new state of things, which make their appearance after every victorious street battle, by a calm and cold-blooded estimate of the conditions and by unconcealed mistrust in the new government. Alongside of the new official governments they must establish simultaneously their own revolutionary workers' governments, whether in the form of municipal committees and municipal councils or in the form of workers' clubs or workers' committees, so that the bourgeois-democratic governments not only immediately lose their backing by the workers but from the outset see themselves supervised and threatened by authorities which are backed by the whole mass of the workers. In a word, from the first moment of victory mistrust must be directed not against the conquered reactionary party, but against the workers' previous allies, against the party that wishes to exploit the common victory for itself alone.

2. But in order to be able energetically and threateningly to oppose this party whose treachery to the workers will begin from the first hour of victory, the workers must be armed and organized. The arming of the whole proletariat with rifles, muskets, cannon and munitions must be put through at once, the revival of the old Citizens' Guard directed against the workers must be opposed. However, where the latter cannot be achieved the workers must attempt to organize themselves independently as a proletarian guard with a commander elected by themselves and with a general staff of their own choosing and put themselves at the command not of the state authority

but of the revolutionary local councils set up by the workers.
. . . Weapons and munitions must not be surrendered on any
pretext; any attempt at disarming must if necessary be frus-
trated by force. Destruction of the influence of the bourgeois
democrats on the workers, immediate independent and armed
organization of the workers and the bringing about of conditions as difficult and compromising as possible for the immediately inevitable rule of bourgeois democracy, these are the
main points which the proletariat and hence the League must
keep in view during the after the coming insurrection.

3. As soon as the new governments have consolidated themselves to some extent, their struggle against the workers will
immediately begin. In order here to oppose the democratic
petty bourgeois by force it is above all necessary that the workers shall be independently organized and centralized through
their clubs. After the overthrow of the existing governments,
the Central Council will, as soon as it is at all possible, betake
itself to Germany, immediately convene a congress and put
before the latter the necessary provisions for the centralization
of the workers' clubs under a leadership established in the chief
seat of the movement. The speedy organization of at least a
provincial union of the workers' clubs is one of the most important points for the strengthening and development of the
Workers' Party; the immediate consequence of the overthrow
of the existing governments will be the election of a National
Assembly. Here the proletariat must see to it:

I. That under no pretext are numbers of workers excluded by
any kind of trickery on the part of local authorities or government commissioners.

II. That everywhere workers' candidates are put up alongside
of the bourgeois-democratic candidates, that they should consist as far as possible of members of the League, and that their
election is promoted by all possible means. Even where there
is no prospect whatsoever of their being elected, the workers
must put up their own candidates in order to preserve their
independence, to count their forces and to bring before the
public their revolutionary attitude and party standpoint. In this
connection they must not allow themselves to be seduced by

the phrases of the democrats, such as, for example, that by this action they are splitting the Democratic Party and giving the reaction the possibility of victory. The final intention of all such phrases is that the proletariat shall be duped. The advance which the proletarian party is bound to make by such an independent action is infinitely more important than the disadvantage that might be caused by the presence of a few reactionaries in the representative body. If the democracy from the outset comes out decisively and with the use of terror against the reaction, then the influence of the latter in the elections will be destroyed in advance.

The first point on which the bourgeois democrats will come into conflict with the workers will be the abolition of feudalism. As in the first French Revolution, the petit bourgeois will give the feudal lands to the peasants as free property, that is to say, try to leave the rural proletariat in existence and form a petit bourgeois peasant class which will go through the same cycle of impoverishment and indebtedness which the French peasant is now going through.

The workers must oppose this plan in the interests of the rural proletariat and in their own interests. They must demand that the confiscated feudal property remain state property and be converted into labor colonies cultivated by the associated rural proletariat with all the advantages of large-scale agriculture, through which the principle of common property immediately obtains a firm basis in the midst of the tottering bourgeois property relations. Just as the democrats combine with the peasants so must the workers combine with the rural proletariat. Further, the democrats will work either directly for the federated republic or, at least, if they cannot avoid the single and indivisible republic, they will attempt to cripple the central government by the utmost possible autonomy and independence on the part of the municipalities and provinces. The workers, in opposition to this plan, must not only strive for the single and indivisible German republic, but also strive in it for the most decisive centralization of power in the hands of the state authority. They must not allow themselves to be led astray by the democratic talk of freedom for the municipalities, of self-government, etc. In a country like Germany where there are so many relics of the Middle Ages to be abolished, where there is so much local and provincial obstinacy to be broken, it must under no circumstances be permitted that every village, every town, and every province should put a new obstacle in the path of revolutionary activity, which can proceed in all its force only from the center. It is not to be tolerated that the present state of things should be renewed, whereby Germans must fight separately for one and the same advance in every town and in every province. . . . As in France in 1793 so today in Germany the carrying through of the strictest centralization is the task of the really revolutionary party.

We have seen how the democrats will come to power with the next movement, how they will be compelled to propose more or less socialist measures. It will be asked what measures the workers ought to propose in reply. At the beginning of the movement, of course, the workers cannot yet propose any directly communist measures. But they can:

1. Compel the democrats to interfere in as many spheres as possible of the existing social order, to disturb its regular course and to compromise themselves, as well as to concentrate the utmost possible productive forces, means to transport, factories, railways, etc., in the hands of the state;

2. They must drive the proposals of the democrats, who in any case will not act in a revolutionary but in a merely reformist manner, to the extreme and transform them into direct attacks against private property; thus, for example, if the petit bourgeois propose purchase of the railways and factories, then the workers must demand that these railways and factories shall be simply confiscated by the state without compensation as being the property of reactionaries. If the democrats propose proportional taxes, the workers must demand progressive taxes; if the democrats themselves put forward a moderate progressive tax, the workers must insist on a tax with rates which rise so steeply that large-scale capital is ruined by it; if the democrats demand the regulation of state debts, the workers demand state bankruptcy. Thus, the demands of the workers must everywhere be governed by the concessions and measures of the democrats.

... The German workers ... will have to do the most for their final victory by becoming enlightened as to their class interests, by taking up their own independent party position as soon as possible and by not allowing themselves for a single moment to be led astray from the independent organizations of the party of the proletariat by the hypocritical phrases of the democratic petit bourgeois. Their battle-cry must be: the permanent revolution.

27. *Critique of Reformist Tendencies*

Marx's letter to Wilhelm Bracke (May 5, 1875) and his far more substantial *Critique of the Gotha Program,* excerpts of which constitute this selection, are both concerned with the program adopted at the Unity Conference of the Social-Democratic Workers' Party of Germany (the so-called Eisenachers) led by Liebknecht and Bebel (parliamentary, i.e., nonrevolutionary, followers of Marx) and the Lassallean party, the General Association of German Workers, held in Gotha in the spring of 1875. In both Marx maintains his position of 1850 (cf. Selection 26) in the face of the reformist and parliamentary emphasis of German socialism. Marx here explicitly reinforces his view of the revolutionary dictatorship of the proletariat as the only means capable of ensuring (a) the complete triumph of the working class over the bourgeoisie and other enemies, and (b) progress towards the final, future development of communism.

London, May 5, 1875

Dear Bracke:

When you have read the following critical marginal notes on the Unity Program, would you be so good as to send them to Geib and Auer, Bebel and Liebknecht for them to see. I am excessively busy and have already had to go a long way beyond the extent of work allowed me by the doctor. Hence it was anything but a "pleasure" to write such a lengthy screed. It was,

From Marx and Engles, *Selected Works,* Vol. II (Moscow, 1935).

however, necessary so that the steps that have to be taken by me later on will not be misinterpreted by our friends in the party for whom this communication is intended. After the Unity Congress has been held, Engels and I will publish a short declaration to the effect that our position is altogether remote from the said program of principles and that we have nothing to do with it.

This is indispensable because the opinion—the entirely erroneous opinion—is held abroad, assiduously nurtured by enemies of the party, that we secretly guide from here the movements of the so-called Eisenach party. . . .

Apart from this, it is my duty not to give recognition, even by diplomatic silence, to what is in my opinion a thoroughly objectionable program tending to demoralize the party.

Every step of real movement is more important than a dozen programs. If, therefore, it was not possible—and the conditions of the time did not permit it—to go *beyond* the Eisenach program, one should simply have concluded an agreement for action against the common enemy. But by drawing up a program of principles (instead of postponing this until it has been prepared for by a considerable period of common activity) one sets up before the whole world a landmark by which the level of the party movement is measured. The Lassallean leaders came because circumstances forced them to come. If they had been told from the beginning that there would be no bargaining about principles, they would have *had* to be content with a program of action or a plan of organization for common action. Instead of this, they have been permitted to arrive armed with mandates, these mandates have been recognized on our part as valid, and thus one surrenders unconditionally to those who are in need of help. . . . One knows that the mere fact of unification is satisfying to the workers, but it would be a mistake to believe that this immediate success is not being bought at too high a price.

For the rest, the program is no good, even apart from its sanctification of the Lassallean articles of faith. . . .

With best wishes,

Yours,

KARL MARX

CRITIQUE OF THE GOTHA PROGRAM: MARGINAL NOTES TO THE PROGRAM OF THE GERMAN WORKERS' PARTY

1. "Labor is the source of all wealth and all culture *and since* useful labor is only possible in society and through society, the proceeds of labor belong undiminished with equal right to all members of society."

First Part of the Paragraph: "Labor is the source of all wealth and all culture."

Labor is *not the source* of all wealth. *Nature* is just as much the source of use values (and it is surely of such that material wealth consists!) as labor, which itself is only the manifestation of a natural force, human labor power. . . .

. . . A socialist program cannot allow such bourgeois phrases to cause the *conditions* that alone give them meaning to be ignored. And in so far as man from the beginning behaves toward nature, the primary source of all instruments and subjects of labor, as her owner, treats her as belonging to him, his labor becomes the source of use values, therefore also of wealth. . . .

Let us now leave the sentence as it stands, or rather limps. What would one have expected as conclusion? Obviously this:

"Since labor is the source of all wealth, in society also no one can appropriate wealth except as the product of labor. Therefore, if he himself does not work, he lives by the labor of others and also acquires his culture at the expense of the labor of others." . . .

Second Part of the Paragraph: "Useful labor is only possible in society and through society."

According to the first proposition, labor was the source of all wealth and all culture, therefore also no society is possible without labor. Now we learn, conversely, that no "useful" labor is possible without society.

One could just as well have said that only in society can useless and even generally harmful labor become a branch of gainful occupation, that only in society can one live by being idle, etc., etc. . . .

And what is "useful" labor? Surely only labor which produces the intended useful effect. A savage—and man was a savage after he had ceased to be an ape—who has killed an animal with a stone, who collects fruits, etc., performs "useful" labor.

Thirdly: The Conclusion: "And since useful work is only possible in society and through society—the proceeds of labor belong undiminished with equal right to all members of society."

A fine conclusion! If useful labor is only possible in society and through society, the proceeds of labor belong to society—and only so much therefrom accrues to the individual workers as is not required to maintain the "condition" of labor, society.

In fact, also, this proposition has at all times been made use of by the champions of the *prevailing state of society*. First come the claims of the government and everything connected with it, since it is the social organ for the maintenance of the social order; then come the claims of the various kinds of private property, for the various kinds of private property are the foundations of society, etc. One sees that such hollow phrases can be twisted and turned as desired.

The first and second parts of the paragraph have some intelligible connection only in the following wording:

"Labor only becomes the source of wealth and culture as social labor," or, what is the same thing, "in and through society."

This proposition is incontestably correct, for although isolated labor (its material conditions presupposed) can also create use values, it can create neither wealth nor culture.

But equally incontestable is this other proposition:

"In proportion as labor develops socially, and becomes thereby a source of wealth and culture, poverty and neglect develop among the workers and wealth and culture among the nonworkers."

This is the law of all history hitherto. What, therefore, had to be done here, instead of making general phrases about "labor" and "society," was to prove concretely how in present capitalist society the material, etc., conditions have at last been created which will enable and compel the workers to lift this social curse. . . .

3. "The emancipation of labor demands the promotion of the instruments of labor to the common property of society and the cooperative regulation of the total labor with equitable distribution of the proceeds of labor."

"Promotion of the instruments of labor to the common property" ought obviously to read their "conversion into the common property," but this only in passing.

What are the "proceeds of labor"? The product of labor or its value? And in the latter case, is it the total value of the product or only that part of the value which labor has newly added to the value of the means of production consumed?

The "proceeds of labor" is a loose notion which Lassalle has put in the place of definite economic conceptions.

What is "equitable distribution"?

Do not the bourgeois assert that the present-day distribution is "equitable"? And is it not, in fact, the only "equitable" distribution on the basis of the present-day mode of production? Are economic relations regulated by legal conceptions or do not, on the contrary, legal relations arise from economic ones? Have not also the socialist sectarians[1] the most varied notions about "equitable" distribution?

To understand what idea is meant in this connection by the phrase "equitable distribution," we must take the first paragraph and this one together. The latter implies a society wherein "the instruments of labor are common property, and

---

1. Marx in 1872 wrote about sectarian socialism in his pamphlet directed against the Bakunists, *Les prétendues scissions dans l'Internationale* [*The Alleged Splits in the International*]: "The first phase in the struggle of the proletariat against the bourgeoisie is marked by the sectarian movement. This is justifiable at a time when the proletariat is not yet sufficiently developed to act as a class. Isolated thinkers subject the social antagonisms to criticism and at the same time give a fantastic solution of them which the mass of the workers have only to accept as complete, to propagate and to put into practical operation. It is in the nature of these sects, which are founded on the initiative of individuals, that they keep themselves aloof and remote from every real activity, from politics, strikes, trade unions, in a word, from every collective movement. The mass of the proletariat always remains indifferent, even hostile, to their propaganda. . . . The sects, at the outset a lever for the movement, become an obstacle as soon as this movement has overtaken them; they then become reactionary. . . . In short, they represented the infancy of the proletarian movement just as astrology and alchemy represented the infancy of science."—*Ed.*

the total labor is cooperatively regulated," and from the first paragraph we learn that "the proceeds of labor belong undiminished with equal right to all members of society."

"To all members of society"? To those who do not work as well? What remains then of the "undiminished proceeds of labor"? Only to those members of society who work? What remains then of the "equal right" of all members of society?

But "all members of society" and "equal right" are obviously mere phrases. The kernel consists in this, that in this communist society every worker must receive the "undiminished" Lassallean "proceeds of labor."

Let us take first of all the words "proceeds of labor" in the sense of the product of labor, then the cooperative proceeds of labor are the *total social product*.

From this is then to be deducted:

Firstly, cover for replacement of the means of production used up.

Secondly, additional portion for expansion of production.

Thirdly, reserve or insurance fund to provide against misadventures, distrubances through natural events, etc.

These deductions from the "undiminished proceeds of labor" are an economic necessity and their magnitude is to be determined by available means and forces, and partly by calculation of probabilities, but they are in no way calculable by equity.

There remains the other part of the total product, destined to serve as means of consumption.

Before this is divided among the individuals, there has to be deducted from it:

Firstly, the general costs of administration not belonging to production.

This part will, from the outset, be very considerably restricted in comparison with present-day society and it diminishes in proportion as the new society develops.

Secondly, that which is destined for the communal satisfaction of needs, such as schools, health services, etc.

From the outset this part is considerably increased in comparison with present-day society and it increases in proportion as the new society develops.

Thirdly, funds for those unable to work, etc., in short, what is included under so-called official poor relief today.

Only now do we come to the "distribution" which the program, under Lassallean influence, alone has in view in its narrow fashion, namely that part of the means of consumption which is divided among the individual producers of the cooperative society.

The "undiminished proceeds of labor" have already quietly become converted into the "diminished" proceeds, although what the producer is deprived of in his capacity as a private individual benefits him directly or indirectly in his capacity as a member of society.

Just as the phrase the "undiminished proceeds of labor" has disappeared, so now does the phrase "proceeds of labor" disappear altogether.

Within the cooperative society based on common ownership of the means of production, the producers do not exchange their products; just as little does the labor employed on the products appear here as *the value* of these products, as a material quality possessed by them, since now, in contrast to capitalist society, individual labor no longer exists in an indirect fashion but directly as a component part of the total labor. The phrase "proceeds of labor," objectionable even today on account of its ambiguity, thus loses all meaning.

What we have to deal with here is a communist society, not as it has *developed* on its own foundations, but, on the contrary, as it *emerges* from capitalist society; which is thus in every respect, economically, morally and intellectually, still stamped with the birthmarks of the old society from whose womb it emerges. Accordingly the individual producer receives back from society—after the deductions have been made—exactly what he gives to it. What he has given to it is his individual amount of labor. For example, the social working day consists of the sum of the individual labor hours; the individual labor time of the individual producer is the part of the social labor day contributed by him, his share in it. He receives a certificate from society that he has furnished such and such an amount of labor (after deducting his labor for the common fund), and with this certificate he draws from the social stock of means of consumption as much as costs the same amount of labor. The same amount of labor which he has given to society in one form, he receives back in another.

Here obviously the same principle prevails as that which regulates the exchange of commodities, as far as this is exchange of equal values. Content and form are changed, because under the altered circumstances no one can give anything except his labor, and because, on the other hand, nothing can pass into the ownership of individuals except individual means of consumption. But, as far as the distribution of the latter among the individual producers is concerned, the same principle prevails as in the exchange of commodity equivalents, so much labor in one form is exchanged for an equal amount of labor in another form.

Hence, *equal right* here is still in principle—*bourgeois right,* although principle and practice are no longer in conflict, while the exchange of equivalents in commodity exchange only exists on the *average* and not in the individual case.

In spite of this advance, this *equal right* is still stigmatized by a bourgeois limitation. The right of the producers is *proportional* to the labor they supply; the equality consists in the fact that measurement is made with an *equal standard,* labor.

But one man is superior to another physically or mentally and so supplies more labor in the same time, or can labor for a longer time; and labor, to serve as a measure, must be defined by its duration or intensity, otherwise it ceases to be a standard of measurement. This *equal* right is an unequal right for unequal labor. It recognizes no class differences, because everyone is only a worker like everyone else; but it tacitly recognizes unequal individual endowment and thus productive capacity as natural privileges. *It is therefore a right of inequality in its content, like every right.* Right by its very nature can only consist in the application of an equal standard; but unequal individuals (and they would not be different individuals if they were not unequal) are only measurable by an equal standard in so far as they are brought under an equal point of view, are taken from one *definite* side only, e.g., in the present case are regarded *only as workers,* and nothing more seen in them, everything else being ignored. Further, one worker is married, another not; one has more children than another and so on and so forth. Thus with an equal output, and hence an equal share in the social consumption fund, one will in fact receive more than another, one will be richer than another, and so on. To avoid all these defects, right instead of being equal would have to be unequal.

But these defects are inevitable in the first phase of communist society as it is when it has just emerged after prolonged birth pangs from capitalist society. Right can never be higher than the economic structure of society and the cultural development thereby determined.

In a higher phase of communist society, after the enslaving subordination of individuals under division of labor, and therewith also the antithesis between mental and physical labor, has vanished, after labor has become not merely a means to live but has become itself the primary necessity of life, after the productive forces have also increased with the all-round development of the individual, and all the springs of cooperative wealth flow more abundantly—only then can the narrow horizon of bourgeois right be fully left behind and society inscribe on its banners: from each according to his ability, to each according to his needs. . . .

Quite apart from the analysis so far given, it was in general incorrect to make a fuss about so-called *distribution* and put the principal stress on it.

The distribution of the means of consumption at any time is only a consequence of the distribution of the conditions of production themselves. The latter distribution, however, is a feature of the mode of production itself. The capitalist mode of production, for example, rests on the fact that the material conditions of production are in the hands of nonworkers in the form of property in capital and land, while the masses are only owners of the personal condition of production, *viz.,* labor power. If the elements of production are so distributed, then the present-day distribution of the means of consumption results automatically. If the material conditions of production are the cooperative property of the workers themselves, then this likewise results in a different distribution of the means of consumption from the present one. Vulgar socialism (and from it in turn a section of democracy) has taken over from the bourgeois economists the consideration and treatment of distribution as independent of the mode of production and hence the presentation of socialism as turning principally on distribution. After the real position has long been made clear, why go back again?

4. "The emancipation of labor must be the work of the working class, in contrast to which all other classes are only . . . *one reactionary mass.*" . . .

In *The Communist Manifesto* it is said: "Of all the classes that stand face to face with the bourgeoisie today, the proletariat alone is a *really revolutionary class.* The other classes decay and finally disappear in the face of modern industry, the proletariat is its special and essential product."

The bourgeoisie is here conceived as a revolutionary class— as the bearer of large-scale industry—in contrast to the feudal lords and middle estates, who desire to maintain all social positions that are the creation of obsolete modes of production. Thus they do not form *together* with the *bourgeoisie* only one reactionary mass.

On the other hand, the proletariat is revolutionary in contrast to the bourgeoisie because, having itself grown up on the basis of large-scale industry, it strives to strip off from production the capitalist character that the bourgeoisie seeks to perpetuate. But the *Manifesto* adds that the "middle class . . . if by chance they are revolutionary, they are so only in view of their impending transfer into the proletariat."

From this point of view, therefore, it is again nonsense to say that they, together with the bourgeoisie, and with the feudal lords into the bargain, "form only one reactionary mass" in relation to the working class. . . .

5. "The working class strives for its emancipation first of all *within the framework of the present-day national state,* conscious that the necessary result of its efforts, which are common

to the workers of all civilized countries, will be the international brotherhood of peoples." . . .

It is altogether self-evident that, to be able to fight at all, the working class must organize itself at home *as a class* and that its own country is the immediate arena of its struggle. In so far as its class struggle is national, not in content, but, as *The Communist Manifesto* says, "in form." But the "framework of the present-day national state," e.g., the German empire, is itself in its turn economically "within the framework" of the world market, politically "within the framework" of the system of states. . . .

And to what does the German Workers' Party reduce its internationalism? To the consciousness that the result of its efforts will be *"the international brotherhood of peoples"*—a phrase borrowed from the bourgeois League of Peace and Freedom, which is intended to pass as equivalent to the international brotherhood of the working classes in the joint struggle against the ruling classes and their governments. Not a word, therefore, *about the international functions* of the German working class! . . .

In fact the international consciousness expressed in the program stands *even infinitely below* that of the Free Trade Party. The latter also asserts that the result of its efforts will be "the international brotherhood of peoples." But it also *does* something to make trade international and by no means contents itself with the consciousness—that all peoples are carrying on trade at home. . . .

"Starting from these basic principles, the German Workers' Party strives by all legal means for the *free state—and—*socialist society; the abolition of the wage system *together with the iron law of wages*—and—exploitation in every form; the removal of all social and political inequality."

I shall return to the "free" state later.

Thus, in future, the German Workers' Party has got to believe in Lassalle's "iron law of wages"! . . .

Quite *apart* from this *false* Lassallean formulation of the law, the truly infuriating retrograde step consists in the following:

Since Lassalle's death the scientific understanding has made progress in *our* party, that wages are not what they *appear* to be, namely, the *value,* or *price, of labor,* but only a masked form for the *value,* or *price, of labor power.* Thereby the whole bourgeois conception of wages hitherto, as well as all the criticism hitherto directed against this conception, was thrown overboard once and for all and it was made clear that the wage worker has permission to work for his own life, i.e., *to live,* only in so far as he works for a certain time gratis for the capitalist (and hence also for the latter's fellow consumers of surplus value); that the whole capitalist system of production turns on the prolongation of this gratis labor by extending the working day or by developing the productivity, or the greater intensity, of labor power, etc., that, consequently, the system of wage labor is a system of slavery, and indeed a slavery which becomes more severe in proportion as the social productive forces of labor develop, whether the worker receives better or worse payment. And after this understanding has more and more made progress in our party, one returns to Lassalle's dogmas, although one must have known that Lassalle *did not know what* wages are, but following in the wake of the bourgeois economists took the appearance for the essence of the matter.

It is as if, among slaves who have at last got behind the secret of slavery and broken out in rebellion, a slave still in thrall to obsolete notions were to inscribe on the program of the rebellion: Slavery must be abolished because the upkeep of slaves in the system of slavery cannot exceed a certain low maximum!

Does not the mere fact that the representatives of our party were capable of perpetrating such a monstrous attack on the understanding that has spread among the mass of our party prove by itself with what criminal levity and with what lack of conscience they set to work in drawing up this compromise program! . . .

I come now to the democratic section.

A. *"The free basis of the state."*

First of all, . . . the German Workers' Party strives for the "free state."

Free state—what is this?

It is by no means the aim of the workers, who have got rid of the narrow mentality of humble subjects, to set the state free. In the German empire the "state" is almost as "free" as in Russia. Freedom consists in converting the state from an organ standing above society into one completely subordinated to it, and today also the forms of the state are more free or less free to the extent that they restrict the "freedom of the state."

The German Workers' Party—at least if it adopts the program—shows that its socialist ideas are not even skin-deep; in that, instead of treating existing society (and this holds good of any future one) as the *basis* of the existing state (or of the future state in the case of future society) it treats the state rather as an independent entity that possesses its own *intellectual, moral and free basis.*

And what of the riotous misuse which the program makes of the words *"present-day state," "present-day society,"* and of the still more riotous misconception that it achieves in regard to the state to which it addresses its demands?

"Present-day society" is capitalist society, which exists in all civilized countries, more or less free from mediaeval admixture, more or less modified by the special historical development of each country and more or less developed. On the other hand, the "present-day state" changes with a country's frontier. It is different in the Prusso-German empire from what it is in Switzerland, it is different in England from what it is in the United States. "The present-day state" is therefore a fiction.

Nevertheless, the different states of the different civilized countries, in spite of their manifold diversity of form, all have this in common that they are based on modern bourgeois society, only one more or less capitalistically developed. They have, therefore, also certain essential features in common. In this sense it is possible to speak of the "present-day state," in contrast to the future in which its present root, bourgeois society, will have died away.

The question then arises: what transformation will the state undergo in communist society? In other words, what social functions will remain in existence there that are analogous to the present function of the state? . . .

Between capitalist and communist society lies the period of the revolutionary transformation of the one into the other. There corresponds to this also a political transition period in which the state can be nothing but *the revolutionary dictatorship of the proletariat.*

28. On the Paris Commune

Marx's *The Civil War in France* (1871) deals with the series of events dating from the Prussian defeat of the French armies in September, 1870, the downfall of Louis Napoleon, the establishment of the Third Republic led by Louis Thiers, that Republic's traitorous dealings with the Prussians, and finally the conquest of the Paris Commune in May, 1871, by the forces of the French Republic. First, Marx traces a brief survey of the political history of France from the Revolution of 1789 in which he portrays the role played by the various social classes and their political representatives for the eighty-two intervening years, and then, in this selection, he describes in detail the characteristics of the Communal organization. It should be emphasized that the Paris Commune represented to Marx the first phase of the successful workers' revolution; that it eventually fell indicated to him only that more such communes would rise in its place.

In the following excerpts, passages enclosed in brackets are taken from Marx's first draft of *The Civil War in France;* those outside the brackets are from the published (third) version.

ON THE DAWN of the 18th of March [1871], Paris arose to the thunderburst of "Vive la Commune!" What is the Commune, that sphinx so tantalizing to the bourgeois mind?

"The proletarians of Paris," said the Central Committee in its manifesto of March 18, "amid the failures and treasons of the

___

From *The Civil War in France* (Peking: Foreign Language Press, 1966).

ruling classes, have understood that the hour has struck for them to save the situation by taking into their own hands the direction of public affairs. . . . They have understood that it is their imperious duty and their absolute right to render themselves masters of their own destinies, by seizing upon the governmental power." But the working class cannot simply lay hold of the ready-made state machinery, and wield it for its own purposes.

The centralized State power, with its ubiquitous organs of standing army, police, bureaucracy, clergy, and judicature—organs wrought after the plan of a systematic and hierarchic division of labor—originates from the days of absolute monarchy, serving nascent middle-class society as a mighty weapon in its struggles against feudalism. Still, its development remained clogged by all manner of medieval rubbish, seignorial rights, local privileges, municipal and guild monopolies and provincial constitutions. The gigantic broom of the French Revolution of the eighteenth century swept away all these relics of bygone times, thus clearing simultaneously the social soil of its last hindrances to the superstructure of the modern State edifice raised under the First Empire [of Napoleon], itself the offspring of the coalition wars of old semifeudal Europe against modern France. During the subsequent regimes the Government, placed under parliamentary control—that is, under the direct control of the propertied classes—became not only a hotbed of huge national debts and crushing taxes; with its irresistible allurements of place, pelf, and patronage, it became not only the bone of contention between the rival factions and adventurers of the ruling classes; but its political character changed simultaneously with the economic changes of society. At the same pace at which the progress of modern industry developed, widened, intensified the class antagonism between capital and labor, the State power assumed more and more the character of the national power of capital over labor, of a public force organized for social enslavement, of an engine of class despotism. After every revolution marking a progressive phase in the class struggle, the purely repressive character of the State power stands out in bolder and bolder relief. The Revolution of

1830, resulting in the transfer of Government from the land-lords to the capitalists, transferred it from the more remote to the more direct antagonists of the working men. The bourgeois Republicans, who, in the name of the Revolution of February [1848], took the State power, used it for the June massacres, in order to convince the working class that "social" republic meant the republic ensuring their social subjection, and in or-der to convince the royalist bulk of the bourgeois and landlord class that they might safely leave the cares and emoluments of government to the bourgeois "Republicans." However, after their one heroic exploit of June, the bourgeois Republicans had, from the front, to fall back to the rear of the "Party of Order" —a combination formed by all the rival fractions and factions of the appropriating class in their now openly declared antago-nism to the producing classes. The proper form of their joint-stock Government was the *Parliamentary Republic*, with Louis Bonaparte for its President. Theirs was a regime of avowed class terrorism and deliberate insult toward the "vile multitude." If the Parliamentary Republic, as M. Thiers said, "divided them (the different fractions of the ruling class) least," it opened an abyss between that class and the whole body of society outside their spare ranks. The restraints by which their own divisions had under former regimes still checked the State power were removed by their union; and in view of the threatening upheaval of the proletariat, they now used that State power mercilessly and ostentatiously as the national war-engine of capital against labor. In their uninterrupted crusade against the producing masses they were, however, bound not only to invest the executive with continually increased powers of repression. . . . The Executive, in the person of Louis Bonaparte, turned them out.[1] The natural offspring of the "Party-of-Order" Republic was the Second Empire.

The empire, with the coup d'état for its certificate of birth, universal suffrage for its sanction, and the sword for its scepter, professed to rest upon the peasantry, the large mass of produc-ers not direcly involved in the struggle of capital and labor. It

1. December 2, 1851—*Ed.*

professed to save the working class by breaking down Parliamentarism, and, with it, the undisguised subserviency of Government to the propertied classes. It professed to save the propertied classes by upholding their economic supremacy over the working class; and, finally, it professed to unite all classes by reviving for all the chimera of national glory. In reality, it was the only form of government possible at a time when the bourgeoisie had already lost, and the working class had not yet acquired, the faculty of ruling the nation. It was acclaimed throughout the world as the savior of society. Under its sway, bourgeois society, freed from political cares, attained a development unexpected even by itself. Its industry and commerce expanded to colossal dimensions; financial swindling celebrated cosmopolitan orgies; the misery of the masses was set off by a shameless display of gorgeous, meretricious and debased luxury. The State power, apparently soaring high above society, was at the same time itself the greatest scandal of that society and the very hotbed of all its corruptions. Its own rottenness, and the rottenness of the society it had saved, were laid bare by the bayonet of Prussia, herself eagerly bent upon transferring the supreme seat of that regime from Paris to Berlin. Imperialism is, at the same time, the most prostitute and the ultimate form of the State power which nascent middle-class society had commenced to elaborate as a means of its own emancipation from feudalism, and which full-grown bourgeois society had finally transformed into a means for the enslavement of labor by capital.

[The 4th of September[2] was only the revindication of the Republic against the grotesque adventurer that had assassinated it. The true antithesis to the *Empire itself*—that is, to the state power, the centralized executive, of which the Second Empire was only the exhausting formula—was *the Commune.* This state power forms in fact the creation of the middle class, first a means to break down feudalism, then a means to crush

---

2. September 4, 1870, the day on which the workingmen of Paris declared the existence of the Third Republic, following the surrender of Napoleon III to Prussia the preceding day—*Ed.*

the emancipatory aspirations of the producers of the working class. All reactions and all revolutions had only served to transfer that organized power—that organized force of the slavery of labor—from one hand to the other, from one fraction of the ruling classes to the other. It had served the ruling classes as a means of subjugation and of pelf. It had sucked new forces from every new change. It had served as the instrument of breaking down every popular rise and served it to crush the working classes after they had fought and been ordered to secure its transfer from one part of its oppressors to the others. This was, therefore, a Revolution not against this or that, legitimate, constitutional, republican or Imperialist form of State Power. It was a Revolution against the *State* itself, of this supernaturalist abortion of society, a resumption by the people for the people of its own social life. It was not a revolution to transfer it from one fraction of the ruling classes to the other, but a Revolution to break down this horrid machinery of class domination itself. It was not one of those dwarfish struggles between the executive and the parliamentary forms of class domination, but a revolt against both these forms, integrating each other, and of which the parliamentary form was only the deceitful bywork of the Executive. The Second Empire was the final form of this State usurpation. The Commune was its definite negation, and, therefore, the initiation of the social revolution of the nineteenth century. Whatever therefore its fate at Paris, it will make *le tour du monde*. It was at once acclaimed by the working class of Europe and the United States as the magic world of delivery. The glories and the antediluvian deeds of the Prussian conqueror seemed only hallucinations of a bygone past.]

The direct antithesis to the empire was the Commune. The cry of "social republic," with which the Revolution of February was ushered in by the Paris proletariat, did but express a vague aspiration after a Republic that was not only to supersede the monarchical form of class rule, but class rule itself. The Commune was the positive form of that Republic.

Paris, the central seat of the old governmental power, and, at the same time, the social stronghold of the French working class, had risen in arms against the attempt of Thiers and the

Rurals[3] to restore and perpetuate that old governmental power bequeathed to them by the empire. Paris could resist only because, in consequence of the siege, it had got rid of the army, and replaced it by a National Guard, the bulk of which consisted of working men. This fact was now to be transformed into an institution. The first decree of the Commune, therefore, was the suppression of the standing army, and the substitution for it of the armed people.

The Commune was formed of the municipal councillors, chosen by universal suffrage in the various wards of the town, responsible and revocable at short terms. The majority of its members were naturally working men, or acknowledged representatives of the working class. The Commune was to be a working, not a parliamentary, body, executive and legislative at the same time. Instead of continuing to be the agent of the Central Government, the police was at once stripped of its political attributes, and turned into the responsible and at all times revocable agent of the Commune. So were the officials of all other branches of the Administration. From the members of the Commune downwards, the public service had to be done at *workmen's wages*. The vested interests and the representation allowances of the high dignitaries of State disappeared along with the high dignitaries themselves. Public functions ceased to be the private property of the tools of the Central Government. Not only municipal administration, but the whole initiative hitherto exercised by the State was laid into the hands of the Commune.

Having once got rid of the standing army and the police, the physical force elements of the old Government, the Commune was anxious to break the spiritual force of repression, the "parson power," by the disestablishment and disendowment of all churches as proprietary bodies. The priests were sent back to the recesses of private life, there to feed upon the alms of the faithful in imitation of their predecessors, the Apostles. The whole of the educational institutions were opened to the people

3. The Parliamentary representatives of the large landowners and provincial bourgeoisie.—*Ed*.

gratuitously, and at the same time cleared of all interference of Church and State. Thus, not only was education made accessible to all, but science itself freed from the fetters which class prejudice and governmental force had imposed upon it.

The judicial functionaries were to be divested of that sham independence which had but served to mask their abject subserviency to all succeeding governments to which, in turn, they had taken, and broken, the oaths of alliegiance. Like the rest of public servants, magistrates and judges were to be elective, responsible and revocable.

The Paris Commune was, of course, to serve as a model to all the great industrial centers of France. The communal regime once established in Paris and the secondary centers, the old centralized Government would in the provinces, too, have to give way to the self-government of the producers. [The Commune—the reabsorption of the State power by society as its own living forces instead of as forces controlling and subduing it, by the popular masses themselves, forming their own force instead of the organized force of their suppression—the political form of their social emancipation, instead of the artificial force (appropriated by their oppressors) (their own force opposed to and organized [one] against them) of society wielded for their oppression by their enemies. The form was simple like all great things.] In a rough sketch of national organization which the Commune had no time to develop, it states clearly that the Commune was to be the political form of even the smallest country hamlet, and that in the rural districts the standing army was to be replaced by a national militia, with an extremely short term of service. The rural communes of every district were to administer their common affairs by an assembly of delegates in the central town, and these district assemblies were again to send deputies to the National Delegation in Paris, each delegate to be at any time revocable and bound by the *mandat impératif* (formal instructions) of his constituents. The few but important functions which still would remain for a central government were not to be suppressed, as has been intentionally misstated, but were to be discharged by Communal, and therefore strictly responsible agents. [The whole sham of state mysteries and state pretensions was done away with by a Commune, mostly consisting of simple working men, organizing the defense of Paris; carrying war against the Pretorians of Bonaparte, securing the approvisionment of that immense town, filling all the posts hitherto divided between Government, police, and Prefecture, doing their work publicly, simply, under the most difficult and complicated circumstances, and doing it . . . for a few pounds, acting in bright daylight, with no pretensions to infallibility, not hiding itself behind circumlocution offices, not ashamed to confess blunders by correcting them. Making in one order the public functions—military, administrative, political— *real workmen's functions,* instead of the hidden attributes of a trained caste (keeping order in the turbulence of civil war and revolution) (initiating measures of general regeneration). Whatever the merits of the single measures of the Commune, its greatest measure was its own organization, extemporized with the Foreign Enemy at one door and the class enemy at the other, proving by its life its vitality, confirming its thesis by its action.] The unity of the nation was not to be broken, but, on the contrary, to be organized by the Communal Constitution, and to become a reality by the destruction of the State power which claimed to be the embodiment of that unity independent of, and superior to, the nation itself, from which it was but a parasitic excrescence. While the merely repressive organs of the old governmental power were to be amputated, its legitimate functions were to be wrested from an authority usurping preeminence over society itself, and restored to the responsible agents of society. Instead of deciding once in three or six years which member of the ruling class was to misrepresent the people, constituted in Communes. . . .

It is generally the fate of completely new historical creations to be mistaken for the counterpart of older and even defunct forms of social life, to which they may bear a certain likeness. Thus, this new Commune, which breaks the modern State power, has been mistaken for a reproduction of the medieval Communes, which first preceded, and afterward became the substratum of, that very State power. The Communal Constitution has been mistaken for an attempt to break up into a federation of small States, as dreamed of by Montesquieu and the Girondins, that unity of great nations which, if originally brought about by political force, has now become a powerful coefficient of social production. The antagonism of the Commune against the State power has been mistaken for an exaggerated form of the ancient struggle against overcentralization. Peculiar historical circumstances may have prevented the classical development, as in France, of the bourgeois form of government, and may have allowed, as in England, to complete the great central State organs by corrupt vestries, jobbing councillors, and ferocious poor-law guardians in the towns, and virtually hereditary magistrates in the counties. The Communal Constitution would have restored to the social body all the forces hitherto absorbed by the State parasite feeding upon, and clogging the free movement of, society. By this one act it would have initiated the regeneration of France. [With all the great towns organized into Communes after the model of Paris, no government could repress the movement by the surprise of sudden reaction. Even by this preparatory step the time of incubation, the guarantee of the movement, came. All France organized into self-working and self-governing communes, the standing army replaced by the popular militias, the army of state parasites removed, the clerical hierarchy displaced by the schoolmaster, the state judge transformed into Communal organs, the suffrage for the National representation not a matter of sleight of hand for an all-powerful government but the deliberate expression of organized communes, the state functions reduced to a few functions for general national purposes.] The provincial French middle class saw in the Commune an attempt to restore the sway their order had held over the country under Louis Philippe,[4] and which, under Louis Napoleon, was supplanted by the pretended rule of the country over the towns. In reality, the Communal Constitution brought the rural producers under the intellectual lead of the central towns of their districts, and there secured to them, in the working men,

4. Refers to the rule of Louis Phillipe, Duc d'Orléans, from July, 1830–February, 1848, sometimes called "July Monarchy."—*Ed*.

the natural trustees of their interests. The very existence of the Commune involved, as a matter of course, local municipal liberty, but no longer as a check upon the now superseded State power. . . . The Commune made that catchword of bourgeois revolutions, cheap government, a reality, by destroying the two greatest sources of expenditure—the standing army and State functionarism. [On its (the National Guard's) existing military organization it grafted a political federation according to a very simple plan. It was the alliance of all the guard nationale, put in connection the one with the other *by the delegates* of each company, appointing in their turn the delegates of the *bataillons*, who in their turn appointed general delegates, generals of legions, who were to represent an arrondissement and to cooperate with the delegates of the 19 other arrondissements. Those 20 delegates, chosen by the majority of the *bataillons* of the National Guard, composed the *Central Committee*, which on March 18 initiated the greatest revolution of this century and still holds its post in the present glorious struggle of Paris. Never were elections more sifted, never delegates fuller representing the masses from which they had sprung. To the objection of the outsiders that they were unknown—in point of fact, that they only were known to the working classes, but no old stagers, no men illustrious by the infamies of their past, by their chase after pelf and place—they proudly answered: "So were the twelve Apostles," and they answered by their deeds.] Its very existence presupposed the nonexistence of monarchy, which, in Europe at least, is the normal incumbrance and indispensable cloak of class rule. It supplied the Republic with the basis of really democratic institutions. But neither cheap government nor the "true Republic" was its ultimate aim; they were its mere concomitants.

The multiplicity of interpretations to which the Commune has been subjected, and the multiplicity of interest which construed it in their favor, show that it was a thoroughly expansive political form, while all previous forms of government had been emphatically repressive. Its true secret was this. It was essentially a working-class government, the produce of the struggle of the producing against the appropriating class, the political form at last discovered under which to work out the economic emancipation of labor.

[Such is the *Commune—the political form of the social emancipation,* of the liberation of labor from the usurpations (slaveholding) of the monopolists of the means of labor, created by the laborers themselves or forming the gift of nature. . . . The Commune is not the social movement of the working class and therefore of a general regeneration of mankind, but the organized means of action. The Commune does not do away with the class struggles, through which the working classes strive to the abolition of all classes and, therefore, of all classes (class rule) (because it does not represent a peculiar interest. It represents the liberation of "labor," that is the fundamental and natural condition of individual and social life which only by usurpation, fraud, and artificial contrivances can be shifted from the few upon the many), but it affords the rational medium in which that class struggle can run through its different phases in the most rational and humane way. It begins the *emancipation of labor*—its great goal—by doing away with the unproductive and mischievous work of the state parasites, by cutting away the springs which sacrifice an immense portion of the national produce to the feeding of the state monster on the one side, by doing, on the other, the real work of administration, local and national, for working men's wages. It begins therefore with an immense saving, with economical reform as well as political transformation.]

Except on this last condition, the Communal Constitution would have been an impossibility and a delusion. The political rule of the producer cannot coexist with the perpetuation of his social slavery. The Commune was therefore to serve as a lever for uprooting the economical foundations upon which rests the existence of classes, and therefore a class rule. With labor emancipated, every man becomes a working man, and productive labor ceases to be a class attribute.

It is a strange fact. In spite of all the tall talk and all the immense literature, for the last sixty years, about Emancipation of Labor, no sooner do the working men anywhere take the subject into their own hands with a will than uprises at once all the apologetic phraseology of the mouthpieces of present society with its two poles of Capital and Wages-slavery (the landlord now is but the sleeping partner of the capitalist), as if capitalist society was still in its purest state of virgin innocence, with its antagonisms still undeveloped, with its delusions still unexploded, with its prostitute realities not yet laid bare. The Commune, they exclaim, intends to abolish property, the basis of all civilization! Yes, gentlemen, the Commune intended to abolish that class property which makes the labor of the many the wealth of the few. It aimed at the expropriation of the expropriators. It wanted to make individual property a truth by transforming the means of production, land and capital, now chiefly the means of enslaving and exploiting labor, into mere instruments of free and associated labor. But this is Communism, "impossible" Communism! Why, those members of the ruling classes who are intelligent enough to perceive the impossibility of continuing the present system—and they are many— have become the obtrusive and full-mouthed apostles of cooperative production. If cooperative production is not to remain a sham and a snare; if it is to supersede the Capitalist system; if united cooperative societies are to regulate national production upon a common plan, thus taking it under their own control, and putting an end to the constant anarchy and periodical convulsions which are the fatality of Capitalist production— what else, gentlemen, would it be but Communism, "possible" Communism?

The working class did not expect miracles from the Commune. They have no ready-made utopias to introduce *par décret du peuple*. They know that in order to work out their own emancipation, and along with it that higher form to which present society is irresistibly tending by its own economical agencies, they will have to pass through long struggles, through a series of historic processes, transforming circumstances and men. They have no ideals to realize, but to set free the elements of the new society with which old collapsing bourgeois society itself is pregnant. . . .

If the Commune was thus the true representative of all the

healthy elements of French society, and therefore the truly national Government, it was, at the same time, as a working men's Government, as the bold champion of the emancipation of labor, emphatically international. [There exists of course in France as in most continental countries a deep antagonism between the townish and rural producers, between the industrial proletariat and the peasantry. The aspirations of the proletariat, the material basis of its movement, is labor organized on a grand scale, although now despotically organized and the means of production centralized, although now centralized in the hands of the monopolist, not only as a means of production, but as a means of the exploitation and enslavement of the producer. What the proletariat has to do is to transform the present capitalist character of that organized labor and those centralized means of labor, to transform them from the means of class rule and class exploitation into forms of free associated labor and social means of production. On the other hand, the labor of the peasant is insulated and the means of production are parceled, dispersed. On these economical differences rests superconstructed a whole world of different social and political views. But this peasantry proprietorship has long since outgrown its normal phase, that is, the phase in which it was a reality, a mode of production and a form of property which responded to the economical wants of society and placed the rural producers themselves into normal conditions of life. It has entered its period of decay. On the one side a large *proletariat foncier* (rural proletariat) has grown out of it whose interests, are identical with those of the townish wages laborers. The mode of production itself has become superannuated by the modern progress of agronomy. Lastly—the peasant proprietorship itself has become nominal, leaving to the peasant the delusion of proprietorship and expropriating him from the fruits of his own labor. The competition of the great farm producers, the bloodtax, the state tax, the usury of the townish mortgagee and the multitudinous pilfering of the judiciary system thrown around him, have degraded him to the position of a Hindu Ryot, while expropriation—even expropriation from his nominal proprietorship—and his degradation into a rural proletarian is an everyday fact. What separates the peasant from the proletarian is, therefore, no longer his real interest, but his delusive prejudice. If the Commune, as we have shown, is the only power that can give him immediate great loans even in its present economical conditions, it is the only form of government that can secure to him the transformation of his present economical conditions, rescue him from expropriation by the landlord on the one hand, save him from grinding, trudging and misery on the pretext of proprietorship on the other, that can convert his nominal proprietorship of the land into real proprietorship of the fruits of his labor, that can combine for him the profits of modern agronomy, dictated by social wants and every day now encroaching upon him as a hostile agency, without annihilating his position as a really independent producer. Being immediately benefited by the Communal Republic, he would soon confide in it.] Within sight of the Prussian army, that had annexed to Germany two French provinces, the Commune annexed to France the working people all over the world.

VI.

The Theoretical Analysis of Capitalism (1857–1883)

Marx devoted the last thirty-five years of his life to preparing his *Critique of Political Economy*. Actually, this work was never completed and was only partially published during Marx's lifetime. As early as 1848 he delivered a series of lectures on the subject of *Wage Labor and Capital* to the German Workers' Association in Brussels (whence he had gone when expelled from Paris in 1845), and in 1859 he published *A Contribution to the Critique of Political Economy*. In 1865 he gave a major address entitled "Value, Price and Profit," and he published the first volume of *Capital* in 1867. In addition, the mass of economic manuscripts which have come to light after Marx's death in 1883 have included his *Grundrisse zu einer Kritik der politischen Ökonomie* (1857–1858), the second and third volumes of *Capital*, edited and published by Engels in 1885 and 1894, as well as a further mass of manuscripts published by Karl Kautsky as *Theories of Surplus Value* (1905–1910). Necessarily, any selection from these writings can do scant justice to Marx's painstaking labors in this field.

The first three selections below present Marx's general analysis of the capitalist process of production as developed in 1857–1858, which was discovered in his papers and subsequently published under the title *Grundrisse der Kritik der politischen Ökonomie*.

In general, the reader might best consider the *Grundrisse* as an outline and draft version of the technical arguments ulti-

mately used in *Capital,* minus the latter work's incisive historical and statistical analyses, as well as its gripping style. On the
other hand, one does find in the *Grundrisse* a discussion of
precapitalist economic systems (cf. Selection 22, above) and of
the capitalistic economic system as a whole, that is, a study
of the interrelations of the component parts of that system,
for example, production, distribution, exchange, and consumption (cf. Selections 29, 30, 31, below).

Marx's major work in the field of economics is, of course, his
three-volume *Capital;* his other works in this area may all be
viewed as preparations for, or popularizations of themes in, the
magnum opus. *Capital* is distinguished from academic treatises
of political economy by its being firmly based upon the Marxian
philosophy, and thus differs radically from the abstract and dis-
interested presentation of material characteristic of "objective"
treatises. The "scientific" aspect of Marx's work lies in (a) its
application of the dialectical and historical, rather than analyti-
cal, method, and (b) its incisive questioning of the very funda-
mentals of capitalism, that is, of critically exposing that system's
philosophical presuppositions and unquestioned assumptions.
Thus, in addition to being an analysis of the capitalist process of
production, *Capital* is equally a *critique* of political economy as
a science. As Marx's approach is predicated upon a commitment
to the overcoming of capitalism, he is primarily interested in
illustrating the dialectical necessity of the transition of that
system into socialism. Because of these fundamental differences
from the academic approach, *Capital* has been consistently
misunderstood as "unscientific" by those who dogmatically assert the purity of their own method; or, alternatively, has been
uncritically accepted by those who, for various reasons, accept
the Marxian philosophy and regard any utterances of Marx as
unquestionably true.

To avoid both these misinterpretations, the selections from
Capital have been chosen to present Marx's theoretical model
of the capitalist production process in its essentials, care having
been taken to avoid all references to complications and subtleties characteristic of actual economic conditions. The reader
who seeks to explore Marx's more detailed formulations is encouraged to refer to the complete text.

29. Production in General

This first selection from the *Grundrisse* discusses the problem of relating the process of production to the stage of social
development of the society in question. This contrasts with
the procedure of the classical political economists, who attempted merely to study production "as such." The latter, in
effect, is only a study of one particular historically given type
of production, namely the capitalist one. Thus Marx is here
criticizing the basically ahistorical character of his predecessors in political economy.

THE SUBJECT of our discussion is first of all *material* production
by individuals as determined by society, naturally constitutes
the starting point. The individual and isolated hunter or fisher
who forms the starting point with Smith and Ricardo belongs
to the insipid illusions of the eighteenth century. They are
Robinsonades which do not by any means represent, as students
of the history of civilization imagine, a reaction against over-
refinement and a return to a misunderstood natural life. They
are no more based on such a naturalism than is Rousseau's
"contrat social," which makes naturally independent individuals come in contact and have mutual intercourse by contract.
They are the fiction and only the aesthetic fiction of the small
and great Robinsonades. They are, moreover, the anticipation of
"bourgeois society," which had been in course of development

From *Grundrisse*, first published in English in Karl Marx, *A Contribution to
the Critique of Political Economy* (Chicago: Charles Kerr, 1904).

since the sixteenth century and made gigantic strides towards maturity in the eighteenth. In this society of free competition the individual appears free from the bonds of nature, etc., which in former epochs of history made him a part of a definite, limited human conglomeration. To the prophets of the eighteenth century, on whose shoulders Smith and Ricardo are still standing, this eighteenth-century individual, constituting the joint product of the dissolution of the feudal form of society and of the new forces of production which had developed since the sixteenth century, appears as an ideal whose existence belongs to the past; not as a result of history, but as its starting point.

Since that individual appeared to be in conformity with nature and [corresponded] to their conception of human nature, [he was regarded] not as a product of history, but of nature. This illusion has been characteristic of every new epoch in the past. ... The further back we go into history, the more the individual and, therefore, the producing individual seems to depend on and constitute a part of a larger whole: at first it is, quite naturally, the family and the clan, which is but an enlarged family; later on, it is the community growing up in its different forms out of the clash and the amalgamation of clans. It is but in the eighteenth century, in "bourgeois society," that the different forms of social union confront the individual as a mere means to his private ends, as an outward necessity. But the period in which this view of the isolated individual becomes prevalent is the very one in which the interrelations of society (general from this point of view) have reached the highest state of development. Man is in the most literal sense of the word a *zoon politikon*, not only a social animal, but an animal which can develop into an individual only in society. Production by isolated individuals outside of society—something which might happen as an exception to a civilized man who by accident got into the wilderness and already dynamically possessed within himself the forces of society—is as great an absurdity as the idea of the development of language without individuals living together and talking to one another. ...

Whenever we speak, therefore, of production, we always have in mind production at a certain stage of social development, or production by social individuals. Hence, it might seem that in order to speak of production at all, we must either trace the historical process of development through its various phases, or declare at the outset that we are dealing with a certain historical period, as, e.g., with modern capitalistic production which, as a matter of fact, constitutes the subject proper of this work. But all stages of production have certain landmarks in common, common purposes. *Production in general* is an abstraction, but it is a rational abstraction, in so far as it singles out and fixes the common features, thereby saving us repetition. Yet these general or common features discovered by comparison constitute something very complex, whose constituent elements have different destinations. Some of these elements belong to all epochs, others are common to a few. Some of them are common to the most modern as well as to the most ancient epochs. No production is conceivable without them; but while even the most completely developed languages have laws and conditions in common with the least developed ones, what is characteristic of their development are the points of departure from the general and common. The conditions which generally govern production must be differentiated in order that the essential point of difference be not lost sight of in view of the general uniformity which is due to the fact that the subject, mankind, and the object, nature, remain the same. The failure to remember this one fact is the source of all the wisdom of modern economists who are trying to prove the eternal nature and harmony of existing social conditions. Thus they say, e.g., that no production is possible without some instrument of production, let that instrument be only the hand; that none is possible without past accumulated labor, even if that labor consists of mere skill which has been accumulated and concentrated in the hand of the savage by repeated exercise. Capital is, among other things, also an instrument of production, also past impersonal labor. Hence capital is a universal, eternal natural phenomenon; which is true if we disregard the specific properties which turn an "instrument of production" and "stored up labor" into capital. . . .

If there is no production in general, there is also no general production. Production is always some special branch of production or an aggregate, as, e.g., agriculture, stock raising, manufactures, etc. . . .

Finally, production is not only a special kind. It is always a certain body politic, a social personality that is engaged on a larger or smaller aggregate of branches of production. . . . [We must thus distinguish between] production in general, special branches of production and production as a whole.

It is the fashion with economists to open their works with a general introduction, which is entitled "production" (see, e.g., John Stuart Mill) and deals with the general "requisites of production."

This general introductory part treats or is supposed to treat: (1) of the conditions without which production is impossible, i.e., of the most essential conditions of production. As a matter of fact, however, it dwindles down, as we shall see, to a few very simple definitions, which flatten out into shallow tautologies; (2) of conditions which further production more or less, as, e.g., Adam Smith's [discussion of] a progressive and stagnant state of society.

In order to give scientific value to what serves with him as a mere summary, it would be necessary to study the *degree of productivity* by periods in the development of individual nations; such a study falls outside of the scope of the present subject, and in so far as it does belong here is to be brought out in connection with the discussion of competition, accumulation, etc. The commonly accepted view of the matter gives a general answer to the effect that an industrial nation is at the height of its production at the moment when it reaches its historical climax in all respects. Or, that certain races, climates, natural conditions, such as distance from the sea, fertility of the soil, etc., are more favorable to production than others. That again comes down to the tautology that the facility of creating wealth depends on the extent to which its elements are present both subjectively and objectively. As a matter of fact a nation is at its industrial height so long as its main object is not gain, but the process of gaining. In that respect the Yankees stand above the English.

But all that is not what the economists are really after in the general introductory part. Their object is rather to represent production in contradistinction to distribution—see Mill, e.g.— as subject to eternal laws independent of history, and then to substitute bourgeois relations, in an underhand way, as immutable natural laws of society *in abstracto*. This is the more or less conscious aim of the entire proceeding. On the contrary, when it comes to distribution, mankind is supposed to have indulged in all sorts of arbitrary action. Quite apart from the fact that they violently break the ties which bind production and distribution together, so much must be clear from the outset: that, no matter how greatly the systems of distribution may vary at different stages of society, it should be possible here, as in the case of production, to discover the common features and to confound and eliminate all historical differences in formulating *general human* laws. E.g., the slave, the serf, the wage worker —all receive a quantity of food, which enables them to exist as slave, serf, and wage worker. The conqueror, the official, the landlord, the monk, or the levite, who respectively live on tribute, taxes, rent, alms, and the tithe—all receive [a part] of the social product which is determined by laws different from those which determine the part received by the slave, etc. The two main points which all economists place under this head, are: first, property; second, the protection of the latter by the administration of justice, police, etc. The objections to these two points can be stated very briefly.

1. All production is appropriation of nature by the individual within and through a definite form of society. In that sense it is a tautology to say that property (appropriation) is a condition of production. But it becomes ridiculous, when from that one jumps at once to a definite form of property, e.g., private property (which implies, besides, as a prerequisite the existence of an opposite form, viz., absence of property). History points rather to common property (e.g., among the Hindus, Slavs, ancient Celts, etc.) as the primitive form, which still plays an important part at a much later period as communal property. The question as to whether wealth grows more rapidly under this or that form of property is not even raised here as yet. But

that there can be no such a thing as production, nor, consequently, society, where property does not exist in any form, is a tautology. Appropriation which does not appropriate is a *contradictio in subjecto.*

2. Protection of property, etc. Reduced to their real meaning, these commonplaces express more than what their preachers know, namely, that every form of production creates its own legal relations, forms of government, etc. The crudity and the shortcomings of the conception lie in the tendency to see but an accidental reflective connection in what constitutes an organic union. The bourgeois economists have a vague notion that it is better to carry on production under the modern police, than it was, e.g., under club law. They forget that club law is also law, and that the right of the stronger continues to exist in other forms even under their "government of law."

When the social conditions corresponding to a certain stage of production are in a state of formation or disappearance, disturbances of production naturally arise, although differing in extent and effect.

To sum up: all the stages of production have certain destinations in common, which we generalize in thought; but the so-called general conditions of all production are nothing but abstract conceptions which do not go to make up any real stage in the history of production.

30. The General Relation of Production to Distribution, Exchange, and Consumption

In this second selection from the *Grundrisse*, Marx presents his thesis that in all historical forms of society the process of production takes precedence over the relations of exchange, distribution, and consumption, and that economic science must concentrate its efforts upon the preeminent role of production (although Marx, of course, indicates certain reciprocal effects). It is the ability to find the determining factor among these four apparently mutually conditioning factors which established Marx's economics as unique within political economy up to his time.

BEFORE GOING into a further analysis of production, it is necessary to look at the various divisions which economists put side by side with it. The most shallow conception is as follows: By production, the members of society appropriate (produce and shape) the products of nature to human wants; distribution determines the proportion in which the individual participates in this production; exchange brings him the particular products into which he wishes to turn the quantity secured by him through distribution; finally, through consumption the products become objects of use and enjoyment, of individual appropriation. Production yields goods adopted to our needs; distribution distributes them according to social laws; exchange distributes

From *Grundrisse*, first published in English in Marx, *A Contribution to the Critique of Political Economy* (Chicago: Charles Kerr, 1904).

further what has already been distributed, according to individual wants; finally, in consumption the product drops out of the social movement, becoming the direct object of the individual want which it serves and satisfies in use. Production thus appears as the starting point; consumption as the final end; and distribution and exchange as the middle; the latter has a double aspect, distribution being defined as a process carried on by society, while exchange, as one proceeding from the individual. In production the person is embodied in things; in [consumption] things are embodied in persons; in distribution, society assumes the part of go-between of production and consumption in the form of generally prevailing rules; in exchange this is acomplished by the accidental make-up of the individual.

Distribution determines what proportion (quantity) of the products the individual is to receive; exchange determines the products in which the individual desires to receive his share allotted to him by distribution.

Production, distribution, exchange, and consumption thus form a perfect connection, production standing for the general, distribution and exchange for the special, and consumption for the individual, in which all are joined together. To be sure this is a connection, but it does not go very deep. Production is determined [according to the economists] by universal natural laws, while distribution depends on social change: distribution can, therefore, have a more or less stimulating effect on production: exchange lies between the two as a formal (?) social movement, and the final act of consumption which is considered not only as a final purpose, but also as a final aim, falls, properly, outside of the scope of economics, except in so far as it reacts on the starting point and causes the entire process to begin all over again.

The opponents of the economists—whether economists themselves or not—who reproach them with tearing apart, like barbarians, what is an organic whole, either stand on common ground with them or are *below* them. Nothing is more common than the charge that the economists have been considering production as an end in itself, too much to the exclusion of everything else. The same has been said with regard to distribution. This accusation is itself based on the economic conception that distribution exists side by side with production as a self-contained, independent sphere. Or [they are accused] that the various factors are not treated by them in their connection as a whole. As though it were the textbooks that impress this separation upon life and not life upon the textbooks; and the subject at issue were a dialectic balancing of conceptions and not an analysis of real conditions.

a. Production is at the same time also consumption. Twofold consumption, subjective and objective. The individual who develops his faculties in production is also expending them, consuming them in the act of production, just as procreation is in its way a consumption of vital powers. In the second place, production is consumption of means of production which are used and used up and partly (as, e.g., in burning) reduced to their natural elements. The same is true of the consumption of raw materials which do not remain in their natural form and state, being greatly absorbed in the process. The act of production is, therefore, in all its aspects an act of consumption as well. But this is admitted by economists. Production as directly identical with consumption, consumption as directly coincident with production, they call productive consumption. . . . But this definition of productive consumption is resorted to just for the purpose of distinguishing between consumption as identical with production and consumption proper, which is defined as its destructive counterpart. Let us then consider consumption proper.

Consumption is directly also production, just as in nature the consumption of the elements and of chemical matter constitutes production of plants. It is clear that in nutrition, e.g., which is but one form of consumption, man produces his own body; but it is equally true of every kind of consumption, which goes to produce the human being in one way or another. [It is] consumptive production. But, say the economists, this production which is identical with consumption is a second production resulting from the destruction of the product of the first. In the first, the producer transforms himself into things; in the second, things are transformed into human beings. Consequently, this

consumptive production—although constituting a direct unity
of production and consumption—differs essentially from production proper. The direct unity in which production coincides
with consumption, and consumption with production, does not
interfere with their direct duality.

Production is thus at the same time consumption, and consumption is at the same time production. Each is directly its
own counterpart. But at the same time an intermediary movement goes on between the two. Production furthers consumption by creating material for the latter which otherwise would
lack its object. But consumption in its turn furthers production,
by providing for the products the individual for whom they are
products. The product receives its last finishing touches in consumption. . . . Without production, no consumption; but, on the
other hand, without consumption, no production; since production would then be without a purpose. Consumption produces
production in two ways.

In the first place, in that the product first becomes a real
product in consumption; e.g., a garment becomes a real garment only through the act of being worn; a dwelling which is
not inhabited is really no dwelling; consequently, a product as
distinguished from a mere natural object proves to be such, first
becomes a product in consumption. Consumption gives the
product the finishing touch by annihilating it, since a product
is the [result] of production not only as the material embodiment of activity, but also as a mere object for the active subject.

In the second place, consumption produces production by
creating the necessity for new production, i.e., by providing the
ideal, inward, impelling cause which constitutes the prerequisite of production. Consumption furnishes the impulse for production as well as its object, which plays in production the part
of its guiding aim. It is clear that while production furnishes the
material object of consumption, consumption provides the ideal
object of production, as its image, its want, its impulse and its
purpose. It furnishes the object of production in its subjective
form. No wants, no production. But consumption reproduces
the want.

In its turn, production:

First, furnishes consumption with its material, its object. Consumption without an object is no consumption, hence production works in this direction by producing consumption.

Second. But it is not only the object that production provides for consumption. It gives consumption its definite outline, its character, its finish. Just as consumption gives the product its finishing touch as a product, production puts the finishing touch on consumption. For the object is not simply an object in general, but a definite object, which is consumed in a certain definite manner prescribed in its turn by production. Hunger is hunger; but the hunger that is satisfied with cooked meat eaten with fork and knife is a different kind of hunger from the one that devours raw meat with the aid of hands, nails, and teeth. Not only the object of consumption, but also the manner of consumption, is produced by production; that is to say, consumption is created by production not only objectively, but also subjectively. Production thus creates the consumers.

Third. Production not only supplies the want with material, but supplies the material with a want. When consumption emerges from its first stage of natural crudeness and directness —and its continuation in that state would in itself be the result of a production still remaining in a state of natural crudeness— it is itself furthered by its object as a moving spring. The want of it which consumption experiences is created by its appreciation of the product. The object of art, as well as any other product, creates an artistic and beauty-enjoying public. Production thus produces not only an object for the individual, but also an individual for the object.

Production thus produces consumption: first, by furnishing the latter with material; second, by determining the manner of consumption; third, by creating in consumers a want for its products as objects of consumption. It thus produces the object, the manner, and the moving spring of consumption. In the same manner, consumption [creates] the *disposition* of the producer by setting (?) him up as an aim and by stimulating wants. The identity of consumption and production thus appears to be a threefold one.

First. Direct identity: production is consumption; consumption is production. Consumptive production. Productive consumption. Economists call both productive consumption, but make one distinction by calling the former reproduction, and the latter productive consumption. All inquiries into the former deal with productive and unproductive labor; those into the latter treat of productive and unproductive consumption.

Second. Each appears as the means of the other and as being brought about by the other, which is expressed as their mutual interdependence; a relation by virtue of which they appear as mutually connected and indispensable, yet remaining outside of each other.

Production creates the material as the outward object of consumption; consumption creates the want as the inward object, the purpose of production. Without production, no consumption; without consumption, no production; this maxim figures in political economy in many forms.

Third. Production is not only directly consumption and consumption directly production; nor is production merely a means of consumption and consumption the purpose of production. . . . Consumption completes the act of production by giving the finishing touch to the product as such, by destroying the latter, by breaking up its independent material form; by bringing to a state of readiness, through the necessity of repetition, the disposition to produce developed in the first act of production; that is to say, it is not only the concluding act through which the product becomes a product, but also [the one] through which the producer becomes a producer. On the other hand, production produces consumption, by determining the manner of consumption, and further, by creating the incentive for consumption, the very ability to consume, in the form of want. . . .

Hence, it is the simplest matter with a Hegelian to treat production and consumption as identical. And this has been done not only by socialist writers of fiction but even by economists, e.g., Say. . . . The important point to be emphasized here is that if production and consumption be considered as activities of one individual or of separate individuals, they appear at any rate as aspects of one process in which production forms the actual starting point and is, therefore, the predominating factor. Consumption, as a natural necessity, as a want, constitutes an internal factor of productive activity, but the latter is the starting point of realization and, therefore, its predominating factor, the act into which the entire process resolves itself in the end. The individual produces a certain article and turns again into himself by consuming it; but he returns as a productive and a self-reproducing individual. Consumption thus appears as a factor of production.

In society, however, the relation of the producer to his product, as soon as it is completed, is an outward one, and the return of the product to the individual depends on his relations to other individuals. He does not take immediate possession of it. Nor does the direct appropriation of the product constitute his purpose, when he produces in society. Between the producer and the product distribution steps in, which determines by social laws his share in the world of products; that is to say, distribution steps in between production and consumption.

Does distribution form an independent sphere standing side by side with and outside of production?

b. Production and Distribution. In perusing the common treatises on economics one can not help being struck with the fact that everything is treated there twice; e.g., under distribution, there figure rent, wages, interest, and profit; while under production we find land, labor and capital as agents of production. As regards capital, it is at once clear that it is counted twice: first, as an agent of production; second, as a source of income; as determining factors and definite forms of distribution, interest and profit figure as such also in production, since they are forms, in which capital increases and grows, and are consequently factors of its own production. Interest and profit, as forms of distribution, imply the existence of capital as an agent of production. They are forms of distribution which have for their prerequisite capital as an agent of production. They are also forms of reproduction of capital.

In the same manner, wages is wage labor when considered under another head; the definite character which labor has in one case as an agent of production appears in the other as a form of distribution. If labor were not fixed as wage labor, its manner of participation in distribution would not appear as wages, as is the case, e.g., under slavery. Finally, rent—to take at once the most developed form of distribution—by means of which landed property receives its share of the products, implies the existence of large landed property (properly speaking, agriculture on a large scale) as an agent of production, and not simply land, no more than wages represents simply labor. The relations and methods of distribution appear, therefore, merely as the reverse sides of the agents of production. An individual who participates in production as a wage laborer receives his share of the products, i.e., of the results of production, in the form of wages. The subdivisions and organization of distribution are determined by the subdivisions and organization of production. Distribution is itself a product of production, not only in so far as the material goods are concerned, since only the results of production can be distributed; but also as regards its form, since the definite manner of participation in production determines the particular form of distribution, the form under which participation in distribution takes place. It is quite an illusion to place land under production, rent under distribution, etc. . . .

To the single individual distribution naturally appears as a law established by society determining his position in the sphere of production, within which he produces, and thus antedating production. At the outset the individual has no capital, no landed property. From his birth he is assigned to wage labor by the social process of distribution. But this very condition of being assigned to wage labor is the result of the existence of capital and landed property as independent agents of production.

From the point of view of society as a whole, distribution seems to antedate and to determine production in another way as well, as a pre-economic fact, so to say. A conquering people divides the land among the conquerors, establishing thereby a certain division and form of landed property and determining the character of production; or, it turns the conquered people into slaves and thus makes slave labor the basis of production. Or, a nation, by revolution, breaks up large estates into small parcels of land and by this new distribution imparts to production a new character. Or, legislation perpetuates land ownership in large families or distributes labor as a hereditary privilege and thus fixes it in castes.

In all of these cases, and they are all historic, it is not distribution that seems to be organized and determined by production, but on the contrary, production by distribution.

In the most shallow conception of distribution, the latter appears as a distribution of products and to that extent as further removed from and quasi-independent of production. But before distribution means distribution of products, it is first, a distribution of the means of production, and second, what is practically another wording of the same fact, it is a distribution of the members of society among the various kinds of production (the subjection of individuals to certain conditions of production). The distribution of products is manifestly a result of this distribution, which is bound up with the process of production and determines the very organization of the latter. To treat of production apart from the distribution which is comprised in it, is plainly an idle abstraction. Conversely, we know the character of the distribution of products the moment we are given the nature of that other distribution which forms originally a factor of production. . . .

All of these questions resolve themselves in the last instance to this: How do general historical conditions affect production and what part does it play at all in the course of history? It is evident that this question can be taken up only in connection with the discussion and analysis of production.

Yet in the trivial form in which these questions are raised above, they can be answered just as briefly. In the case of all conquests three ways lie open. The conquering people may impose its own methods of production upon the conquered (e.g., the English in Ireland in the nineteenth century, partly also in India); or, it may allow everything to remain as it was contenting itself with tribute (e.g., the Turks and the Romans); or, the two systems by mutually modifying each other may result in something new, a synthesis (which partly resulted from the Germanic conquests). In all of these conquests the method of production, be it of the conquerors, the conquered, or the one resulting from a combination of both, determines the nature of the new distribution which comes into play. Although the latter appears now as the prerequisite condition of the new period of production, it is in itself but a product of production, not of production belonging to history in general, but of production relating to a definite historical period. The Mongols with their devastations in Russia, e.g., acted in accordance with their system of production, for which sufficient pastures on large uninhabited stretches of country are the main prerequisite. The Germanic barbarians, with whom agriculture carried on with the aid of serfs was the traditional system of production and who were accustomed to lonely life in the country, could introduce the same conditions in the Roman provinces so much easier since the concentration of landed property which had taken place there, did away completely with the older systems of agriculture. There is a prevalent tradition that in certain periods robbery constituted the only source of living. But in order to be able to plunder, there must be something to plunder, i.e., there must be production. And even the method of plunder is determined by the method of production. A stockjobbing nation, e.g., cannot be robbed in the same manner as a nation of shepherds. . . .

c. Exchange and Circulation. Circulation is but a certain aspect of exchange, or it may be defined as exchange considered as a whole. Since *exchange* is an intermediary factor between production and its dependent, distribution, on the one hand, and consumption, on the other; and since the latter appears but as a constituent of production, exchange is manifestly also a constituent part of production.

In the first place, it is clear that the exchange of activities and abilities which takes place in the sphere of production falls directly within the latter and constitutes one of its essential elements. In the second place, the same is true of the exchange of products, in so far as it is a means of completing a certain product, designed for immediate consumption. To that extent exchange constitutes an act included in production. Thirdly, the so-called exchange between dealers and dealers is by virtue of its organization determined by production, and is itself a species of productive activity. Exchange appears to be independent of and indifferent to production only in the last stage when products are exchanged directly for consumption. But in the first place, there is no exchange without a division of labor, whether natural or as a result of historical development; secondly, private exchange implies the existence of private production; thirdly, the intensity of exchange, as well as its extent and character are determined by the degree of development and organization of production, as, e.g., exchange between city and country, exchange in the country, in the city, etc. Exchange thus appears in all its aspects to be directly included in or determined by production.

The result we arrive at is not that production, distribution, exchange and consumption are identical, but that they are all members of one entity, different sides of one unit. Production predominates not only over production itself in the opposite sense of that term, but over the other elements as well. With it the process constantly starts over again. That exchange and consumption cannot be the predominating elements is self-evident. The same is true of distribution in the narrow sense of distribution of products; as for distribution in the sense of distribution of the agents of production, it is itself but a factor of production. A definite [form of] production thus determines the [forms of] consumption, distribution, exchange and *also the mutual relations between these various elements.* Of course, production *in its one-sided form* is in its turn influenced by other elements; e.g., with the expansion of the market, i.e., of the sphere of exchange, production grows in volume and is subdivided to a greater extent. . . .

31. The Method of Political Economy

In this third selection from the *Grundrisse*, Marx continues his arguments of the preceding two selections. Here he explicitly states his case against classical political economy, citing the abstract concepts with which it deals and which make it impossible for it to deal with the nature of capitalist production. Marx's viewpoint, of course, involves the study of the category of labor as basic to production, the historical bases of capitalist production, and the dialectical method as utilized especially in bringing out the conflict between bourgeoisie and proletariat as the fundamental feature of capitalism. The details of the study will emerge in the selections following this one.

WHEN WE consider a given country from a politico-economic standpoint, we begin with its population, then analyze the latter according to its subdivision into classes, location in city, country, or by the sea, occupation in different branches of production; then we study its exports and imports, annual production and consumption, prices of commodities, etc. It seems to be the correct procedure to commence with the real and concrete aspect of conditions as they are; in the case of political economy, to commence with population which is the basis and the author of the entire productive activity of society. Yet, on closer consideration it proves to be wrong. Population is an

From *Grundrisse*, first published in English in Marx, *A Contribution to the Critique of Political Economy* (Chicago: Charles Kerr, 1904).

abstraction, if we leave out, e.g., the classes of which it consists. These classes, again, are but an empty word, unless we know what are the elements on which they are based, such as wage labor, capital, etc. These imply, in their turn, exchange, division of labor, prices, etc. Capital, e.g., does not mean anything without wage labor, value, money, price, etc. If we start out, therefore, with population, we do so with a chaotic conception of the whole, and by closer analysis we will gradually arrive at simpler ideas; thus we shall proceed from the imaginary concrete to less and less complex abstractions, until we get at the simplest conception. This once attained, we might start on our return journey until we would finally come back to population, but this time not as a chaotic notion of an integral whole, but as a rich aggregate of many conceptions and relations. The former method is the one which political economy had adopted in the past at its inception. The economists of the seventeenth century, e.g., always started out with the living aggregate: population, nation, state, several states, etc., but in the end they invariably arrived, by means of analysis, at certain leading, abstract general principles, such as division of labor, money, value, etc. As soon as these separate elements had been more or less established by abstract reasoning, there arose the systems of political economy which start from simple conceptions, such as labor, division of labor, demand, exchange value, and conclude with state, international exchange and world market. The latter is manifestly the scientifically correct method. The concrete is concrete, because it is a combination of many objects with different destinations, i.e., a unity of diverse elements. In our thought, it therefore appears as a process of synthesis, as a result, and not as a starting point, although it is the real starting point and, therefore, also the starting point of observation and conception. By the former method the complete conception passes into an abstract definition; by the latter, the abstract definitions lead to the reproduction of the concrete subject in the course of reasoning. . . .

Labor is quite a simple category. The idea of labor in that sense, as labor in general, is also very old. Yet, "labor" thus simply defined by political economy is as much a modern category as the conditions which have given rise to this simple abstraction. The monetary system, e.g., defines wealth quite objectively, as a thing [outside itself] in money. Compared with this point of view, it was a great step forward when the industrial or commercial system came to see the source of wealth not in the object but in the activity of persons, viz., in commercial and industrial labor. But even the latter was thus considered only in the limited sense of a money-producing activity. The physiocratic system [marks still further progress] in that it considers a certain form of labor, viz., agriculture, as the source of wealth, and wealth itself not in the disguise of money, but as a product in general, as the general result of labor. But corresponding to the limitations of the activity, this product is still only a natural product. Agriculture is productive, land is the source of production *par excellence.* It was a tremendous advance on the part of Adam Smith to throw aside all limitations which mark wealth-producing activity and [to define it] as labor in general, neither industrial, nor commercial, nor agricultural, or one as much as the other. Along with the universal character of wealth-creating activity we have now the universal character of the object defined as wealth, viz., product in general, or labor in general, but as past incorporated labor. How difficult and great was the transition is evident from the way Adam Smith himself falls back from time to time into the physiocratic system. Now, it might seem as though this amounted simply to finding an abstract expression for the simplest relation into which men have been mutually entering as producers from times of yore, no matter under what form of society. In one sense this is true. In another it is not.

The indifference as to the particular kind of labor implies the existence of a highly developed aggregate of different species of concrete labor, none of which is any longer the predominant one. So do the most general abstractions commonly arise only where there is the highest concrete development, where one feature appears to be jointly possessed by many, and to be common to all. Then it cannot be thought of any longer in one particular form. On the other hand, this abstraction of labor is but the result of a concrete aggregate of different kinds of labor. The indifference to the particular kind of labor corresponds to a form of society in which individuals pass with ease from one kind of work to another, which makes it immaterial to them what particular kind of work may fall to their share. Labor has become here, not only categorically but really, a means of creating wealth in general and is no longer grown together with the individual into one particular destination. This state of affairs has found its highest development in the most modern of bourgeois societies, the United States. It is only here that the abstraction of the category "labor," "labor in general," labor *sans phrase*, the starting point of modern political economy, becomes realized in practice. Thus, the simplest abstraction which modern political economy sets up as its starting point, and which expresses a relation dating back to antiquity and prevalent under all forms of society, appears in this abstraction truly realized only as a category of the most modern society. . . .

This example of labor strikingly shows how even the most abstract categories, in spite of their applicability to all epochs —just because of their abstract character—are by the very definiteness of the abstraction a product of historical conditions as well, and are fully applicable only to and under those conditions.

The bourgeois society is the most highly developed and most highly differentiated historical organization of production. The categories which serve as the expression of its conditions and the comprehension of its own organization enable it at the same time to gain an insight into the organization and the conditions of production which had prevailed under all the past forms of society, on the ruins and constituent elements of which it has arisen, and of which it still drags along some unsurmounted remnants, while what had formerly been mere intimation has now developed to complete significance. . . . The bourgeois economy furnishes a key to ancient economy, etc. This is, however, by no means true of the method of those economists who blot out all historical differences and see the bourgeois form in all forms of society. One can understand the nature of tribute, tithes, etc., after one has learned the nature of rent. But they must not be considered identical.

Since, furthermore, bourgeois society is but a form resulting from the development of antagonistic elements, some relations belonging to earlier forms of society are frequently to be found in it but in a crippled state or as a travesty of their former self, as, e.g., communal property. While it may be said, therefore, that the categories of bourgeois economy contain what is true of all other forms of society, the statement is to be taken *cum grano salis.* They may contain these in a developed, or crippled, or caricatured form, but always essentially different. The so-called historical development amounts in the last analysis to this, that the last form considers its predecessors as stages leading up to itself and perceives them always one-sidedly, since it is very seldom and only under certain conditions that it is capable of self-criticism. . . . In the same way bourgeois political economy first came to understand the feudal, the ancient, and the oriental societies as soon as the self-criticism of the bourgeois society had commenced. . . .

In the study of economic categories, as in the case of every historical and social science, it must be borne in mind that as in reality so in our mind the subject, in this case modern bourgeois society, is given and that the categories are therefore but forms of expression, manifestations of existence, and frequently but one-sided aspects of this subject, this definite society; and that, therefore, the origin of [political economy] *as a science* does not by any means date from the time to which it is referred *as such.* This is to be firmly held in mind because it has an immediate and important bearing on the matter of the subdivisions of the science.

For instance, nothing seems more natural than to start with rent, with landed property, since it is bound up with land, the source of all production and all existence, and with the first form of production in all more or less settled communities, viz., agriculture. But nothing would be more erroneous. Under all forms of society there is a certain industry which predominates over all the rest and whose condition therefore determines the rank and influence of all the rest. . . .

Let us take for example pastoral nations (mere hunting and fishing tribes are not as yet at the point from which real development commences). They engage in a certain form of agriculture, sporadically. The nature of landownership is determined thereby. It is held in common and retains this form more or less according to the extent to which these nations hold on to traditions; such, e.g., is landownership among the Slavs. Among nations whose agriculture is carried on by a settled population—the settled state constituting a great advance—where agriculture is the predominant industry, such as in ancient and feudal societies, even the manufacturing industry and its organization, as well as the forms of property which pertain to it, have more or less the characteristic features of the prevailing system of landownership; [society] is then either entirely dependent upon agriculture, as in the case of ancient Rome, or, as in the Middle Ages, it imitates in its city relations the forms of organization prevailing in the country. Even capital, with the exception of pure money capital, has, in the form of the traditional working tool, the characteristics of landownership in the Middle Ages.

The reverse is true of bourgeois society. Agriculture comes to be more and more merely a branch of industry and is completely dominated by capital. The same is true of rent. In all the forms of society in which landownership is the prevalent form, the influence of the natural element is the predominant one. In those where capital predominates the prevailing element is the one historically created by society. Rent cannot be understood without capital, nor can capital without rent. Capital is the all-dominating economic power of bourgeois society. It must form the starting point as well as the end and be developed before landownership is. After each has been considered separately, their mutual relation must be analyzed.

It would thus be impractical and wrong to arrange the economic categories in the order in which they were the determining factors in the course of history. Their order of sequence is rather determined by the relation which they bear to one another in modern bourgeois society, and which is the exact opposite of what seems to be their natural order or the order of their historical development. What we are interested in is not the place which economic relations occupy in the historical succession of different forms of society. Still less are we interested in the order of their succession "in idea" *(Proudhon)*, which is but a hazy conception of the course of history. We are interested in their organic connection within modern bourgeois society. . . .

The order of treatment must manifestly be as follows: first, the general abstract definitions which are more or less applicable to all forms of society, but in the sense indicated above. Second, the categories which go to make up the inner organization of bourgeois society and constitute the foundations of the principal classes; capital, wage labor, landed property; their mutual relations; city and country; the three great social classes, the exchange between them; circulation, credit (private). Third, the organization of bourgeois society in the form of a state, considered in relation to itself; the "unproductive" classes; taxes; public debts; public credit; population; colonies; emigration. Fourth, the international organization of production; international division of labor; international exchange; import and export; rate of exchange. Fifth, the world market and crises.

32. The Commodity

Marx begins his analysis in *Capital* with a discussion of the nature of the *commodity*, starting from the basic distinction between a commodity's *use value* and its *exchange value*. The use value of a commodity refers to the subjectively based desire a person has to obtain a certain commodity; for example, when I have not drunk any liquids for three hours I am "thirsty," and thus a glass of water has a certain "use value" for me. Once I've sated my thirst, the use value of all the rest of the water in the world is, temporarily, reduced to zero. On an occasion when I've spent a full day in the desert without a drink, the use value (as the measure of my desire and need or, alternatively, of the commodity's "importance" to me) becomes enormous. As a result of the variation in the "use value" of the water for me on these three occasions, the amount of other commodities (including money; cf. below) I would be willing to exchange for this glass of water varies dramatically.

Use values are created solely by the fact that commodities are available in any given society, that is, that they have been brought out of their pure state in nature by the power of human labor (including all applications of science), whereas it is the amount of this labor power (taking into account the varying degrees of training which make, say, the labor of the

From *Capital*, trans. by Samuel Moore and Edward Aveling, ed. by Frederick Engels (Chicago: Charles H. Kerr & Co., 1906, 1909). In subsequent references, this edition is referred to as "Kerr edition." This selection is taken from Vol. I, pp. 41–81.

engineer more valuable than that of his construction worker) which determines the specific exchange value of any given commodity (within any given society). Thus, the exchange value of any given commodity does not depend on any subjectively based factor such as desire, but is a quantitative measure of the relations (in terms of the amount of labor power contained therein) among all commodities available in the market.

Because they ultimately refer to amounts of an equivalent commodity (the labor power required for their production), all commodities can become equivalents of one another according to the proportions of labor power they contain, and one such commodity, because of certain conveniences of portability and uniform divisibility, can come to serve universally as a recognized *medium* of commodity exchange (i.e., as *money*). Because, however, of the fluctuations in use value, the *demand* (a term of the bourgeois economists) for a certain commodity may vary considerably, and thus commodities need not exchange at their exact equivalents. As a simplifying assumption, useful at this stage of his study, Marx, however, will *assume* that they do so. This assumption, necessary to give us a quantitative measure of the relative values of commodities, is subsequently corrected by Marx as the theory (to be developed) is adjusted to actual conditions in the third volume of *Capital*.

THE WEALTH of those societies in which the capitalist mode of production prevails presents itself as an immense accumulation of commodities, its unit being a single commodity. Our investigation must therefore begin with the analysis of a commodity.

A commodity is, in the first place, an object outside us, a thing that by its properties satisfies human wants of some sort or another. The nature of such wants, whether, for instance, they spring from the stomach or from fancy, makes no difference. Neither are we here concerned to know how the object satisfies these wants, whether directly as means of subsistence, or indirectly as means of production. . . .

The utility of a thing makes it a use value. But this utility is not a thing of air. Being limited by the physical properties of the commodity, it has no existence apart from that commodity. A commodity, such as iron, corn, or a diamond, is therefore, so far as it is a material thing, a use value, something useful. This property of a commodity is independent of the amount of labor required to appropriate its useful qualities. When treating of use value, we always assume to be dealing with definite quantities, such as dozens of watches, yards of linen, or tons of iron. The use values of commodities furnish the material for a special study, that of the commercial knowledge of commodities. Use values become a reality only by use or consumption: they also constitute the substance of all wealth, whatever may be the social form of that wealth. In the form of society we are about to consider, they are, in addition, the material depositories of exchange value.

Exchange value, at first sight, presents itself as a quantitative relation, as the proportion in which values in use of one sort are exchanged for those of another sort, a relation constantly changing with time and place. Hence exchange value appears to be something accidental and purely relative, and consequently an intrinsic value, i.e., an exchange value that is inseparably connected with, inherent in commodities, seems a contradiction in terms. Let us consider the matter a little more closely. . . .

Let us take two commodities, e.g., corn and iron. The proportions in which they are exchangeable, whatever those proportions may be, can always be represented by an equation in which a given quantity of corn is equated to some quantity of iron: e.g., 1 quarter corn = x cwt. iron. What does this equation tell us? It tells us that in two different things—in 1 quarter of corn and x cwt. of iron, there exists in equal quantities something common to both. The two things must therefore be equal to a third, which in itself is neither the one nor the other. Each of them, so far as it is exchange value, must therefore be reducible to this third. . . .

This common "something" cannot be either a geometrical, a chemical, or any other natural property of commodities. Such properties claim our attention only in so far as they affect the utility of those commodities, make them use values. But the exchange of commodities is evidently an act characterized by a total abstraction from use value. Then one use value is just as good as another, provided only it be present in sufficient quantity. . . . As use values, commodities are, above all, of different qualities, but as exchange values they are merely different quantities, and consequently do not contain an atom of use value.

If then we leave out of consideration the use value of commodities, they have only one common property left, that of being products of labor. But even the product of labor itself has undergone a change in our hands. If we make abstraction from its use value, we make abstraction at the same time from the material elements and shapes that make the product a use value; we see in it no longer a table, a house, yarn, or any other useful thing. Its existence as a material thing is put out of sight. Neither can it any longer be regarded as the product of the labor of the joiner, the mason, the spinner, or of any other definite kind of productive labor. Along with the useful qualities of the products themselves, we put out of sight both the useful character of the various kinds of labor embodied in them, and the concrete forms of that labor; there is nothing left but what is common to them all; all are reduced to one and the same sort of labor, human labor in the abstract.

Let us now consider the residue of each of these products; it consists of the same unsubstantial reality in each, a mere congelation of homogeneous human labor, of labor power expended without regard to the mode of its expenditure. All that these things now tell us is that human labor power has been expended in their production, that human labor is embodied in them. When looked at as crystals of this social substance, common to them all, they are—Values. . . .

A use value, or useful article, therefore, has value only because human labor in the abstract has been embodied or materialized in it. How, then, is the magnitude of this value to be measured? Plainly, by the quantity of the value-creating substance, the labor, contained in the article. The quantity of labor, however, is measured by its duration, and labor time in its turn finds its standard in weeks, days, and hours.

Some people might think that if the value of a commodity is determined by the quantity of labor spent on it, the more idle and unskillful the laborer, the more valuable would his commodity be, because more time would be required in its production. The labor, however, that forms the substance of value, is homogeneous human labor, expenditure of one uniform labor power. The total labor power of society, which is embodied in the sum total of the values of all commodities produced by that society, counts here as one homogeneous mass of human labor power, composed though it be of innumerable individual units. Each of these units is the same as any other, so far as it has the character of the average labor power of society, and takes effect as such; that is, so far as it requires for producing a commodity, no more time than is needed on an average, no more than is socially necessary. The labor time socially necessary is that required to produce an article under the normal conditions of production, and with the average degree of skill and intensity prevalent at the time. . . .

Productive activity, if we leave out of sight its special form, viz., the useful character of the labor, is nothing but the expenditure of human labor power. Tailoring and weaving, though qualitatively different productive activities, are each a productive expenditure of human brains, nerves, and muscles, and in this sense are human labor. They are but two different modes of expending human labor power. Of course, this labor power, which remains the same under all its modifications, must have attained a certain pitch of development before it can be expended in a multiplicity of modes. But the value of a commodity represents human labor in the abstract, the expenditure of human labor in general. . . . It is the expenditure of simple labor power, i.e., of the labor power which, on an average, apart from any special development, exists in the organism of every ordinary individual. Simple average labor, it is true, varies in character in different countries and at different times, but in a particular society it is given. Skilled labor counts only as simple labor intensified, or rather, as multiplied simple labor, a given quantity of skilled being considered equal to a greater quantity of simple labor. Experience shows that this reduction is constantly being made. A commodity may be the product of the most skilled labor, but its value, by equating it to the product of simple unskilled labor, represents a definite quantity of the latter labor alone. . . . For simplicity's sake we shall henceforth account every kind of labor to be unskilled, simple labor; by this we do no more than save ourselves the trouble of making the reduction.

In the first place, the relative expression of value is incomplete because the series representing it is interminable. The chain of which each equation of value is a link, is liable at any moment to be lengthened by each new kind of commodity that comes into existence and furnishes the material for a fresh expression of value. In the second place, it is a many-colored mosaic of disparate and independent expressions of value. . . .

The expanded relative value form is, however, nothing but the sum of the elementary relative expressions or equations of the first kind, such as

$$20 \text{ yards of linen} = 1 \text{ coat}$$
$$20 \text{ yards of linen} = 10 \text{ pounds of tea, etc.}$$

Each of these implies the corresponding inverted equation,

$$1 \text{ coat} = 20 \text{ yards of linen}$$
$$10 \text{ pounds of tea} = 20 \text{ yards of linen, etc.}$$

In fact, when a person exchanges his linen for many other commodities, and thus expresses its value in a series of other commodities, it necessarily follows, that the various owners of the latter exchange them for the linen, and consequently express the value of their various commodities in one and the same third commodity, the linen. If then, we reverse the series, 20 yards of linen = 1 coat or = 10 pounds of tea, etc., that is to say, if we give expression to the converse relation already implied in the series, we get: *C. the general form of value.*

$$\left. \begin{array}{l} 1 \text{ coat} \\ 10 \text{ pounds of tea} \\ 40 \text{ pounds of coffee} \\ 1 \text{ quarter of corn} \\ 2 \text{ ounces of gold} \\ \tfrac{1}{2} \text{ ton of iron} \\ x \text{ commodity A., etc.} \end{array} \right\} = 20 \text{ yards of linen}$$

The last developed form expresses the values of the whole world of commodities in terms of a single commodity set apart for the purpose, namely, the linen, and thus represents to us their values by means of their equality with linen. The value of every commodity is now, by being equated to linen, not only differentiated from its own use value, but from all other use values generally, and is, by that very fact, expressed as that which is common to all commodities. By this form, commodities are, for the first time, effectively brought into relation with one another as values, or made to appear as exchange values. . . .

The general form of value C results from the joint action of the whole world of commodities, and from that alone. A commodity can acquire a general expression of its value only by all other commodities, simultaneously with it, expressing their values in the same equivalent; and every new commodity must follow suit. It thus becomes evident that, since the existence of commodities as values is purely social, this social existence can be expressed by the totality of their social relations alone, and consequently that the form of their value must be a socially recognized form. . . .

The general form of relative value, embracing the whole world of commodities, converts the single commodity that is excluded from the rest, and made to play the part of equivalent —here the linen—into the universal equivalent. The bodily form of the linen is now the form assumed in common by the value of all commodities; it therefore becomes directly exchangeable with all and every of them. . . .

The universal equivalent form is a form of value in general. It can, therefore, be assumed by any commodity. . . .

The particular commodity, with whose bodily form the equivalent form is thus socially identified, now becomes the money commodity, or serves as money. It becomes the special social function of that commodity, and consequently its social monopoly, to play within the world of commodities the part of the universal equivalent. Among the commodities which, first, figure as particular equivalents of the linen, and in form C, express in common their relative values in linen, this foremost place has been attained by one in particular—namely, gold. If, then, in form C we replace the linen by gold, we get: *D. the money form*.

$$
\left.
\begin{array}{l}
\text{20 yards of linen} \quad = \\
\text{1 coat} \qquad\qquad\; = \\
\text{10 pounds of tea} \quad = \\
\text{40 pounds of coffee} = \\
\text{1 quarter of corn} \;\; = \\
\text{½ ton of iron} \qquad = \\
\text{x commodity A} \quad\; =
\end{array}
\right\}
\quad \text{2 ounces of gold}
$$

. . . There is no difference between forms C and D, except that, in the latter, gold has assumed the equivalent form in the place of linen. Gold is in form D what linen was in form C—the universal equivalent. The progress consists in this alone, that the character of direct and universal exchangeability—in other words, that the universal equivalent form—has now, by social custom, become finally identified with the substance, gold.

Gold is now money with reference to all other commodities only because it was previously, with reference to them, a simple commodity. Like all other commodities, it was also capable of serving as an equivalent, either as simple equivalent in isolated exchanges, or as particular equivalent by the side of others. Gradually it began to serve, within varying limits, as universal equivalent. So soon as it monopolizes this position in the expression of value for the world of commodities, it becomes the money commodity, and then, and not till then, does form D become distinct from form C, and the general form of value become changed into the money form. . . .

33. The Fetishism of Commodities

In this famous section devoted to "The Fetishism of Commodities and the Secret Thereof," Marx has occasion to apply the Feuerbachian argument to the study of the role of commodities in a capitalist (i.e., "commodity-dominated") economy. The "secret" of the commodity is that it is an objective economic expression of the social relations among the members of society, and thus that it is the relationship of labor rather than of any property (e.g., chemical or physical property) of the commodity itself which determines the relative exchange value of commodities.

It is thus, argues Marx, that the question of the relationship among commodities has for so long puzzled political economists because they have failed to see the social role of human labor as the basis of the (exchange-) value of commodities and have instead sought the answer in some properties of the commodities themselves. It is interesting to note that this section, which deals with a basic "mystery" of a capitalistic economy, could, with but little alteration, be applied with equal force to a critique of the "fetishism of the Plan" of a state-capitalistic economy, such as that of the U.S.S.R., which equally mysteriously reflects the real social relations of a population lying in thrall to an authoritarian state.

A COMMODITY appears, at first sight, a very trivial thing, and easily understood. Its analysis shows that it is, in reality, a very

From the Kerr edition, Vol. I, pp. 81–96.

queer thing, abounding in metaphysical subtleties and theological niceties. So far as it is a value in use, there is nothing mysterious about it, whether we consider it from the point of view that by its properties it is capable of satisfying human wants, or from the point that these properties are the product of human labor. It is as clear as noonday that man, by his industry, changes the forms of the materials furnished by nature, in such a way as to make them useful to him. The form of wood, for instance, is altered by making a table out of it. Yet, for all that the table continues to be that common, everyday thing, wood. But, so soon as it steps forth as a commodity, it is changed into something transcendent. It not only stands with its feet on the ground, but, in relation to all other commodities, it stands on its head, and evolves out of its wooden brain grotesque ideas, far more wonderful than "table-turning" ever was.

The mystical character of commodities does not originate, therefore, in their use value. Just as little does it proceed from the nature of the determining factors of value. For, in the first place, however varied the useful kinds of labor, or productive acitivities, may be, it is a physiological fact that they are functions of the human organism, and that each such function, whatever may be its nature or form, is essentially the expenditure of human brain, nerves, muscles, etc. Secondly, with regard to that which forms the groundwork for the quantitative determination of value, namely, the duration of that expenditure, or the quantity of labor, it is quite clear that there is a palpable difference between its quantity and quality. In all states of society, the labor time that it costs to produce the means of subsistence must necessarily be an object of interest to mankind, though not of equal interest in different stages of development. And lastly, from the moment that men in any way work for one another, their labor assumes a social form.

Whence, then, arises the enigmatical character of the product of labor, so soon as it assumes the form of commodities? Clearly from this form itself. The equality of all sorts of human labor is expressed objectively by their products all being equally values; the measure of the expenditure of labor power, by the duration of that expenditure, takes the form of the quantity of value of the products of labor; and finally, the mutual relations of the producers, within which the social character of their labor affirms itself, take the form of a social relation between the products.

A commodity is therefore a mysterious thing, simply because in it the social character of men's labor appears to them as an objective character stamped upon the product of that labor; because the relation of the producers to the sum total of their own labor is presented to them as a social relation, existing not between themselves, but between the products of their labor. This is the reason why the products of labor become commodities, social things whose qualities are at the same time perceptible and imperceptible by the senses. . . . The existence of the things *qua* commodities, and the value relation between the products of labor which stamps them as commodities, have absolutely no connection with their physical properties and with the material relations arising therefrom. There it is a definite social relation between men, that assumes, in their eyes, the fantastic form of a relation between things. In order, therefore, to find an onology, we must have recourse to the mist-enveloped regions of the religious world. In that world the productions of the human brain appear as independent beings endowed with life, and entering into relation both with one another and the human race. So it is in the world of commodities with the products of men's hands. This I call the Fetishism which attaches itself to the products of labor, so soon as they are produced as commodities, and which is therefore inseparable from the production of commodities.

This Fetishism of commodities has its origin, as the foregoing analysis has already shown, in the peculiar social character of the labor that produces them.

As a general rule, articles of utility become commodities, only because they are products of the labor of private individuals or groups of individuals who carry on their work independently of each other. The sum total of the labor of all these private individuals forms the aggregate labor of society. Since the producers do not come into social contact with each other until they exchange their products, the specific social character of each producer's labor does not show itself except in the act of exchange. In other words, the labor of the individual asserts itself as a part of the labor of society, only by means of the relations which the act of exchange establishes directly between the products, and indirectly, through them, between the producers. To the latter, therefore, the relations connecting the labor of one individual with that of the rest appear, not as direct social relations between individuals at work, but as what they really are, material relations between persons and social relations between things. It is only by being exchanged that the products of labor acquire, as values, one uniform social status, distinct from their varied forms of existence as objects of utility. This division of a product into a useful thing and a value becomes pratically important only when exchange has acquired such an extension that useful articles are produced for the purpose of being exchanged, and their character as values has therefore to be taken into account, beforehand, during production. From this moment the labor of the individual producer acquires socially a twofold character. On the one hand, it must, as a definite useful kind of labor, satisfy a definite social want, and thus hold its place as part and parcel of the collective labor of all, as a branch of a social division of labor that has sprung up spontaneously. On the other hand, it can satisfy the manifold wants of the individual producer himself, only in so far as the mutual exchangeability of all kinds of useful private labor is an established social fact, and therefore the private useful labor of each producer ranks on an equality with that of all others. The equalization of the most different kinds of labor can be the result only of an abstraction from their inequalities, or of reducing them to their common denominator, viz., expenditure of human labor power or human labor in the abstract. The twofold social character of the labor of the individual appears to him, when reflected in his brain, only under those forms which are impressed upon that labor in everyday practice by the exchange of products. In this way, the character that his own labor possesses of being socially useful takes the form of the condition, that the product must be not only useful, but useful for others, and the social character that his particular labor has of being the equal of all other particular kinds of labor takes the form that all the physically different articles that are the products of labor have one common quality, viz., that of having value.

Hence, when we bring the products of our labor into relation with each other as values, it is not because we see in these articles the material receptacles of homogeneous human labor. Quite the contrary; whenever, by an exchange, we equate as values our different products, by that very act, we also equate, as human labor, the different kinds of labor expended upon them. We are not aware of this; nevertheless we do it. Value, therefore, does not stalk about with a label describing what it is. It is value, rather, that converts every product into a social hieroglyphic. Later on, we try to decipher the hieroglyphic, to get behind the secret of our own social products; for to stamp an object of utility as a value is just as much a social product as language. . . .

What, first of all, practically concerns producers when they make an exchange, is the question, how much of some other product they get for their own? in what proportions the products are exchangeable? When these proportions have, by custom, attained a certain stability, they appear to result from the nature of the products, so that, for instance, one ton of iron and two ounces of gold appear as naturally to be of equal value as a pound of gold and a pound of iron in spite of their different physical and chemical qualities appear to be of equal weight. The character of having value, when once impressed upon products, obtains fixity only by reason of their acting and reacting upon each other as quantities of value. These quantities vary continually, independently of the will, foresight and action of the producers. To them, their own social action takes the form of the action of objects, which rule the producers instead of being ruled by them. It requires a fully developed production of commodities before, from accumulated experience alone, the scientific conviction springs up that all the different kinds of private labor, which are carried on independently of each other, and yet as spontaneously developed branches of the social division of labor, are continually being reduced to the quantitive proportions in which society requires them. And why?

Because, in the midst of all the accidental and ever fluctuating exchange relations between the products, the labor time socially necessary for their production forcibly asserts itself like an overriding law of nature. The law of gravity thus asserts itself when a house falls about our ears. The determination of the magnitude of value by labor time is therefore a secret, hidden under the apparent fluctuations in the relative values of commodities. Its discovery, while removing all appearance of mere accidentality from the determination of the magnitude of the values of products, yet in no way alters the mode in which that determination takes place.

Man's reflections on the forms of social life, and consequently, also, his scientific analysis of those forms, take a course directly opposite to that of their actual historical development. He begins, post festum, with the results of the process of development ready to hand before him. The characters that stamp products as commodities, and whose establishment is a necessary preliminary to the circulation of commodities, have already acquired the stability of natural, self-understood forms of social life, before man seeks to decipher, not their historical character, for in his eyes they are immutable, but their meaning. Consequently it was the analysis of the prices of commodities that alone led to the determination of the magnitude of value, and it was the common expression of all commodities in money that alone led to the establishment of their characters as values. It is, however, just this ultimate money form of the world of commodities that actually conceals, instead of disclosing, the social character of private labor, and the social relations between the individual producers. When I state that coats or boots stand in a relation to linen, because it is the universal incarnation of abstract human labor, the absurdity of the statement is self-evident. Nevertheless, when the producers of coats and boots compare those articles with linen, or, what is the same thing, with gold or silver, as the universal equivalent, they express the relation between their own private labor and the collective labor of society in the same absurd form.

The categories of bourgeois economy consist of such like forms. They are forms of thought expressing with social validity the conditions and relations of a definite, historically deter-mined mode of production, viz., the production of commodi-ties. The whole mystery of commodities, all the magic and necromancy that surrounds the products of labor as long as they take the form of commodities, vanishes therefore, so soon as we come to other forms of production.

Since Robinson Crusoe's experiences are a favorite theme with political economists, let us take a look at him on his island. Moderate though he be, yet some few wants he has to satisfy, and must therefore do a little useful work of various sorts, such as making tools and furniture, taming goats, fishing and hunt-ing. Of his prayers and the like we take no account, since they are a source of pleasure to him, and he looks upon them as so much recreation. In spite of the variety of his work, he knows that his labor, whatever its form, is but the activity of one and the same Robinson, and consequently, that it consists of nothing but different modes of human labor. Necessity itself compels him to apportion his time accurately between his different kinds of work. Whether one kind occupies a greater space in his general activity than another depends on the difficulties, greater or less as the case may be, to be overcome in attaining the useful effect aimed at. This our friend Robinson soon learns by experience, and having rescued a watch, ledger, and pen and ink from the wreck, commences, like a true-born Briton, to keep a set of books. His stock-book contains a list of the objects of utility that belong to him, of the operations necessary for their production; and lastly, of the labor time that definite quan-tities of those objects have, on an average, cost him. All the relations between Robinson and the objects that form this wealth of his own creation are here so simple and clear as to be intelligible without exertion. . . . And yet those relations contain all that is essential to the determination of value.

Let us now transport ourselves from Robinson's island bathed in light to the European middle ages shrouded in darkness. Here, instead of the independent man, we find everyone de-pendent, serfs and lords, vassals and suzerains, laymen and clergy. Personal dependence here characterizes the social rela-tions of production just as much as it does the other spheres of life organized on the basis of that production. But for the very reason that personal dependence forms the groundwork of society, there is no necessity for labor and its products to assume a fantastic form different from their reality. They take the shape, in the transactions of society, of services in kind and payments in kind. Here the particular and natural form of labor, and not, as in a society based on production of commodities, its general abstract form, is the immediate social form of labor. Compulsory labor is just as properly measured by time as commodity-producing labor; but every serf knows that what he expends in the service of his lord is a definite quantity of his own personal labor power. The tithe to be rendered to the priest is more matter of fact than his blessing. No matter, then, what we may think of the parts played by the different classes of people themselves in this society, the social relations between individuals in the performance of their labor appear at all events as their own mutual personal relations, and are not disguised under the shape of social relations between the products of labor.

For an example of labor in common or directly associated labor, we have no occasion to go back to that spontaneously developed form which we find on the threshold of the history of all civilized races. We have one close at hand in the patriarchal industries of a peasant family that produces corn, cattle, yarn, linen, and clothing for home use. These different articles are, as regards the family, so many products of its labor, but as between themselves, they are not commodities. The different kinds of labor, such as tillage, cattle tending, spinning, weaving and making clothes, which result in the various products, are in themselves, and such as they are, direct social functions, because functions of the family, which just as much as a society based on the production of commodities, possesses a spontaneously developed system of division of labor. The distribution of the work within the family, and the regulation of the labor time of the several members, depend as well upon differences of age and sex as upon natural conditions varying with the seasons. The labor power of each individual, by its very nature, operates in this case merely as a definite portion of the whole labor power of the family, and therefore, the measure of the expenditure of individual labor power by its duration appears here by its very nature as a social character of their labor.

Let us now picture to ourselves, by way of change, a community of free individuals, carrying on their work with the means of production in common, in which the labor power of all the different individuals is consciously applied as the combined labor power of the community. All the characteristics of Robinson's labor are here repeated, but with this difference, that they are social, instead of individual. Everything produced by him was exclusively the result of his own personal labor, and therefore simply an object of use for himself. The total product of our community is a social product. One portion serves as fresh means of production and remains social. But another portion is consumed by the members as means of subsistence. A distribution of this portion among them is consequently necessary. The mode of this distribution will vary with the productive organization of the community, and the degree of historical development attained by the producers. We will assume, but merely for the sake of a parallel with the production of commodities, that the share of each individual producer in the means of subsistence is determined by his labor time. Labor time would, in that case, play a double part. Its apportionment in accordance with a definite social plan maintains the proper proportion between the different kinds of work to be done and the various wants of the community. On the other hand, it also serves as a measure of the portion of the common labor borne by each individual and of his share in the part of the total product destined for individual consumption. The social relations of the individual producers, with regard both to their labor and to its products, are in this case perfectly simple and intelligible, and that with regard not only to production but also to distribution. . . .

The life process of society, which is based on the process of material production, does not strip off its mystical veil until it is treated as production by freely associated men, and is consciously regulated by them in accordance with a settled plan. This, however, demands for society a certain material groundwork or set of conditions of existence which in their turn are the spontaneous product of a long and painful process of development.

Political economy has indeed analyzed, however incompletely, value and its magnitude, and has discovered what lies beneath these forms. But it has never once asked the question why labor is represented by the value of its product and labor time by the magnitude of that value. These formulas, which bear stamped upon them in unmistakable letters that they belong to a state of society in which the process of production has the mastery over man, instead of being controlled by him, such formulas appear to the bourgeois intellect to be as much a self-evident necessity imposed by nature as productive labor itself. Hence forms of social production that preceded the bourgeois form are treated by the bourgeoisie in much the same way as the Fathers of the Church treated pre-Christian religions.

To what extent some economists are misled by the Fetishism inherent in commodities, or by the objective appearance of the social characteristics of labor, is shown, among other ways, by the dull and tedious quarrel over the part played by Nature in the formation of exchange value. Since exchange value is a definite social manner of expressing the amount of labor bestowed upon an object, Nature has no more to do with it than it has in fixing the course of exchange.

The mode of production in which the product takes the form of a commodity, or is produced directly for exchange, is the most general and most embryonic form of bourgeois production. It therefore makes its appearance at an early date in history, though not in the same predominating and characteristic manner as nowadays. Hence its Fetish character is comparatively easy to be seen through. But when we come to more concrete forms, even this appearance of simplicity vanishes. Whence arose the illusions of the monetary system? To it gold and silver, when serving as money, did not represent a social relation between producers, but were natural objects with strange social properties. And modern economy, which looks down with such disdain on the monetary system, does not its superstition come out as clear as noonday, whenever it treats of capital? How long is it since economy discarded the physiocratic illusion that rents grow out of the soil and not out of society?

But not to anticipate, we will content ourselves with yet another example relating to the commodity form. Could commodities themselves speak, they would say: Our use value may be a thing that interests men. It is no part of us as objects. What, however, does belong to us as objects is our value. Our natural intercourse as commodities proves it. In the eyes of each other we are nothing but exchange values. Now listen how those commodities speak through the mouth of the economist. "Value"—(i.e., exchange value) "is a property of things, riches" —(i.e., use value) "of man. Value, in this sense, necessarily implies exchanges, riches do not." "Riches" (use value) "are the attribute of men, value is the attribute of commodities. A man or a community is rich, a pearl or a diamond is valuable. . . . A pearl or a diamond is valuable" as a pearl or diamond. So far no chemist has ever discovered exchange value either in a pearl or a diamond. The economical discoverers of this chemical element, who, by the bye, lay special claim to critical acumen, find however that the use value of objects belongs to them independently of their material properties, while their value, on the other hand, forms a part of them as objects. What confirms them in this view, is the peculiar circumstances that the use value of objects is realized without exchange, by means of a direct relation between the objects and man, while, on the other hand, their value is realized only by exchange, that is, by means of a social process. . . .

34. Exchange and Money

In this short selection Marx describes the simple circulation of commodities within the market as a series of individual actions in which the commodity owner first exchanges his commodity for money (in *selling*, which can be schematically represented as C—M) and then, in a separate transaction, exchanges this money for a second commodity (in *purchasing*, schematically represented as M—C). The whole process of circulation may be represented (allowing for the distinction between the first and second commodities) as C_1—M—C_2.

EVERY OWNER of a commodity wishes to part with it in exchange only for those commodities whose use value satisfies some want of his. Looked at in this way, exchange is for him simply a private transaction. On the other hand, he desires to realize the value of his commodity, to convert it into any other suitable commodity of equal value, irrespective of whether his own commodity has or has not any use value for the owner of the other. From this point of view, exchange is for him a social transaction of a general character. But one and the same set of transactions cannot be simultaneously for all owners of commodities both exclusively private and exclusively social and general. . . .

Up to this point, however, we are acquainted only with one function of money, namely, to serve as the form of manifestation of the value of commodities, or as the material in which the magnitudes of their values are socially expressed. An adequate form of manifestation of value, a fit embodiment of abstract, undifferentiated, and therefore equal human labor, that material alone can be whose every sample exhibits the same uniform qualities. On the other hand, since the difference between the magnitudes of value is purely quantitative, the money commodity must be susceptible of merely quantitative differences, must therefore be divisible at will, and equally capable of being reunited. Gold and silver possess these properties by nature.

The use value of the money commodity becomes twofold. In addition to its special use value as a commodity (gold, for instance, serving to stop teeth, to form the raw material of articles of luxury, etc.), it acquires a formal use value, originating in its specific social function. . . .

A commodity strips off its original commodity form on being alienated, i.e., on the instant its use value actually attracts the gold, that before existed only ideally in its price. The realization of a commodity's price, or of its ideal value form, is therefore at the same time the realization of the ideal use value of money; the conversion of a commodity into money is the simultaneous conversion of money into a commodity. The apparently single process is in reality a double one. From the pole of the commodity owner it is a sale, from the opposite pole of the money owner, it is a purchase. In other words, a sale is a purchase, C—M is also M—C. . . .

We will assume that the two gold pieces, in consideration of which our weaver has parted with his linen, are the metamorphosed shape of a quarter of wheat. The sale of the linen, C—M, is at the same time its purchase, M—C. But the sale is the first act of a process that ends with a transaction of an opposite nature, namely, the purchase of a Bible; the purchase of the linen, on the other hand, ends a movement that began with a transaction of an opposite nature, namely, with the sale of the wheat. C—M (linen—money), which is the first phase of C—M—C (linen—money—Bible), is also M—C (money—linen), the last phase of another movement C—M—C (wheat—money—

linen). The first metamorphosis of one commodity, its transformation from a commodity into money, is therefore also invariably the second metamorphosis of some other commodity, the retransformation of the latter from money into a commodity. . . .

The circulation of commodities differs from the direct exchange of products (barter), not only in form, but in substance. Only consider the course of events. The weaver has, as a matter of fact, exchanged his linen for a Bible, his own commodity for that of someone else. But this is true only so far as he himself is concerned. The seller of the Bible, who prefers something to warm his inside, no more thought of exchanging his Bible for linen than our weaver knew that wheat had been exchanged for his linen. B's commodity replaces that of A, but A and B do not mutually exchange those commodities. It may, of course, happen that A and B make simultaneous purchases, the one from the other; but such exceptional transactions are by no means the necessary result of the general conditions of the circulation of commodities. We see here, on the one hand, how the exchange of commodities breaks through all local and personal bounds inseparable from direct barter, and develops the circulation of the products of social labor; and on the other hand, how it develops a whole network of social relations spontaneous in their growth and entirely beyond the control of the actors. It is only because the farmer has sold his wheat that the weaver is enabled to sell his linen, only because the weaver has sold his linen that our Hotspur is enabled to sell his Bible, and only because the latter has sold the water of everlasting life that the distiller is enabled to sell his *eau-de-vie,* and so on. . . .

35. *The General Formula for Capital*

Marx begins his analysis of "The General Formula for Capital" by noting, alongside the formula for the circulation of commodities, C—M—C, another transformation, M—C—M. It is this new transformation which describes the activity of the capitalist as distinguished from the person who sells certain commodities in order to purchase an equivalent amount of other commodities (e.g., the peasant who brings his crops to market and sells them so as to be able to buy clothing, tools, etc., with which to provide for the needs and comfort of his family). That is, the transformation C—M—C refers to individuals whose concern is the satisfying of their needs and wants, whereas the transformation M—C—M refers to the capitalist, whose sole aim is to seek an increase in the size of his capital. This latter situation would be satisfied if the amount of money with which the capitalist begins, M_1, is increased upon his purchase and subsequent sale of a commodity or commodities for an amount of money, M_2. Thus, in M_1—C—M_2, if M_2 is greater than M_1 the capitalist has made a profit, if M_1 and M_2 are equal he has neither profited not lost by the transaction, and if M_2 is less than M_1 he has suffered a loss of capital. The capitalist's problem, then, is to ensure himself a profit, and Marx brings out the impossibility of so profiting if he confines himself to the mere exchange of equivalent values.

From the Kerr edition, Vol. I, pp. 163–185.

THE CIRCULATION of commodities is the starting point of capital. The production of commodities, their circulation, and that more developed form of their circulation called commerce, these form the historical groundwork from which it rises. The modern history of capital dates from the creation in the sixteenth century of a world-embracing commerce and a world-embracing market. . . .

All new capital, to commence with, comes on the stage, that is, on the market, whether of commodities, labor, or money, even in our days, in the shape of money that by a definite process has to be transformed into capital.

The first distinction we notice between money that is money only, and money that is capital, is nothing more than a difference in their form of circulation.

The simplest form of the circulation of commodities is C—M —C, the transformation of commodities into money, and the change of the money back again into commodities; or selling in order to buy. But alongside of this form we find another specifically different form: M—C—M, the transformation of money into commodities, and the change of commodities back again into money; or buying in order to sell. Money that circulates in the latter manner is thereby transformed into, becomes capital, and is already potentially capital.

Now let us examine the circuit M—C—M a little closer. It consists, like the other, of two anithetical phases. In the first phase, M—C, or the purchase, the money is changed into a commodity. In the second phase, C—M, or the sale, the commodity is changed back again into money. The combination of these two phases constitutes the single movement whereby money is exchanged for a commodity and the same commodity is again exchanged for money; whereby a commodity is bought in order to be sold, or, neglecting the distinction in form between buying and selling, whereby a commodity is bought with money, and then money is bought with a commodity. The result, in which the phases of the process vanish, is the exchange of money for money, M—M. If I purchase 2,000 pounds of cotton for £100, and resell the 2,000 pounds of cotton for £110, I have, in fact, exchanged £100 for £110, money for money.

Now it is evident that the circuit M—C—M would be absurd and without meaning if the intention were to exchange by this means two equal sums of money, £100 for £100. The miser's plan would be far simpler and surer; he sticks to his £100 instead of exposing it to the dangers of circulation. And yet, whether the merchant who has paid £100 for his cotton sells it for £110, or lets it go for £100, or even £50, his money has, at all events, gone through a characteristic and original movement, quite different in kind from that which it goes through in the hands of the peasant who sells corn, and with the money thus set free buys clothes. . . .

Let us see, in the first place, what the two forms have in common.

Both circuits are resolvable into the same two antithetical phases, C—M, a sale, and M—C, a purchase. In each of these phases the same material elements—a commodity, and money, and the same economical dramatis personae, a buyer and a seller—confront one another. Each circuit is the unity of the same two antithetical phases, and in each case this unity is brought about by the intervention of three contracting parties, of whom one only sells, another only buys, while the third both buys and sells.

What, however, first and foremost distinguishes the circuit C—M—C from the circuit M—C—M, is the inverted order of succession of the two phases. The simple circulation of commodities begins with a sale and ends with a purchase, while the circulation of money as capital begins with a purchase and ends with a sale. In the one case both the starting point and the goal are commodities, in the other they are money. In the first form the movement is brought about by the intervention of money, in the second by that of a commodity.

In the circulation C—M—C, the money is in the end converted into a commodity, that serves as a use value; it is spent once for all. In the inverted form, M—C—M, on the contrary, the buyer lays out money in order that, as a seller, he may recover money. By the purchase of his commodity he throws money into circulation, in order to withdraw it again by the sale of the same commodity. He lets the money go, but only with the sly intention of getting it back again. The money, therefore, is not spent, it is merely advanced. . . .

The circuit C—M—C starts with one commodity, and finishes with another, which falls out of circulation and into consumption. Consumption, the satisfaction of wants, in one word, use value, is its end and aim. The circuit M—C—M, on the contrary, commences with money and ends with money. Its leading motive, and the goal that attracts it, is therefore mere exchange value. . . .

The circulation M—C—M at first sight appears purposeless, because tautological. Both extremes have the same economic form. They are both money, and therefore are not qualitatively different use values; for money is but the converted form of commodities, in which their particular use values vanish. To exchange £100 for cotton, and then this same cotton again for £100, is merely a roundabout way of exchanging money for money, the same for the same, and appears to be an operation just as purposeless as it is absurd. One sum of money is distinguishable from another only by its amount. The character and tendency of the process M—C—M is therefore not due to any qualitative difference between its extremes, both being money, but solely to their quantitative difference. More money is withdrawn from circulation at the finish than was thrown into it at the start. The cotton that was bought for £100 is perhaps resold for £100 + £10 or £110. The exact form of this process is therefore M—C—M', where $M' = M + \triangle M =$ the original sum advanced, plus an increment. This increment or excess over the original value I call "surplus value." The value originally advanced, therefore, not only remains intact while in circulation, but adds to itself a surplus value or expands itself. It is this movement that converts it into capital. . . .

If now, the £110 be spent as money, they cease to play their part. They are no longer capital. Withdrawn from circulation, they become petrified into a hoard, and though they remained in that state till doomsday, not a single farthing would accrue to them. If, then, the expansion of value is once aimed at, there is just the same inducement to augment the value of the £110 as that of the £100; for both are but limited expressions for exchange value, and therefore both have the same vocation to approach, by quantitative increase, as near as possible to absolute wealth. . . . The simple circulation of commodities—selling in order to buy—is a means of carrying out a purpose unconnected with circulation, namely, the appropriation of use values, the satisfaction of wants. The circulation of money as capital is, on the contrary, an end in itself, for the expansion of value takes place only within this constantly renewed movement. The circulation of capital has therefore no limits. Thus the conscious representative of this movement, the possessor of money, becomes a capitalist. . . . The expansion of value, which is the objective basis or mainspring of the circulation M—C—M, becomes his subjective aim, and it is only in so far as the appropriation of ever more and more wealth in the abstract becomes the sole motive of his operations, that he functions as a capitalist, that is, as capital personified and endowed with consciousness and a will. Use values must therefore never be looked upon as the real aim of the capitalist; neither must the profit on any single transaction. The restless never-ending process of profit making alone is what he aims at. This boundless greed after riches, this passionate chase after exchange value, is common to the capitalist and the miser; but while the miser is merely a capitalist gone mad, the capitalist is a rational miser. The never-ending augmentation of exchange value, which the miser strives after, by seeking to save his money from circulation, is attained by the more acute capitalist, by constantly throwing it afresh into circulation. . . .

A may be clever enough to get the advantage of B or C without their being able to retaliate. A sells wine worth £40 to B, and obtains from him in exchange corn to the value of £50. A has converted his £40 into £50, has made more money out of less, and has converted his commodities into capital. Let us examine this a little more closely. Before the exchange we had £40 worth of wine in the hands of A, and £50 worth of corn in those of B, a total value of £90. After the exchange we have still the same total value of £90. The value in circulation has not increased by one iota, it is only distributed differently between A and B. What is a loss of value to B is surplus value to A; what is "minus" to one is "plus" to the other. The same change would have taken place, if A, without the formality of an exchange, had directly stolen the £10 from B. The sum of the values in circulation can clearly not be augmented by any change in their distribution. . . .

Turn and twist then as we may, the fact remains unaltered. If equivalents are exchanged, no surplus value results, and if nonequivalents are exchanged, still no surplus value. Circulation, or the exchange of commodities, begets no value. . . .

We have shown that surplus value cannot be created by circulation, and, therefore, that in its formation, something must take place in the background, which is not apparent in the circulation itself. . . .

It is therefore impossible for capital to be produced by circulation, and it is equally impossible for it to originate apart from circulation. It must have its origin both in circulation and yet not in circulation.

We have, therefore, got a double result.

The conversion of money into capital has to be explained on the basis of the laws that regulate the exchange of commodities in such a way that the starting point is the exchange of equivalents. Our friend, Moneybags, who as yet is only an embryo capitalist, must buy his commodities at their value, must sell them at their value, and yet at the end of the process must withdraw more value from circulation than he threw into it at starting. His development into a full-grown capitalist must take place, both within the sphere of circulation and without it. These are the conditions of the problem.

36. *The Sale of Labor Power*

The source of the extra, or surplus, value (accounting for the difference between the capitalist's M_2 and M_1) must lie in some other realm than that of the simple exchange of commodities. Rather, such a source of surplus value lies in the peculiar characteristic of the commodity of labor power, which is found on the market because the laborer has no other commodity to offer for sale to provide himself and his dependents with the means to exist. His only available source of income lies in precisely his power to perform labor for another man, who agrees to compensate him with a wage to which both parties agree in advance.

THE CHANGE of value that occurs in the case of money intended to be converted into capital cannot take place in the money itself, since in its function of means of purchase and of payment, it does no more than realize the price of the commodity it buys or pays for; and, as hard cash, it is value petrified, never varying. Just as little can it originate in the second act of circulation, the resale of the commodity, which does no more than transform the article from its bodily form back again into its money form. The change must, therefore, take place in the commodity bought by the first act, M—C, but not in its value, for equivalents are exchanged, and the commodity is paid for at its full value. We are, therefore, forced to the conclusion that the change originates in the use value, as such, of the commodity,

From the Kerr edition, Vol. I, pp. 185–191.

i.e., in its consumption. In order to be able to extract value from the consumption of a commodity, our friend, Moneybags, must be so lucky as to find, within the sphere of circulation, in the market, a commodity whose use value possesses the peculiar property of being a source of value, whose actual consumption, therefore, is itself an embodiment of labor, and, consequently, a creation of value. The possessor of money does find on the market such a special commodity in capacity for labor or labor power.

By labor power or capacity for labor is to be understood the aggregate of these mental and physical capabilities existing in a human being, which he exercises whenever he produces a use value of any description. . . .

Labor power can appear upon the market as a commodity only if, and so far as, its possessor, the individual whose labor power it is, offers it for sale, or sells it, as a commodity. In order that he may be able to do this, he must have it at his disposal, must be the untrammeled owner of his capacity for labor, i.e., of his person. He and the owner of money meet in the market, and deal with each other as on the basis of equal rights, with this difference alone, that one is buyer, the other seller; both, therefore, equal in the eyes of the law. The continuance of this relation demands that the owner of the labor power should sell it only for a definite period, for if he were to sell it rump and stump, once for all, he would be selling himself, converting himself from a free man into a slave, from an owner of a commodity into a commodity. He must constantly look upon his labor power as his own property, his own commodity, and this he can only do by placing it at the disposal of the buyer temporarily, for a definite period of time. . . .

The second essential condition to the owner of money finding labor power in the market as a commodity is this—that the laborer instead of being in the position to sell commodities in which his labor is incorporated, must be obliged to offer for sale as a commodity that very labor power, which exists only in his living self. . . .

The question why this free laborer confronts him in the market, has no interest for the owner of money, who regards the labor market as a branch of the general market for commodities. And for the present it interests us just as little. We cling to the fact theoretically, as he does practically. One thing, however, is clear—nature does not produce on the one side owners of money or commodities, and on the other men possessing nothing but their own labor power. This relation has no natural basis, neither is its social basis one that is common to all historical periods. It is clearly the result of a past historial development, the product of many economical revolutions, of the extinction of a whole series of older forms of social production. . . .

We must now examine more closely this peculiar commodity, labor power. Like all others it has a value. How is that value determined?

The value of labor power is determined, as in the case of every other commodity, by the labor time necessary for the production, and consequently also the reproduction, of this special article. So far as it has value, it represents no more than a definite quantity of the average labor of society incorporated in it. Labor power exists only as a capacity , or power of the living individual. Its production consequently presupposes his existence. Given the individual, the production of labor power consists in his reproduction of himself or his maintenance. For his maintenance he requires a given quantity of the means of subsistence. Therefore the labor time requisite for the production of labor power reduces itself to that necessary for the production of those means of subsistence; in other words, the value of labor power is the value of the means of subsistence necessary for the maintenance of the laborer. . . . If the owner of labor power works today, tomorrow he must again be able to repeat the same process in the same conditions as regards health and strength. His means of subsistence must therefore be sufficient to maintain him in his normal state as a laboring individual. His natural wants, such as food, clothing, fuel, and housing, vary according to the climatic and other physical conditions of his country. On the other hand, the number and extent of his so-called necessary wants, as also the modes of satisfying them, are themselves the product of historical development, and depend therefore to a great extent on the degree of civilization of a country, more particularly on the conditions under which, and consequently on the habits and degree of comfort in which, the class of free laborers has been formed. In contradistinction therefore to the case of other commodities, there enters into the determination of the value of labor power a historical and moral element. Nevertheless, in a given country, at a given period, the average quantity of the means of subsistence necessary for the laborer is practically known.

The owner of labor power is mortal. If then his appearance in the market is to be continuous, and the continuous conversion of money into capital assumes this, the seller of labor power must perpetuate himself, "in the way that every living individual perpetuates himself, by procreation." The labor power withdrawn from the market by wear and tear and death must be continually replaced by, at the very least, an equal amount of fresh labor power. Hence the sum of the means of subsistence necessary for the production of labor power must include the means necessary for the laborer's substitutes, i.e., his children, in order that this race of peculiar commodity owners may perpetuate its appearance in the market.

In order to modify the human organism, so that it may acquire skill and handiness in a given branch of industry, and become labor power of a special kind, a special education or training is requisite, and this, on its part, costs an equivalent in commodities of a greater or less amount. This amount varies according to the more or less complicated character of the labor power. The expenses of this education (excessively small in the case of ordinary labor power), enter pro tanto into the total value spent in its production. . . .

37. The Labor Process

The following selection, in which Marx analyzes the nature of the labor process, brings together the roles of the laborer, the raw materials, the tools and machinery which comprise the process of production. This discussion brings to the fore the respective roles of the capitalist and laborer, and leads to the next section, which illustrates the way in which the laborer creates surplus value.

THE CAPITALIST buys labor power in order to use it; and labor power in use is labor itself. The purchaser of labor power consumes it by setting the seller of it to work. By working, the latter becomes actually, what before he only was potentially, labor power in action, a laborer. In order that his labor may reappear in a commodity, he must, before all things, expend it on something useful, on something capable of satisfying a want of some sort. Hence, what the capitalist sets the laborer to produce is a particular use value, a specified article. The fact that the production of use values, or goods, is carried on under the control of a capitalist and on his behalf does not alter the general character of that production. We shall, therefore, in the first place, have to consider the labor process independently of the particular form it assumes under given social conditions.

Labor is, in the first place, a process in which both man and Nature participate, and in which man of his own accord starts, regulates, and controls the material reactions between himself

From the Kerr edition, Vol. I, pp. 197–206.

and Nature. He opposes himself to Nature as one of her own forces, setting in motion arms and legs, head and hands, the natural forces of his body, in order to appropriate Nature's productions in a form adapted to his own wants. By thus acting on the external world and changing it, he at the same time changes his own nature. He develops his slumbering powers and compels them to act in obedience to his sway. We are now dealing with those primitive instinctive forms of labor that remind us of the mere animal. An immeasurable interval of time separates the state of things in which a man brings his labor power to market for sale as a commodity, from that state in which human labor was still in its first instinctive stage. We presuppose labor in a form that stamps it as exclusively human. A spider conducts operations that resemble those of a weaver, and a bee puts to shame many an architect in the construction of her cells. But what distinguishes the worst architect from the best of bees is this, that the architect raises his structure in imagination before he erects it in reality. At the end of every labor process, we get a result that already existed in the imagination of the laborer at its commencement. He not only effects a change of form in the material on which he works, but he also realises a purpose of his own that gives the law to his *modus operandi,* and to which he must subordinate his will. And this subordination is no mere momentary act. Besides the exertion of the bodily organs, the process demands that, during the whole operation, the workman's will be steadily in consonance with his purpose. This means close attention. The less he is attracted by the nature of the work and the mode in which it is carried on, and the less, therefore, he enjoys it as something which gives play to his bodily and mental powers, the more close his attention is forced to be.

The elementary factors of the labor process are 1. the personal activity of man, i.e., work itself; 2. the subject of that work; and 3. its instruments.

The soil (and this, economically speaking, includes water) in the virgin state in which it supplies man with necessaries or the means of subsistence ready to hand, exists independently of him, and is the universal subject of human labor. All those things which labor merely separates from immediate connection with their environment are subjects of labor spontaneously provided by Nature. Such are fish which we catch and take from their element, water, timber which we fell in the virgin forest, and ores which we extract from their veins. If, on the other hand, the subject of labor has, so to say, been filtered through previous labor, we call it raw material; such is ore already extracted and ready for washing. All raw material is the subject of labor, but not every subject of labor is raw material; it can only become so after it has undergone some alteration by means of labor.

An instrument of labor is a thing, or a complex of things, which the laborer interposes between himself and the subject of his labor, and which serves as the conductor of his activity. He makes use of the mechanical, physical, and chemical properties of some substances in order to make other substances subservient to his aims. Leaving out of consideraton such ready-made means of subsistence as fruits, in gathering which a man's own limbs serve as the instruments of his labor, the first thing of which the laborer possesses himself is not the subject of labor but its instrument. Thus Nature becomes one of the organs of his activity, one that he annexes to his own bodily organs, adding stature to himself in spite of the Bible. As the earth is his original larder, so too it is his original tool house. It supplies him for instance, with stones for throwing, grinding, pressing, cutting, etc. The earth itself is an instrument of labor, but when used as such in agriculture implies a whole series of other instruments and a comparatively high development of labor. No sooner does labor undergo the least development, than it requires specially prepared instruments. Thus in the oldest caves we find stone implements and weapons. In the earliest period of human history domesticatcd animals, i.e., animals which have been bred for the purpose, and have undergone modifications by means of labor, play the chief part as instruments of labor along with specially prepared stones, wood, bones, and shells. The use and fabrication of instruments of labor although existing in the germ among certain species of animals, is specifically characteristic of the human labor process, and Franklin therefore defines man as a tool-making animal. Relics of bygone instruments of labor possess the same importance for the investigation of extinct economical forms of society as do fossil bones for the determination of extinct species of animals. It is not the articles made, but how they are made, and by what instruments, that enables us to distinguish different economical epochs. Instruments of labor not only supply a standard of the degree of development to which human labor has attained, but they are also indicators of the social conditions under which that labor is carried on. Among the instruments of labor, those of a mechanical nature, which, taken as a whole, we may call the bone and muscles of production, offer much more decided characteristics of a given epoch of production than those which, like pipes, tubs, baskets, jars, etc., serve only to hold materials for labor, which latter class we may in a general way call the vascular system of production. The latter first begins to play an important part in the chemical industries.

In a wider sense we may include among the instruments of labor, in addition to those things that are used for directly transferring labor to its subject, and which therefore, in one way or another, serve as conductors of activity, all such objects as are necessary for carrying on the labor process. These do not enter directly into the process, but without them it is either impossible for it to take place at all, or possible only to a partial extent. Once more we find the earth to be a universal instrument of this sort, for it furnishes a locus standi to the laborer and a field of employment for his activity. Among instruments that are the result of previous labor and also belong to this class, we find workshops, canals, roads, and so forth.

In the labor-process, therefore, man's activity, with the help of the instruments of labor, effects an alteration, designed from the commencement, in the material worked upon. The process disappears in the product; the latter is a use value, Nature's material adapted by a change of form to the wants of man. Labor has incorporated itself wth its subject: the former is materialized, the latter transformed. That which in the laborer appeared as movement, now appears in the product as a fixed quality without motion. The blacksmith forges and the product is a forging.

If we examine the whole process from the point of view of its result, the product, it is plain that both the instruments and the subject of labor are means of production, and that the labor itself is productive labor.

Though a use value, in the form of a product, issues from the labor process, yet other use values, products of previous labor, enter into it as means of production. The same use value is both the product of a previous process and a means of production in a latter process. Products are therefore not only results, but also essential conditions of labor.

With the exception of the extractive industries, in which the material for labor is provided immediately by nature, such as mining, hunting, fishing, and agriculture (so far as the latter is confined to breaking up virgin soil), all branches of industry manipulate raw material, objects already filtered through labor, already products of labor. Such is seed in agriculture. Animals and plants, which we are accustomed to consider as products of nature, are in their present form not only products of, say last year's labor, but the result of a gradual transformation, continued through many generations, under man's superintendence, and by means of his labor. But in the great majority of cases, instruments of labor show even to the most superficial observer, traces of the labor of past ages. . . .

Hence we see that whether a use value is to be regarded as raw material, as instrument of labor, or as product, this is determined entirely by its function in the labor process, by the position it there occupies: as this varies, so does its character.

Whenever therefore a product enters as a means of production into a new labor process, it thereby loses its character of product, and becomes a mere factor in the process. A spinner treats spindles only as implements for spinning, and flax only as the material that he spins. Of course it is impossible to spin without material and spindles; and therefore the existence of these things as products, at the commencement of the spinning operation, must be presumed; but in the process itself, the fact that they are products of previous labor, is a matter of utter indifference; just as in the digestive process, it is of no importance whatever that bread is the produce of the previous labor of the farmer, the miller, and the baker. . . .

A machine which does not serve the purposes of labor is useless. In addition, it falls a prey to the destructive influence of natural forces. Iron rusts and wood rots. Yarn with which we neither weave nor knit is cotton wasted. Living labor must seize upon these things and rouse them from their death-sleep, change them from mere possible use values into real and effective ones. Bathed in the fire of labor, appropriated as part and parcel of labor's organism, and, as it were, made alive for the performance of their functions in the process, they are in truth consumed, but consumed with a purpose, as elementary constituents of new use values, of new products, ever ready as means of subsistence for individual consumption, or as means of production for some new labor process.

If then, on the one hand, finished products are not only results, but also necessary conditions, of the labor process, on the other hand, their assumption into that process, their contact with living labor, is the sole means by which they can be made to retain their character of use values, and be utilized.

Labor uses up its material factors, its subject and its instruments, consumes them, and is therefore a process of consumption. Such productive consumption is distinguished from individual consumption by this, that the latter uses up products, as means of subsistence for the living individual; the former, as means whereby alone labor, the labor power of the living individual, is enabled to act. The product, therefore, of individual consumption is the consumer himself; the result of productive consumption is a product distinct from the consumer.

In so far then, as its instruments and subjects are themselves products, labor consumes products in order to create products, or in other words, consumes one set of products by turning them into means of production for another set. But, just as in the beginning, the only participators in the labor process were man and the earth, which latter exists independently of man, so even now we still employ in the process many means of production, provided directly by nature, that do not represent any combination of natural substances with human labor.

The labor process, resolved as above into its simple elementary factors, is human action with a view to the production of use values, appropriation of natural substances to human requirements; it is the necessary condition for effecting exchange of matter between man and Nature; it is the everlasting nature-imposed condition of human existence, and therefore is independent of every social phase of that existence, or rather, is common to every such phase. It was, therefore, not necessary to represent our laborer in connection with other laborers; man and his labor on one side, Nature and its materials on the other, sufficed. As the taste of the porridge does not tell you who grew the oats, no more does this simple process tell you of itself what are the social conditions under which it is taking place, whether under the slave-owner's brutal lash, or the anxious eye of the capitalist, whether Cincinnatus carries it on in tilling his modest farm or a savage in killing wild animals with stones.

Let us now return to our would-be capitalist. We left him just after he had purchased, in the open market, all the necessary factors of the labor process; its objective factors, the means of production, as well as its subjective factor, labor power. With the keen eye of an expert, he had selected the means of production and the kind of labor power best adapted to his particular trade, be it spinning, bootmaking, or any other kind. He then proceeds to consume the commodity, the labor power that he has just bought, by causing the laborer, the impersonation of that labor power, to consume the means of production by his labor. The general character of the labor process is evidently not changed by the fact that the laborer works for the capitalist instead of for himself; moreover, the particular methods and operations employed in bootmaking or spinning are not immediately changed by the intervention of the capitalist. He must begin by taking the labor power as he finds it in the market, and consequently be satisfied with labor of such a kind as would be found in the period immediately preceding the rise of the capitalists. Changes in the methods of production by the subordination of labor to capital can take place only at a later period, and therefore will have to be treated of in a later chapter.

The labor process, turned into the process by which the capitalist consumes labor power, exhibits two characteristic phenomena. First, the laborer works under the control of the capitalist to whom his labor belongs; the capitalist taking good care that the work is done in a proper manner, and that the means of production are used with intelligence, so that there is no unnecessary waste of raw material, and no wear and tear of the implements beyond what is necessarily caused by the work.

Secondly, the product is the property of the capitalist and not that of the laborer, its immediate producer. Suppose that a capitalist pays for a day's labor power at its value; then the right to use that power for a day belongs to him, just as much as the right to use any other commodity, such as a horse that he has hired for the day. To the purchaser of a commodity belongs its use, and the seller of labor power, by giving his labor, does no more, in reality, than part with the use value that he has sold. From the instant he steps into the workshop, the use value of his labor power, and therefore also its use, which is labor, belongs to the capitalist. By the purchase of labor power, the capitalist incorporates labor, as a living ferment, with the lifeless constituents of the product. From his point of view, the labor process is nothing more than the consumption of the commodity purchased, i.e., of labor power; but this consumption cannot be effected except by supplying the labor power with the means of production. The labor process is a process between things that the capitalist has purchased, things that have become his property. The product of this process also belongs, therefore, to him. . . .

38. *The Production of Surplus Value*

Marx's analysis of the production of surplus value is based upon the independence of two factors: (1) the value of labor power (as seen by the laborer in terms of the amount of wages he can obtain) and (2) the amount of value which that labor power can create once it is in the employ of the capitalist. As Marx puts it, the unique feature of the commodity of labor power lies in its "being a source not only of value, but of more value than it has itself." In terms of our two factors above, the key to the entire process of capitalistic production lies in the fact that the capitalist can ensure that the second factor accounts for the creation of more value than is represented by the cost of the labor power, the first factor.

OUR CAPITALIST has two objects in view: in the first place, he wants to produce a use value that has a value in exchange, that is to say, an article destined to be sold, a commodity; and secondly, he desires to produce a commodity whose value shall be greater than the sum of the values of the commodities used in its production, that is, of the means of production and the labor power, that he purchased with his good money in the open market. His aim is to produce not only a use value, but a commodity also; not only use value, but value; not only value, but at the same time surplus value. . . .

The fact that half a day's labor is necessary to keep the laborer alive during 24 hours does not in any way prevent him from working a whole day. Therefore, the value of labor power, and the value which that labor power creates in the labor process, are two entirely different magnitudes; and this difference of the two values was what the capitalist had in view when he was purchasing the labor power. The useful qualities that labor power possess, and by virtue of which it makes yarn or boots, were to him nothing more than a *conditio sine qua non;* for in order to create value, labor must be expended in a useful manner. What really influenced him was the specific use value which this commodity possesses of being *a source not only of value, but of more value than it has itself.* This is the special service that the capitalist expects from labor power. . . . The owner of the money has paid the value of a day's labor power; his, therefore, is the use of it for a day; a day's labor belongs to him. The circumstance that on the one hand the daily sustenance of labor power costs only half a day's labor, while on the other hand the very same labor power can work during a whole day, that consequently the value which its use during one day creates, is [for example] double what he pays for that use, this circumstance is, without doubt, a piece of good luck for the buyer, but by no means an injury to the seller. . . .

If we now compare the two processes of producing value and of creating surplus value, we see that the latter is nothing but the continuation of the former beyond a definite point. If on the one hand the process be not carried beyond the point, where the value paid by the capitalist for the labor power is replaced by an exact equivalent, it is simply a process of producing value; if, on the other hand, it be continued beyond that point, it becomes a process of creating surplus value.

If we proceed further, and compare the process of producing value with the labor process, pure and simply, we find that the latter consists of the useful labor, the work, that produces use values. Here we contemplate the labor as producing a particular article; we view it under its qualitative aspect alone, with regard to its end and aim. But viewed as a value-creating process, the same labor process presents itself under its quantitative aspect alone. Here it is a question merely of the time occupied by the laborer in doing the work; of the period during which the labor power is usefully expended. Here, the commodities that take part in the process do not count any longer as necessary adjuncts of labor power in the production of a definite, useful object. They count merely as depositaries of so much absorbed or materialized labor; that labor, whether previously embodied in the means of production or incorporated in them for the first time during the process by the action of labor power, counts in either case only according to its duration; it amounts to so many hours or days as the case may be.

Moreover, only so much of the time spent in the production of any article is counted, as, under the given social conditions, is necessary. The consequences of this are various. In the first place, it becomes necessary that the labor should be carried on under normal conditions. If a self-acting mule is the implement in general use for spinning, it would be absurd to supply the spinner with a distaff and spinning wheel. The cotton too must not be such rubbish as to cause extra waste in being worked, but must be of suitable quality. Otherwise the spinner would be found to spend more time in producing a pound of yaɪd than is socially necessary, in which case the excess of time would create neither value nor money. But whether the material factors of the process are of normal quality or not depends not upon the laborer, but entirely upon the capitalist. Then again, the labor power itself must be of average efficacy. In the trade in which it is being employed, it must possess the average skill, handiness and quickness prevalent in that trade, and our capitalist took good care to buy labor power of such normal goodness. This power must be applied with the average amount of exertion and with the usual degree of intensity; and the capitalist is as careful to see that this is done, as that his workmen are not idle for a single moment. He has bought the use of the labor power for a definite period, and he insists upon his rights. He has no intention of being robbed. Lastly, and for this purpose our friend has a penal code of his own, all wasteful consumption of raw material or instruments of labor is strictly forbidden, because what is so wasted represents labor superfluously expended, labor that does not count in the product or enter into its value.

We now see that the difference between labor, considered on the one hand as producing utilities, and on the other hand, as creating value, a difference which we discovered by our analysis of a commodity, resolves itself into a distinction between two aspects of the process of production.

The process of production, considered on the one hand as the unity of the labor process and the process of creating value, is production of commodities; considered on the other hand as the unity of the labor process and the process of producing surplus value, it is the capitalist process of production, or capitalist production of commodities.

We stated, on a previous page, that in the creation of surplus value it does not in the least matter whether the labor appropriated by the capitalist be simple unskilled labor of average quality or more complicated skilled labor. All labor of a higher or more complicated character than average labor is expenditure of labor power of a more costly kind, labor power whose production has cost more time and labor, and which therefore has a higher value, than unskilled or simple labor power. This power being of higher value, its consumption is labor of a higher class, labor that creates in equal times proportionally higher values than unskilled labor does. Whatever difference in skill there may be between the labor of a spinner and that of a jeweler, the portion of his labor by which the jeweler merely replaces the value of his own labor power does not in any way differ in quality from the additional portion by which he creates surplus value. In the making of jewelry, just as in spinning, the surplus value results only from a quantitative excess of labor, from a lengthening-out of one and the same labor process, in the one case, of the process of making jewels, in the other of the process of making yarn.

But on the other hand, in every process of creating value, the reduction of skilled labor to average social labor, e.g., one day of skilled to six days of unskilled labor, is unavoidable. We therefore save ourselves a superfluous operation, and simplify our analysis, by the assumption, that the labor of the workman employed by the capitalist is unskilled average labor.

39. *The Rate of Surplus Value*

The next group of selections deals with the problem of calculating the rate of surplus value, the single most important factor involved in capitalistic production. Marx first makes the distinction between (1) *constant capital* (i.e., the means of production—exclusive of labor power—which are used up in the production process and whose value is merely transferred to the finished product) and (2) *variable capital* (i.e., wages, the expense of the process whereby the laborer adds value to the raw materials of production as they are transformed into the finished product). The crucial step for the capitalist, of course, lies in having the laborer transfer more value to the raw materials than is covered in the cost of his wages.

The rate of surplus value is then calculated as the amount of surplus value produced divided by the amount of variable capital (i.e., wages) involved in the process.

Marx finds an equivalent way of expressing this rate of surplus value. Beginning from the distinction between *necessary labor* (that portion of the working day in which the laborer replaces the value which is paid to him in wages) and *surplus labor* (that portion of the working day in which the worker, having already created a value equivalent to his wages during the "necessary" labor time, now continues to create value for the capitalist—which is to create surplus value), Marx is able to express the rate of surplus value in

---

terms of the ratio of surplus labor divided by necessary labor. Thus, "the rate of surplus value is . . . an exact expression for the degree of exploitation of labor power by capital, or of the laborer by the capitalist."

CONSTANT CAPITAL AND VARIABLE CAPITAL

The various factors of the labor process play different parts in forming the value of the product.

The laborer adds fresh value to the subject of his labor by expending upon it a given amount of additional labor, no matter what the specific character and utility of that labor may be. On the other hand, the values of the means of production used up in the process are preserved, and present themselves afresh as constituent parts of the value of the product; the values of the cotton and the spindle, for instance, reappear again in the value of the yarn. The value of the means of production is therefore preserved, by being transferred to the product. This transfer takes place during the conversion of those means into a product, or in other words, during the labor process. It is brought about by labor; but how? . . .

Since, however, the addition of new value to the subject of his labor, and the preservation of its former value, are two entirely distinct results, produced simultaneously by the laborer, during one operation, it is plain that this twofold nature of the result can be explained only by the twofold nature of his labor; at one and the same time, it must in one character create value, and in another character preserve or transfer value.

Now, in what manner does every laborer add new labor and consequently new value? Evidently, only by laboring productively in a particular way; the spinner by spinning, the weaver by weaving, the smith by forging. But, while thus incorporating labor generally, that is value, it is by the particular form alone of the labor, by the spinning, the weaving and the forging respectively, that the means of production, the cotton and spindle, the yarn and loom, and the iron and anvil become constituent elements of the product, of a new use value. Each use value disappears, but only to reappear under a new form in a new use value. Now, we saw, when we were considering the process of creating value, that, if a use value be effectively consumed in the production of a new use value, the quantity of labor expended in the production of the consumed article forms a portion of the quantity of labor necessary to produce the new use value; this portion is therefore labor transferred from the means of production to the new product. Hence, the laborer preserves the values of the consumed means of production, or transfers them as portions of its value to the product, not by virtue of his additional labor, abstractedly considered, but by virtue of the particular useful character of that labor, by virtue of its special productive form. In so far then as labor is such specific productive activity, in so far as it is spinning, weaving, or forging, it raises, by mere contact, the means of production from the dead, makes them living factors of the labor process, and combines with them to form the new products. . . .

We have seen that the means of production transfer value to the new product, so far only as during the labor process they lose value in the shape of their old use value. The maximum loss of value that they can suffer in the process is plainly limited by the amount of the original value with which they came into the process, or in other words, by the labor time necessary for their production. Therefore the means of production can never add more value to the product than they themselves possess independently of the process in which they assist. However useful a given kind of raw material, or a machine, or other means of production may be, though it may cost £150, or, say 500 days' labor, yet it cannot, under any circumstances, add to the value of the product more than £150. Its value is determined not by the labor process into which it enters as a means of production, but by that out of which it has issued as a product. In the labor process it only serves as a mere use value, a thing with useful properties, and could not, therefore, transfer any value to the product, unless it possessed such value previously.

As regards the means of production, what is really consumed is their use value, and the consumption of this use value by labor results in the product. There is no consumption of their value, and it would therefore be inaccurate to say that it is reproduced. It is rather preserved; not by reason of any operation it undergoes itself in the process; but because the article in which it originally exists, vanishes, it is true, but vanishes into some other article. Hence, in the value of the product, there is a reappearance of the value of the means of production, but there is, strictly speaking, no reproduction of that value. That which is produced is a new use value in which the old exchange value reappears.

It is otherwise with the subjective factor of the labor process, with labor power in action. While the laborer, by virtue of his labor being of a specialized kind that has a special object, preserves and transfers to the product the value of the means of production, he at the same time, by the mere act of working, creates each instant an additional or new value. Suppose the process of production to be stopped just when the workman has produced an equivalent for the value of his own labor power, when, for example, by six hours' labor, he has added a value of three shillings. This value is the surplus, of the total value of the product, over the portion of its value that is due to the means of production. It is the only original bit of value formed during this process, the only portion of the value of the product created by this process. Of course, we do not forget that this new value only replaces the money advanced by the capitalist in the purchase of the labor power, and spent by the laborer on the necessaries of life. With regard to the money spent, the new value is merely a reproduction; but, nevertheless, it is an actual, and not, as in the case of the value of the means of production, only an apparent, reproduction. The substitution of one value for another is here effected by the creation of new value.

We know, however, from what has gone before, that the labor process may continue beyond the time necessary to reproduce and incorporate in the product a mere equivalent for the value of the labor power. Instead of the six hours that are sufficient for the latter purpose, the process may continue for twelve hours. The action of labor power, therefore, not only reproduces its own value, but produces value over and above it. This surplus value is the difference between the value of the product and the value of the elements consumed in the formation of that product, in other words, of the means of production and the labor power. . . .

That part of capital then, which is represented by the means of production, by the raw material, auxiliary material and the instruments of labor, does not, in the process of production, undergo any quantitative alteration of value. I therefore call it the constant part of capital, or, more shortly, *constant capital.*

On the other hand, that part of capital represented by labor power does, in the process of production, undergo an alteration of value. It both reproduces the equivalent of its own value, and also produces an excess, a surplus value, which may itself vary, may be more or less according to circumstances. This part of capital is continually being transformed from a constant into a variable magnitude. I therefore call it the variable part of capital, or, shortly, *variable capital.* The same elements of capital which, from the point of view of the labor process, present themselves respectively as the objective and subjective factors, as means of production and labor power, present themselves, from the point of view of the process of creating surplus value, as constant and variable capital. . . .

The Rate of Surplus Value

The capital C is made up of two components, one, the sum of money c laid out upon the means of production, and the other, the sum of money v expended upon the labor power; c represents the portion that has become constant capital, and v the portion that has become variable capital. At first then, $C = c + v$: for example, if £500 is the capital advanced, its components may be such that the £500 = £410 const. + £90 var. When the process of production is finished, we get a commodity whose value $= (c + v) + s$, where s is the surplus value; or taking our former figures, the value of this commodity may be (£410 const. + £90 var.) + £90 surpl. The original capital has now changed from C to C', from £500 to £590. The difference is s or a surplus value of £90. . . .

Now we have seen how that portion of the constant capital

which consists of the instruments of labor transfers to the product only a fraction of its value, while the remainder of that value continues to reside in those instruments. Since this remainder plays no part in the formation of value, we may at present leave it on one side. . . .

We know that the value of the constant capital is transferred to, and merely reappears in, the product. The new value actually created in the process, the value produced, or value product, is therefore not the same as the value of the product; it is not, as it would at first sight appear $(c+v)+s$ or £410 const. + £90 var. + £90 surpl.; but $v+s$ or £90 var. + £90 surpl., not £590 but £180. . . .

If we look at the means of production, in their relation to the creation of value, and to the variation in the quantity of value, apart from anything else, they appear simply as the material in which labor power, the value creator, incorporates itself. Neither the nature nor the value of this material is of any importance. The only requisite is that there be a sufficient supply to absorb the labor expended in the process of production. That supply once given, the material may rise or fall in value, or even be, as land and the sea, without any value in itself; but this will have no influence on the creation of value or on the variation in the quantity of value.

In the first place then we equate the constant capital to zero. The capital advanced is consequently reduced from $c+v$ to v, and instead of the value of the product $(c+v)+s$ we have now the value produced $(v+s)$. Given the new value produced = £180, which sum consequently represents the whole labor expended during the process, then subtracting from it £90, the value of the variable capital, we have remaining £90, the amount of the surplus value. This sum of £90 of s expresses the absolute quantity or surplus value produced. The relative quantity produced, or the increase per cent of the variable capital, is determined, it is plain, by the ratio of the surplus value to the variable capital, or is expressed by $\frac{s}{v}$. In our example this ratio is $\frac{90}{90}$, which gives an increase of 100%. This relative increase in the value of the variable capital, or the relative magnitude of the surplus value, I call, "The rate of surplus value."

We have seen that the laborer, during one portion of the labor process, produces only the value of his labor power, that is, the value of his means of subsistence. Now since his work forms part of a system, based on the social division of labor, he does not directly produce the actual necessaries which he himself consumes; he produces instead a particular commodity, yarn for example, whose value is equal to the value of those necessaries or of the money with which they can be bought. The portion of his day's labor devoted to this purpose, will be greater or less, in proportion to the value of the necessaries that he daily requires on an average, or, what amounts to the same thing, in proportion to the labor time required on an average to produce them. If the value of those necessaries represents on an average the expenditure of six hours' labor, the workman must on an average work for six hours to produce that value. If instead of working for the capitalist, he worked independently on his own account, he would, other things being equal, still be obliged to labor for the same number of hours, in order to produce the value of his labor power, and thereby to gain the means of subsistence necessary for his conservation or continued reproduction. But as we have seen, during that portion of his day's labor in which he produces the value of his labor power, say three shillings, he produces only an equivalent for the value of his labor power already advanced by the capitalist; the new value created only replaces the variable capital advanced. It is owing to this fact that the production of the new value of three shillings take the semblance of a mere reproduction. That portion of the working day, then, during which this reproduction takes place, I call *"necessary"* labor time, and the labor expended during that time I call *"necessary"* labor. Necessary, as regards the laborer, because independent of the particular social form of his labor; necessary, as regards capital, and the world of capitalists, because on the continued existence of the laborer depends their existence also.

During the second period of the labor process, that in which his labor is no longer necessary labor, the workman, it is true, labors, expends labor power; but his labor, being no longer necessary labor, he creates no value for himself. He creates surplus value which, for the capitalist, has all the charms of a creation out of nothing. This portion of the working day, I name surplus labor time, and to the labor expended during that time, I give the name of surplus labor. . . .

Since, on the one hand, the values of the variable capital and of the labor power purchased by that capital are equal, and the value of this labor power determines the necessary portion of the working day; and since, on the other hand, the surplus value is determined by the surplus portion of the working day, it follows that surplus value bears the same ratio to variable capital that surplus labor does to necessary labor, or in other words, the rate of surplus value $\frac{s}{v} = \frac{\text{surplus labor}}{\text{necessary labor}}$. Both ratios, $\frac{s}{v}$ and $\frac{\text{surplus labor}}{\text{necessary labor}}$ express the same thing in different ways; in the one case by reference to materialized, incorporated labor, in the other by reference to living, fluent labor.

The rate of surplus value is therefore an exact expression for the degree of exploitation of labor power by capital, or of the laborer by the capitalist.

We assumed in our example, that the value of the product= £410 const.+ £90 var.+ £90 surpl., and that the capital advanced= £500. Since the surplus value= £90, and the advanced capital= £500, we should, according to the usual way of reckoning, get as the rate of surplus value (generally confounded with rate of profits) 18%, a rate so low as possibly to cause a pleasant surprise to Mr. Carey and other harmonizers. But in truth, the rate of surplus value is not equal to $\frac{s}{c}$ or $\frac{s}{cv}$ but to $\frac{s}{v}$: thus it is not $\frac{90}{500}$ but $\frac{90}{90}$ or 100%, which is more than five times the apparent degree of exploitation. Although, in the case we have supposed, we are ignorant of the actual length of the working day, and of the duration in days or weeks of the labor process, as also of the number of laborers employed, yet the rate of surplus value $\frac{s}{v}$ accurately discloses to us, by means of its equivalent expression $\frac{\text{surplus labor}}{\text{necessary labor}}$ the relation between the two parts of the working day. This relation is here one of equality, the rate being 100%. Hence, it is plain, the laborer, in our example, works one half of the day for himself, the other half for the capitalist. .·. .

At first, capital subordinates labor on the basis of the technical conditions in which it historically finds it. It does not, therefore, change immediately the mode of production. The production of surplus value—in the form hitherto considered by us—by means of simple extension of the working day, proved, therefore, to be independent of any change in the mode of production itself. If was not less active in the old-fashioned bakeries than in the modern cotton factories.

If we consider the process of production from the point of view of the simple labor process, the laborer stands in relation to the means of production, not in their quality as capital, but as the mere means and material of his own intelligent productive activity. In tanning, e.g., he deals with the skins as his simple object of labor. It is not the capitalist whose skin he tans. But it is different as soon as we deal with the process of production from the point of view of the process of creation of surplus value. The means of production are at once changed into means for the absorption of the labor of others. It is now no longer the laborer that employs the means of production, but the means of production that employ the laborer. Instead of being consumed by him as material elements of his productive activity, they consume him as the ferment necessary to their own life process, and the life process of capital consists only in its movement as value constantly expanding, constantly multiplying itself. Furnaces and workshops that stand idle by night, and absorb no living labor, are "a mere loss" to the capitalist. Hence, furnaces and workshops constitute lawful claims upon the night labor of the workpeople. The simple transformation of money into the material factors of the process of production, into means of production, transforms the latter into a title and a right to the labor and surplus labor of others. . . .

40. The Struggle Between Capitalist and Laborer

Following the discussion of the distinction between "necessary" and "surplus" labor time, Marx presents a historical survey of some seventy-five pages devoted to the struggle between capital and labor concerning such items as the length of the working day, child and female labor, and the conditions within the factories. The overall picture is clearly one of the continued effort of employers to assure the legal sanctioning of the most blatant exploitative practices; it was not until the Factory Act of 1833 in Great Britain that even the most meager guarantees against such practices were won for the workers.

After this interlude Marx introduces the concept of relative surplus value, of which we include a few passages, which indicate that the new struggle is over the *division* of the working day (between "necessary" and "surplus" working time) now that its *length* is effected by statutory limitations.

There then follows a detailed discussion of some two hundred fifty pages dealing with the process by which large-scale industry was developed on the basis of a division of labor according to the functions of the machine (not human activities) and which has thus reduced the modern worker to an appendage of the machine (cf. the passage dealing with the "inversion" of the relationship between dead and living labor), and the various efforts by the capitalists to increase

From the Kerr edition, Vol. I, pp. 342–581.

productivity by placing ever greater burdens upon the worker (e.g., piece wages and the depression of normal wages *below* the subsistence minimum, which forces the worker to work overtime simply to obtain a barely sufficient wage).

The selections which follow serve only to summarize Marx's often exciting observations in these areas.

THAT PORTION of the working day which merely produces an equivalent for the value paid by the capitalist for his labor power, has, up to this point, been treated by us as a constant magnitude; and such in fact it is, under given conditions of production and at a given stage in the economical development of society. Beyond this, his necessary labor time, the laborer, we saw, could continue to work for 2, 3, 4, 6, etc., hours. The rate of surplus value and the length of the working day depended on the magnitude of this prolongation. Though the necessary labor time was constant, we saw, on the other hand, that the total working day was variable. Now suppose we have a working day whose length, and whose apportionment between necessary labor and surplus labor, are given. Let the whole line a c, a————————b—c, represent, for example, a working day of 12 hours; the portion of a b 10 hours of necessary labor, and the portion b c 2 hours of surplus labor. How now can the production of surplus value be increased, i.e., how can the surplus labor be prolonged, without, or independently of, any prolongation of a c?

Although the lengh of a c is given, b c appears to be capable of prolongation, if not by extension beyond its end c, which is also the end of the working day a c, yet, at all events, by pushing back its starting point b in the direction of a. Assume that b'—b in the line a b' b c is equal to half of b c

a————————b'—b————c

or to one hour's labor time. If now, in a c, the working day of 12 hours, we move the point b to b', b c becomes b' c; the surplus labor increases by one-half, from 2 hours to 3 hours, although the working day remains as before at 12 hours. This extension of the surplus labor time from b c to b' c, from 2 hours to 3 hours, is, however, evidently impossible, without a simultaneous contraction of the necessary labor time from a b into a b , from 10 hours to 9 hours. The prolongation of the surplus labor would correspond to a shortening of the necessary labor; or a portion of the labor time previously consumed, in reality, for the laborer's own benefit, would be converted into labor time for the benefit of the capitalist. There would be an alteration, not in the length of the working day, but in its division into necessary labor time and surplus labor time. . . .

The surplus value produced by prolongation of the working day, I call *absolute surplus value.* On the other hand, the surplus value arising from the curtailment of the necessary labor time, and from the corresponding alteration in the respective lengths of the two components of the working day, I call *relative surplus value.*

The shortening of the working day is, therefore, by no means what is aimed at, in capitalist production, when labor is economized by increasing its productiveness. It is only the shortening of the labor time, necessary for the production of a definite quantity of commodities, that is aimed at. The fact that the workman, when the productiveness of his labor has been increased, produces, say 10 times as many commodities as before, and thus spends one-tenth as much labor time on each, by no means prevents him from continuing to work 12 hours as before, nor from producing in those 12 hours 1,200 articles instead of 120. Nay, more, his working day may be prolonged at the same time, so as to make him produce, say 1,400 articles in 14 hours. . . . The object of all development of the productiveness of labor, within the limits of capitalist production, is to shorten that part of the working day during which the workman must labor for his own benefit, and by that very shortening, to lengthen the other part of the day, during which he is at liberty to work gratis for the capitalist. . . .

Increased productiveness and greater intensity of labor both have a like effect. They both augment the mass of articles produced in a given time. Both, therefore, shorten that portion of the working day which the laborer needs to produce his means of subsistence or their equivalent. The minimum length of the working day is fixed by this necessary but contractile portion of it. If the whole working day were to shrink to the length of this portion, surplus labor would vanish, a consummation utterly impossible under the regime of capital. Only by suppressing the capitalist form of production could the length of the working day be reduced to the necessary labor time. But, even in that case, the latter would extend its limits. On the one hand, because the notion of "means of subsistence" would considerably expand, and the laborer would lay claim to an altogether different standard of life. On the other hand, because a part of what is now surplus labor would then count as necessary labor; I mean the labor of forming a fund for reserve and accumulation.

The more the productiveness of labor increases, the more can the working day be shortened; and the more the working day is shortened, the more can the intensity of labor increase. From a social point of view, the productiveness increases in the same ratio as the economy of labor, which, in its turn; includes not only economy of the means of production, but also the avoidance of all useless labor. The capitalist mode of production, while on the one hand, enforcing economy in each individual business, on the other hand, begets, by its anarchical system of competition, the most outrageous squandering of labor power and of the social means of production, not to mention the creation of a vast number of employments, at present indispensable, but in themselves superfluous.

The intensity and productiveness of labor being given, the time which society is bound to devote to material production is shorter, and as a consequence, the time at its disposal for the free development, intellectual and social, of the individual is greater, in proportion as the work is more and more evenly divided among all the able-bodied members of society, and as a particular class is more and more deprived of the power to shift the natural burden of labor from its own shoulders to those of another layer of society. In this direction, the shortening of the working day finds at last a limit in the generalization of labor. In capitalist society spare time is acquired for one class by converting the whole lifetime of the masses into labor time.

41. *The Conversion of Surplus Value into Capital*

Marx has hitherto pursued two apparently diverse lines of argument: first he established the general formula of capitalist enterprise as represented in the formula M—C—M, and then he entered into the long discourse on the value-creating role of labor power. It should be of no surprise to the reader, then, to see in the chapter entitled "Conversion of Surplus Value into Capital" that the surplus value created by the worker is speedily transformed by the capitalist into *profit*, a new capital which now begins its own course of M—C—M alongside that of the original capital. This is succinctly described in the passages which follow.

HITHERTO WE have investigated how surplus value emanates from capital; we have now to see how capital arises from surplus value. Employing surplus value as capital, reconverting it into capital, is called accumulation of capital.

First let us consider this transaction from the standpoint of the individual capitalist. Suppose a spinner to have advanced a capital of £10,000, of which four-fifths (£8,000) are laid out in cotton, machinery, etc., and one-fifth (£2,000) in wages. Let him produce 240,000 pounds of yarn annually, having a value of £12,000. The rate of surplus value being 100%, the surplus value lies in the surplus or net product of 40,000 pounds of yarn,

From the Kerr edition, Vol. I, pp. 634–637.

one-sixth of the gross product, with a value of £2,000 which will be realized by a sale. . . .

It is the old story: Abraham begat Isaac, Isaac begat Jacob, and so on. The original capital of £10,000 brings in a surplus value of £2,000, which is capitalized. The new capital of £2,000 brings in a surplus value of £400, and this, too, is capitalized, converted into a second additional capital, which, in its turn, produces a further surplus value of £80. And so the ball rolls on.

We here leave out of consideration the portion of the surplus value consumed by the capitalist. Just as little does it concern us, for the moment, whether the additional capital is joined on to the original capital, or is separated from it to function independently; whether the same capitalist, who accumulated it, employs it, or whether he hands it over to another. This only we must not forget, that by the side of the newly formed capital, the original capital continues to reproduce itself, and to produce surplus value, and that this is also true of all accumulated capital, and the additional capital engendered by it. . . .

42. *The General Law of Capitalist Accumulation*

The chapter which constitutes the climax of the first volume of *Capital* is entitled "The General Law of Capitalist Accumulation." In it all the elements developed thus far are integrated. The three separate selections from this crucial chapter are essential for understanding Marx's analysis.

A. *The "Organic Composition" of Capital*

In Section 1 of this chapter Marx begins by defining another key term, the *organic composition of capital,* defined as the ratio of constant capital to the total capital, i.e., a measure of the degree to which capital has been invested in such items as plant, equipment, and machinery. Furthermore, all historical evidence points to the working of a "law of the progressive increase in constant capital" relative to variable capital, and this is shown in the progressive development of the process known today as "automation."

THE COMPOSITION of capital is to be understood in a twofold sense. On the side of value, it is determined by the proportion in which it is divided into constant capital or value of the means of production, and variable capital or value of labor power, the sum total of wages. On the side of material, as it functions in the process of production, all capital is divided into means of pro-

From the Kerr edition, Vol. I, pp. 671–673.

duction and living labor power. This latter composition is determined by the relation between the mass of the means of production employed, on the one hand, and the mass of labor necessary for their employment, on the other. I call the former the *value composition*, the latter the *technical composition*, of capital. Between the two there is a strict correlation. To express this, I call the value composition of capital, in so far as it is determined by its technical composition and mirrors the changes of the latter, the *organic composition* of capital. Wherever I refer to the composition of capital, without further qualification, its organic composition is always understood.

The many individual capitals invested in a particular branch of production have, one with another, more or less different compositions. The average of their individual compositions gives us the composition of the total capital in this branch of production. Lastly, the average of these averages, in all branches of production, gives us the composition of the total social capital of a country, and with this alone are we, in the last resort, concerned in the following investigation.

Growth of capital involves growth of its variable constituent or of the part invested in labor power. A part of the surplus value turned into additional capital must always be retransformed into variable capital, or additional labor fund. . . . Since the capital produces yearly a surplus value, of which one part is yearly added to the original capital; since this increment itself grows yearly along with the augmentation of the capital already functioning; since lastly, under special stimulus to enrichment, such as the opening of new markets, or of new spheres for the outlay of capital in consequence of newly developed social wants, etc., the scale of accumulation may be suddenly extended, merely by a change in the division of the surplus value or surplus product into capital and revenue, the requirements of accumulating capital may exceed the increase of labor power or of the number of laborers; the demand for laborers may exceed the supply, and, therefore, wages may rise. This must, indeed, ultimately be the case if the conditions supposed above continue. For since in each year more laborers are employed than in its predecessor, sooner or later a point must be reached, at which the requirements of accumulation begin to surpass the customary supply of labor, and, therefore, a rise of wages takes place. . . . The more or less favorable circumstances in which the wage-working class supports and multiplies itself in no way alter the fundamental character of capitalist production. As simple reproduction constantly reproduces the capital-relation itself, i.e., the relation of capitalists on the one hand, and wage workers on the other, so reproduction on a progressive scale, i.e., accumulation, reproduces the capital relation on a progressive scale, more capitalists or larger capitalists at this pole, more wage workers at that. The reproduction of a mass of labor power, which must incessantly reincorporate itself with capital for that capital's self-expansion; which cannot get free from capital, and whose enslavement to capital is only concealed by the variety of individual capitalists to whom it sells itself, this reproduction of labor power forms, in fact, an essential of the reproduction of capital itself. Accumulation of capital is, therefore, increase of the proletariat. . . .

B. The "Concentration" of Capital

In the second section of the chapter on "The General Law of Capitalist Accumulation," Marx argues that as the amount of constant capital required to compete successfully in a field rises, there occurs a *concentration of capital* as smaller, less efficient capitalists are thrown out of business or absorbed by their larger rivals, and it becomes nearly impossible for new capitalists to amass a sufficiently large amount of constant capital to enter an established field. The theoretical limit of this process is, of course, monopoly. Marx also touches upon the role of credit in this process, as well as upon the role, only just begun at the time of writing *Capital*, of the joint-stock company in facilitating the concentration of capital.

APART FROM natural conditions, such as fertility of the soil, etc., and from the skill of independent and isolated producers

---

From the Kerr edition, Vol. I, pp. 681–688.

(shown rather qualitatively in the goodness than quantitatively in the mass of their products), the degree of productivity of labor, in a given society, is expressed in the relative extent of the means of production that one laborer, during a given time, with the same tension of labor power, turns into products. The mass of the means of production which he thus transforms, increases with the productiveness of his labor. . . . The increase of the latter appears, therefore, in the diminution of the mass of labor in proportion to the mass of means of production moved by it, or in the diminution of the subjective factor of the labor process as compared with the objective factor.

This change in the technical composition of capital, this growth in the mass of means of production, as compared with the mass of the labor power that vivifies them, is reflected again in its value composition, by the increase of the constant constituent of capital at the expense of its variable constituent. There may be, e.g., originally 50 per cent of a capital laid out in means of production, and 50 per cent in the labor power; later on, with the development of the productivity of labor, 80 per cent in means of production, 20 per cent in labor power, and so on. This law of the progressive increase in constant capital, in proportion to the variable, is confirmed at every step (as already shown) by the comparative analysis of the prices of commodities, whether we compare different economic epochs or different nations in the same epoch. . . .

But, if the progress of accumulation lessens the relative magnitude of the variable part of capital, it by no means, in doing this, excludes the possibility of a rise in its absolute magnitude. Suppose that a capital value at first is divided into 50 per cent of constant and 50 per cent of variable capital; later into 80 per cent of constant and 20 per cent of variable. If in the meantime the original capital, say £6,000 has increased to £18,000, its variable constituent has also increased. It was £3,000, it is now £3,600. But whereas formerly an increase of capital by 20 per cent would have sufficed to raise the demand for labor 20 per cent, now this latter rise requires a tripling of the original capital.

It [has been] shown how the development of the productiveness of social labor presupposes cooperation on a large scale;

how it is only upon this supposition that division and combination of labor can be organized, and the means of production economized by concentration on a vast scale; how instruments of labor which, from their very nature, are only fit for use in common, such as a system of machinery, can be called into being; how huge natural forces can be pressed into the service of production; and how the transformation can be effected of the process of production into a technological application of science. On the basis of the production of commodities, where the means of production are the property of private persons, and where the artisan therefore either produces commodities, isolated from and independent of others, or sells his labor power as a commodity, because he lacks the means for independent industry, cooperation on a large scale can realize itself only in the increase of individual capitals, only in proportion as the means of social production and the means of subsistence are transformed into the private property of capitalists. The basis of the production of commodities can admit of production on a large scale in the capitalistic form alone. A certain accumulation of capital, in the hands of individual producers of commodities, forms therefore the necessary preliminary of the specifically capitalistic mode of production. We had, therefore, to assume that this occurs during the transition from handicraft to capitalistic industry. It may be called primitive accumulation, because it is the historic basis instead of the historic result of specifically capitalist production. . . . All methods for raising the social productive power of labor that are developed on this basis are at the same time methods for the increased production of surplus value or surplus product, which in its turn is the formative element of accumulation. They are, therefore, at the same time methods of the production of capital by capital, or methods of its accelerated accumulation. . . .

The laws of this centralization of capitals, or of the attraction of capital by capital, cannot be developed here. A brief hint at a few facts must suffice. The battle of competition is fought by cheapening of commodities. The cheapness of commodities depends on the productiveness of labor, and this again on the scale of production. Therefore, the larger capitals beat the smaller.

It will further be remembered that, with the development of the capitalist mode of production, there is an increase in the minimum amount of individual capital necessary to carry on a business under its normal conditions. The smaller capitals, therefore, crowd into spheres of production which Modern Industry has only sporadically or incompletely got hold of. Here competition rages in direct proportion to the number, and in inverse proportion to the magnitudes, of the antagonistic capitals. It always ends in the ruin of many small capitalists, whose capitals partly pass into the hand of their conquerors, partly vanish. Apart from this, with capitalist production an altogether new force comes into play—the credit system.

In its beginnings, the credit system sneaks in as a modest helper of accumulation and draws by invisible threads the money resources scattered all over the surface of society into the hands of individual or associated capitalists. But soon it becomes a new and formidable weapon in the competitive struggle, and finally it transforms itself into an immense social mechanism for the centralization of capitals. . . .

Centralization in a certain line of industry would have reached its extreme limit if all the individual capitals invested in it would have been amalgamated into one single capital. This limit would not be reached in any particular society until the entire social capital would be united, either in the hands of one single capitalist or in those of one single corporation.

Centralization supplements the work of accumulation, by enabling the industrial capitalists to expand the scale of their operations. The economic result remains the same, whether this consummation is brought about by accumulation or centralization, whether centralization is accomplished by the violent means of annexation, by which some capitals become such overwhelming centers of gravitation for others as to break their individual cohesion and attract the scattered fragments, or whether the amalgamation of a number of capitals, which already exist or are in process of fermation, proceeds by the smoother road of forming stock companies. The increased volume of industrial establishments forms everywhere the point of departure for a more comprehensive organization of the cooperative labor of many, for a wider development of their material powers, that is, for the progressive transformation of isolated processes of production carried on in accustomed ways into socially combined and scientifically managed processes of production. . . .

C. The "Industrial Reserve Army"

In the third section of his discussion of "The General Law of Capitalist Accumulation," Marx develops his famous concept of the industrial reserve army, which, by growing along with the accumulation and concentration of capital, serves to maintain a downward pressure on wages. Thus, despite the claims of the ideologists of capitalism and of "progress," the worker's lot does not improve along with that of the capitalist, even though it is true that his position does deteriorate more rapidly than that of the capitalist in periods of depressed business activity. With the progressive increase in the organic composition of capital, there is a decreasing need for additional workers, and thus the industrial reserve army grows even in times of capitalist expansion, thereby ensuring that conditions rapidly worsen for the proletariat as a whole. This "increasing misery" is the "absolute law of capitalist accumulation," i.e., the "negation" of the humanity of the overwhelming portion of mankind. The historical tendency of such a situation, Marx argues, cannot be anything but the eventual "negation of the negation," i.e., the overthrow of capitalism, followed by the establishment of cooperative and communal possession of the means of production.

THE ACCUMULATION of capital, though originally appearing as its quantitative extension only, is effected, as we have seen, under a progressive qualitative change in its composition, under a constant increase of its constant, at the expense of its variable constitutent.

From the Kerr edition, Vol. I, pp. 689–837.

The specifically capitalist mode of production, the development of the productive power of labor corresponding to it, and the change thence resulting in the organic composition of capital, do not merely keep pace with the advance of accumulation, or with the growth of social wealth. They develop at a much quicker rate, because mere accumulation, the absolute increase of the total social capital, is accompanied by the centralization of the individual capitals of which that total is made up; and because the change in the technological composition of the additional capital goes hand in hand with a similar change in the technological composition of the original capital. With the advance of accumulation, therefore, the proportion of constant to variable capital changes. It was originally say 1:1, it now becomes successively 2:1, 3:1, 4:1, 5:1, 7:1, etc., so that, as the capital increases, instead of ½ of its total value, only ⅓, ¼, ⅕, ⅙, ⅛, etc., is transformed into labor power, and, on the other hand, ⅔, ¾, ⅘, ⅚, ⅞ into means of production. Since the demand for labor is determined not by the amount of capital as a whole, but by its variable constituent alone, that demand falls progressively with the increase of the total capital, instead of, as previously assumed, rising in proportion to it. It falls relatively to the magnitude of the total capital, and at an accelerated rate, as this magnitude increases. . . . The rapidity of the change in the organic composition of capital, and in its technical form increases, and an increasing number of spheres of production becomes involved in this change. . . . The laboring population therefore produces, along with the accumulation of capital produced by it, the means by which itself is made relatively superfluous, is turned into a relative surplus population; and it does this to an always increasing extent. . . .

The mass of social wealth, overflowing with the advance of accumulation, and transformable into additional capital, thrusts itself frantically into old branches of production, whose market suddenly expands, or into newly formed branches, such as railways, etc., the need for which grows out of the development of the old ones. In all such cases, there must be the possibility of throwing great masses of men suddenly on the decisive points without injury to the scale of production in other spheres. Overpopulation supplies these masses. The course characteristic of modern industry, viz., a decennial cycle (interrupted by smaller oscillations), of periods of average activity, production at high pressure, crisis and stagnation, depends on the constant formation, the greater or less absorption, and the re-formation of the industrial reserve army of surplus population. In their turn, the varying phases of the industrial cycle recruit the surplus population, and become one of the most energetic agents of its reproduction. . . . The expansion by fits and starts of the scale of production is the preliminary to its equally sudden contraction; the latter again evokes the former, but the former is impossible without disposable human material, without an increase in the number of laborers independently of the absolute growth of the population. This increase is effected by the simple process that constantly "sets free" a part of the laborers; by methods which lessen the number of laborers employed in proportion to the increased production. The whole form of the movement of modern industry depends, therefore, upon the constant transformation of a part of the laboring population into unemployed or half-employed hands. . . .

The overwork of the employed part of the working class swells the ranks of the reserve, while conversely the greater pressure that the latter by its competition exerts on the former, forces these to submit to overwork and to subjugation under the dictates of capital. The condemnation of one part of the working class to enforced idleness by the overwork of the other part, and the converse, becomes a means of enriching the individual capitalists, and accelerates at the same time the production of the industrial reserve army on a scale corresponding with the advance of social accumulation. . . .

Taking them as a whole, the general movements of wages are exclusively regulated by the expansion and contraction of the industrial reserve army, and these again correspond to the periodic changes of the industrial cycle. They are, therefore, not determined by the variations of the absolute number of the working population, but by the varying proportions in which the working class is divided into active and reserve army, by the increase of diminution in the relative amount of the surplus population, by the extent to which it is now absorbed, now set free. . . .

The industrial reserve army, during the periods of stagnation and average prosperity, weighs down the active labor army; during the periods of overproduction and paroxysm, it holds its pretensions in check. Relative surplus population is therefore the pivot upon which the law of demand and supply of labor works. . . .

The greater the social wealth, the functioning capital, the extent and energy of its growth, and, therefore, also the absolute mass of the proletariat and the productiveness of its labor, the greater is the industrial reserve army. The same causes which develop the expansive power of capital, develop also the labor power at its disposal. The relative mass of the industrial reserve army increases therefore with the potential energy of wealth. But the greater this reserve army in proportion to the active labor army, the greater is the mass of a consolidated surplus population, whose misery is in inverse ratio to its torment of labor. The more extensive, finally, the Lazurus layers of the working class, and the industrial reserve army, the greater is official pauperism. *This is the absolute general law of capitalist accumulation.* Like all other laws it is modified in its working by many circumstances, the analysis of which does not concern us here. . . .

We saw . . . when analyzing the production of relative surplus value: within the capitalist system all methods for raising the social productiveness of labor are brought about at the cost of the individual laborer; all means for the development of production transform themselves into means of domination over, and exploitation of, the producers; they mutilate the laborer into a fragment of a man, degrade him to the level of an appendage of a machine, destroy every remnant of charm in his work and turn it into a hated toil; they estrange from him the intellectual potentialities of the labor process in the same proportion as science is incorporated in it as an independent power; they distort the conditions under which he works, subject him during the labor process to a despotism the more hateful for its meanness; they transform his lifetime into working time, and drag his wife and child beneath the wheels of the Juggernaut of capital. But all methods for the production of surplus value are at the same time methods of accumulation; and every extension of accumulation becomes again a means for the development of those methods. It follows therefore that in proportion as capital accumulates, the lot of the laborer, be his payment high or low, must grow worse. The law, finally, that always equilibrates the relative surplus population, or industrial reserve army, to the extent and energy of accumulation, this law rivets the laborer to capital more firmly than the wedges of Vulcan did Prometheus to the rock. It establishes an accumulation of misery, corresponding with accumulation of capital. Accumulation of wealth at one pole is, therefore, at the same time accumulation of misery, agony of toil, slavery, ignorance, brutality, mental degradation, at the opposite pole, i.e., on the side of the class that produces its own product in the form of capital. . . .

As soon as this process of transformation has sufficiently decomposed the old society from top to bottom, as soon as the laborers are turned into proletarians, their means of labor into capital, as soon as the capitalist mode of production stands on its own feet, then the further socialization of labor and further transformation of the land and other means of production into socially exploited and, therefore, common means of production, as well as the further expropriation of private proprietors, takes a new form. That which is now to be expropriated is no longer the laborer working for himself, but the capitalist exploiting many laborers. This expropriation is accomplished by the action of the immanent laws of capitalistic production itself, by the centralization of capital. One capitalist always kills many. Hand in hand with this centralization, or this expropriation of many capitalists by few, develop, on an ever extending scale, the cooperative form of the labor process, the conscious technical application of science, the methodical cultivation of the soil, the transformation of the instruments of labor into instruments of labor only usable in common, the economizing of all means of production by their use as the means of production of combined, socialized labor, the entanglement of all peoples in the net of the world market, and this, the international character of the capitalistic regime. Along with the constantly diminishing number of the magnates of capital, who usurp and monopolize all advantages of this process of transformation, grows the mass of misery, oppression, slavery, degradation, exploitation; but with this too grows the revolt of the working class, a class always increasing in numbers, and disciplined, united, organized by the very mechanism of the process of capitalist production itself. The monopoly of capital becomes a fetter upon the mode of production, which has sprung up and flourished along with, and under it. Centralization of the means of production and socialization of labor at last reach a point where they become incompatible with their capitalist integument. This integument is burst asunder. The knell of capitalist private property sounds. The expropriators are expropriated.

The capitalist mode of appropriation, the result of the capitalist mode of production, produces capitalist private property. This is the first negation of individual private property, as founded on the labor of the proprietor. But capitalist production begets, with the inexorability of a law of Nature, its own negation. It is the negation of negation. This does not reestablish private property for the producer, but gives him individual property based on the acquisitions of the capitalist era: i.e., on cooperation and the possession in common of the land and of the means of production. . . .

43. The Law of the Tendency of the Rate of Surplus Value to Fall

In presenting the broad range of Marx's thought and its philosophical grounding it is necessary to omit large masses of material of an extremely complex and technical economic nature. However, before we can turn to the more important sections of the third volume of *Capital*, a brief survey of the omitted material is in order.

Only the first volume of *Capital* was published by Marx. The collections of Marx's notes which we know as Volumes II and III were edited and published by Engels following his friend's death, and are of a far more technical and less philosophical and historical nature than Marx's first volume. The second volume and the first two parts of the third are concerned entirely with the problem of making the general formulas of the first volume apply to actual economic fact. Thus, one by one, we see complicating but empirical considerations introduced into the general formula M_1—C—M_2. These items include, but are not limited to, such factors as turnover time, cost price, factors tending to defray the selling price from the commodity's exchange value, the inexact and variable conversion of surplus value to profit, the formation of an average rate of profit first in an enterprise, then in an industry, and finally in the national economy as a whole.

This first selection from the third volume is from Marx's vital discussion of "The Law of the Tendency of the Rate of

From the Kerr edition, Vol. III, pp. 247–271.

Profit to Fall." This section essentially continues that of the first volume's chapter on "The General Law of Capitalist Accumulation" (cf. Selection 42), although now Marx brings out the crucial distinction between the *rate* and the *mass* of surplus value. It is the former quantity which is the key to capitalist planning and development; as it falls, more and more extreme methods have to be adopted to at least keep the mass of profit at a satisfactory level. These "counteracting causes" are taken up in the next group of selections.

WITH A given wage and working day, a certain variable capital, for instance of 100, represents a certain number of employed laborers. It is the index of this number. For instance, let 100 p.st. be the wages of 100 laborers for one week. If these laborers perform the same amount of necessary as of surplus labor, in other words, if they work daily as much time for themselves as they do for the capitalist, or, in still other words, if they require as much time for the reproduction of their wages as they do for the production of surplus value for the capitalist, then they would produce a total value of 200 p.st., and the surplus value would amount to 100 p.st. The rate of surplus value, $\frac{s}{v}$, would be 100%. But we have seen that this rate of surplus value would express itself in considerably different volumes of constant capitals c and consequently of total capitals C. For the rate of profit is calculated by the formula $\frac{s}{C}$.

Take it that the rate of surplus value is 100%. Now, if

$$c = 50, \text{ and } v = 100, \text{ then } p' = \tfrac{100}{150}, \text{ or } 66\tfrac{1}{3}\%.$$
$$c = 100, \text{ and } v = 100, \text{ then } p' = \tfrac{100}{200}, \text{ or } 50\%.$$
$$c = 200, \text{ and } v = 100, \text{ then } p' = \tfrac{100}{300}, \text{ or } 33\tfrac{1}{3}\%.$$
$$c = 300, \text{ and } v = 100, \text{ then } p' = \tfrac{100}{400}, \text{ or } 25\%.$$
$$c = 400, \text{ and } v = 100, \text{ then } p' = \tfrac{100}{500}, \text{ or } 20\%.$$

In this way, the same rate of surplus value, with the same degree of labor exploitation, would express itself in a falling rate of profit, because the material growth of the constant capital, and consequently of the total capital, implies their growth in value, although not in the same proportion.

If it is furthermore assumed that this gradual change in the composition of capital is not confined to some individual spheres of production, but occurs more or less in all, or at least in the most important ones, so that they imply changes in the organic average composition of the total capital of a certain society, then the gradual and relative growth of the constant over the variable capital must necessarily lead to *a gradual fall of the average rate of profit,* so long as the rate of surplus value, or the intensity of exploitation of labor by capital, remain the same. Now we have seen that it is one of the laws of capitalist production that its development carries with it a relative decrease of variable as compared with constant capital, and consequently as compared to the total capital, which it sets in motion. This is only another way of saying that the same number of laborers, the same quantity of labor power set in motion by a variable capital of a given value, consume in production an ever increasing quantity of means of production, such as machinery and all sorts of fixed capital, raw and auxiliary materials, and consequently a constant capital of ever increasing value and volume, during the same period of time, owing to the peculiar methods of production developing within the capitalist system. This progressive relative decrease of the variable capital as compared to the constant, and consequently to the total, capital is identical with the progressive higher organic composition of the average social capital. It is, in another way, but an expression of the progressive development of the productive powers of society, which is manifested by the fact that the same number of laborers, in the same time, convert an ever growing quantity of raw and auxiliary materials into products, thanks to the growing application of machinery and fixed capital in general, so that less labor is needed for the production of the same, or of more, commodities. This growing value and volume of constant capital corresponds to a progressive cheapening of products, although the increase in the value of the constant capital indicates but imperfectly the growth in the actual mass of use values represented by the material of the constant capital. Every individual product, taken by itself, contains a smaller quantity of labor than the same product did on a lower scale of production, in which the capital invested in wages occupies a far greater space compared to the capital invested in means of production. The hypothetical series placed at the beginning of this chapter expresses, therefore, the actual tendency of capitalist production. This mode of production produces a progressive decrease of the variable capital as compared to the constant capital, and consequently a continuously rising organic composition of the total capital. The immediate result of this is that the rate of surplus value, at the same degree of labor exploitation, expresses itself in a continually falling average rate of profit. . . . This progressive tendency of the average rate of profit to fall is, therefore, but a peculiar expression of capitalist production for the fact that the social productivity of labor is progressively increasing. This is not saying that the rate of profit may not fall temporarily for other reasons. But it demonstrates at least that it is the nature of the capitalist mode of production, and a logical necessity of its development, to give expression to the average rate of surplus value by a falling rate of average profit. Since the mass of the employed living labor is continually on the decline compared to the mass of materialized labor incorporated in productively consumed means of production, it follows that that portion of living labor, which is unpaid and represents surplus value, must also be continually on the decrease compared to the volume and value of the invested total capital. Seeing that the proportion of the mass of surplus value to the value of the invested total capital forms the rate of profit, this rate must fall continuously. . . .

The law of the falling tendency of the rate of profit, which is the expression of the same, or even of a higher, rate of surplus value, says in so many words: If you take any quantity of the average social capital, say a capital of 100, you will find that an ever larger portion of it is invested in means of production, and an ever smaller portion in living labor. Since, then, the aggregate mass of the living labor operating the means of production decreases in comparison to the value of these means of production, it follows that the unpaid labor, and that portion of value in which it is expressed, must decline as compared to the value of the advanced total capital. Or, an ever smaller aliquot part of the invested total capital is converted into living labor, and this capital absorbs in proportion to its magnitude less and less surplus labor, although the proportion of the unpaid part of the employed labor may simultaneously grow as compared with the paid part. The relative decrease of the variable, and the relative increase of the constant, capital, while both parts may grow absolutely in magnitude, is but another expression for the increased productivity of labor. . . .

The law of the falling tendency of the rate of profit, or of the relative decline of the appropriated surplus labor compared to the mass of materialized labor set in motion by living labor does not argue in any way against the fact that the absolute mass of the employed and exploited labor set in motion by the social capital, and consequently the absolute mass of the surplus-labor appropriated by it, may grow. Nor does it argue against the fact that the capitals controlled by individual capitalists may dispose of a growing mass of labor and surplus labor, even though the number of the laborers employed by them may not grow.

Take for illustration's sake a certain population of working people, for instance, two millions. Assume, furthermore, that the length and intensity of the average working day, and the level of wages, and thereby the proportion between necessary and surplus labor, are given. In that case the aggregate labor of these two millions, and their surplus labor expressed in surplus value, represent always the same magnitude of values. But with the growth of the mass of the constant (fixed and circulating) capital, which this labor manipulates, the proportion of this produced quantity of values declines as compared to the value of this total capital. . . . This proportion changes, not because the mass of living labor decreases, but because the mass of the materialized labor set in motion by living labor increases. It is a relative decrease, not an absolute one, and has really nothing to do with the absolute magnitude of the labor and surplus labor set in motion. The fall of the rate of profit is not due to an absolute, but only to a relative decrease of the variable part of the total capital, that is, its decrease as compared with the constant part.

The capitalist process of production is essentially a process of accumulation. We have shown that the mass of values, which must be simply reproduced and maintained, increases progressively with the development of capitalist production to the extent that the productivity of labor grows, even if the employed labor power should remain constant. . . . The progress of the process of production and accumulation *must*, therefore, be accompanied by a growth of the mass of available and appropriated surplus labor, and consequently by a growth of the absolute mass of profit appropriated by the social capital. But the same laws of production and accumulation increase the volume and value of the constant capital in a more rapid progression than those of the variable capital invested in living labor. The same laws, then, produce for the social capital an increase in the absolute mass of profit and a falling rate of profit. . . .

The development of capitalist production and accumulation lifts the processes of labor to a higher scale and gives them greater dimensions, which imply larger investments of capital for each individual establishment. A growing concentration of capitals (accompanied by a growing number of capitalists, though not to the same extent) is therefore one of the material requirements of capitalist production as well as one of the results produced by it. Hand in hand with it, and mutually interacting, goes a progressive expropriation of the more or less direct producers. It is, then, a matter of course for the capitalists that they should control increasing armies of laborers (no matter how much the variable capital may relatively decrease in comparison to the constant capital), and that the mass of surplus value, and of profit, appropriated by them, should grow simultaneously with the fall of the rate of profit, and in spite of it. The same causes which concentrate masses of laborers under the control of capitalists are precisely those which also swell the mass of fixed capital, auxiliary and raw materials in a growing proportion as compared to the mass of the employed living labor. . . .

A fall in the rate of profit by 50% means its fall by one-half. If the mass of profit is to remain the same, the capital must be doubled. In order that the mass of profit made at a declining rate of profit may remain the same as before, the multiplier indicating the growth of the total capital must be equal to the divisor indicating the fall of the rate of profit. If the rate of profit falls from 40 to 20, the total capital must rise at the rate of 20 to 40, in order that the result may remain the same. If the rate of profit had fallen from 40 to 8, the capital would have to increase at the rate of 8 to 40, or five times its value. A capital of 1,000,000 at a rate of 40% produces 400,000, and a capital of 5,000,000 at a rate of 8% likewise produces 400,000. This applies, so long as the result is to remain the same. But if the result is to be higher, then the capital must grow at a faster rate than the rate of profit falls. In other words, in order that the variable portion of the total capital may not only remain the same, but may also increase absolutely, although its percentage in the total capital falls, the total capital must grow at a higher rate than the percentage of the variable capital falls. It must grow at such a rate that it requires in its new composition not merely the same old variable capital, but more than it for the purchase of labor power. . . .

In short, the same development of the social productivity of labor expresses itself in the course of capitalist production on the one hand in a tendency to a progressive fall of the rate of profit, and on the other hand in a progressive increase of the absolute mass of the appropriated surplus value, or profit; so that on the whole a relative decrease of variable capital and profit is accompanied by an absolute increase of both. This twofold effect, as we have seen, can express itself only in a growth of the total capital at a ratio more rapid than that expressed by the fall in the rate of profit. In order that an absolutely increased variable capital may be employed in a capital of higher composition, that is, a capital in which the constant capital has relatively increased still more than the variable, the total capital must not only grow in proportion to its higher composition, but even still more rapidly. It follows, then, that an ever larger quantity of capital is required in order to employ the same, and still more an increased amount of labor power, to the extent that the capitalist mode of production develops. The increasing productivity of labor thus creates necessarily and permanently an apparent overpopulation of laboring people. If the variable capital forms only one-sixth of the total capital instead of one-half, as before, then the total capital must be trebled in order to employ the same amount of labor power. And if the labor power to be employed is doubled, then the total capital must be multiplied by six. . . .

Since the development of the productive powers and the higher composition of capital corresponding to it set in motion an ever increasing quantity of means of production with an ever decreasing quantity of labor, every aliquot part of the total product, every single commodity, or every particular quantity of commodities in the total mass of products absorbs less living labor, and also contains less materialized labor, both as to the wear and tear of fixed capital and to the raw and auxiliary materials consumed. Every single commodity, then, contains a smaller amount of labor materialized in means of production and of labor newly added during production. Hence the price of the individual commodity falls. . . . The mass of profit on each individual commodity will decrease considerably with the development of the productive power of labor, in spite of the increase of the rate of surplus value. And this reduction, the same as the fall in the rate of profits, is only delayed by the cheapening of the elements of constant capital and the other circumstances mentioned in the first part of this volume, which increase the rate of profit at a stable, or even falling, rate of surplus value. . . .

Since everything appears inverted under competition, the individual capitalist may imagine that he is reducing his profit on the individual commodity by cutting its price, but still making a greater profit on account of the larger quantity of commodities which he is selling. . . .

A capitalist working with improved methods of production that have not yet become general sells below the market price, but above his individual price of production. In this way his rate of profit rises until competition levels it down. During this leveling period the second requisite puts in its appearance, namely the expansion of the invested capital. According to the degree of this expansion the capitalist will be enabled to employ a part of his former laborers under the new conditions, and eventually all of them or more, in other words, he will be enabled to produce the same or a greater mass of profits.

44. Means of Counteracting the Law

The following group of selections deals with the various ways in which the capitalists are able to forestall many of the effects of the Law of Capitalist Accumulation. It should be emphasized that Marx formulates the Law as one of the *tendency* of the rate of profit to fall, and it is indeed possible that such a tendency may be thwarted over the short and even intermediate terms. Thus it would be to miss Marx's point entirely to claim that his "predictions" have simply "failed"; although, indeed, a full century seems to be sufficient time to await corroboration.

What has really occurred since Marx's day has been a steady *modification* of the capitalist system in many of its basic traits. This modification has developed in part along the lines foreseen by Marx, especially in the formation of large joint-stock companies, the enormous power of credit, and the accelerating rate of the consolidation ("concentration") of capitals into oligopolistic (and in some cases outright monopolistic) forms.

Among the many factors effecting this evolution the foremost has been the effectiveness with which the bourgeoisie has outgrown its dependence upon the philosophy of limited government (this is not to claim that it has outgrown such *rhetoric*, however). Today government (of all types) plays the

First part from the Kerr edition, Vol. III, pp. 272–280; second part from Marx's essay "Future Results of British Rule in India," in Marx and Engels, Selected Works (Moscow, 1935).

largest single role in maintaining the expansion of the economy, and it openly intervenes when needed to support entire industries when they may be threatened by such problems as foreign competition, labor disputes, and sagging sales. Not the least of these factors have been those listed by Marx as "counteracting causes" to the Law: for example, increasing productivity (i.e., the "level of exploitation"); the depression of wages (although this has tended to occur by depressing total wages rather than the wages of the individual union-protected employee), including the direct exploitation of millions of workers in foreign, wage-depressed countries; the cheapening of the elements of constant capital (in terms of cost per unit of product); the governmental policies of aiding domestic migration from rural to urban areas (Marx's "relative overpopulation") and, of course, vastly increased foreign trade.

Under the latter heading must also be included colonial and neocolonial (i.e., economic domination without the trappings of political rule) foreign policies, which have tended to increase foreign trade in an especially exploitative (because uncompetitive) manner. To this point the short selection from an article of Marx's on future British rule in India may be considered as indicative of the role of colonialization as a means of capitalist development.

To the list of such "counteracting causes" can also be added two which do not appear on Marx's list, because they have been developed only since Marx's day: first, modern warfare, whether real or threatened, is the single most effective means by which a government can continually and decisively support its economy; and second, advertising, the incessant creation of entirely new and often imaginary "needs" in the populace for the crassest pecuniary motives.

IF WE consider the enormous development of the productive powers of labor, even comparing but the last 30 years with all former periods; if we consider in particular the enormous mass of fixed capital, aside from machinery in the strict meaning of the term, passing into the process of social production as a whole, then the difficulty, which has hitherto troubled the vulgar economists, namely that of finding an explanation for the falling rate of profit, gives way to its opposite, namely to the question: How is it that this fall is not greater and more rapid? There must be some counteracting influences at work, which thwart and annul the effects of this general law, leaving to it merely the character of a tendency. For this reason we have referred to the fall of the average rate of profit as a tendency to fall.

The following are the general counterbalancing causes:

RAISING THE INTENSITY OF EXPLOITATION

The rate at which labor is exploited, the appropriation of surplus labor and surplus value, is raised by a prolongation of the working day and an intensification of labor. These two points have been fully discussed in Volume I as incidents to the production of absolute and relative surplus value. There are many ways of intensifying labor which imply an increase of the constant capital as compared to the variable, and consequently a fall in the rate of profit, for instance setting a laborer to watch a larger number of machines. In such cases—and in the majority of manipulations serving to produce relative surplus value—the same causes, which bring about an increase in the rate of surplus value, may also imply a fall in the mass of surplus value, looking upon the matter from the point of view of the total quantities of invested capital. . . . It is particularly the prolongation of the working day, this invention of modern industry, which increases the mass of appropriated surplus labor without essentially altering the proportion of the employed labor power to the constant capital set in motion by it, and which tends to reduce this capital relatively, if anything. . . . The manipulations made for the purpose of producing relative surplus value amount on the whole to this: That on one side as much as possible of a certain quantity of labor is transformed into surplus value, and that on the other hand as little labor as possible is employed in proportion to the invested capital, so that the same causes which permit the raising of the intensity of exploitation forbid the exploitation of the same quantity of labor by the same capital as before. These are the warring tendencies, which, while aiming at a raise in the rate of surplus value, have at the same time a tendency to bring about a fall in the mass of surplus value, and therefore of the rate of surplus value produced by a certain capital. . . .

DEPRESSION OF WAGES BELOW THEIR VALUE

This is mentioned only empirically at this place, since it, like many other things, which might be enumerated here, has nothing to do with the general analysis of capital, but belongs in a presentation of competition, which is not given in this work. However, it is one of the most important causes checking the tendency of the rate of profit to fall.

CHEAPENING OF THE ELEMENTS OF CONSTANT CAPITAL

. . . This applies particularly to the fact that, from the point of view of the total capital, the value of the constant capital does not increase in the same proportion as its material volume. For instance, the quantity of cotton which a single European spinning operator works up in a modern factory has grown in a colossal degree compared to the quantity formerly worked up by a European operator with a spinning wheel. But the value of the worked-up cotton has not grown in proportion to its mass. The same holds good of machinery and other fixed capital. In short, the same development which increases the mass of the constant capital relatively over that of the variable reduces the value of its elements as a result of the increased productivity of labor. In this way the value of the constant capital, although continually increasing, is prevented from increasing at the same rate as its material volume, that is, the material volume of the means of production set in motion by the same amount of labor power. . . .

This is another one of the causes which by their constant effects tend to check the fall of the rate of profit, although it may under certain circumstances reduce the mass of profit by reducing the mass of capital yielding a profit. This shows once more that the same causes which bring about a tendency of the rate of profit to fall also check the realization of this tendency.

RELATIVE OVERPOPULATION

The production of a relative surplus population is inseparable from the development of the productivity of labor expressed by a fall in the rate of profit, and the two go hand in hand. The relative overpopulation becomes so much more apparent in a certain country, the more the capitalist mode of production is developed in it. This, again, is on the one hand a reason, which explains why the imperfect subordination of labor to capital continues in many lines of production, and continues longer than seems at first glance compatible with the general stage of development. This is due to the cheapness and mass of the disposable or unemployed wage laborers, and to the greater resistance, which some lines of production, by their nature, oppose to a transformation of manufacture into machine production. On the other hand, new lines of production are opened up, especially for the production of luxuries, and these lines take for their basis this relative overpopulation set free in other lines of production by the increase of their constant capital. These new lines start out with living labor as their predominating element, and go by degrees through the same evolution as the other lines of production. In either case the variable capital constitutes a considerable proportion of the total capital and wages are below the average, so that both the rate and mass of surplus value are exceptionally high. Since the average rate of profit is formed by leveling the rates of profit in the individual lines of production, the same cause which brings about a falling tendency of the rate of profit once more produces a counterbalance to this tendency and paralyzes its effects more or less.

FOREIGN TRADE

To the extent that foreign trade cheapens partly the elements of constant capital, partly the necessities of life for which the variable capital is exchanged, it tends to raise the rate of profit by raising the rate of surplus value and lowering the value of the constant capital. It exerts itself generally in this direction by permitting an expansion of the scale of production. But by this means it hastens on one hand the process of accumulation, on the other the reduction of the variable as compared to the constant capital, and thus a fall in the rate of profit. In the same way the expansion of foreign trade, which is the basis of the capitalist mode of production in its stages of infancy, has become its own product in the further progress of capitalist development through its innate necessities, through its need of an ever expanding market. . . .

Capitals invested in foreign trade are in a position to yield a higher rate of profit, because, in the first place, they come in competition with commodities produced in other countries with lesser facilities of production, so that an advanced country is enabled to sell its goods above their value even when it sells them cheaper than the competing countries. To the extent that the labor of the advanced countries is here exploited as a labor of a higher specific weight, the rate of profit rises, because labor which has not been paid as being of a higher quality is sold as such. The same condition may obtain in the relations with a certain country, into which commodities are exported and from which commodities are imported. This country may offer more materialized labor in goods than it receives, and yet it may receive in return commodities cheaper than it could produce them. . . . On the other hand, capitals invested in colonies, etc., may yield a higher rate of profit for the simple reason that the rate of profit is higher there on account of the backward development, and for the added reason that slaves, coolies, etc., permit a better exploitation of labor. . . . These higher rates of profit realized by capitals invested in certain lines and sent home by them enter as elements into the average rate of profit and tend to keep it up to that extent. . . . The favored country recovers more labor in exchange for less labor, although this difference, this surplus, is pocketed by a certain class, as it is in any exchange between labor and capital. So far as the rate of profit is higher, because it is generally higher in the colonial country, it may go hand in hand with a low level of prices, if the natural conditions are favorable. . . .

However, this same foreign trade devlops the capitalist mode of production in the home country. And this implies the relative decrease of the variable as compared to the constant capital, while it produces, on the other hand, an overproduction for the foreign market, so that it has once more the opposite effect in its further course.

COLONIALISM

. . . England has to fulfill a double mission in India: one destructive, and the other regenerating—the annihilation of old Asiatic society, and the laying the material foundations of Western society in Asia.

Arabs, Turks, Tartars, Moguls, who had successively overrun India, soon become *Hinduized*, the barbarian conquerors being, by an eternal law of history, conquered themselves by the superior civilization of their subjects. The British were the first conquerors superior, and therefore inaccessible to Hindu civilization. They destroyed it by breaking up the native communities, by uprooting the native industry, and by leveling all that was great and elevated in the native society. The historic pages of their rule in India report hardly anything beyond that destruction. The work of regeneration hardly transpires through a heap of ruins. Nevertheless it has begun.

The political unity of India, more consolidated, and extending farther than it ever did under the Great Moguls, was the first condition of its regeneration. That unity, imposed by the British sword, will now be strengthened and perpetuated by the electric telegraph. The native army, organized and trained by the British drill sergeant, was the *sine qua non* of Indian self-emancipation, and of India ceasing to be the prey of the first foreign intruder. The free press, introduced for the first time into Asiatic society, and managed principally by the common offspring of Hindus and Europeans, is a new and powerful agent of reconstruction. The *Zemindaree*[1] and *Ryotwar*[2] themselves, abominable as they are, involve two distinct forms to private property in land—the great *desideratum* of Asiatic society. From the Indian natives, reluctanly and sparingly educated at Calcutta, under English superintendence, a fresh class is springing, endowed with the requirements for government and imbued with European science. Steam has brought India into regular and rapid communication with Europe, has connected its chief ports with those of the whole southeastern ocean, and has revindicated it from the isolated position which was the prime law of its stagnation. The day is not far distant when, by a combination of railways and steam vessels, the distance between England and India, measured by time, will be shortened to eight days, and when that once fabulous country will thus be actually annexed to the Western world.

The ruling classes of Great Britain have had, till now, but an accidental, transitory and exceptional interest in the progress of India. The aristocracy wanted to conquer it, the moneyocracy to plunder it and the millocracy to undersell it. But now the tables are turned. The millocracy have discovered that the transformation of India into a reproductive country has become of vital importance to them, and that, to that end, it is necessary above all to gift her with means of irrigation and of internal communication. They intend now drawing a net of railroads over India. And they will do it. The results must be inappreciable.

It is notorious that the productive powers of India are paralyzed by the utter want of means for conveying and exchanging its various produce. Nowhere, more than in India, do we

1. *Zemindars.* Landowners in Bengal who were established by the British from former tax collectors who subsequently become merchants and usurers. Thus, instead of coming under the old expropriated feudal landowners, the Indian peasant came under the yoke of the new landlord-usurer–*Ed.*

2. *Ryotwar.* From the word *ryot* or peasant cultivator. Under the ryotwari system the peasant cultivator pays land tax directly to the state.–*Ed.*

meet with social destitution in the midst of natural plenty, for want of the means of exchange. It was proved before a Committee of the British House of Commons which sat in 1848 that "when grain was selling from 6s. to 8s. a quarter at Kandeish, it was sold at 64s. to 70s. at Poonah, where the people were dying in the streets of famine, without the possibility of gaining supplies from Kandeish, because the clay roads were impracticable."

The introduction of railroads may be easily made to subserve agricultural purposes by the formation of tanks, where ground is required for embankment, and by the conveyance of water along the different lines. Thus irrigation, the *sine qua non* of farming in the East, might be greatly extended, and the frequently recurring local famines, arising from the want of water, would be averted. The general importance of railways, viewed under this head, must become evident, when we remember that irrigated lands, . . . pay three times as much in taxes, afford ten or twelve times as much employment, and yield twelve or fifteen times as much profit as the same area without irrigation. . . .

We know that the municipal organization and the economical basis of the village communities has been broken up, but their worst feature, the dissolution of society into sterotype and disconnected atoms, has survived their vitality.

The village isolation produced the absence of roads in India, and the absence of roads perpetuated the village isolation. On this plan a community existed with a given scale of low conveniences, almost without intercourse with other villages, without the desires and efforts indispensable to social advance. The British having broken up this self-sufficient *inertia* of the villages, railways will provide the new want of communication and intercourse. Besides, "one of the effects of the railway system will be to bring into every village affected by it such knowledge of the contrivances and appliances of other countries, and such means of obtaining them, as will first put the hereditary and stipendiary village artisanship of India to full proof of its capabilities, and then supply its defects" (Chapman, *The Cotton and Commerce of India*).

I know that the English millocracy intend to endow India with railways with the exclusive view of extracting at diminished expenses the cotton and other raw materials for their manufactures. But when you have once introduced machinery into the locomotion of a country which possesses iron and coals, you are unable to withold it from its fabrication. You cannot maintain a net of railways over an immense country without introducing all those industrial processes necessary to meet the immediate and current wants of railway locomotion, and out of which there must grow the application of machinery to those branches of industry not immediately connected with railways. The railway system will therefore become, in India, truly the forerunner of modern industry. This is the more certain as the Hindus are allowed by British authorities themselves to possess particular aptitude for accommodating themselves to entirely new labor, and acquiring the requisite knowledge of machinery. Ample proof of this fact is afforded by the capacities and expertness of the native engineers in the Calcutta mint, where they have been for years employed in working the steam machinery, by the natives attached to the several steam engines in the Hurdwar coal districts, and by other instances. Mr. Campbell himself, greatly influenced as he is by the prejudices of the East India Company,[3] is obliged to avow "that the great mass of the Indian people possesses a great *industrial energy,* is well fitted to accumulate capital, and remarkable for a mathematical clearness of head, and talent for figures and exact sciences." "Their intellects," he says, "are excellent." Modern industry, resulting from the railway system, will dissolve the hereditary divisions of labor, upon which rest the Indian castes, those decisive impediments to Indian progress and Indian power.

All the English bourgeoisie may be forced to do will neither emancipate nor materially mend the social condition of the mass of the people, depending not only on the development of

3. The British East India Company was formed in 1599 for monopoly trade with India. Under the pretext of "trade" operations, the company conquered India for British capitalism and ruled it for many years. After the Indian rising of 1857, the company was dissolved and the British government took over directly the administration and exploitation of India.–Ed.

the productive power, but of their appropriation by the people. But what they will not fail to do is to lay down the material premises for both. Has the bourgeoisie ever done more? Has it ever effected a progress without dragging individuals and people through blood and dirt, through misery and degradation?

The Indians will not reap the fruits of the new elements of society scattered among them by the British bourgeosie till in Great Britain itself the now ruling classes shall have been supplanted by the industrial proletariat, or till the Hindus themselves shall have grown strong enough to throw off the English yoke altogether. At all events, we may safely expect to see, at a more or less remote period, the regeneration of that great and interesting country, whose gentle natives are, to use the expression of Prince Saltykov, even in the most inferior classes, *"plus fins et plus adroits que les Italiens,"* whose submission even is counterbalanced by a certain clam nobility, who, notwithstanding their natural languor, have astonished the British officers by their bravery, whose country has been the source of our languages, our religions, and who represent the type of the ancient German in the *Jat* and the type of the ancient Greek in the Brahmin.[4] . . .

The devastating effects of English industry, when contemplated with regard to India, a country as vast as Europe and containing 150 million acres, are palpable and confounding. But we must not forget that they are only the organic results of the whole system of production as it is now constituted. That production rests on the supreme rule of capital. The centralization of capital is essential to the existence of capital as an independent power. The destructive inflence of that centralization upon the markets of the world but reveal, in the most gigantic dimensions, the inherent organic laws of political economy now at work in every civilized town. The bourgeois period of history has to create the material basis of the new world—on the one hand universal intercourse founded upon the mutual dependency of mankind, and the means of that intercourse; on the

4. *Jats.* A race of peasants in Northwest India, supposed to be Indo-Aryan origin.—*Ed.*

other hand the development of the productive powers of man and the transformation of material production into a scientific domination of natural agencies. Bourgeois industry and commerce create these material conditions of a new world in the same way as geological revolutions have created the surface of the earth. When a great social revolution shall have mastered the results of the bourgeois epoch, the market of the world and the modern powers of production, and subjected them to the common control of the most advanced peoples, then only will human progress cease to resemble that hideous pagan idol who would not drink the nectar but from the skulls of the slain.

45. The Dialectic of Capitalist Production

Our last selection, taken from near the end of the third volume of *Capital*, presents a brief summary and evaluation of the historical role of capitalism, and ends with one of Marx's most ringing reiterations of the Communist ideal. Whereas such pronouncements had been, in 1844, the result of Marx's philosophical investigations, here, in his last writings, we see that the ideal of "the true realm of freedom" has remained constant despite Marx's wanderings on the often arid terrain of political economy; and this constancy is perhaps some real testimony to the strength of its appeal.

And so we have seen in a general way that the same causes which produce a falling tendency in the rate of profit also call forth countereffects, which check and partly paralyze this fall. This law is not suspended, but its effect is weakened. Otherwise it would not be the fall of the average rate of profit, which would be unintelligible, but rather the relative slowness of this fall. The law therefore shows itself only as a tendency whose effects become clearly marked only under certain conditions and in the course of long periods. . . .

It must never be forgotten that the production of this surplus value—and the reconversion of a portion of it into capital, or accumulation, forms an indispensable part of this production of surplus value—is the immediate purpose and the compelling motive of capitalist production. It will not do to represent capi-

From the Kerr edition, Vol. III, pp. 280, 285–312, 952–954.

talist production as something which it is not, that is to say, as a production having for its immediate purpose the consumption of goods, or the production of means of enjoyment for capitalists. This would be overlooking the specific character of capitalist production, which reveals itself in its innermost essence.

The creation of this surplus value is the object of the direct process of production, and this process has no other limits but those mentioned above. As soon as the available quantity of surplus value has been materialized in commodities, surplus value has been produced. But this production of surplus value is but the first act of the capitalist process of production, it merely terminates the act of direct production. Capital has absorbed so much unpaid labor. With the development of the process, which expresses itself through a falling tendency of the rate of profit, the mass of surplus value thus produced is swelled to immense dimensions. Now comes the second act of the process. The entire mass of commodities, the total product, which contains a portion which is to reproduce the constant and variable capital as well as a portion representing surplus value, must be sold. If this is not done, or only partly accomplished, or only at prices which are below the prices of production, the laborer has been none the less exploited, but his exploitation does not realize as much for the capitalist. It may yield no surplus value at all for him, or only realize a portion of the produced surplus value, or it may even mean a partial or complete loss of his capital. The conditions of direct exploitation and those of the realization of surplus value are not identical. They are separated logically as well as by time and space. The first are only limited by the productive power of society, the last by the proportional relations of the various lines of production and by the consuming power of society. This last-named power is not determined either by the absolute productive power or by the absolute consuming power, but by the consuming power based on antagonistic conditions of distribution, which reduces the consumption of the great mass of the population to a variable minimum within more or less narrow limits. The consuming power is furthermore restricted by the tendency to accumulate, the greed for an expansion of capital and a production of surplus value on an enlarged scale. This is a law of capitalist production imposed by incessant revolutions in the methods of production themselves, the resulting depreciation of existing capital, the general competitive struggle and the necessity of improving the product and expanding the scale of production, for the sake of self-preservation and on penalty of failure. The market must, therefore be continually extended, so that its interrelations and the conditions regulating them assume more and more the form of a natural law independent of the producers and become ever more uncontrollable. This internal contradiction seeks to balance itself by an expansion of the outlying fields of production. But to the extent that the productive power develops, it finds itself at variance with the narrow basis on which the condition of consumption rests. On this self-contradictory basis it is no contradiction at all that there should be an excess of capital simultaneously with an excess of population. For while a combination of these two would indeed increase the mass of the produced surplus value, it would at the same time intensify the contradiction between the conditions under which this surplus value is produced and those under which it is realized. . . .

The real barrier of capitalist production is capital itself. It is the fact that capital and its self-expansion appear as the starting and closing point, as the motive and aim of production; that production is merely production for *capital*, and not vice versa, the means of production mere means for an ever expanding system of the life process for the benefit of the *society* of producers. The barriers, within which the preservation and self-expansion of the value of capital resting on the expropriation and pauperization of the great mass of producers can alone move, these barriers come continually in collision with the methods of production, which capital must employ for its purposes, and which steer straight toward an unrestricted extension of production, toward production for its own self, toward an unconditional development of the productive forces of society. The means, this unconditional development of the productive forces of society, comes continually into conflict with the limited end, the self-expansion of the existing capital. Thus, while the capitalist mode of production is one of the historical means by which the material forces of production are developed and the world market required for them created, it is at the same time in continual conflict with this historical task and the conditions of social production corresponding to it.

With the fall of the rate of profit grows the lowest limit of capital required in the hands of the individual capitalist for the productive employment of labor, required both for the exploitation of labor and for bringing the consumed labor time within the limits of the labor time necessary for the production of the commodities, the limits of the average social labor time required for the production of the commodities. Simultaneously with it grows the concentration, because there comes a certain limit where large capital with a small rate of profit accumulates faster than small capital with a large rate of profit. This increasing concentration in its turn brings about a new fall in the rate of profit at a certain climax. The mass of the small divided capitals is thereby pushed into adventurous channels, speculation, fraudulent credit, fraudulent stocks, crises. The so-called plethora of capital refers always essentially to a plethora of that class of capital which finds no compensation in its mass for the fall in the rate of profit. . . . This plethora of capital proceeds from the same causes which call forth a relative overpopulation. It is therefore a phenomenon supplementing this last one, although they are found at opposite poles, unemployed capital on the one hand, and unemployed laboring population on the other. . . .

As soon as capital would have grown to such a proportion compared with the laboring population that neither the absolute labor time nor the relative surplus labor time could be extended any further . . . as soon as a point is reached where the increased capital produces no larger, or even smaller, quantities of surplus value than it did before its increase, there would be an absolute overproduction of capital. That is to say, the increased capital $C + \triangle C$ would not produce any more profit, or even less profit, than capital C before its expansion by $\triangle C$. In both cases there would be a strong and sudden fall in the average rate of profit, but it would be due to a change in the composition of capital which would not be caused by the development of the productive forces, but by a rise in the money value of the variable capital (on account of the increased wages) and the corresponding reduction in the proportion of surplus labor to necessary labor.

In reality the matter would amount to this, that a portion of the capital would lie fallow completely or partially (because it would first have to crowd some of the active capital out before it could take part in the process of self-expansion), while the active portion would produce values at a lower rate of profit, owing to the pressure of the unemployed or but partly employed capital. . . . The fall in the rate of profit would then be accompanied by an absolute decrease in the mass of profits, since under the conditions assumed by us the mass of the employed labor power could not be increased and the rate of surplus value not raised, so that there could be no raising of the mass of surplus value. And the reduced mass of profits would have to be calculated on an increased total capital. But even assuming that the employed capital were to continue producing value at the old rate, the mass of profits remaining the same, this mass would still be calculated on an increased total capital, and this would likewise imply a fall in the rate of profits. . . .

It is evident that this actual depreciation of the old capital could not take place without a struggle, that the additional capital $\triangle$ C could not assume the functions of capital without an effort. The rate of profit would not fall on account of competition due to the overproduction of capital. The competitive struggle would rather begin, because the fall of the rate of profit and the overproduction of capital are caused by the same conditions. The capitalists who are actively engaged with their old capitals would keep as much as the new additional capitals as would be in their hands in a fallow state, in order to prevent a depreciation of their original capital and a crowding of its space within the field of production. Or they would employ it for the purpose of loading, even at a momentary loss, the necessity of keeping additional capital fallow upon the shoulders of new intruders and other competitors in general.

That portion of $\triangle$ C which would be in new hands would seek to make room for itself at the expense of the old capital, and would accomplish this in part by forcing a portion of the old capital into a fallow state. The old capital would have to give up its place to the new and retire to the place of the completely or partially unemployed additional capital. . . .

The mode of settlement . . . implies the necessity of making unproductive, or even partially destroying, some capital, amounting either to the complete value of the additional capital $\triangle$ C, or to a part of it. But a graphic presentation of this conflict shows that the loss is not equally distributed over all the individual capitals, but according to the fortunes of the competitive struggle, which assigns the loss in very different proportions and in various shapes by grace of previously captured advantages or positions, so that one capital is rendered unproductive, another destroyed, a third but relatively injured or but momentarily depreciated, etc.

But under all circumstances the equilibrium is restored by making more or less capital unproductive or destroying it. This would affect to some extent the material substance of capital, that, is, a part of the means of production, fixed and circulating capital, would not perform any service as capital; a portion of the running establishments would then close down. Of course, time would corrode and depreciate all means of production (except land), but this particular stagnation would cause a far more serious destruction of means of production. . . .

This interference and stagnation paralyzes the function of money as a medium of payment, which is conditioned on the development of capital and the resulting price relations. The chain of payments due at certain times is broken in a hundred places, and the disaster is intensified by the collapse of the credit system. Thus violent and acute crises are brought about, sudden and forcible depreciations, an actual stagnation and collapse of the process of reproduction, and finally a real falling off in reproduction.

At the same time still other agencies would have been at work. The stagnation of production would have laid off a part of the laboring class and thereby placed the employed part in a condition in which they would have to submit to a reduction of wages, even below the average. . . .

On the other hand, the fall in the rate of profit connected with accumulation necessarily creates a competitive struggle. The compensation of the fall in the rate of profit by a rise in the mass of profit applies only to the total social capital and to the great capitalists who are firmly installed. The new additional capital, which enters upon its functions, does not enjoy any such compensating conditions. It must conquer them for itself, and so the fall in the rate of profit calls forth the competitive struggle among capitalists, not vice versa. This competitive struggle is indeed accompanied by a transient rise in wages and a resulting further fall of the rate of profit for a short time. The same thing is seen in the overproduction of commodities, the overstocking of markets. Since the aim of capital is not to minister to certain wants, but to produce profits, and since it accomplishes this purpose by methods which adapt the mass of production to the scale of production, not vice versa, conflict must continually ensue between the limited conditions of consumption on a capitalist basis and a production which forever tends to exceed its immanent barriers. Moreover, capital consists of commodities, and therefore the overproduction of capital implies an overproduction of commodities. . . .

It is not a fact that too much wealth is produced. But it is true that there is periodical overproduction of wealth in its capitalistic and self-contradictory form.

The barrier of the capitalist mode of production becomes apparent:

1) In the fact that the development of the productive power of labor creates in the falling rate of profit a law which turns into an antagonism of this mode of production at a certain point and requires for its defeat periodical crises.

2) In the fact that the expansion or contraction of production is determined by the appropriation of unpaid labor, and by the proportion of this unpaid labor to materialized labor in general, or, to speak the language of the capitalists, is determined by profit and by the proportion of this profit to the employed

capital, by a definite rate of profit, instead of being determined by the relations of production to social wants to the wants of socially developed human beings. The capitalist mode of production, for this reason, meets with barriers at a certain scale of production which would be inadequate under different conditions. It comes to a standstill at a point determined by the production and realization of profit, not by the satisfaction of social needs. . . .

The rate of profit, that is, the relative increment of capital, is above all important for all new offshoots of capital seeking an independent location. And as soon as the formation of capital were to fall into the hands of a few established great capitals, which are compensated by the mass of profits for the loss through a fall in the rate of profits, the vital fire of production would be extinguished. It would fall into a dormant state. The rate of profit is the compelling power of capitalist production, and only such things are produced as yield a profit. . . .

We have seen that the growing accumulation of capital implies its growing concentration. Thus the power of capital, the personification of the conditions of social production in the capitalist, grows over the heads of the real producers. Capital shows itself more and more as a social power, whose agent the capitalist is, and which stands no longer in any possible relation to the things which the labor of any single individual can create. Capital becomes a strange, independent, social power, which stands opposed to society as a thing, and as the power of capitalists by means of this thing. The contradiction between capital as a general social power and as a power of private capitalists over the social conditions of production develops into an ever more irreconcilable clash, which implies the dissolution of these relations and the elaboration of the conditions of production into universal, common, social conditions. This elaboration is performed by the development of the productive powers under capitalist production, and by the course which this development pursues.

No capitalist voluntarily introduces a new method of production, no matter how much more productive it may be, and how much it may increase the rate of surplus value, so long as it reduces the rate of profit. But every new method of production of this sort cheapens the commodities. Hence the capitalist sells them originally above their prices of production, or, perhaps, above their value. He pockets the difference, which exists between these prices of production and the market prices of the other commodities produced at higher prices of production. He can do this, because the average labor time required socially for the production of these other commodities is higher than the labor time required under the new methods of production. His method of production is above the social average. But competition generalizes it and subjects it to the general law. Then follows a fall in the rate of profit—perhaps first in this sphere of production, which gradually brings the others to its level—which is, therefore, wholly independent of the will of the capitalist. . . .

As soon as the new mode of production begins to expand, and thereby to furnish the tangible proof that these commodities can actually be produced more cheaply, the capitalists working under the old methods of production must sell their product below their full prices of production, because the value of these commodities has fallen, because the labor time required by these capitalists for the production of these commodities is longer than the social average. In one word—this appears as the effect of competition—these capitalists are compelled to introduce the new method of production, under which the proportion of the variable to the constant capital has been reduced.

All circumstances which bring about the cheapening of commodities by the employment of improved machinery amount in the last analysis to a reduction of the quantity of labor absorbed by the individual commodities; in the second place, to a reduction of the wear and tear portion of machinery transferred to the value of the individual commodity. To the extent that the wear and tear of machinery is less rapid, it is distributed over more commodities and displaces more living labor during its period of reproduction. In both cases the quantity and value of the fixed constant capital are increased

The following three principal facts of capitalist production must be kept in mind:

1) Concentration of means of production in a few hands, whereby they cease to appear as the property of the immediate laborers and transform themselves into social powers of production. It is true, they first become the private property of capitalists. These are the trustees of bourgeois society, but they pocket the proceeds of their trusteeship.

2) Organization of labor itself into social labor, by social cooperation, division of labor, and combination of labor with natural sciences.

In both directions, the capitalist mode of production abolishes private property and private labor, even though it does so in contradictory forms.

3) Creation of the world market. . . .

We have seen that the capitalist process of production is a historically determined form of the social process of production in general. This process is on the one hand the process by which the material requirements of life are produced, and on the other hand a process which takes place under specific historical and economic conditions of production and which produces and reproduces these conditions of production themselves, and with them the human agents of this process, their material conditions of existence and their mutual relations, that is, their particular economic form of society. For the aggregate of these relations, in which the agents of this production live with regard to nature and to themselves, and in which they produce, is precisely their society, considered from the point of view of its economic structure. Like all its predeccessors, the capitalist process of production takes place under definite material conditions, which are at the same time the bearers of definite social relations maintained toward one another by the individuals in the process of producing their life's requirements. These conditions and these relations are on the one hand prerequisites, on the other hand results and creations of the capitalist process of production. They are produced and reproduced by it. We have also seen that capital (the capitalist is merely capital personified and functions in the process of production as the agent of capital), in the social process of production corresponding to it, pumps a certain quantity of surplus labor out of the direct producer, or laborer. It extorts this surplus without returning an equivalent. This surplus labor always remains forced labor in essence, no matter how much it may seem to be the result of free contract. This surplus labor is represented by a surplus value, and this surplus value is materialized in a surplus product. It must always remain surplus labor in the sense that it is labor performed above the normal requirements of the producer. In the capitalist system as well as in the slave system, etc., it merely assumes an antagonistic form and is supplemented by the complete idleness of a portion of society. A certain quantity of surplus labor is required for the purpose of discounting accidents, and by the necessary and progressive expansion of the process of reproduction in keeping with the development of the needs and the advance of population, called accumulation from the point of view of the capitalist. It is one of the civilizing sides of capital that it enforces this surplus labor in a manner and under conditions which promote the development of the productive forces, of social conditions, and the creation of the elements for a new and higher formation better than did the proceding forms of slavery, serfdom, etc. Thus it leads on the one hand to a stage in which the coercion and the monopolization of the social development (including its material and intellectual advantages) by a portion of society at the expense of the other portion are eliminated; on the other hand it creates the material requirements and the germ of conditions which make it possible to combine this surplus labor in a higher form of society with a greater reduction of the time devoted to material labor. . . . The actual wealth of society, and the possibility of a continual expansion of its process of reproduction, do not depend upon the duration of the surplus labor, but upon its productivity and upon the more or less fertile conditions of production, under which it is performed. In fact, the realm of freedom does not commence until the point is passed where labor under the compulsion of necessity and of external utility is required. In the very nature of things it lies beyond the sphere of material production in the strict meaning of the term. Just as the savage must wrestle with nature, in order to satisfy his wants, in order to maintain his life and reproduce it, so civilized man has to do it, and he must do it in all forms of society and under all possible modes of production. With his development the realm of natural necessity expands, because his wants increase; but at the same time the forces of production increase, by which these wants are satisfied. The freedom in this field cannot consist of anything else but of the fact that socialized man, the associated producers, regulate their interchange with nature rationally, bring it under their common control, instead of being ruled by it as by some blind power; that they accomplish their task with the least expenditure of energy and under conditions most adequate to their human nature and most worthy of it. But it always remains a realm of necessity. Beyond it begins that development of human power which is its own end, the true realm of freedom, which, however, can flourish only upon that realm of necessity as it basis. . . .

Suggestions for Further Reading

The works listed below have been selected for the use of the reader who wishes to further pursue his studies of Marxist thought. For the sake of convenience, the list has been limited to sources available in English. Items of special interest are indicated with an asterisk.

Works by Marx and Engels

Unfortunately, there is at present no complete English edition of the works of Marx and Engels. A forthcoming edition has, however, been announced to be published jointly by International Publishers (New York) and Lawrence and Wishart (London).

MARX, KARL. *Early Writings. Trans. and ed. by T. B. Bottomore. New York: McGraw-Hill, 1964.

_____. *Writings of the Young Marx on Philosophy and Society. Trans. and ed. by Loyd D. Easton and Kurt H. Guddat. Garden City: Doubleday, 1967.

_____. *Capital. Three vol. Moscow: Progress Publishers, 1965–66.

_____. On Colonialism and Modernization. Ed. by Shlomo Avineri. Garden City: Doubleday, 1968.

_____. A Contribution to the Critique of Political Economy. Trans. by N. I. Stone. Chicago: Charles H. Kerr Co., 1904.

_____. Letters to Kugelman. New York: International Publishers, 1934.

_____. The Poverty of Philosophy. Moscow: Progress Publishers, 1968.

_____. Pre-Capitalist Economic Formations. Trans. and ed. by Eric Hobsbawm. London: Lawrence and Wishart, 1964.

ENGELS, FRIEDRICH. *Herr Eugen Dühring's Revolution in Science (the so-called "Anti-Dühring"). Moscow: Foreign Languages Publishing House, 1962.

_____. The Condition of the Working Class in England in 1844. London: George Allen and Unwin, 1955.

————. *Dialectics of Nature.* Moscow: Foreign Languages Publishing House, 1966.

————. *The Origin of the Family, Private Property and the State.* New York: International Publishers, 1964.

MARX AND ENGELS. *Basic Writings on Politics and Philosophy.* Ed. by Lewis F. Feuer. Garden City: Doubleday, 1959.

————. **Selected Works.* Two vols. New York: International Publishers, 1936.

————. *Selected Correspondence.* Moscow: Progress Publishers, 1965.

————. *On Britain.* Moscow: Progress Publishers, 1962.

————. *On Colonialism.* Moscow: Progress Publishers, 1968.

————. **The German Ideology.* Moscow: Progress Publishers, 1968.

————. *The Holy Family.* Trans. by R. Dixon. Moscow: Foreign Languages Publishing House, 1956.

Secondary Sources

1. Biographies

MEHRING, FRANZ. **Karl Marx: The Story of His Life.* Ann Arbor: University of Michigan Press, 1962. The standard biography by a Social Democrat and great admirer of Marx. Dated, especially as regards the early Marx.

PAYNE, ROBERT. **Marx.* London: W. H. Allen, 1968. A rather critical biography which concentrates more on the man than on his thought. A valuable source on the many personal controversies involving Marx.

2. The Philosophical Background of Marxism

DUPRE, LOUIS. **The Philosophical Foundations of Marxism.* New York: Harcourt Brace Jovanovich, 1966. A good introduction to the subject. Strong on relating Marx to Hegel.

FEUERBACH, LUDWIG. ** The Essence of Christianity.* Trans. by George Eliot (pseud.). New York: Harper and Row, 1957. Crucial for grasping Marx's concept of alienation.

————. *Lectures on the Essence of Religion.* Trans. by Ralph Manheim. New York: Harper and Row, 1967. Feuerbach on the role of nature in religion; an aspect of his thought seldom discussed.

————. *Principles of the Philosophy of the Future.* Trans. by Manfred Vogel. Indianapolis: Bobbs-Merrill, 1966. Documents Feuerbach's break with Hegel and develops his ethics of community.

HEGEL, G. W. F. *On Christianity: Early Theological Writings*. Trans. and ed. by T. M. Knox. New York: Harper and Row, 1961. When Hegel's early writings were first published at the beginning of this century they revolutionized Hegel scholarship. Unfortunately, this edition does not contain translations of the full text.

_____. *The Phenomenology of Mind*. Trans. by J. B. Baillie. New York: Harper and Row, 1967. Crucial. Hegel's first major published work.

_____. *The Philosophy of History*. Trans. by J. Sibree. New York: Dover, 1956. Hegel's lectures on the subject as edited by his disciples from students' notes. Hegel's most popular work.

_____. *The Philosophy of Right*. Trans. by T. M. Knox. Oxford: The Oxford University Press, 1965. Crucial. Hegel on civil society and the state.

_____. *The Science of Logic*. Two vols. Trans. by W. H. Johnston and L. G. Struthers. New York: Humanities Press, 1966. The first part of Hegel's mature system. A philosophically revolutionary, if often obscure, classic.

HOOK, SIDNEY. *From Hegel to Marx*. Ann Arbor: University of Michigan Press, 1962. For a long time the only book on the Young Hegelians readily available in English. Still the most detailed such study, although incorrect on some details.

HYPPOLITE, JEAN. *Studies in Marx and Hegel*. New York: Basic Books, 1969. A collection of essays by one of the foremost French scholars of Hegel.

KAMENKA, EUGENE. *The Ethical Foundations of Marxism*. New York: Frederick A. Praeger Co., 1962. A study of the early Marx emphasizing his relation to the traditional problems of ethics.

LOWITH, KARL. *From Hegel to Nietzsche*. New York: Holt, Rinehart and Winston, 1964. An insightful history of nineteenth-century German thought, often ranging far beyond the material included in this anthology.

MCLELLAN, DAVID. *The Young Hegelians and Karl Marx*. London: Macmillan, 1969. A recent work of considerable scholarly interest, superseding Hook, *op. cit.*

MARCUSE, HERBERT. *Reason and Revolution*. Boston: Beacon Press, 1966. Still the best introduction to Hegel's thought available in English. Somewhat weak on Marx.

POPPER, KARL R. *The Open Society and Its Enemies: Volume Two*. Princeton: Princeton University Press, 1971. A book which has earned a reputation among positivistic philosophers. It suffers directly from the prejudices of its author, and thus it is an often-quoted source for anti-Marxist commentators.

3. Studies of Marx's Thought

AVINERI, SHLOMO. *The Social and Political Thought of Karl Marx.* Cambridge: Cambridge University Press, 1969. One of the outstanding works on Marx. It stresses the unity of his earlier and later works.

FROMM, ERICH (ed.). *Marx's Concept of Man.* New York: Frederick Ungar, 1961. An anthology with a long introduction by the distinguished psychologist and advocate of Marxist humanism.

MESZAROS, ISTVAN. *Marx's Theory of Alienation.* London: Merlin Press, 1970. A new work which sets high standards for further Marx scholarship in English. Not to be attempted by the novice.

SWEEZY, PAUL M. *The Theory of Capitalist Development.* New York: Monthly Review Press, 1964. A thoroughly readable commentary on Marx's *Capital* with reference to the United States economy.

TUCKER, ROBERT. *Philosophy and Myth in Karl Marx.* Cambridge: Cambridge University Press, 1961. A controversial study which attempts to place Marx in the mainstream of German Idealism and psychoanalyze the "inner drama" *(sic!)* of Marx's thought.

4. Marxism as a Political Movement

JORDAN, Z. A. *The Evolution of Dialectical Materialism.* New York: St. Martin's Press, 1967. A thorough and detailed study of the fate of Marx's thought at the hands of the more influential of his erstwhile disciples.

LENIN, V. I. *Selected Works.* Three vols. New York: International Publishers. Although equal in originality to the works of Marx himself, this collection of Lenin's works provides the most suitable introduction to the latter's contributions to Marxism.

————. *Philosophical Notebooks* (Collected Works, Vol. 38). Moscow: Foreign Languages Publishing House, 1960. An interesting glimpse into Lenin's philosophical development. Especially interesting are his comments on Hegel's *Logic*.

LICHTHEIM, GEORGE. *Marxism: An Historical and Critical Study.* New York: Frederick A. Praeger, 1961. A basic work on the development of Marxism.

Ed

WOLFE, BERTRAM D. *Marxism: One Hundred Years in the Life of a Doctrine*. New York: Dell, 1967. A historical study by an opponent of Marxism which nevertheless covers the material with a minimum of distortion.

5. Problems of Contemporary Marxism

DJILAS, MILOVAN. *The New Class*. New York: Frederick A. Praeger, 1962. This classical study of bureaucratizing trends in a Marxist society which earned a prison sentence for its author, once second in the Yugoslav Communist hierarchy, remains controversial today, although modern "revisionism" has moved further theoretically since Djilas's work.

DUNAYEVSKAYA, RAYA. *Marxism and Freedom*. New York: Twayne, 1964. A challenging attempt to relate Marxist theory to the problems of the United States' working class in the sixties, written by a former secretary to Leon Trotsky.

FROMM, ERICH (ed.). *Socialist Humanism*. Garden City: Doubleday, 1966. A wide-ranging collection of essays of the mid-sixties presenting Marxism as a humanist philosophy. Strongly anti-Soviet in orientation.

KOLAKOWSKI, LESZEK. *Toward a Marxist Humanism*. Trans. by J. Z. Peel. New York: Grove Press, 1968. A collection of essays written while the author was still a member of the Polish Communist party dealing with the problems of revising obsolete dogmas in the light of current realities.

LOBKOWICZ, NICHOLAS (ed.). *Marx and the Western World*. Notre Dame, Ind.: Notre Dame University Press, 1967. A general selection of essays of interest to social scientists and historians as well as philosophers.

PETROVIC, GAJO. **Marx in the Mid-Twentieth Century*. Garden City: Doubleday, 1967. A leading work of contemporary Eastern European "revisionism."

SCHAFF, ADAM. *A Philosophy of Man*. New York: Monthly Review Press, 1963. A Marxist critique of existentialism, especially that of Jean-Paul Sartre.

Index

American Studies: General

HENRY ADAMS Degradation of the Democratic Dogma. ‡ *Introduction by Charles Hirschfeld.* TB/1450

LOUIS D. BRANDEIS: Other People's Money, *and How the Bankers Use It. Ed. with Intro, by Richard M. Abrams* TB/3081

HENRY STEELE COMMAGER, Ed.: The Struggle for Racial Equality TB/1300

CARL N. DEGLER: Out of Our Past: *The Forces that Shaped Modern America* CN/2

CARL N. DEGLER, Ed.: Pivotal Interpretations of American History
Vol. I TB/1240; Vol. II TB/1241

A. S. EISENSTADT, Ed.: The Craft of American History: *Selected Essays*
Vol. I TB/1255; Vol. II TB/1256

LAWRENCE H. FUCHS, Ed.: American Ethnic Politics TB/1368

MARCUS LEE HANSEN: The Atlantic Migration: 1607-1860. *Edited by Arthur M. Schlesinger. Introduction by Oscar Handlin* TB/1052

MARCUS LEE HANSEN: The Immigrant in American History. *Edited with a Foreword by Arthur M. Schlesinger* TB/1120

ROBERT L. HEILBRONER: The Limits of American Capitalism TB/1305•

JOHN HIGHAM, Ed.: The Reconstruction of American History TB/1068

ROBERT H. JACKSON: The Supreme Court in the American System of Government TB/1106

JOHN F. KENNEDY: A Nation of Immigrants. *Illus. Revised and Enlarged. Introduction by Robert F. Kennedy* TB/1118

LEONARD W. LEVY, Ed.: American Constitutional Law: *Historical Essays* TB/1285

LEONARD W. LEVY, Ed.: Judicial Review and the Supreme Court TB/1296

LEONARD W. LEVY: The Law of the Commonwealth and Chief Justice Shaw: *The Evolution of American Law, 1830-1860* TB/1309

GORDON K. LEWIS: Puerto Rico: *Freedom and Power in the Caribbean. Abridged edition* TB/1371

GUNNAR MYRDAL: An American Dilemma: *The Negro Problem and Modern Democracy. Introduction by the Author.*
Vol. I TB/1443; Vol. II TB/1444

GILBERT OSOFSKY, Ed.: The Burden of Race: *A Documentary History of Negro-White Relations in America* TB/1405

ARNOLD ROSE: The Negro in America: *The Condensed Version of Gunnar Myrdal's* An American Dilemma. *Second Edition* TB/3048

JOHN E. SMITH: Themes in American Philosophy: *Purpose, Experience and Community* TB/1466

WILLIAM R. TAYLOR: Cavalier and Yankee: *The Old South and American National Character* TB/1474

American Studies: Colonial

BERNARD BAILYN: The New England Merchants in the Seventeenth Century TB/1149

ROBERT E. BROWN: Middle-Class Democracy and Revolution in Massachusetts, 1691-1780. *New Introduction by Author* TB/1413

JOSEPH CHARLES: The Origins of the American Party System TB/1049

WESLEY FRANK CRAVEN: The Colonies in Transition: 1660-1712† TB/3084

CHARLES GIBSON: Spain in America † TB/3077

CHARLES GIBSON, Ed.: The Spanish Tradition in America + HR/1351

LAWRENCE HENRY GIPSON: The Coming of the Revolution: 1763-1775. † *Illus.* TB/3007

JACK P. GREENE, Ed.: Great Britain and the American Colonies: 1606-1763. + *Introduction by the Author* HR/1477

AUBREY C. LAND, Ed.: Bases of the Plantation Society + HR/1429

PERRY MILLER: Errand Into the Wilderness TB/1139

PERRY MILLER & T. H. JOHNSON, Ed.: The Puritans: *A Sourcebook of Their Writings*
Vol. I TB/1093; Vol. II TB/1094

EDMUND S. MORGAN: The Puritan Family: *Religion and Domestic Relations in Seventeenth Century New England* TB/1227

WALLACE NOTESTEIN: The English People on the Eve of Colonization: 1603-1630. † *Illus.* TB/3006

LOUIS B. WRIGHT: The Cultural Life of the American Colonies: 1607-1763. † *Illus.* TB/3005

YVES F. ZOLTVANY, Ed.: The French Tradition in America + HR/1425

American Studies: The Revolution to 1860

JOHN R. ALDEN: The American Revolution: 1775-1783. † *Illus.* TB/3011

MARTIN HEIDEGGER: Discourse on Thinking. *Translated with a Preface by John M. Anderson and E. Hans Freund. Introduction by John M. Anderson* TB/1459
IMMANUEL KANT: Religion Within the Limits of Reason Alone. § *Introduction by Theodore M. Greene and John Silber* TB/FG
H. RICHARD NIERUHR: Christ and Culture TB/3
H. RICHARD NIEBUHR: The Kingdom of God in America TB/49
JOHN H. RANDALL, JR.: The Meaning of Religion for Man. *Revised with New Intro. by the Author* TB/1379

Science and Mathematics

W. E. LE GROS CLARK: The Antecedents of Man: *An Introduction to the Evolution of the Primates.* ° *Illus.* TB/559
ROBERT E. COKER: Streams, Lakes, Ponds. *Illus.* TB/586
ROBERT E. COKER: This Great and Wide Sea: *An Introduction to Oceanography and Marine Biology. Illus.* TB/551
F. K. HARE: The Restless Atmosphere TB/560
WILLARD VAN ORMAN QUINE: Mathematical Logic TB/558

Science: Philosophy

J. M. BOCHENSKI: The Methods of Contemporary Thought. *Tr. by Peter Caws* TB/1377
J. BRONOWSKI: Science and Human Values. *Revised and Enlarged. Illus.* TB/505
WERNER HEISENBERG: Physics and Philosophy: *The Revolution in Modern Science. Introduction by F. S. C. Northrop* TB/549
KARL R. POPPER: Conjectures and Refutations: *The Growth of Scientific Knowledge* TB/1376
KARL R. POPPER: The Logic of Scientific Discovery TB/576

Sociology and Anthropology

REINHARD BENDIX: Work and Authority in Industry: *Ideologies of Management in the Course of Industrialization* TB/3035
BERNARD BERELSON, Ed., The Behavioral Sciences Today TB/1127
KENNETH B. CLARK: Dark Ghetto: *Dilemmas of Social Power. Foreword by Gunnar Myrdal* TB/1317
KENNETH CLARK & JEANNETTE HOPKINS: A Relevant War Against Poverty: *A Study of Community Action Programs and Observable Social Change* TB/1480
LEWIS COSER, Ed.: Political Sociology TB/1293
ROSE L. COSER, Ed.: Life Cycle and Achievement in America ** TB/1434
ALLISON DAVIS & JOHN DOLLARD: Children of Bondage: *The Personality Development of Negro Youth in the Urban South* || TB/3049
ST. CLAIR DRAKE & HORACE R. CAYTON: Black Metropolis: *A Study of Negro Life in a Northern City. Introduction by Everett C. Hughes. Tables, maps, charts, and graphs* Vol. I TB/1086; Vol. II TB/1087

PETER F. DRUCKER: The New Society: *The Anatomy of Industrial Order* TB/108
LEON FESTINGER, HENRY W. RIECKEN, STANLEY SCHACHTER: When Prophecy Fails: *A Social and Psychological Study of a Modern Group that Predicted the Destruction of the World* TB/113
CHARLES Y. GLOCK & RODNEY STARK: Christian Beliefs and Anti-Semitism. *Introduction by the Authors* TB/1454
L. S. B. LEAKEY: Adam's Ancestors: *The Evolution of Man and His Culture. Illus.* TB/1019
KURT LEWIN: Field Theory in Social Science: *Selected Theoretical Papers.* || *Edited by Dorwin Cartwright* TB/1135
RITCHIE P. LOWRY: Who's Running This Town? *Community Leadership and Social Change* TB/1383
R. M. MACIVER: Social Causation TB/1153
GARY T. MARX: Protest and Prejudice: *A Study of Belief in the Black Community* TB/1435
ROBERT K. MERTON, LEONARD BROOM, LEONARD S COTTRELL, JR., Editors: Sociology Today: *Problems and Prospects* || Vol. I TB/1173; Vol. II TB/1174
GILBERT OSOFSKY, Ed.: The Burden of Race: *A Documentary History of Negro-White Relations in America* TB/1405
GILBERT OSOFSKY: Harlem: The Making of a Ghetto: *Negro New York 1890-1930* TB/1381
TALCOTT PARSONS & EDWARD A. SHILS, Editors: Toward a General Theory of Action: *Theoretical Foundations for the Social Sciences* TB/1083
PHILIP RIEFF: The Triumph of the Therapeutic: *Uses of Faith After Freud* TB/1360
JOHN H. ROHRER & MUNRO S. EDMONSON, Eds.: The Eighth Generation Grows Up: *Cultures and Personalities of New Orleans Negroes* || TB/3050
ARNOLD ROSE: The Negro in America: *The Condensed Version of Gunnar Myrdal's An American Dilemma. Second Edition* TB/3048
GEORGE ROSEN: Madness in Society: *Chapters in the Historical Sociology of Mental Illness.* || *Preface by Benjamin Nelson* TB/1337
PHILIP SELZNICK: TVA and the Grass Roots: *A Study in the Sociology of Formal Organization* TB/1230
PITIRIM A. SOROKIN: Contemporary Sociological Theories: *Through the First Quarter of the Twentieth Century* TB/3046
MAURICE R. STEIN: The Eclipse of Community: *An Interpretation of American Studies* TB/1128
FERDINAND TONNIES: Community and Society: *Gemeinschaft und Gesellschaft. Translated and Edited by Charles P. Loomis* TB/1116
SAMUEL E. WALLACE: Skid Row as a Way of Life TB/1367
W. LLOYD WARNER and Associates: Democracy in Jonesville: *A Study in Quality and Inequality* || TB/1129
W. LLOYD WARNER: Social Class in America: *The Evaluation of Status* TB/1013
FLORIAN ZNANIECKI: The Social Role of the Man of Knowledge. *Introduction by Lewis A. Coser* TB/1372

942   522